Man and his salvation

In memoriam Samueli G. F. Brandon

qui obiit a.d. IV Kalendas Novembres MCMLXXI

ecclesiae Anglicanae sacerdos, artis et scientiae cultus ac religiones hominum inter se comparandi viginti annos in Academia Mamuciensi professor, aliquamdiu officiis Vicecancellarii diligenter perfunctus et nuper societatis omnium per orbem terrarum religionum historiae studentium praeses electus; qui indefesso labore et immensa eruditione de religionibus omnium gentium a Gadibus usque ad Auroram et Gangem habitantium disseruit, discipulos studiosos et audiendi cupidos undique attraxit necnon transatlanticos invenit sectatores; qui ausus est de historia Iudaeorum deque iudicio et condemnatione Iesus Nazareni novas promulgare hypotheses; qui denique qua erat eximia doctrina, humanitate, benevolentia academicam iuventutem bonis artibus erudivit consiliisque adiuvit; cuius igitur amici, collegae, discipuli mortem repentinam lugentes pia vota his opusculis testificanda esse voluerunt

A. N. Marlow

S. G. F. Brandon

Man and his salvation

Studies in memory of S. G. F. Brandon

edited by Eric J. Sharpe and John R. Hinnells

[redacted]

Manchester University Press

Rowman & Littlefield Publishers

Published by the University of Manchester
at the University Press
316–24 Oxford Road, Manchester M13 9NR

UK ISBN 0 7190 0537 X

USA
Rowman & Littlefield Publishers
81 Adams Drive, Totowa, N.J. 07512
US ISBN 0 87471 181 9

Library of Congress cataloguing-in-publication data

Main entry under title:

Man and his salvation

CONTENTS: *Snape, H. C. Samuel George Frederick Brandon: a personal appreciation.—James, E. O. Professor Brandon's contribution to scholarship.—Oxtoby, W. G. Reflections on the idea of salvation.* [*etc.*]
Includes bibliographical references.
1. *Salvation—Addresses, essays, lectures.* 2. *Brandon, Samuel George Frederick.* 3. *Brandon, Samuel George Frederick—Bibliography.* I. *Sharpe, Eric J., 1933– , ed.* II. *Hinnells, John R., ed.* III. *Brandon, Samuel George Frederick.*

BL476.M35 1973 291.2′2 73–2814
UK ISBN 0 7190 0537 X
US ISBN 0 87471 181 9

Printed in Great Britain
by Butler & Tanner Ltd, Frome and London

Contents

Editors' foreword

In an article published in 1969 S. G. F. Brandon wrote that

> . . . Man's consciousness of Time causes him always to be aware that he is immersed in an unceasing process of change—that he can never stay and rest in the present; that what seems to be here and now is inexorably moving into the past as he seeks to apprehend it, while a new situation is ever confronting him as it emerges to present reality from its state of non-being in the future. But this is not all. Man also knows that he is no mere spectator of an ever changing phenomenal world which the Time-process presents to him—for he is, himself, part of that process and is himself subject to that change of being through which Time manifests itself. He knows that he has been, that he now is, and that he will be—but for how long?[1]

It was shortly after these words were written that some of Professor Brandon's colleagues first began to discuss the possibility of presenting him with a volume of essays in celebration of his sixty-fifth birthday, which would have fallen in October 1972. We little realised at that moment exactly what the Time-process would have in store, and that the proposed *Festschrift* would, when published, have to take the form of a memorial volume.

Professor Brandon's death occurred in an aircraft over the Mediterranean on 29th October 1971. He had been in Egypt on a research and study tour, and there contracted an infection which could not be controlled, and led to his tragic death. These are the bald facts. Their implications we are only now beginning to realise. The world of scholarship was deprived of an outstanding historian of religion, the range of whose activities was increasing, rather than diminishing, with the years; the International Association for the History of Religions was deprived of its newly appointed Secretary-General, who had set about his new tasks with characteristic energy and thoroughness; many colleagues lost a close and valued guide, philosopher and friend, and countless students, a committed teacher and compassionate mentor. Most of all, the loss was felt by Mrs Brandon, who had been with Professor Brandon throughout his last journey, and by his son, David.

1 'A new awareness of time and history', in *Religious Pluralism and World Community*, ed. Jurji, p. 227.

It was clear that the proposed *Festschrift* should be produced, and dedicated to Professor Brandon's memory. What was less clear was whether the editors should attempt to provide, in its pages, a complete critical account of his life and scholarly work. After a good deal of heart-searching, it was decided not to do so. First, because of the vast range of territory which such an account would have to cover if it was to be worthy of the man and his mind; and second, because it was genuinely felt to be too soon to place his work in its proper perspective. Eventually the task should be—indeed, must be—undertaken; but it must not be undertaken lightly.

The first two essays in this volume—those by the Rev. H. C. Snape and the late Professor E. O. James—do indeed survey Professor Brandon's life and work; both writers were close friends of Professor Brandon over many years. After an article on methodology the remaining articles, in alphabetical order of author, deal in various ways with aspects of a problem to which Professor Brandon devoted much of his scholarly career, the problem of man and his salvation. It is hoped that as well as being a fitting tribute to the memory of an outstanding scholar, the volume as a whole will contribute to the ongoing debate concerning the nature and conditions of religion in the life of mankind.

It is an additional sadness for the editors to have to record the death of the Rev. Professor E. O. James as a result of a motor car accident on 6 July 1972, after the completion of his tribute to Professor Brandon but before the volume went to press.

Easter 1973

Eric J. Sharpe
John R. Hinnells

I

H. C. Snape

Samuel George Frederick Brandon: a personal appreciation

Samuel George Frederick Brandon was by birth a Devonian, whose father was a seaman in the merchant navy. Professor Brandon used to say that he knew little of his forebears. The *Dictionary of National Biography* records two men of this name, one the first Duke of Suffolk, who was raised to the peerage by Henry VIII; the other was the executioner of Charles I. There is also supposed to have been a Jewish family who came over from Portugal in the eighteenth century and adopted the name of Brandon. Educated at the local grammar school, he was noticed by the incumbent of the parish, on whose advice he proceeded to join the Community of the Resurrection at Mirfield, with a view to ordination.

Although Professor Brandon appeared to retain little of the ecclesiastical and theological outlook peculiar to Mirfield, it was doubtless there that he learned of the authority possessed by a pattern of ceremony and ritual, and its power to communicate that sense of solemnity, awe and reverence which is the essence of religion. Probably unconsciously these early influences provoked him to turn his attention from the theological beliefs of the world's religions to their images and pictorial expressions. Towards the end of his life he introduced the study of iconography as a separate subject into the Department of Comparative Religion in the University of Manchester, and had also completed a book on the subject. While training for the ministry at Mirfield he was also a student at the University of Leeds, where he graduated in Ancient History in 1930. There he discovered where his life's interests lay.

My own observations have led me to think that some men are given such a clear call that they know what to do in life from their earliest years—why they become scientists, artists or historians cannot be rationally explained. Professor Brandon used to recall how as a small boy he diligently collected a series of cigarette cards depicting ancient monuments such as the pyramids, the Sphinx and the Colosseum.

Ordained in 1932, he served curacies at St Mark's, Devonport, and Westward Ho! In 1939 he enlisted as an army chaplain, with the hope of being despatched to Egypt and seeing the Sphinx and the pyramids at first hand. However, instead he probably gained a first-hand acquaintance with tactics and strategy which stood him in good stead when he came to write his account of the Jewish war, culminating in the siege of Jerusalem and its fall in A.D. 70. It is noteworthy in this connection that he was for a time chairman of the Manchester Tactical Society, and was a contributor to the society's volume entitled *The Fourth Dimension of Warfare* (1970).

But war was also for him an experience which revealed depths and heights in himself and in the world, and compelled a revision of philosophies and religions. He related how, when with the British Expeditionary Force in France, waiting on the shores at Dunkirk in 1940, bereft of his equipment, communion vessels and vestments, and possessing only a copy of the *Meditations* of Marcus Aurelius, he realised that for him henceforth none of the externals of religion was necessary for the profession of faith. Although for some years he continued to exercise a pastoral ministry within the traditional structure in which he had been nurtured, he became increasingly absorbed in the study of religion as an expression of man's attitude towards life—in a word, as a humane study. He had already obtained his Leeds B.D. in 1936 with a thesis which was later to appear as a book under the title *Time and Mankind*. That this theme was to be a continuing interest with him is shown by his Wilde lectures, published in 1962 as *Man and his Destiny in the Great Religions*, and by his Forwood lectures, published in 1965 as *History, Time and Deity*. Furthermore, he was one of the founder members of the International Society for the Study of Time, which held its first conference in 1969.

For his M.A. at Leeds he made a study of Herod the Great. This was the outcome of what was to be another continuing interest, the political context in which Christian origins are set. The late Professor E. O. James, in the next essay, sets out Brandon's basic thesis, which he maintained consistently over the years, that Jesus as crucified under Pontius Pilate was inevitably involved in Judaean politics, and that the destruction of Jerusalem and the Jewish State, in a larger measure than the New Testament documents would lead one to suppose, prevented the infant Church from perishing as a sect within Judaism and enabled it to become a world religion. While Professor Brandon never claimed that his thesis was entirely original, yet it could justifiably be maintained that the exact scholarship, scrupulous investigation of the evidence and single-minded regard for historical truth, irrespective of any confessional prejudices with which he pursued his researches, have made it impossible to continue to divorce discussion of Jesus and the origins of Christianity from their political context. British New Testament scholars, with their customary caution, have tended either to ignore his contentions or to give them a cool reception, but Brandon was one of the few Anglican scholars whose work is well known both in Germany and in North America. Roman Catholic and Jewish scholars have given his thesis special attention, the former perhaps because it deals a fresh blow at the liberal Protestant image of Jesus, and the latter because it makes it possible to think of Jesus as a patriotic revolutionary. Others, building upon Brandon's hypothesis, have assumed that Jesus himself was a Zealot, but Brandon never went beyond suggesting that Jesus had the closest sympathy with the Zealots.

Despite what we have said earlier, Professor Brandon never ceased to be active as an ordained minister in the Church of England. During his service in North Africa, from 1943 to 1945, he organised through the army postal services a study scheme for officers and men of various denominations who were contemplating ordination. And after his retirement from the army in 1951 he continued to assist his friends from among the pastoral clergy as occasion demanded. While on service in North Africa he came into touch with John Pearce Higgins, an active member of the Modern Churchmen's Union, who persuaded him to contribute a paper to its annual conference in 1945. From then until his death he was an active member of the Union, always ready to participate in its endeavours to maintain the Anglican tradition of liberality and sound learning, chiefly by contributions—both articles and reviews—to its journal, *The Modern Churchman*. In 1949 he organised and chaired the Modern Churchmen's annual conference, the theme of which was 'Life and death'. For him man's consciousness of death and change creates the riddle and tragedy which man attempts to meet by the practice of religion. He divided religions into two groups: first, those, such as Christianity, which refuse to accept death as natural and necessary, and take it as a consequence of sin, to be reversed by divine action; and second, those, like Buddhism, which accept death and decay, no less than life and growth, as unavoidable facets of the human condition. Brandon's study of the world's religions led him to believe that no religion by itself—not even Christianity—could claim to be exclusively true and final. We may perhaps quote the conclusion of the paper with which he brought this outstanding conference to an end:

That the latter group of religions ascribe to God, as ground of all existence, the dual character of Creator and Destroyer is consistent with this realism, and is not the product of superstition and ignorance. The witness of this ascription by so many great and ancient religious traditions is of immense significance, because it represents what a large part of the human race down the centuries has come to believe about the nature of the power that has produced, sustains and governs the universe. It is, accordingly, the duty of Christian thinkers to ponder the significance of this fact, and then to ask whether the traditional Christian conception of God adequately accounts for the whole of human experience. This is not to say that the Christian estimate is wrong or seriously defective when compared with that of other religions. It may, rather, mean that those who have been responsible for moulding the Christian doctrine of God have been so inspired to exalt the providence of God as only benevolent to the short-term interests of men, that they have failed to see that his providence, in the totality of its manifestations, must involve the destruction of certain patterns of being in order to create others. Perhaps the time has come for Christian theology to move towards a greater synthesis of man's religious experience, and to appreciate a truth which finds expression in what is surely an inspired mistranslation of a verse from the *Book of Job*: 'Though he slay me, yet will I trust in him.'[1]

It is, of course, obvious that two spheres of interest became Professor Brandon's preoccupation: (1) the bearing of the contemporary political environment on the origins of Christianity; and (2) the history of the world's religions in so far as they can be studied without confessional prejudice as a human activity.

Samuel Butler said of Darwin that he brought us all round to evolution. Professor Brandon brought us round to accepting that Jesus of Nazareth was politically involved in the life of his time in Judaea, and that the history of the Christian Church in the first century cannot be studied without taking into consideration the effects of the Jewish war and the fall of Jerusalem on the religious thought and the practices of the Judaeo-Hellenic world. He expounded this theme not only in works of pure scholarship such as *The Fall of Jerusalem and the Christian Church* but also in works and studies intended for the general reader, such as *The Trial of Jesus of Nazareth* and the articles published in *History Today* and collected into the volume *Religion in Ancient History* (1969).

He used every opportunity to establish comparative religion as an

1 *The Modern Churchman*, new series, III, No. 1, pp. 107f.

accepted branch of the humanities. As a separate subject for the first degree in the University of Manchester it is attracting an increasingly large number of students. At the same time, he played a full part in the promotion and co-ordination of the study of comparative religion at an international level, particularly in reconciling the varying approaches to the subject belonging to each national tradition, ranging from the highly academic Continental approach to the pragmatic North American. In 1965 he became a member of the executive committee of the International Association for the History of Religions. In 1970 he was appointed Secretary-General of the Association, and would have been responsible for organizing the international congress to be held at Manchester in 1975. He had also recently been appointed to the *comité de direction* of the Centre de Recherches d'Histoire des Religions in the University of Strasbourg.

All Brandon's studies were animated by a passionate desire and regard for truth. Every statement was supported by tested evidence; every reference was verified. Caution and imaginativeness went hand in hand. He repeatedly pointed out that, if Christians maintain that their faith has a prior claim over others because it is grounded in history, then they must be prepared to accept the conclusions of historical research, however uncomfortable and disturbing they may prove to be. If, at the same time, religion should be found in awe and wonder rather than in explicit professions of faith, what the great French scholar Maurice Goguel wrote of himself might be adapted and applied to Samuel George Frederick Brandon: he felt himself to be more a Catholic than an Anglican, more a Christian than a Catholic, and more a religious man than a Christian.

2

E. O. James
Professor Brandon's contribution to scholarship

It is greatly to be regretted that this collection of essays in honour of Professor S. G. F. Brandon, from being a *Festschrift* for his sixty-fifth birthday in October 1972, of necessity has become a memorial volume by his colleagues owing to his premature tragic death on 29th October 1971. Nevertheless, sad as the cause is, it provides an appropriate occasion for a personal appreciation and assessment of his outstanding contribution to his field of comparative religious studies. In my own case it is especially a privilege, as I have had a very intimate acquaintance with him since the time of his ordination in 1932, intermittently during his parochial work and subsequently as a regular army chaplain with the British Expeditionary Force in Belgium, France, North Africa and Austria.

It was then that he began his investigation of a new awareness of the consciousness of time, its definition, deification, and other human reactions to it. It has been, in fact, this consciousness of time that in his judgment has been the primary premise from which religion has emerged in a great variety of connotations, past, present and future. Indeed, it may have been this, he suggested, that was inherent and efficacious in the sacred dance portrayed in the so-called 'dancing sorcerer' in the palaeolithic cave of Trois Frères in Ariège, and in other magical paintings, as an attempt to depict a being personifying the relations between man and the animals, and the transitoriness of mundane occurrences, notably in the cult of the dead, and underlying the idea of immortality. Similarly, the representation of female figures such as that at Laussel, in the Dordogne, and other palaeolithic sites, could be indicative of the conception of the cyclic progress of life and death in which birth and death and survival were conceived in terms of time, present, past and future. Even man's tool-making, he thought, involved these three temporal categories, envisaging the production of implements determined by past knowledge and experience of human workmanship in these skills, how to improve upon them, and render them better adapted to future use, thereby increasing man's powers and attainments in his precarious struggle for survival.

It was to *Time and Mankind* that Brandon's first book, published in 1951, was devoted, and opened the way for his subsequent study of the subject in his later works in much greater detail and documentation. Thus when he was appointed to give the Wilde Lectures in Natural and Comparative Religion in the University of Oxford in 1954–7 he undertook an historical and comparative survey of the concept of man as it has found expression in the higher religions, with special reference to his destiny. These he greatly expanded when he published the course six years later under the title *Man and his Destiny in the Great Religions* (1962). In over 400 pages the evidence and its theme were pursued through the principal cultures everywhere and at all times, beginning with the emergence of *homo sapiens* under palaeolithic conditions. New light having been thrown on this initial phase, the inquiry was carried on in the food-producing civilisations in ancient Egypt, Mesopotamia, Israel, Greece, India, Iran, China and in Christendom and Islam. The work constitutes one of the most ambitious and widespread surveys ever attempted in this field, with remarkable success, the vast documentation and extensive bibliographies making it a work of reference of permanent value for further future research.

Moreover, Professor Brandon had already had a long-standing interest in New Testament studies, going back to his army days, when just before he resigned his commission in the forces, he had completed the manuscript of his *Fall of Jerusalem and the Christian Church* while he was at Catterick and in Austria, before it was published in 1951. How this was accomplished under the conditions of army life in war-time passes comprehension. Be that as it may, Brandon had followed the lead of B. H. Streeter, who had stressed the importance and significance of the destruction of Jerusalem in A.D. 70 in its effects on the origins and development of the Christian Church. As a result he arrived at the conclusion that the fall of the city was a dominant factor in the Church's survival in the new era. Hitherto, he maintained, this had been greatly neglected by New Testament scholars and canonists, notwithstanding, and perhaps because of, the Tübingen hypothesis and its rejection. Therefore he undertook a thorough investigation of the relevant ancient documents in search of the significance for Christianity of the catastrophic events of A.D. 70 which involved the destruction of the Jewish State and its aftermath.

It was in the last decades of the second temple period that Roman dominion gave rise to an organised group working for the restoration of Herodian rule, among whom were those Jewish patriots who were known as *Siccarii*, or Zealots, and who were prepared to go to any lengths in guerrilla rebellion to secure freedom from Roman rule. Most of our information about this little known organisation, its identity and its alliance with the Essenes and other groups, has been very conjectural, deriving from Josephus, by no means a reliable and unbiased source. This was recognised in the last century by Jost, Salvadore, Kitto and subsequent writers, who made it clear that Zealot nationalism was very deeply grounded in the Jewish background and social structure of the first century A.D., which was very different from that portrayed by Josephus. Since in the Gospels the epithet 'Zealot' was applied in Aramaic to the apostle Simon (Luke 6: 15), it suggests that he belonged to the Zealots. Brandon was led to the investigation of the place and function of the faction in apostolic tradition, and to the extent to which it was involved in the movement. As a result of this inquiry, published in his book *Jesus and the Zealots* (1967), he came to the conclusion not only that the Zealots' involvement was much greater than has been supposed but also that Jesus himself was a Zealotic figure, regarded as such in his messianic capacity. Brandon realised that in making this suggestion he would give offence to orthodox practising Christians, and incur the strenuous opposition of the majority of theologians, treading as he was on very sacred and insecure ground and making use of precarious data. Representing the crucified Christ as a victim of a Jewish political insurrection was exceedingly difficult to equate with the devotional and theological conception of the Saviour of mankind, however much it might receive some support from the Passion narratives.

Nothing daunted, however, he engaged in a study of the complex historical political problem of the execution of Jesus on a charge of sedition against the Roman government in Judaea as attested in all the New Testament documents. In the light of the evidence now available he had come to the conclusion that it demanded re-examination as a sequel to his book *The Fall of Jerusalem*, working backwards from A.D. 70. This he considered necessary to the understanding of the historical Jesus, who, he said, 'chose a Zealot for an apostle, and who died between two men, probably resistance fighters, who challenged Rome's sovereignty over Israel'. With this end in mind, he investigated the origin and ideals of the Zealots coincident with the birth, upbringing and ministry of Jesus in Galilee and Judaea, and their cause against Rome. To become acquainted at first hand with the Zealot environment he visited the great fortress at Masada, and included some illuminating illustrations of this important site, with its fragments of scrolls of Qumranic type, Zealot relics, and Roman coins, indicative of the Zealots' last stand in Palestine in A.D. 73.

It is clear, as he stressed, that the Christian movement was not an isolated phenomenon in Judaea under the Roman rule. This is confirmed by the Qumran documents, the fate of the 'Teacher of Righteousness' anticipating that of the Founder of Christianity. Moreover, as Brandon contended in his book *The Trial of Jesus of Nazareth* (1969), Jesus was crucified by the Romans rather than, as the Evangelists asserted, through the Jewish authorities' putting pressure on Pilate because they had no power to put a man to death. This, it is pointed out, could have been done on several charges, whereas the Passion narratives are agreed that it was for sedition that he was condemned, as is manifest by the title on the cross. In fact it would appear to have been a joint condemnation in which both the Roman and the Jewish authorities were involved in their respective capacities, the subject having been long in debate, as is here shown, with documentation, interpreted in terms of Brandon's Zealot theme.

In *The Saviour God*, a number of comparative studies in the concept of salvation presented to me in 1963, which Professor Brandon edited and collected as a symposium on soteriology, he dealt with 'The ritual technique of salvation in the ancient Near East'. In this essay he demonstrated that with a few exceptions the quest has been the assurance of *post mortem* security. The earliest example of this is in the texts inscribed on the walls of the royal pyramids in Egypt in the third millennium B.C. to enable the *ba* of the pharaoh buried in the sepulchre to join his *ka* in the after-life, thereby obtaining salvation as the son of the sun god. The climax of the ritual was reached in the mummification of the body and reanimation ('opening of the mouth') ceremonies. Furthermore, the Osiris mortuary mythology was centred on a saviour god of the dying–rising type. The relevant texts are quoted, and their pattern described and interpreted, including the later democratised versions in the coffin texts, in the *Book of the Dead* and in a papyrus from the late Ptolemaic era.

In this concise summary of the Egyptian evidence it is very skilfully shown how the solar and Osirian myth and ritual became a *post mortem* judgment of the dead before the concept recurred in other religions.

In the parallel Mesopotamian civilisation the practice of the ritual is examined in the cult of Tammuz. Here, however, the deity's becoming a saviour god is precluded, salvation being confined to relief from the ills of this life. In the Hellenic Eleusinian mysteries the *dromena* affords a better example of the ritual soteriological assimilation, though it did not afford a personal death and resurrection mythos like that of the Osirian tradition, or of its Christian counterpart, which is briefly discussed.

This analysis of the ritual technique of salvation led Professor Brandon in 1967 to make the first comprehensive study in English of *The Judgment of the Dead.* In this volume he elaborated the idea of a *post mortem* judgment approached historically and comparatively in the major religions from their earliest assumption in ancient Egypt. Special attention was paid to the Egyptian data as man's first confrontation with conscience, constituting both the earliest and most elaborate evidence of the idea of judgment after death. In striking contrast was its absence in Mesopotamia, while in Hinduism and Buddhism it has been conditioned by the doctrine of the transmigration of the soul and its mundane rebirth in higher or lower species and status. In Israel the situation was shown to be very different, when Yahweh was recognised to be the national deity with whom his 'chosen people' stood in a covenant relationship. In pre-exilic times, however, Sheol was regarded as a cul-de-sac outside his interest and care until in apocalyptic Judaism retributive justice with *post mortem* rewards and punishments was introduced. This Yahwist eschatology, as it is here discussed and evaluated in Hebrew literature in general, is of importance for Old Testament scholarship. In its last expression, in the Enochian phase, Egyptian affinities were detected in the descriptions of human destiny in Sheol, in which the weighing of the soul recurred, recorded in Brandon's contribution to the *Festschrift* for Eliade. In the *Studies in Honour of C. J. Bleeker* (1969) the similarity of phenomenological ambivalence between Osiris and Christ as Saviour and Judge was reviewed by him in this context.

Turning next to the problem of a non-theistic judgment in Graeco-Roman culture, the data were examined, going back to the Aegean Hellenic period before the arrival of the Indo-Europeans in the middle of the second millennium B.C. Awaiting further evidence from the Linear B tablets, the scene on the Minoan sarcophagus found at Hagia Triada in Crete is indicative, it is suggested, of the deceased making a journey by sea, presumably to the land of the dead. The notion of some heroes having been transported to the Isles of the Blest, as is pointed out, is preserved in the Hesiodic *Theogony* and the *Odyssey*. It is also recalled that miniature balances found in Mycenaean tombs suggest the continuance of life of heroes before an Elysium was situated in the nether regions inhabited by witless shades. These scales, and those represented on Greek vase paintings, if they determine the fate of two heroes in the after-life, could, as Brandon says, have Egyptian influence behind them, since this is not an isolated instance of such contacts in Cretan and Mycenaean culture.

In the Eleusinian mysteries one of the purposes of initiation was to escape the darkness of Hades and to enjoy the *post mortem* beatitude of the initiated. In the Homeric literature judgment is shown to be irrelevant for the wraiths in their shadowy conscious survival of the dead in their gloomy abode. Evil-doers, however, were punished and tortured by Minos and his tribunal, and eventually an effort was made by Lucretius to reinterpret the traditional view of Hades as a place of retribution eliminating human survival altogether. It remained for the Orphio-Pythagorean doctrine of the destiny of man, and its Platonic interpretation, to introduce justice beyond the grave in terms of metempsychosis. As Brandon has shown, salvation, judgment and the destiny of man have been determined similarly in Hinduism and Buddhism by reincarnation, transmigration and the law of *karma*, whereas in the theistic religions, notably in Judaism, Christianity and Islam, a final judgment has been a theological and ethical necessity.

Since in no faith has this been more basic than in Christianity, the Christian section of the inquiry is of outstanding importance, examined as it has been with expert knowledge, accuracy and sympathetic understanding of a belief which, as is rightly asserted, has been 'a factor of basic significance for the evaluation of man's life in the past, and is still regarded as such by millions all over the world'. In Christendom it has always been *de fide*, appearing as such in the Nicene Creed and the *Quicunque vult*, though in the Gospels it is assumed and affirmed rather than vindicated as a new and independent doctrine along Pauline lines. But, as Professor Brandon says, while the Jewish apocalyptic was adapted to the views of Jewish Christians, there are other incidental indications of a conception of human destiny which envisaged a *post mortem* judgment where the verdict would be decided by the individual's own actions, as in the parable of the tares. It was, however, the Great Assize in the Johannine Apocalypse, described in considerable detail, that influenced most strongly the later eschatological and soteriological imagery in its cosmological setting and interpretation centred on a final judgment at the consummation of the cosmic order.

Considerable attention has been given here to the development of the doctrine of Purgatory and the suffering of holy souls, indistinguishable from the torments of the damned in hell in the medieval literature, including the *Divina Commedia* of Dante, and demonstrated in the dooms in the fresco in the Campo Santo at Pisa, the Byzantine Last Judgment at Tortello, that on the tympanus at Autun, and on the mural paintings at Chaldon in Surrey. Their purpose, it is contended, was 'to keep Christians ever mindful of the awful Judgment of God', as proclaimed in the *Dies Irae* at Reims, and in such morality plays as *Everyman*. In Michelangelo's magnificent presentation of the Last Judgment in the Sistine chapel in the Vatican a combination of medieval symbolism and Renaissance humanism is discerned, marking an epoch in the life of its creator, and heralding the dawn of a new era.

It is recognised that when this was brought to an end at the Reformation the decline in belief in the traditional eschatology since the seventeenth century has raised very difficult problems for Christian soteriology in the attempts that have been made to re-state the doctrine of judgment, heaven and hell. These have been duly considered, and the excellent illustrations of the dooms are a valuable asset in the account of this aspect of medieval eschatology and the destiny of man, to which hitherto little attention has been paid in their historical and comparative conceptions.

Michelangelo's anthropomorphic portrayal of the creation of man in the fresco in the Sistine chapel in Rome led Professor Brandon to concentrate attention upon the Hebrew cosmogonies and the creation legends of other peoples in the ancient Near East; as he says, 'while the Hebrew creation story has now lost much of its former prestige, for our understanding of our common humanity there has been much gain'. In seeking to do this, in *Creation Legends of the Ancient Near East* (1963), he recorded these early speculations about the origin of the world in which its peoples found themselves in their respective habitations and movements. Following his usual comprehensive pattern, in the introductory chapter the dawning concept of creativity before the legends were formulated in the ancient Near East is surveyed in the light of his former conclusions as to how the idea of creation first arose in the mind of early man; it was suggested, he contends, by the phenomenon of biological birth indicating the initial conception of 'beginning' and of time-consciousness. Together with this it is conjectured that the palaeolithic artist conceived of himself as a personal creator, giving rise to the notion of creativity without stimulating cosmological speculations about the origin of the world and the development of the physical environment and its contents, as in the neolithic period in the middle of the third millennium B.C., when cosmogonies began to appear in Egypt and Mesopotamia, conditioned by the physical features of the universe as it was then known.

In the pyramid texts in the Nile valley, compiled by the Heliopolitan priests in the Fifth and Sixth Dynasties, a primordial state is envisaged, with its watery Chaos of Nun and the annual fructifying inundation of the Nile, equated with the culture hero Osiris and the Heliopolitan genealogical Ennead derived from Atum, the Creator. This is contrasted with the Memphite imagery and the Hermopolitan Ogdoad tradition, and that of Amun at Thebes in the New Kingdom. The absence of a struggle with the primeval forces of Chaos, so conspicuous in the Mesopotamian cosmogony, is explained by the predictable beneficence of the inundation of the Nile as against the incalculable turbulence of the Tigris and Euphrates. In both the Egyptian and the Babylonian cosmologies the numerous texts are quoted in abundance, the Sumerian literary compositions dealing with creation being primarily aetiological, whereas those in Egypt are dominated by a theological motif. In their later developments, however, they were concerned with ultimate destinies, human and cosmic, with *Endzeit* and *Urzeit*, though at both ends a deeply laid pessimism has characterised Mesopotamian thought and speculation eschatologically.

In the examination of the Hebrew cosmogony set against this background, while the debt to Babylonia and Assyria is recognised, the absence of a struggle between the personified forces of good and evil leading to the creation of the universe and of man is shown to be a distinctive feature of the Genesis stories. In the Yahwist tradition the origin of all things, and particularly of the world and of man and his destiny, is an integral part of the teleological process of history, culminating in the settlement of the 'chosen people' in their Palestinian 'Promised Land' as a unified federation of tribes. This, it is suggested, 'set forth an account of human nature that would accord with Yahwist theology', and implied the suppression of the mortuary cults to facilitate *post mortem* existence—the creation of man from the clay of the ground animated by the breath of life but destined to return to dust from which he was fashioned. The story of the Fall, centred on the 'tree of the knowledge of good and evil', and in the context of the decree of death, is discussed in relation to sexual consciousness in its various aspects. Stress is laid on the lucidity of the Hebrew cosmogony and its freedom from primitive imagery by comparison with the Egyptian and Mesopotamian counterparts. In resolving the Yahwist and priestly traditions into a continuous narrative in accord with the ethical monotheism and creativity of the prophetic movement, and of post-exilic theology, however, the discovery of their deeper significance has been rendered more difficult, as is here pointed out in a most illuminating chapter.

To bring the cosmogonic thought of Greece within the purview of this inquiry, mention can now be made of the Near Eastern influences in the Aegean in the Bronze Age becoming more apparent. As is demonstrated, the Hesiodic *Theogony* was greatly indebted to Anatolian and Indo-European sources, though neither Homer nor Hesiod was really concerned with the origin of the universe or of mankind, still less of any doctrine of soteriology. Similarly, what remains of contemporary Hellenic art is devoid of any evidence of a conception of the beginning of things. No attempt was made to go beyond Zeus and the remote 'age of the Olympian gods', or that of local folk tradition, rather than to actual primordial creation, though the basic ideas of other cosmogonies were incorporated in the Hesiodic poems. The crude Kronos castration myth was derived ultimately from Asia Minor, and was displaced by the Indo-European Zeus in a Cretan guise in the setting of a primeval conflict between the forces of order and disorder, as in that with the Titan gods. But the *Theogony* contains no account of the creation of man. The Greeks were interested in the past, but, as Professor Brandon maintains, so far as mankind was concerned the evaluation of the past seems to have been ambivalent and devoid of any view of the beginning of things. In Iran, on the other hand, a serious effort was made in the *Avesta*, as he shows, to deal with the intractable problem of the origin of evil by postulating the basic unity of Ahura Mazdah with the two opposed spirits, the one beneficent and the other malign. Zoroaster, as the founder of Zoroastrianism, regarded Ahura Mazdah, the Wise Lord, as the sole Creator, the twin spirits Spenta Mainyu and Angra Mainyu having been responsible for the Better and the Bad in thought, word and deed, and of light and darkness since the beginning of time at the dawn of creation.

After the death of Zoroaster the solution of this unsolved problem of good and evil was sought in the absolute dualism which emerged in

Mazdaeism in the personification of time in the 'high god' Zurvan with a twofold aspect or nature, perhaps going back ultimately to the twelfth century B.C. It has also been suggested that the Vedic deity Varuna was behind Ahura Mazdah, together with his partner Mithra, who became an attribute or son of the Wise Lord, dispensing rain and fertility on earth, and having been originally a twin of Yima, the primal man, whose original sin is obscure. It was out of this complex Iranian dualism that Mithraism emerged as a popular mystery cult, and to some extent it seems to have been a rival to Christianity in the later Roman empire.

In this erudite cosmological study of Near Eastern creation legends, with its impressive documentation, bibliographies, photographs, illustrations and line drawings, Professor Brandon made an outstanding contribution to scholarship in a wide, interrelated field of inquiry based on the concept of creativity. This may be regarded as constituting the climax of his interpretation of man and his destiny, the soteriology and eschatological investigations of saviour and judge, and the rise and development of the Christian Church and its Christology centred on the effects of the fall of Jerusalem in A.D. 70 and its aftermath. Having achieved so much in the history and comparative study of religion, he was turning his interest to iconography as a primary source for this field of learning. In his academic department in the University of Manchester he had helped institute a new honours degree in Religious Studies, with comparative religion as one major subject, and having the expression of religion in art and ritual illustrated by slides as an integral element of the course. He had just finished a book for Scribner's of New York, to be entitled *Man and God in Art and Ritual*, with 350 illustrations.

In addition to these literary achievements it was in the International Association for the History of Religions that his interest was becoming concentrated, and in 1970 he was appointed to succeed Professor Bleeker of Amsterdam as its Secretary-General. This afforded him an opportunity to make his diverse stores of knowledge internationally accessible in collaboration with so many other scholars engaged in this field of learning, which was essentially his own.

3

Willard G. Oxtoby

Reflections on the idea of salvation

Salvation has been treated as a key concept in religion. It has been central in the thought of particular religions, so that any discussion of it must include at least some particulars as data. But salvation as a general term has come to be applied to different religions, suggesting that the user of the term recognises in them something familiar. Besides the level of data we thus have a level of comparison.

This essay proposes to proceed at both levels. In the first two sections I hope to trace some ancient sources of the concept of salvation, and the manner in which the Christian tradition drew on them. In the third I shall inquire into some implications of the extension of the concept by the West to identify elements of other religions as salvation.

1 *Pre-Christian backgrounds*

The modern West owes its traditional concept of salvation to the Mediterranean world of antiquity. The word 'salvation' is of Latin derivation. To the ancient Romans, the noun *salūs* designated the condition of anyone or anything who was *salvus*, that is, intact. A person could be *salvus*, in good health, as the expression *salvus sīs*, 'may you be well', testifies. The greeting *salvē* likewise expresses such a wish. To voice such a wish was 'to speak health', *salūtem dīcere*. But things as well as persons could be *salvum*, particularly the institutions of law.

To the ancient Romans such a condition was not without its religious implications, even if in conversational formulae the word *salvus* became routine in a manner analogous to 'Bless you' after a sneeze in today's English. The idea of wholeness or safety was personified as a goddess, Salūs, 'the giver of health'.[1]

In the history of the Latin language, the word *salūs* is an example

1 Macrobius, *Saturnalia* I: 16, 8.

of a word with old religious connotations which passed into daily language, and was then taken up in the usage of the Christian Church, which gave a new religious sense to it.[2] The verb *salvāre*, 'to save', and the nouns *salvātor*, 'saviour', and *salvātiō*, 'salvation', enter after the classical literature, appearing in Christian Latin by the time of Augustine. Thus, while the old religious sense of the Latin *salūs* as health and good fortune became secularised in a variety of words for salutation and greeting, a new religious sense of *salūs* as a transcendence of man's condition came into play in a number of words for salvation in Christian Latin.[3]

Though our word itself is of Latin derivation, it was employed in the early Christian era to express ideas which had been derived from Semitic, Hellenistic and Iranian sources.

Semitic. Much of the West's sense of salvation can be seen as rooted in the religious literature of ancient Israel. The Old Testament refers to a variety of situations in which life or safety is threatened, and in which God is either thanked for deliverance received or petitioned for deliverance still hoped for.[4]

The principal Hebrew root which figures in Scripture with a meaning 'to save' is *yšʿ*. The etymological meaning of this root involves breadth or spaciousness, hence ease or lack of constraint. Many of the most striking contexts of 'salvation' in the Old Testament imply an escape from, or a victory over, a military enemy. The well known Song of Moses in Exod. 15 describes the escape of the Israelites from Egypt in these terms:

> I will sing to [Yahweh], for he has triumphed gloriously;
> The horse and his rider he has thrown into the sea.

2 Ernout and Meillet, *Dictionnaire étymologique de la langue latine*, fourth edition (1959), s.v. '*saluus, -a, um*', pp. 591–2. The authors, on p. 592, compare the development of a new religious sense with the history of the word *fidēs*. See also Walde, *Lateinisches etymologisches Wörterbuch*, ed. Hofmann, third edition (1938–54), s.v. '*salvus*', pp. 472–3.

3 This contrast between salutation and salvation persists in European vocabularies derived from Latin, whereas in German *Heil* retains the whole range of meanings. The senses of *Heil* will be mentioned *à propos* of G. van der Leeuw in the third portion of this essay.

4 Hirsch, 'Salvation', in *The Jewish Encyclopedia* (1901–6), X, pp. 663–4; Verghese, 'Salvation: the meanings of a biblical word', *International Review of Missions* LVII (1968), pp. 399–416; Westermann, 'Salvation and healing in the community: the Old Testament understanding', *International Review of Mission* LXI (1972), pp. 9–19.

[Yahweh] is my strength and my song,
And he has become my salvation. [Exod. 15: 1, 2; RSV]

The apparatus of war therefore makes an important contribution to biblical imagery: horses and chariots (Hab. 3: 8, where the Revised Standard Version translates *yᵉšûʿāh* as 'victory'), a shield of salvation (Ps. 18: 35), a helmet of salvation (Isa. 59: 17). Salvation is an enduring security, and God is identified with that security in the expressions:

He is a tower of salvation to his king
[One reading of 2 Sam. 22: 51]

He sets up salvation as walls and bulwarks [Isa. 26: 1]

Thou art . . . the rock of my salvation [Ps. 89: 26]

He only is my rock, and my salvation [Ps. 62: 2]

Thus a root involving openness has, paradoxically, come to be used of fortifications and enclosures; but the fortifications make possible the ultimate ease and freedom of the defenders.[5]

While salvation in the Old Testament may begin with deliverance from a military enemy, it does not end there. In certain passages in the Psalms and prophets it is associated with righteousness, which one may interpret as the deliverance of the people from the evils afflicting society.

My mouth will tell of thy righteous acts,
of thy deeds of salvation all the day [Ps. 71: 15]

He has clothed me with the garments of salvation,
he has covered me with the robe of righteousness
[Isa. 61: 10][6]

The call for immediate salvation or national deliverance appears to have become a liturgical formula during the Israelite monarchy and to have taken on a more distant messianic and eschatological character after its fall. *Hôšîʿāh-nā* ('save, we pray', Ps. 118: 25) is familiar in its untranslated form *hosanna* from the Jewish world of New Testament times.

The author of Isa. 45: 21, optimistic over the prospect of return from exile in Babylonia, sees God both as creator of the earth and as

5 Pedersen, *Israel: its Life and Culture* (1926–40), I–II, pp. 330–1, similarly compares the twin relationships of salvation to the perils from which one is delivered and the power of the deliverer: 'The positive: to acquire victory, is the all-important thing.'

6 On this subject see Smith, *The Bible Doctrine of Salvation: a Study of the Atonement* (1941).

its deliverer. Creation and salvation are two parts of the same order, as can be seen also in the celebrated picture of Yahweh as the slayer of the primeval monster of Semitic mythology:

> Yet God my king is from of old, working salvation in the midst of the earth.
> Thou didst divide the sea by thy might; thou didst break the heads of the dragons on the waters.
> Thou didst crush the heads of Leviathan. [Ps. 74: 12–14]

While salvation in the history of Israel is a victory of God's moral order to his people, 'salvation' in the context of the creation of the world appears as a victory of order over chaos.

Hellenistic. The Greek verb *sōzein*, together with its noun forms *sōtēria* and *sōtērion*, is the translation equivalent for the Hebrew scriptures' uses of *yšʿ* which we have just characterised. But a number of other Hebrew words are also rendered by the Greek *sōzein*, accounting for nearly 40 per cent of the instances of *sōzein* and its derivatives in the Septuagint. These other Hebrew roots include: *mlṭ*, 'to deliver'; *nṣl*, 'to rescue'; *plṭ*, 'to escape'; *śrd*, 'to survive'; *ḥyh*, 'to keep alive'; and *ʿzr*, 'to help'.[7] If the old familiar saying 'The Greeks had a word for it' is intended to mean that for each subtle nuance of meaning Greek had a different vocabulary item, then on the subject of salvation that saying does not hold; for the contribution of the Greek *sōzein* appears to have been the reverse: the fusion of a number of subtle nuances of escape and deliverance which the Hebrew of the Old Testament had already associated with Yahweh.

Well before that Alexandrian translation of the Old Testament, however, the Greek *sōzein* was used of divine action or influence. Zeus was often referred to as *sōtēr*, saviour, as was also Korē, the grain maiden, daughter of Demeter.[8]

As in the case of the Old Testament world, the perils from which one might be saved were often quite specific threats of illness, military danger or oppression. Civic festivals called *sōtēria* were sacrificial observances petitioning or commemorating the deliverance of the community from a major threat. Perhaps the prototype of such festivals was the Eleutheria, quinquennial games at Plataea dedicated to Zeus

7 Siedl, 'Salvation', in *Bauer Encyclopedia of Biblical Theology*, ed. Bauer, III (1970), pp. 807–8.

8 Rose, 'Soter, Soteira', in *The Oxford Classical Dictionary*, ed. Hammond and Scullard, second edition (1970), p. 1005. For Zeus, Rose cites Xenophon, *Anabasis* I: 8, 16, and for Korē, Aristophanes, *Frogs*, 379.

Eleutherios in honour of the warriors who had fallen in battle against the Achaemenid Persians there in 479 B.C. As the number of festivals of this sort increased during Hellenistic times, some were named after military leaders, such as the Diogeneia at Athens, about 229 B.C. At least sixteen festivals came to be called *sōtēria* (festival of deliverance), of which the best documented is the *sōteria* at Delphi, held to commemorate the defeat of the Celtic invaders by the Aetolians in 279–278 B.C.[9]

Just how strong a religious element such festivals may be said to have preserved is a matter for evaluation; both the event of deliverance and the celebration of it can be seen as political. The Hellenistic world also witnessed a claim of divinity by kings—Alexander and his successors—which, while claiming the religious support of Near Eastern traditions familiar to their Egyptian and Persian subjects, must surely have been political in their intent.[10] In Macedonia, Antigonus III, who ruled in 229–221 B.C., was called Dōson, 'the one who will give', but also Euergetēs, 'benefactor', during his lifetime and Sōtēr, 'saviour', after his death. The title *Sōtēr* was more common; in Egypt both Ptolemy I (305–283 B.C.) and Ptolemy VIII (116–108 B.C.) were styled *Sōtēr* during their reigns, as in Syria were Antiochus I (280–261 B.C.) and Seleucus III (226–223 B.C.) likewise. In Asia Minor, Attalus I of Pergamum took the title of king and received the surname Sōtēr after defeating the Galatians in 230 B.C. In Smyrna and Alabdana in the early second century B.C. the majesty of Rome (personified as a goddess) was worshipped for salvation, which was a deliverance from the Seleucid ruler Antiochus III.

Hellenistic ideas of salvation may be traced in the personal as well as in the political realm. That the salvation preached by the early Christians, to whom we shall return presently, was a deliverance not from a specific political condition of bondage to Rome but from the human condition of bondage to selfishness, sin and death leads historians of philosophy and religion to look for similar messages in other cults and teachings of the Roman imperial world. Hans Jonas, for example, speaking of the 'Oriental wave' in the Hellenistic world

9 Nilsson, *A History of Greek Religion*, second edition (1952), pp. 257–8; *The Oxford Classical Dictionary*, second edition (1970), s.v. 'Soteria', p. 1005. On a related topic: Becher, 'Antike Heilgötter und die römische Staatsreligion', *Philologus* CXIV (1970), pp. 211–55.

10 Tarn, *Hellenistic Civilisation*, third edition (1952), pp. 49–55; Dornseiff, 'Sōtēr', *Paulys Real-Encyclopädie der classischen Altertumswissenschaft*, ed. Wissowa (1894–1967), II: 5, cols. 1211–21.

(meaning Alexandrian Jewish philosophy, Babylonian astrology and magic, the Eastern mystery cults, and transcendental philosophies such as neo-Pythagoreanism and neo-Platonism), says, 'all these currents have in some way to do with *salvation*: the general religion of the period is a religion of salvation'.[11]

The Gnostics, heirs to this 'Oriental wave' in the second and third centuries A.D., tended to interpret Christian teaching as the myth of a primal heavenly man or divine redeemer who comes to earth to redeem mankind from its entrapment in the material world.[12] The world itself they viewed as evil, the result of the original fall of the godhead through demonic temptation or conflict; the task of the believer was to extricate himself from worldly existence through the *gnosis* or saving knowledge imparted by the redeemer. The salvation of mankind consisted, for the Gnostics, in the perfection of fallen man to the state of existence before the Fall.

Iranian. The pattern of the Gnostic redeemer figure leads us to an area of both fascination and frustration in history-of-religions research: the extent to which elements from Iran figure along with the Semitic and Hellenistic in the formation of Christendom's notion of salvation. Scholarship has for a century been willing to consider as a hypothesis the influence of Iran on the religion either of post-exilic Israel or of the Hellenistic world.[13] It is a plausible enough hypothesis, given the contiguity of these cultures in time and space; but the frustration is that from the fragmentary records of ancient Iran not enough evidence has yet come to light to rule out the also plausible hypothesis that Jewish and Christian ideas of salvation developed internally from the relatively well documented Hebrew biblical views.[14]

We lack many of the specific details of vocabulary correspondence and the like (apart from *pairidaēza*, 'pleasant garden', whence Greek

11 Jonas, *The Gnostic Religion: the Message of the Alien God and the Beginnings o, Christianity*, second edition (1963), p. 31; italics his.

12 For an introduction to relationships between Gnostic teachings and the New Testament, see Richardson, 'Salvation, Savior', in *The Interpreter's Dictionary of the Bible* IV, ed. Buttrick (1962), pp. 168–81; Grant, *Gnosticism and Early Christianity* (1959).

13 The problem is reviewed by Winston, 'The Iranian component in the Bible, Apocrypha and Qumran: a review of the evidence', *History of Religions* V (1965–6), pp. 183–216.

14 Glasson, *Greek Influence in Jewish Eschatology*, SPCK Biblical Monographs, I (1961).

paradeisos, 'paradise', and *razah*, 'secret', comparable with Semitic *rāz*, there is hardly anything suggestive) which would be convincing proof of a common source. In their absence, it is chiefly general features on which a case for Iran's contribution to the West must be built: Iran offers an eschatology, with a judgment and a future life; it offers a view of the struggle between good and evil, and an angelology and demonology. To the extent that our idea of salvation is not simply the escape from particular physical and political perils but rather an escape from built-in limitations of the human condition, it parallels our picture of the Zoroastrian ethic and eschatology in general. That eschatology is recorded in sources of varying date, some as late as the ninth century A.D., but it may be surmised that many of its features were in circulation by late Achaemenid and Parthian times contemporary with the Hellenistic world. Salvation, from the inception of Zoroastrianism as we know it, is the future reward of the righteous. But the correspondences with the West are fairly unspecific; amid them there is simply some final conflict, some last judgment, some ultimate reward of salvation for the righteous.

It may be useful to ask not whether ancient Iran offered to the West a conception of salvation in general but whether it said anything specific about an individual figure as saviour or redeemer. In this case one can see in Zoroastrian teachings, particularly in the Pahlavi literature, a fairly well developed doctrine of a saviour figure, Sōšyant, 'he who brings benefits'. Sōšyant—who would be born of a virgin of the preserved seed of Zoroaster before the end of the world—would restore the state of living beings in the world and smite the demons, resurrect the dead, and mete out the final judgment, thus bringing about the return of the primeval paradise and the condition of life as it existed at the beginning.[15] I know of no other single redeemer in Greek or Jewish literature prior to the New Testament for whom quite this list of claims is made.

The Iranian case is not closed. Many problems remain as regards whether such saviour imagery actually influenced the very similar assemblage of thought which Christianity made from Hellenistic and Jewish sources. We may never be able to assign a precise time or place to an Iranian contact, though the Parthian era seems particularly plausible. But one thing is clear: the above features of Iranian development

15 These points follow the important article of J. R. Hinnells, 'Zoroastrian saviour imagery and its influence on the New Testament', *Numen* XVI (1969), pp. 161–85.

of a saviour figure were compatible with the type of portrayal which the early Christians sought to provide for the salvation offered in Jesus, including a new world order, a new creation, a new condition of existence for man.

2 *Christian usage*

The streams of Semitic, Greek and Iranian usage converge in the New Testament, where the notion of salvation is indeed central.[16] During the lifetime of Jesus it must have been the profound expectation of his followers that Yahweh's salvation was at hand in a quite specific political and possibly military sense. The New Testament's understanding of salvation springs from those moments in time (at the latest, not long after the crucifixion of Jesus) when the early Christians came to see in the self-sacrificing life of Jesus the fulfilment of the more individual and eschatological aspects of Jewish expectations of the time.

In the New Testament epistles, which provide evidence of an early stage of Christian thought, there is already ample reference to Jesus as saviour. Particularly in Titus and 2 Peter the expression 'the Lord and Saviour Jesus Christ' becomes a recurring formula. Salvation becomes the destiny of the believer, which in the thought of Paul is obtained 'in Christ Jesus' (e.g. 2 Tim. 2: 10). Salvation, in the preaching of the early Church, was becoming a doctrine.[17]

It is surprising how little, in comparison with the rest of the New Testament, the Gospels use the actual words *sōtēr*, 'saviour', and *sōtēria*, *sōtērion*, 'salvation'. The Gospels are, after all, interpretative biographies, written from the perspective of the early Christian preaching of Jesus as saviour. The angels announce to the shepherds in Luke 2: 11 that a saviour has been born in Bethlehem, but otherwise it is chiefly in John's theological account that the Messiah is saviour (John 4: 42) and that the world through him is saved (John 3:17). And yet the Gospels, though they mention the word salvation less

16 For an extensive discussion governing many aspects of the subject, see Foerster and Fohrer, 'Sōzō, sōtēria, sōtēr, sōtērios', in *Theological Dictionary of the New Testament*, ed. Kittel and Friedrich (1964–), VII, pp. 965–1024. Also important is Nock, 'Early gentile Christianity and its Hellenistic background', in *Essays on the Trinity and the Incarnation by Members of the Anglican Community*, ed. Rawlinson (1928), pp. 53–156.

17 Stanley, 'The conception of salvation in primitive Christian preaching', *Catholic Biblical Quarterly* XVIII (1956), pp. 231–54; *id.*, *Christ's Resurrection in Pauline Soteriology*, Analecta Biblica, 13 (1961).

explicitly than the epistles, actually represent a stage of development in which additional themes are associated with the *kērygma* ('preaching') of the early apostles. What the synoptic Gospels contribute in their design is a more complex theology of the death of Christ for man's sins, a use of the miracle stories of Jesus' ministry in Galilee as evidence of his saving power, and a treatment of Jesus' birth as the incarnation of a saviour. This trend, implicit in the synoptic Gospels' treatment of narrative detail, is developed in John's Gospel into a full theology of the present and ultimate saving work of Jesus.[18]

However much today we may be tempted to view such a soteriology as but one of the possibilities open to the ancient world, reflection on the meaning of salvation as a Christian concept for more than a millennium between Constantine and the Enlightenment will lead one to see that the dominant question of what we may call classical Christendom in that period is not how many paths to salvation there may be but how the individual can travel the one path. The question 'What must I do to be saved?' is a question which figures most importantly in Christian discussions of religion throughout the tradition's history. If one were to be saved, of course, it would be salvation through Christ.[19]

The modern world sees in the proposition 'Outside the Church there is no salvation' a rejection of other religions, as though Christianity's concerns had always been competitive, as they were at the end of the second century, when Origen of Alexandria employed the phrase. It might now seem that the Christian community, surrounded by the pagan cults of Rome at its inception, has had more or less consistently ever since to compete with non-Christian promises of relief for man's condition. It has not been so very long in the European West, however, since that proposition 'Outside the Church there is no salvation' would generate not an inter-religious but an intra-Christian discussion: whether salvation in Christ was available to those who, as a result of the Protestant Reformation, had broken with the authority of the Church in Rome.

The discussion of salvation was at the very centre of Reformation

18 Stanley, 'The conception of salvation in the synoptic Gospels', *Catholic Biblical Quarterly* XVIII (1956), pp. 345–63; Lesquivit and Grelot, 'Salvation, in *Dictionary of Biblical Theology*, ed. Léon-Dufour (1967), pp. 457–61.

19 A representative discussion in this area is Lafon, *Essai sur la signification du salut* (1964). See also Borovy, 'What is salvation? An Orthodox statement', *International Review of Mission* LXI (1972), pp. 29–45, where individual personal salvation is grounded in an ontological universal salvation through Christ.

theology. To be sure, earlier ages of Christendom had not ignored it, for the delights of the blessed and the torments of the damned had been spelled out by medieval Christians in painstaking and often vivid detail. But for Martin Luther the compelling issue was his certainty of personal, individual salvation. In his view, to achieve salvation man must become aware that God, in his grace and justice, had already given it to him. Man's works do not effect salvation, God's do; man is asked to perform an act not of righteousness but of faith.

In a sense Luther represents the middle of a spectrum of Protestant thinking concerning salvation. Some have reasoned about what it is in God's power to do, while others have reported on the feeling of what God has done for them. The Calvinist tradition in Protestantism focuses more attention on a scripturally based discussion of the nature and character of God; salvation is seen as God's act, and an affirmation of God's power to damn as well as to save is one of the corollaries which follow from an emphasis on God as sovereign.[20] In the other direction, the Wesleyan, Quaker and Pentecostal emphases in Protestantism focus more attention than did Luther on the nature and character of man's experience; salvation is seen as the content of an often vivid personal awareness. In recent years of *rapprochement* between Protestant and Catholic Christianity there have been attempts to demonstrate points in common between the Reformation and medieval theologians, including Aquinas on the subject of man's confidence in a hope of salvation.[21] Catholic Christianity, too, manifests a spectrum in which the speculative thinkers may be ranged at one end and the intensely devotional emphases at the other. But all bands of the spectrum, in both its Catholic and its Protestant forms, trace their roots to Paul and Augustine.

While Christianity's principal controversy concerning salvation—*viz.* the Reformation discussion of the individual believer's certainty of it—dealt with the means to salvation, Christianity has also had a variety of things to say about the content of salvation. These may be grouped under several heads.

Paradise. Part of salvation is the victory over death. In a sense all religions contribute an answer to the question of what happens to the

20 See, for example, Warfield, *The Plan of Salvation* (c. 1915; reprinted 1966); Bloesch, *The Christian Life and Salvation* (1967).

21 Pfurtner, *Luther and Aquinas: a Conversation* (1964), also published as *Luther and Aquinas on Salvation* (1965).

individual personality upon death. It may be recycled in another birth; it may be preserved in the identity and memory of posterity; or, as in Christianity, it may enter into a realm of comfort and fulfilment. To be saved, for the traditional Christian, is in its simplest terms to be saved for heaven and to be saved from hell.

Redemption. Part of salvation is the victory over sin and evil. In a sense all religions provide a code of ritual or moral conduct and specify punishments for its infraction. What the status of responsibility for wrongdoing is will vary from one tradition to another, but it is pretty much the general consensus that nobody is perfect. Pure selfishness may be well-nigh universally wicked in religions, and in any event it is for several the principal problem with the human condition. In Christianity the power of evil, both in its individual form of personal selfishness and in its cosmic form of demonic or satanic conflict with the purposes of God, is seen as vanquished through Christ's self-giving as an atoning sacrifice.[22]

History. Part of salvation is the victory over purposelessness. All religions offer at least some part of an answer to the question 'Why am I?' or 'Why am I here?'. The Christian tradition, like the pattern of Jewish apocalyptic before it, is eschatological; it builds the future on the model of the past, and sees the end as a reflection of the beginning. God is credited with the creation of the world, and with a sequence of saving acts in the biblical interpretation of history; likewise he is expected to continue to make his will felt in human history and to sum the whole thing up in the end of the world. Man's purpose, in the light of this overall divine design, is to discern the will of God in the course of events and to participate with God in bringing about the ultimate goal of salvation.[23]

3 *Salvation as a generic concept*

'Salvation' as a term for man's fulfilment has migrated from Western Christendom's religion into the description of various themes in

22 A general discussion, with extensive references to theological literature, will be found in Rahner *et al.*, 'Salvation', in *Sacramentum Mundi: an Encyclopedia of Theology* v, ed. Rahner (1970), pp. 405–38. See also *The Theology of the Atonement: Readings in Soteriology*, ed. Sheets (1967).

23 Cullmann, *Salvation in History* (1967); Rust, *Salvation History: a Biblical Interpretation* (1962); *Mysterium Salutis, Grundriss heilsgeschichtlicher Dogmatik*, ed. Feiner and Löhrer (1965), especially vol. I.

modern Western philosophy, and in other religions. In most cases it implies man's mastery over, or reconciliation to, the limitations of his condition.

In philosophy the term seems particularly to describe certain nineteenth century positions, in contrast perhaps to the description of the goal of a number of ancient teachings (particularly the post-Socratic ethical schools) as 'happiness'. For Schopenhauer salvation is deliverance from the sequence of unfulfilled wishes, from the restless, unhappy life of the average person, through an absorption of our self-interest into aesthetic, ascetic or other self-denying efforts. For Freud, likewise, salvation consisted in facing up to the illusory and futile character of the self, its wishes and strivings. Freud offers a stark self-knowledge of our own nature and thus a deliverance from our unconscious anxieties. These are forms of individual salvation; for other modern philosophers salvation has been corporate. In the thought of the Utilitarians, or of Positivism, salvation resides in the improving of the sum total of society, a deliverance of society at large from ignorance as well as from the consequence of individual selfishness. A social goal is present also in the system of Marxism; here, salvation is a rational ordering of inter-personal relationships towards the ideal of material social benefit.[24]

If 'salvation' as a term seems less applicable to twentieth century philosophy it may be because of the twin directions which much twentieth century philosophy has taken: logical analysis, and the movement of existentialism and phenomenology. In each of these, the notion of a value which transcends the self seems less present: logical analysis furnishes little ground to suggest that a basis of knowledge transcends the self, while existentialism does little to suggest that any basis of value transcends the self. From the inappropriateness of the word 'salvation' in the context of these two lines of thought we can be reminded that part of the West's central conception of salvation is the transcendence of the limitations of the self.

We move next to the subject of salvation as a category for the description by the Christian West of religious teachings outside its own scheme of salvation. If, for Christendom, salvation is the accomplish-

24 A recent theological review of salvation themes in modern philosophy and literature is provided by Padovano, *American Culture and the Quest for Christ* (1970). See also De Ropp, *Science and Salvation: a Scientific Appraisal of Religion's Central Theme* (1962); Moeller, *Man and Salvation in Literature* (1970); Barnes, 'Literature as salvation in the work of Jean Paul Sartre', *Proceedings of the American Catholic Philosophical Association* XXXIX (1968), pp. 53–68.

ment of Christ for the faithful, what reference can the term have for the destiny or experience of anyone else?

This question was a fairly immediate one for the early Church Fathers, in as much as the New Testament was new indeed from their perspective in history. To the intellectual, exclusiveness could be a liability; the Fathers' task was to explain how men living in past centuries, including much-admired pagans of the recent as well as the distant past, might be held accountable for faith in the Gospel. One of the favourite patristic authorities for an answer to this question was Paul's epistle to the Romans, 1: 20: 'Ever since the creation of the world his invisible nature, namely, his eternal power and deity, has been clearly perceived in the things that have been made.' By this token, men other than God's elect might share in his plan of salvation.

With the fourth century establishment of Christianity and the Christianisation of Mediterranean civilisation, the exclusiveness of the Church's claim on salvation shifted to being an asset in apologetics and doctrine. Augustine, in arguing against Pelagius, could make much of the role of the Church as mediator both of man's faith and of God's grace, both of which were held essential for salvation. The non-Christian world receded into the past and became less and less of a problem; when Islam arose, it could be handled within Christian terms as an explicit rejection of Christianity—a heresy. Denying Christian faith, the Muslims had denied themselves God's salvation. The problem of the pagan to whom the Gospel had not been preached did not recur until Europe's voyages of discovery and trade, when previously unknown populations in America, Africa and Asia were discovered; but by this time Catholic theology had developed the notions of invincible ignorance, and of *in voto* (implicit) faith in Christ which would be sufficient for the salvation of the heathen on whose ears the Gospel had not fallen.[25] The Protestant reformers were actually much more ready than the Catholic theologians to think of pagans as having been explicitly denied salvation.

For Christian theology, in effect, salvation is not a comparative category at all, but a unique one. The Christian assertion that non-Christians (at least those in contact with Christians) do not have it implies, in effect, that there is nothing non-Christian describable by the word 'salvation'.[26]

25 Eminyan, 'Salvation, necessity of the Church for', *New Catholic Encyclopedia* (1967) XII, pp. 995–7.

26 Limitations of space do not permit us to examine here the status (in logic) of

Theologians and missionaries discuss salvation largely within the circle of individual and corporate Christian experience. For a type of theological position which for convenience I shall call orthodoxy, salvation is so uniquely Christian that it is hardly worth one's effort to look for instances of it in religions other than the Christian; indeed, for the Barthian statement of this view, Christianity is not a religion at all but true faith—the gift of God, different from 'the religions', which are the attempts of man. A view which for convenience I shall call liberalism is perfectly willing to see Christianity as one of the religions; comparable, indeed, but the victor in any comparison. Such was the bias of comparative-religion efforts, especially two and three generations ago.

The bias need not be blatant. An interesting example is the book *Enlightenment and Salvation*, by R. D. M. Shaw, an Anglican professor of Old Testament studies in Tokyo. Shaw's review of the religions groups them into two categories: the Hindu, Buddhist, Confucian and Shintō religions of discovery, knowledge and enlightenment; and the Jewish, Christian and Muslim religions of revelation, personal relationship and salvation. For the Eastern group, salvation amounts to enlightenment; for the Western, enlightenment amounts to salvation.[27] Shaw is at pains to indicate the force and attractiveness of each approach. But he is also at pains to show how Christianity, though being rooted in the tradition of intuitive revelation, incorporated into itself elements of the way of intellectual discovery, thus having more to offer mankind than at least some of its rivals. Shaw's attitudes may have been liberal for his day, sympathetically receptive to the potentialities of other religions, but he does not avoid his preference for Christianity before he has finished.

Similar positions continue to be voiced, albeit hesitantly, in Protestant ecumenical circles today. The World Council of Churches' Commission on World Mission and Evangelism addressed the theme 'Salvation today' in preparation for its 1972 meeting.[28] Discussing it,

salvation as a set with only one member in assertions of this sort. For a treatment of a similar question—whether mention of a god in another religion contravenes the assertion that there is only one god—see Durrant, 'Professor Geach and the gods of the heathen', *Religious Studies* VII (1971), pp. 227–31.

27 Shaw, *Enlightenment and Salvation* (1930), pp. 178–9.

28 Samartha, 'The quest for salvation and the dialogue between religions', *International Review of Missions* LVII (1968), pp. 424–32; de Silva, 'Good news of salvation to the Buddhists', *ibid.*, 448–58.

Thomas Wieser writes, 'While the ancient phrase "outside the Church there is no salvation" is today seldom expicitly defended, it tends nevertheless to divide those for whom the Church is the exclusive bearer of the message of salvation in Word and Sacrament from those for whom . . . the universal significance of salvation in Christ becomes manifest in many situations.' Wieser's own conclusion is that 'the Church can at best be one of the groups manifesting salvation today'.[29] But, significantly, the Christian understanding of salvation seems to remain for him the norm by which to decide whether anything else in another religion can be salvation at all.

The rise of the modern comparative study of religion, since the middle of the nineteenth century, has been characterised by an emphasis on the human character of religion. 'Religion' in general is a virtually universal phenomenon, a constant of culture, even if there may be no specific detail which all the religions, on examination, can be said to manifest. But if anything is common to all the religions, it is man himself, and his limited and uncertain condition. Whereas the comparative study of religion may see salvation in specific primitive and ancient contexts as deliverance from particular perils or uncertainties, the quest for salvation at its most general is seen as the quest for relief from the human condition.[30]

For the purposes of this discussion I wish to divide the history of comparative religion since 1850 into two principal periods or phases: the period prior to about 1915, and the period since. In large measure, the primary growth of the field up to World War I was antithetical to Christian theology and proceeded from humanistic assumptions. Religion was a product of human culture, and to be explained as a mechanism for the satisfaction of man's psychic or social needs. By choosing the date of 1915 I do not mean to imply that the momentum of this approach was dissipated overnight; in social scientific theories of religion it has continued actively to the present, and in the history-of-religions school's approach to Christian origins it was influential through the 1920s. But what emerged in the years after World War I

29 Wieser, 'The experience of salvation today', *International Review of Mission* LX (1971), pp. 382–94, especially p. 383. See also Takenaka, 'Salvation in the Japanese context', *International Review of Missions* LXI (1972), pp. 79–89, especially p. 87, where Takenaka observes, with disapproval, 'Japanese easily adopt Western Christianity as one of the ways of life, rather than as the definitive way of life.'

30 Brandon, Smith and Smart, 'Salvation', in *A Dictionary of Comparative Religion*, ed. Brandon (1970), pp. 552–3.

to alter the field, as seen from today's perspective, was a cluster of religious approaches to the nature of religion, in which the content of religion was seen not simply as the product of human culture but as a response to a transcendent power. The phenomenology of religion, for example, has as an enterprise sought to delineate the general patterns of man's response; and while suspending endorsement of any religion as compared with another in particular, it has endorsed religion in general as compared with secularity.

Having characterised the above two phases of modern comparative religion, I wish now to suggest that reflection on 'salvation' as a general topic in comparative religion has been more at home in the second phase than the first. I do not find, looking at work in comparative religion published before the first world war, that reflection on 'salvation' played as large a part as I had at first been tempted to suspect. It does not seem to figure as a central term in the great late nineteenth century ethnological theories of religion—in the manner, for example, in which 'myth' or 'magic' or 'spirits' appear. My suspicion is that in the anti-theological approach of the time 'salvation' was a term with too much theological baggage to be pressed into service. Durkheim in 1912 could speak of 'the sacred', and draw on Western Christendom's sense of this word; but to speak of 'the sacred' was to use in noun form, as a category, a concept which in Christian theology had been adjectival only, and one which did not therefore as automatically suggest Christian doctrine.[31] To speak of salvation, on the other hand, would be to employ a concept which had been substantive in Christianity, and central to it, and exhaustively discussed by it, from its inception. That this should be the situation is borne out in Hastings's monumental *Encyclopaedia of Religion and Ethics*, where there is no general article on salvation, in contrast, for example, with the presence of an important general article on 'holiness'. In the *Encyclopaedia*, salvation receives a variety of rather unrelated short treatments for several of the religions, and a long article on salvation in Christianity which, if a monument to anything at all, demonstrates the insularity of the traditional Christian understanding of salvation.[32]

In our second half-century of modern comparative religion, since

31 I have discussed the emergence of 'the sacred' as a noun and a category in 'The Holy (the Sacred)', in *Dictionary of the History of Ideas*, ed. Wiener (forthcoming).

32 Kilpatrick, 'Salvation (Christian)', in *Encyclopaedia of Religion and Ethics*, ed. Hastings (1908–26), XI, pp. 110–31.

World War I, it is possible to discern movement towards the use of salvation as a comparative category.[33] One important aspect of this movement was the history-of-religions school, especially as it related to New Testament studies: this school drew heavily on the presence of saviour figures and their cults in the Hellenistic world for parallels with (and, it was held, therefore, explanations of) the early Christian veneration of Jesus as saviour. By the end of the 1920s the term 'salvation religions' can be said to have become a category, and those with historical training in the religions of the ancient world, particularly the Hellenistic era, could ill afford to ignore salvation as a category in religion.[34] Thus, while the theological implications of the history-of-religions school's liberalism were viewed as threateningly secularist by some of the increasingly influential dialectical theologians, this school did nonetheless help to make a central place for the Christian concept 'salvation' in comparative studies.

Another aspect of the emergence of salvation as a comparative category was provided by the phenomenology of religion, whose status as not a secular but a religious theory of religion we have already mentioned. The sympathetic-observer stance of the phenomenologist, willing to let the phenomenon speak to him on its own terms but then confident to describe the phenomenon in *his* own terms, means that Christian theological terminology would be used by a Christian phenomenologist in a manner which consciously left open the possibility of making religious affirmations without consciously restricting such affirmations to Christian ones. Thus Brede Kristensen could employ, in describing non-Christian phenomena, a range of traditional meanings of salvation: ritual purification, the sacrifice of a victim as saviour, the sun god as maintainer of the cosmic order, and the salvation of metaphysical insight.[35] And while Kristensen's work did not make

33 Examples include Parker, *The Idea of Salvation in the World's Religions* (1935); Braden, *Man's Quest for Salvation* (1941); *id.*, 'Salvation', in *Encyclopedia of Religion*, ed. Ferm (1945), pp. 682–4.

34 Wach, 'Erlösungsreligionen', in *Die Religion in Geschichte und Gegenwart, Handwörterbuch für Theologie und Religionswissenschaft*, ed. Gunkel, *et al.*, second edition (1927–32), II, cols. 285–6; Wach *et al.*, 'Erlösung', in *ibid.*, cols. 266–85; Kitagawa, '*Verstehen* and *Erlösung*: some remarks on Joachim Wach's work', *History of Religions* XI (1971–2), pp. 31–53, especially p. 45; see also Bammel *et al.*, 'Erlöser', 'Erlösung', 'Erlösungsreligionen', in *Die Religion in Geschichte und Gegenwart*, ed. Galling, third edition (1957–65), II, cols. 576–84, 584–99, 599–600.

35 Kristensen, *The Meaning of Religion: Lectures in the Phenomenology of Religion* (1960), pp. 446, 111, 69, 238.

salvation a central matter for discussion, Gerardus van der Leeuw's did; he associates salvation with beneficent power, saying, 'When felicity thus comes from without, from some potent situation, it is termed *Salvation* . . . Salvation therefore is Power, experienced as Good.' Capitalising on the semantic range of the German *Heil* (which covers salutation as well as salvation), van der Leeuw states that he wishes to imply 'such concepts as whole, complete, perfect, healthy, strong, vigorous, welfare, well-being, as contrasted with suffering and misery, and in some connections bliss, both earthly and heavenly'.[36] The category of salvation, as well as the category of salvation religions, is thus available for use.

In the past decade the more precise study of salvation as a comparative topic has been the focus of several corporate academic ventures. The Centre d'Étude des Religions in the University of Brussels focused during the 1960–1 session on the notion of salvation. These papers, published in 1962 under the title *Religions de salut*, push the geographical horizons of the subject to the western hemisphere and to China, the chronological horizons to ancient Egypt, and the intellectual horizons to Heidegger and Sartre.[37] Almost as wide a range emerged the following year in the *Festschrift* edited by S. G. F. Brandon for the seventy-fifth birthday of the late Professor E. O. James: *The Saviour God: Comparative Studies in the Concept of Salvation*.[38] In each of these cases the discussion of the overall category was implicit rather than explicit; the planners and organisers had set forth a useful category or rubric, with the collected papers introducing material from various sources and specialisms. In these collections salvation was not so much defined as illustrated; but the illustrations may be used as evidence for the kinds of definition the organisers had in mind, and as a corpus against which to test the accuracy and adequacy of any descriptive definition.

It is, in my view, worth mentioning that in both these volumes the concept of salvation is largely defined by the ancient world: the Hellenistic saviour cults, Semitic and Iranian eschatology, and early Christianity's fusion of these into the concept to which modern Chris-

36 Van der Leeuw, *Religion in Essence and Manifestation* (1938), p. 101; italics his.

37 Abel *et al.*, *Religions de salut*, Annales du Centre d'Étude des Religions, 2 (1962).

38 *The Saviour God: Comparative Studies in the Concept of Salvation presented to Edwin Oliver James . . . by Colleagues and Friends to Commemorate his Seventy-fifth Birthday*, ed. Brandon (1963).

tendom is heir. It is reasonable to expect that a scholar of the ancient world and early Christianity such as S. G. F. Brandon should be interested in a topic of this nature.

More recently, since the two volumes mentioned, the concept of salvation has received more explicit discussion. The 1967 study conference of the International Association for the History of Religions, attended in Jerusalem by S. G. F. Brandon among others, addressed the theme 'Types of redemption'. An informative review of that conference by U. M. Vesci makes the observation that redemption, as a means to salvation in which some form of sacrifice may play a particularly important part, was perceived as a concept which was particularly appropriate to Christianity. Various of the religions bordering the ancient Mediterranean were seen to have one or another of the Christian features, but the question was then raised whether religions from other culture areas manifest these features in a manner sufficient for anything in them to be spoken of as redemption.[39] Shintō, African and ancient Mexican religions have mythological figures who may share narrative details with the Christian saviour but who do not have the same salvific role; Hinduism and Buddhism, on the other hand, offer a deliverance or release from the human condition which may be spoken of as salvation but is not necessarily achieved through the mediation of a redeemer figure.[40] Even the role of the Messiah in Judaism and the Mahdi in Islam as restorers of the cosmic order does not seem to provide an analogue to Christianity's expectation of power for individual deliverance available to the believer.

In my judgment, salvation is still in the early stages of becoming a term with an adequate semantic range for comparative religion. We have begun to take into account the manner in which our concept has been shaped by particular circumstances in the West. We recognize that 'salvation' may be useful as a description of (for example) Hindu *mokṣa* only if the differences of *mokṣa* from the weight of Christian

39 Vesci, 'Man's salvation: the goal of all religions', *Journal of Ecumenical Studies* VII (1970), pp. 102–8.

40 In neo-Platonism salvation is also achieved by an impersonal principle: Armstrong, 'Salvation, Plotinian and Christian', *Downside Review* LXXV (1957), pp. 126–39. On Hindu and Buddhist equivalents to salvation, in addition to standard works, see von Glasenapp, *Immortality and Salvation in Indian Religions* (1963); Williams, 'Selflessness in the pattern of salvation', *Religious Studies* VII (1971), pp. 153–67; Joshi, 'Social perspective of Buddhist soteriology', *Religion and Society* XVIII (1971), No. 3, pp. 59–68.

impressions of salvation have a chance to appear.[41] Christianity may have blessed our efforts by giving currency and a connotation of urgency to the category, even if it has cursed them by treating it as filled. If the category remains susceptible of expansion, much may be accomplished through its use in the comparison of religions. And it is neither in the interest of the non-theological comparativist to restrict man's search for salvation, nor should it be in the interest of the theologically inclined to restrict the divine gift of it.

A description's integrity and usefulness are enhanced if its criteria are identified. Practitioners of the academic study of religion are in a particularly sensitive situation here, because of the sometimes conflicting appeals for sympathy and impartiality. It is now widely agreed that we should not show partiality towards one religion to the detriment of another; it is far less clear whether we should be advocates of religion, or religious faith, in general. In the times in which we live, we shall likely have occasion to express attitudes on the question of whether religious faith in general (as contrasted with faith in some specific religious tradition) is sufficient to 'save' twentieth or twenty-first century man. To answer this question would be to make a religious, not merely a descriptive, statement: a statement of faith, not a statement about faith. Comparative religion may now be in an 'identity crisis' because of the desire of many of its personnel to make statements which imply, or at least leave open, the possibility of faith. Are we obliged to speak of salvation as simply man's quest? To posit such an obligation is the legacy of nineteenth century comparative religion, when its conflict with Christian theology was clear. Or must we leave our description open to the possibility that salvation—any salvation—is God's act? To posit this obligation may entail maintaining a religious understanding of religion.

The situation which we face in the field today boils down to a basic dialectic of approaches to religion. Given the present backgrounds and allegiances of individual scholars, both the secular and the religious views of religion will be represented in our academic life for the foreseeable future. It is not my intention to assert that either view ought to prevail, for I believe that each of these two alternatives can be maintained with integrity. Depending on the context or audience, I and

41 A substantial Catholic phenomenological study which attempts this is Manthey, *Das Problem der Erlösung in den Religionen der Menschheit* (1964). [See also, in the present volume, Parrinder, 'The salvation of other men'—Eds.]

others have at different times spoken from the perspective of each approach. But I would contend nevertheless that an unconscious oscillation between the two approaches, mixing their assumptions in the *same* description, is untenable and indeed constitutes a major threat to the integrity of the discipline. This is why words rich in theological connotations, such as the word 'salvation', must be used with sophistication and care.

The day may be past when comparative religion treated all religions as false. The day is also past when comparison would successfully treat only one religion as true. We have yet to decide whether comparative religion must assert that all religions are in some sense true. The manner in which we conduct discussions touching on the applicability of the concept of salvation to the world's religions may be an indicator of the direction in which we tend to proceed.

4

James Barr

An aspect of salvation in the Old Testament

The question which I propose to discuss belongs to the field of the typology of religions. Within such a typology one might perhaps establish as one type of religion the religions within which salvation is central, in which therefore the structure of the religion is to a considerable extent built around concepts such as that of salvation or of a saviour. New Testament Christianity, for instance, belongs to such a type; Gnosticism or Manichaeism would be another agreed example. Some stages or aspects of Zoroastrianism furnish yet another illustration. But how far, we ask, is the religion of the Old Testament one which should be classified as a salvation religion? In what sense, if any, is salvation central to it? To what areas and strata within it does the interest in salvation belong? Is salvation structurally essential to it? The question, I submit, is one in which our late colleague Professor Brandon would have found much interest.

There is, however, no straight and simple way in which the question can be answered. It is interesting, perhaps, as a first approach to the collection of material, that the various modern *Theologies* of the Old Testament and *Religions* of ancient Israel, all of them works which in some degree or other have tried to disengage the essential underlying structure of Old Testament religion or theology, appear not to have taken salvation as one of their main organising concepts. This can be discerned from well known books, such as those of Eichrodt, Jacob, Vriezen, Rowley and von Rad among the *Theologies*, and those of Ringgren and Vriezen among the *Religions*. Naturally, in all these works terms like 'salvation' occur, but it does not appear to have been made a general organising concept. Perhaps the closest one comes to it is the central position sometimes assumed by the concept of *Heilsgeschichte*, often rendered in English as 'history of salvation'; but that does not seem to be quite the same thing. The one work among the genres mentioned which does make considerable use of salvation as an organising concept is the *Theology* written by L. Köhler.[1] This was, however, one of the earliest attempts at an Old Testament *Theology* in the modern sense of the word, and it can hardly be said to belong to the mainstream of modern scholarship in the matter. Moreover, Köhler's use of the categories of salvation and redemption formed one of the less happy aspects of his book. He was particularly embarrassed by cultic practices such as sacrifice, and saw them in very negative terms as human attempts at self-redemption or self-salvation[2] —a judgment which, one must feel, had its basis in later Christian ideas. In general, among the main currents of Old Testament scholarship in this century the concept of salvation—at least as expressed in just this way—has not been given central prominence in descriptions of the religion.

It may be profitable to look at the question by considering the relation between two things: on the one hand themes, stories and narratives the content of which appears to suggest salvation, deliverance, rescue and the like, and on the other hand the use of linguistic terms which themselves more or less mean 'save', 'deliver' and 'salvation'.[3] The mere collection of such words, and the semantic analysis of those thus found, are not in themselves decisive. Themes and images may speak of salvation even where the obvious surface terminology is lacking. Conversely, even when the surface terminology is present, the statistics of it do not necessarily give a picture of the inner structural relations of man and his salvation in the religion.

We may make a start with the observation that explicit salvation

1 Köhler, *Theologie des Alten Testaments* (1935; third and revised edition 1953); English translation, Koehler (name so spelt), *Old Testament Theology* (1957). Part III of the work is entitled 'Judgement and salvation'. Readers should be warned that the English translation is full of errors and misconstructions for most of which Köhler is not to blame.

2 See Köhler's chapter 52, 'Man's expedient for his own redemption: the cult', English translation, pp. 181–98.

3 On all this I would refer to the much more thorough study of J. F. A. Sawyer, at the time of writing shortly to be published as *Semantics in Biblical Research: New Methods of Defining Hebrew Words for Salvation* (1972). I have had the opportunity of consulting this work in its earlier stage as a Ph.D. thesis but was not able to have it at hand in the actual writing of this article. I apologise for points at which I trespass on Dr Sawyer's territory and for failure to give him credit at specific points where my argument may follow his. I would refer also to his two articles, 'What was a *mošiaʿ*?', *Vetus Testamentum* XV (1965), pp. 475–86, and 'Spaciousness', *Annual of the Swedish Theological Institute* VI (1968), pp. 20–34.

terminology is far from equally distributed in the Old Testament. For salvation of man by God, the most central and characteristic designation is that through the root morpheme *y-š-ʿ*, found in the corresponding verb and in the noun forms *yešaʿ*, *yᵉšuʿa* and *tᵉšuʿa*. In some parts of the Hebrew Bible, such as the Psalms, these terms are very frequent; the verb, for instance, appears over fifty times in this book. In the Pentateuch, on the other hand, the same term is strikingly uncommon. In the entirety of this quite central literature the verb *y-š-ʿ* occurs only a handful of times (hiphil in effect twice, Exod. 14: 30 and Deut. 20: 4; niphal also twice, Num. 10: 9 and Deut. 33: 29. Exod. 2: 17, being of Moses rescuing some girls from ill-treatment, is not quite a case in point). Of these cases most can probably be attributed to a rather late and stereotyped Deuteronomising phraseology; if this is so, then the use of the verb 'save' for salvation of men by God in the older Pentateuchal traditions is quite minimal. The noun *yᵉšuʿa* also appears rarely, thrice in all (Gen. 49: 18; Exod. 15: 2; Deut. 32: 15), and the other nouns not at all. Moreover, all these passages which use the noun are poetic passages, embedded in the Pentateuch but in genre belonging to the psalm literature; they are thus exceptions which prove the rule that in the main prose narrative of the Pentateuch the term is rare.

This sort of uneven distribution of terms over various strata of the Hebrew Bible is in fact nothing unfamiliar, and other instances have often been remarked. A good example is that of the term 'covenant' (*bᵉrit*). This is extremely frequent in the historical books but is sparsely represented in the prophets, especially the earlier strata of them. The interpretation of this has long been controversial. One school of opinion held that the covenant idea was a late innovation; more recently it has often been argued that, even if the *term* 'covenant' was lacking, the covenant idea was omnipresent; more recently opinion once again seems to be veering towards the view that, if the *term* is rarely used, that must have serious significance for the religious structure of the sources concerned. The case of covenant is in fact a good parallel to our own subject of salvation, for here also the question is that of the *structural* place of covenant in the religion. Many scholars have maintained that the covenant is in fact the structural principle of Old Testament religion—a position given its most imposing formulation by Eichrodt.[4] If the parallel is a valid one, then we may expect that

4 Eichrodt, *Theologie des Alten Testaments* (three volumes, 1933–9; revised edition, two volumes, 1957 and 1961); English translation, *Theology of the*

there will be *some* sort of relation between the use of explicit terms for salvation and the importance of the theme of salvation within the structure of Old Testament religion.

In proceeding farther from this point, we may give notice that matters of the etymology of *y-š-ʿ* will be ignored. It has been widely customary to hold that behind the Hebrew words the basic meaning 'width', 'spaciousness', lies (cf. Arabic *wasiʿa*, 'be wide'); but this connection, even if phonologically well based, must be judged to be semantically insignificant.[5] It remains true, however, that the group of Hebrew terms related to salvation contains a number of associations with 'enlargement', 'spaciousness', etc, as opposed to 'restriction', 'narrowness'. These words have been studied in this regard by Sawyer and I shall not return to the subject here. In any case, one would not claim that these 'spaciousness' terms constitute the central core of the salvation vocabulary.

When we turn to the other salvation terms which scholars would usually quote, the observation which we made about *y-š-ʿ* appears still to stand. Other salvation terms are also rare in the Pentateuch; or, if they are not formally rare, they are words which belong only partially or equivocally to the semantic field of divine salvation. Thus words like *m-l-ṭ* and *p-l-ṭ*, 'cause to escape; deliver', and even the very common *ʿ-z-r*, 'help', are rare or of negligible significance in the prose of the Pentateuch. To the Hebraist the fact that the verb *ʿ-z-r* does not occur at all in Pentateuchal prose is little short of astounding, and must have something to say about the stilistics of this literature.

Among other terms which one might consider there is *p-d-h*, traditionally 'redeem'. This word, however, is associated with one special sphere of religious action, namely the use of a substitute or of a monetary payment for the commutation of an offering; through this substitution the life of something which otherwise would be owed to God (and given to him through putting to death) is 'redeemed'. Though the word came to be used for the 'redemption' of man in a general sense, carrying associations with sacrificial commutation but in general coming close to 'salvation', in the Pentateuch this is still not generally so except for Deuteronomy. It is there only that this shift of usage is apparent, and indeed it is quite striking there (about six cases, of types such as Deut. 9: 26, 'your people . . . which you re-

Old Testament (two volumes, 1961 and 1967). See on this especially vol. 1, pp. 36–69, of the English edition.

5 See Sawyer, 'Spaciousness', p. 20.

deemed by your great power'). Otherwise in the Pentateuch *p-d-h* remains in the sphere of commutation and similar practices. We may at the same time mention *g-ʾ-l*, later widely used, in the salvation theology of Deutero-Isaiah, and elsewhere, of God as 'Redeemer'. In the Pentateuch this word is used quite considerably in the social institutions of 'redeeming' land, blood, losses to the family and the like; but of salvation of men by God it is used only very sparingly. In the basic prose narrative the only instance is Exod. 6: 6, 'I will redeem you with arm outstretched', NEB; Gen. 48: 16 is abnormal, and Exod. 15: 13 is in effect psalm literature.

The commonest term, in fact, which might be set alongside of *y-š-ʿ* is *n-ṣ-l* (*hiṣṣil*), and this word is indeed commonly used in salvation statements in Hebrew. But though it is so used, it is in many ways equivocal. It is used of 'removing', 'getting out of the way' all sorts of things, like cattle or riches, other than men. Correspondingly, its subject is quite often not God but some character in the story or even a casual passer-by; it is even used, negatively, to say that there is no deliverance *from* the actions of God (Deut. 32: 39).[6] Thus, though it is often used in contexts of salvation of men by God, it is far from univocal in this sense; and it is not surprising that no nominalisation of this verb, so as to produce a noun 'salvation', takes place, apart from the lone and inconsiderable instance in the late source Esther 4: 14 (*haṣṣala*: 'relief and deliverance for the Jews will appear from another quarter', NEB). Even in post-biblical times this did not become a general and usual term for salvation.[7] Though the morpheme *n-ṣ-l* is not uncommon in the Pentateuch, and though it is certainly much more frequent than *y-š-ʿ*, only a fairly small proportion of the cases (perhaps seven or eight) refer to God's saving of men; and of these no fewer than five are concentrated in one chapter, Exod. 18, where they appear in the conversation of Moses with his father-in-law Jethro. This frequent use of *n-ṣ-l* must be considered as a stylistic idiosyncrasy of this particular chapter, which has, of course, other obvious peculiarities. Typical instances of *n-ṣ-l* which remain, once this chapter has been set apart, are Exod. 3: 8 ('I have come down

6 Cf. Sawyer, 'Mošiaʿ', p. 479 and note 7; as he says, in contrast with *mošiaʿ* '*maṣṣil* does not invariably represent justice'.

7 Cf. Jastrow, *Dictionary* (1903), p. 363b. The instances there cited suggest that in rabbinic usage the sense is less 'salvation' and rather 'relief' (cf. the association at Esther 4: 14 with *rewaḥ*, whence NEB 'relief and deliverance', as quoted above), or else 'rescue' in the sense of life-saving, rescue from accidents or drowning, etc.

to rescue it from the hand of Egypt'), 6: 6 (where successive sentences have the verbs 'bring out', 'rescue' (*n-ṣ-l*) and 'redeem' (*g-ʾ-l*)). But, all in all, *n-ṣ-l* used of God's action towards men is still not common in the Pentateuch.

In general, then, the actions of God as reported in the Pentateuchal stage are not normally or definitively characterised by terms like 'save', 'deliver' or 'salvation'. It is much more common for them to be characterised in purely external or locomotive terms, such as 'he brought them out' (from Egypt).

This paucity of explicit salvation terminology in the Pentateuch stands in some contrast with the well evidenced narrative themes suggesting some sort of salvation or deliverance. Noah and his immediate family are saved from the flood because they have been instructed to build the ark; Lot and his daughters escape the destruction of Sodom; Abraham and Sarah escape from several dangerous situations with local potentates; by a divine intervention Isaac is miraculously saved from impending sacrifice; Joseph is repeatedly preserved when on the point of disaster; and the people of Israel, deeply oppressed in Egypt, are delivered. It seems, then, that narratives of salvation can and do exist without explicit salvation terminology. When these same narratives are cited in later times, for instance in the New Testament, the writers find it natural to epitomise them in salvation language (e.g. Noah, Heb. 11: 7; Lot, 2 Pet. 2: 7).

The contrast in terminology with the typical poetical (and generally non-narrative) literature like the Psalms is very striking. It is here that the central nouns for 'salvation', the group *yešaʿ* and *yᵉšuʿa*, are deeply rooted. Of the former there seem to be no cases at all in prose, and the great majority are in psalm-type texts. Of the latter there are few genuine instances in prose (we shall shortly in another connection mention cases like 1 Sam. 14: 45 and 2 Sam. 10: 11, where the word occurs in the context of a military success), and by far the greatest concentration is in the psalm literature, with the next significant block in Isaiah. Among the verbs the common form from *y-š-ʿ*, i.e. the hiphil *hošiaʿ*, is also strongly represented in the Psalms and similar poetic literature. This literature also has a strong representation of *n-ṣ-l*, while in the statistics of *p-l-ṭ*, hiph. 'make to escape', it has a quite overwhelming preponderance. It is, if we take the Pentateuch and the psalm literature as the points of contrast, clear that the latter rather than the former is the locus of salvation vocabulary. Much attention has been given in recent study to the fact that Hebrew poetical vocabulary (like that of some other comparable languages) has its own peculiar shapes and patterns; and not only this, but also in respect of subject-matter there is in Hebrew a divergence between the sort of things that are said in prose and those that are said in verse.[8]

We shall return to make some further observations about the terminology; but can we meanwhile form some kind of preliminary hypothesis about the facts as we have described them so far? First, we may suggest this: the presence of narrative themes concerned with some sort of deliverance does not in itself show that the religion of the Pentateuch was in structure a religion of salvation. This depends on the way in which the incidents reported are regarded, and the way in which they bear upon the relation between God and man. Basically, it would seem that the deliverances in the Pentateuch do not alter the relationship between the men saved and their God; on the contrary, they confirm and re-establish the relationship already existing. Noah was a righteous and blameless man, and therefore was instructed how he must avoid the destruction which fell upon all others. In Sodom, as the story emphasises, Lot was uniquely honest and decent. Abraham and Joseph were always in the right in all essential points; among the major figures of the patriarchal story the one who is set in a much more ambiguous light is Jacob; but he is not particularly depicted as the object of an act of 'salvation'. It is stated in the Exodus story that Israel are to *become* God's people and he to be their God (Exod. 6: 7; NEB has 'I will adopt you as my people, and I will become your God', in which the 'become' perhaps goes a little too far); but they were, expressly, his people already. The deliverance from Egypt is on the one hand a confirmation of this fact; on the other, it is a necessary step towards the realisation of purposes which God has for his people—the constitution of them on a special basis as a special people, the giving of the law, the start on the travels to the land they were to occupy. It is, as the Pentateuch sees it, in these matters, rather than in the act of deliverance itself, that the new step in their relation to God lies.

In other words, though the Pentateuch contains a number of notable acts of deliverance, and though some of these in some later stages came to be regarded as prime examples of 'salvation', the inner structure of

8 For observations on this, within the framework of comparative literary studies rather than technical Old Testament scholarship, and with reference to Auerbach's influential work *Mimesis* (1953), see Whallon, *Formula, Character and Context: Studies in Homeric, Old English and Old Testament Poetry* (1969), especially pp. 173–210.

the Pentateuch is not particularly that of a religion of salvation; it can be read otherwise. In particular, it can be read as the document of a religion of law.

Any religion in which 'salvation' is central must give some kind of specification of that from which one is to be saved. It is notorious that in the Pentateuch this is not done; and the fact has long been a source of embarrassment to theologies which have tried to find in the early chapters of Genesis a doctrine of 'sin' or of 'original sin'. Gen. 3 clearly indicates a disturbance in the relation between God and man and specifies that man has done what God forbade; but the disturbance is not defined as 'sin', nor indeed is it described by any of the numerous terms later found in the Old Testament and glossed as 'rebellion', 'wickedness', etc. After the crisis human life went on—contrary to the assertion of God, who had said that man would die in the day he ate of the tree, and in agreement with the words of the serpent, who had said that nothing of the kind would happen. Conditions of life, it is hinted, were in part higher (NEB: 'the man has become like one of us, knowing good and evil') and in part worse, with trouble to come on the agricultural, the domestic and the obstetric levels, plus *eventual* death. 'Sin' is not mentioned, nor is anything said about 'salvation'; the so-called *protevangelium* of Gen. 3: 15 is too vague for anything of this magnitude to be drawn from it.

As is well known, Gen. 3 comes from only one of the several sources used in the make-up of Genesis. The other main account of increasing trouble and deterioration, found in Gen. 6, talks of the amount of 'evil' in the world, but offers no 'salvation' from evil; for God decides to wipe out mankind, exempting only Noah and such others as did not partake in the prevailing evil. After the recovery of the world from the flood no attempt is made to express or conceptualise the ultimate evil from which one might need to have 'salvation'. Terms like 'sin' do occur, but (as is notably the case in Gen. 4: 7) are not clearly attached to any universal framework; and while in the Levitical code of sacrifice, ostensibly given in the Mosaic stage of revelation at Sinai, offerings for the removal of 'sin' are provided for, the 'sin' in question is mainly a ritual uncleanness, and there is no question of a 'salvation' from such 'sin' other than the sacrifice prescribed for it.

We cannot, however, go further without mentioning another area of the prose literature, other than the Pentateuch, in which some have looked for the basic locus of the salvation concept. This area is the military narratives of the historical books—the 'Former Prophets'—

the wars of the Judges against the oppressors of Israel, and to a lesser extent the later battles of the kings against the neighbouring peoples.[9] Here once again the material is of terminological interest. Here, for instance, the noun *yᵉšuʿa* (cf. above, p. 41) is sometimes found (*a*) in prose and (*b*) used with reference to military successes. Thus in 1 Sam. 14: 45 we hear of Jonathan, 'who has effected this great *yᵉšuʿa* in Israel' (NEB: 'who has won this great victory in Israel'; cf. below); and in 2 Sam. 10: 11 Joab makes plans with Abishai as follows: 'if the Aramaeans prove too strong for me, you must come to my relief [*yᵉšuʿa*]; and if the Ammonites prove too strong for you, then I will come to relieve [*lᵉhošiaʿ*] you' (NEB, modified by me). The 'Judges' of the book so named were notoriously not—or were not primarily, if at all—experts in jurisprudence; rather, they were men of war, and the term which is often applied to them in this respect is *mošiaʿ*, participle of this same verb, and said to mean 'deliverer' or 'saviour'. Such 'Judges' thus 'saved' Israel from the oppression of Ammonites or other foreigners; and this salvation came about, according to the Deuteronomic framework of the book, as soon as the Israelites ceased following other gods and cried out to their own true God for help.

It is possible, however, to exaggerate the degree to which terms of the root *y-š-ʿ* are truly anchored in this military background. It is true that the 'Judges' who acted as deliverers for Israel were called by the term *mošiaʿ* and were in many cases, like Ehud or Gideon, military victors. It is also true that a military success for Israel could be called a *yᵉšuʿa*. We have cited just above an instance where the NEB translates with 'this great victory'; and in this the NEB follows a long tradition of scholarship which has said that this word meant 'victory'—e.g. Brown, Driver and Briggs, *Lexicon*, s.v., p. 447b. But this probably extends the sense too far. What we today might call a 'victory' would be a *yᵉšuʿa* only in so far as it was regarded as a relief, a rescue, a deliverance. The incident may have been in fact a victory, indeed it must so have been; from a referential standpoint this can be agreed. But this does not mean that 'victory' was the essential and characteristic *information* conveyed by the use of this word.[10] The same is true

9 On this see the basic work of van Rad, *Der heilige Krieg im alten Israel* (1951). Von Rad attributes a great deal, religiously speaking, to the institution of the 'holy war'. Thus (p. 31) it is 'as good as certain that the idea of faith, i.e. that confident trust in the action of Yahweh, had its real origin in the holy war'. Cf. also von Rad, *Old Testament Theology* I (1962), p. 17.

10 On the difference between reference and information in this sort of matter, cf. my *Comparative Philology and the Text of the Old Testament* (1968), pp. 291f.

of *t^e^šu'a*; and as for the third noun, *yeša'*, the case hardly needs to be argued. It is unlikely, therefore, that the military use, even in the case of holy wars or 'wars of the Lord', in spite of its clear occurrence at many points in prose narrative, formed in any way the source or point of origin from which the term spread into soteriology generally; the reverse is more probable. Incidentally, similar arguments can be deployed about the word group *ṣedeq*, etc, basically 'right' and 'righteousness' but sometimes alleged, on the basis of similar evidence, to have the sense of 'victory' or 'triumph'.[11] Finally, as for *mošia'* itself, it is not at all clear that this must have a military *Sitz im Leben*; Sawyer argues that the term is basically rather a forensic one.

Thus, although in the historical books 'salvation' terminology is quite frequently used in military applications, it is unlikely that this is the original setting from which the terms came to be extended to cover divine salvation of man in general. It is rather the reverse: the chances and insecurities of war are conceptualised as threats and emergencies, and any means of overcoming these dangers, whether by human aid or divine, is regarded as 'rescue', 'deliverance' or 'salvation'. We do not doubt that the powerful and widespread traditions of Yahweh as a god who wins wars for his people had a great effect in later times, for instance in the poetry of Deutero-Isaiah, and encouraged the application of titles such as 'saviour' to him; but it remains doubtful whether the basic theme of salvation derives from that early military experience.

The basic development of salvation language, and its application to the basic relations between God and man, appear, then, not to lie within the main prose tradition of the Old Testament, whether in the Pentateuch or in the succeeding historical books. The real locus of salvation language, we shall submit, lay in the poetic tradition. Here, as we have seen, was to be found the statistical concentration of words meaning 'salvation'. Moreover, the framework within which this material is set is very different. There is indeed some common ground between the prose historical writing and the poetic; but for the most part the styles are different. Circumstantial reports of particular 'deliverances' are now rather uncommon; in this sense, the texts are no longer 'historical'. We hear of enemies who are characteristically undefined, of 'the wicked', of 'my pursuers'; the one who prays is in the neighbourhood of Sheol, of the underworld, of death, of sickness, of

11 For a brief mention of this matter, cf. Hill, *Greek Words and Hebrew Meanings* (1967), and my discussion in *Biblica* XLIX (1968), p. 380.

lies and false accusations. Such threats put in question the relation between the one who prays and his God. Salvation is *sought*, because it is not automatic that it will come. The situations are recurrent; they do not apply only to one named individual or group at some stage of history, they can apply to anyone at one time or another. This universalisation of the situation is a reason for the use of general salvation terminology. The language does not *report*: it is rather a language of prayer *for* salvation, of glad confession that prayer has been heard, of joyful assurance that God has 'saved'.

Thus the poetic language tends to do something that the prose texts do not do: it indicates what it is, other than mere concrete human enemies, that one must be saved *from*. The 'enemies' in the poetry are more than the physical military foes; they are associated with a whole range of powers and manifestations of evil, of lies, of sickness and death, of separation from God. Thus, though the Psalter comes no nearer than Genesis does to defining the nature of 'sin', it nevertheless does much more to bring to expression what is the fundamental reality from which man as man has to find 'salvation'.

This fundamental concern with salvation is very likely not derived from the peculiar experience of Israel; it derives also from patterns current more widely in the ancient Near East. As is well known, patterns and associations of Hebrew poetry can often be widely paralleled, and many of them may have been the common property of Canaanite poetic technique. If we look still more widely afield, something of the atmosphere of the prayers in the Psalms can be illustrated from the inscriptions of dedication in South Arabia, set up by a man to his god because he protected him on a journey, healed his sons, saved him from attacks or otherwise prospered him on his way.

It is in this latter aspect, as expressed in the poetic literature, that the religion of the Old Testament, we suggest, is much more a salvation religion. It is here that salvation seems to be conceptualised, here that the nouns for it are concentrated.

What are the relations between the different strands and currents of Old Testament religion which we have tried to distinguish here? I have sought to avoid an evolutionistic picture—not because such pictures are necessarily wrong, but because in this case it does not seem to fit. The religious ethos of the poetic literature is not *derived* from that of the prose, nor is the reverse the case; nor, again, do they represent temporally succeeding stages. The content of the prose literature belonged more fully to Israel's peculiar experience and memory. But through much of the Old Testament period the two lay side by side in the total religious consciousness.

Some illustration of this can perhaps be given from the sphere of Israelite personal names.[12] As is well known, many or most Hebrew names in the central historical period were intelligible sentences or phrases—'God gave' (Elnathan), 'God strengthened', etc. In names of this kind we find plentiful examples of the words which occur in the salvation language of Hebrew—notably, for instance, *p-l-ṭ* and *ʿ-z-r*.[13] The names of Israelites seem to have been based within their personal piety rather than within the historical and narrative material of the prose literature. Names which unequivocally refer to the historical events of the prose narrative are rare or lacking; thus we do not find names of the type 'God-brought-us-out-of-Egypt', although such names would be linguistically possible and names of comparable length and complexity (though hardly of the same religious content) are found in Mesopotamia. The 'help', 'rescue' and 'salvation' referred to in the personal names is generally understood by Noth, and doubtless rightly, to be a relief in personal circumstances, whether in birth or in later life; its theological analogy lies rather in the religion of the Psalms than in the narrative of the Pentateuch.

Thus far we have disengaged two main contrasting areas in the Old Testament in which the place of salvation in the religion seems to be different. In conclusion we must mention a third, and it is in this third that something is drawn from each of the other two and something fresh is created. I refer to the place of salvation in the prophets, and the growth of an eschatological hope for salvation. In the prophets, and especially in their later sections and in their poetic material, salvation language appears in proportions which sometimes begin to approximate to those of the Psalms. Some of this, indeed, is rather 'anti-salvation' language: the prophets had to struggle against false hopes and assurances of divine help before they were able to announce their own assurance. The earlier prophetic movement has a more negative, the later a more positive, emphasis. The role of the foreign nations, their place in relation to the purpose of God, can be said to constitute

12 For a general consideration of some of the questions, see my 'The symbolism of names in the Old Testament', *Bulletin of the John Rylands Library* LII (1969), pp. 11–29.

13 See Noth, *Die israelitischen Personennamen* (1928)—still the basic work on the matter—and on names involving salvation or deliverance pp. 154*ff*., 175*f*., 180, 199*f*.

the epochs, the turning points, in the history of prophecy as a whole. We have mentioned the older tradition of a military salvation vouchsafed by the Lord in the wars of his people. This tradition and its terminology are in part appropriated by the prophets; but at the same time they begin in the classical period to speak against, rather than for, this kind of simple assurance, this belief that God *must* fight for his people. Rather, it is the foreign nations who can be his instrument for the chastisement of his own. Accordingly, there can be false hopes, and true hopes, for salvation. It is in Jeremiah that salvation language in the prophetic sense becomes most rich and profound. It is in his time that the work of the foreign nations is carried to its furthest point in the destruction of Jerusalem by the Babylonians; but just from this point onwards an increasingly positive expectation of salvation for Israel begins to be proclaimed. The foreign peoples have carried out their part in God's work, but they in their turn are now ripe for judgment and punishment. The God of Israel will vindicate after all the hopes and expectations of his people. The idea of salvation for the people and institutions of Israel, the return of the Davidic kingship and the restoration of the Temple, set on an international scale, is typical of prophecy in the exilic period. In Deutero-Isaiah and some of the other contemporary prophetic fragments this hope for salvation on a national level, set against an international scene, is further elaborated into a 'theology of salvation'[14], integrated with the cosmic dimension through the emphasis on creation. This later prophecy, and the apocalyptic movement which followed still later, are forms of Judaism which seek salvation and have an articulated picture of that which they seek. The later heritage of such a position could naturally take its place within the longings for salvation so common in the Graeco-Roman world.

The question with which we began, how far the religion of the Old Testament is a religion of salvation, can thus be answered only ambiguously: it depends how you read the Old Testament, and what authority and what importance you attach to one element as against another. The Jewish view of scripture, as is well known, ranged the Pentateuch higher in authority than the Prophets, and the Prophets higher than the Writings. Christianity, conscious of itself as a fulfilment of the prophets, tended to set the Old Testament on one level but to follow the prophetic pattern in the reading of the whole. The

14 I take the words from the title of Ulrich Simon's commentary on Deutero-Isaiah, *A Theology of Salvation* (1953).

comparative religionist of today, tied by no view of canonical authority, and reading the text against a wide background of extra-canonical texts, may perhaps be able to see values which the ancient religions in their developed forms were not able to discern.

5

Ugo Bianchi

Psyche and destiny

On the question of correspondences between Gnostic soteriology and Orphic–Platonic soteriology

A recent book by K.-W. Tröger, *Mysterienglaube und Gnosis in Corpus Hermeticum XIII* (1971), is devoted to a comparative consideration of the soteriology of Gnosticism and the soteriology of the mystery cults—an important question for the religious history of the ancient world.

Is it a matter of the soul again becoming what it once was as it returns to a higher world from which it has fallen; or is it a matter of the soul attaining for the first time a higher sphere of existence? What is the attitude of Gnosticism to this question, and what is the attitude which characterised the mysteries? Over the years the question has been answered in two ways. H.-M. Schenke,[1] in insisting on the essential difference between these two soteriological perspectives, has affirmed the heterogeneity of two important forms of religion in antiquity: (1) gnosis, and (2) the mystery cults. While the soteriology of the mysteries would imply the final divinisation of the soul (it might be more prudent to say, at least as far as the Eleusinian mysteries are concerned, the incorporation of the individual into the circle of the gods of the underworld), Gnostic soteriology, according to Schenke, contemplates the restoration of the soul to its proper nature and its original condition, which was divine. E. von Ivánka[2] disagrees: in his opinion, Gnostic soteriology may be envisaged as a kind of pseudomorphosis of the soteriology of the mysteries; for one may in fact discover in this certain elements which speak in favour of a soteriological cycle implying an original divine condition of the soul, separated from its original milieu and fallen into a world ruled by the cycle of rebirth, death and fate. Tröger's book[3] tends towards conclusions similar to Schenke's.

1 In *Umwelt des Urchristentums* I, ed. Leipoldt and Grundmann (1965), pp. 371*ff*.

2 In *Le origini dello gnosticismo*, ed. Bianchi, Studies in the History of Religions, supplements to *Numen* XII (1967), pp. 317ff.

3 *Op. cit.*, p. 170.

In our opinion, the choice which we have set out cannot be decided without having recourse to another category, not less historical than phenomenological, to which we have attempted to draw attention on a number of other occasions:[4] the category of 'mysteriosophy', as distinct from the category of 'mystery cult'. An example (or perhaps *the* example) of this mysteriosophy is to be found—in Greece—in the 'Orphic' current; an 'example within the example' is provided by the religious experience of Empedocles of Agrigentum, with his dualistic and anti-somatic understanding of the presence of man, a fallen *daimon*, in this world and in the 'foreign tunic of the flesh'.[5]

The category of 'mysteriosophy', as it is expressed in the Orphic experience, implies a reinterpretation of the spirituality of the mystery cults, on the basis of a distinctive feeling about the destiny of the soul, which is regarded as the subject of the vicissitudes of fall, the assumption of flesh, and reintegration. The soul is divine by nature and by origin; it has fallen, fatally and culpably,[6] into bodily existence and into a material world made up of birth, destiny, death and impurity, and is bound to that world by a sorrowful series of reincarnations. To escape from this 'wheel', which is at one and the same time the sign and the means of 'punishment' (*kolasis*, *poina*, *timoria*), is the goal of a purification involving the use of certain sufficient means, most important among them being abstention from the *empsycha*.

This mysteriosophical experience, as we have described it, is nourished by many elements of the spirituality, the imagery and the terminology of the mysteries; nevertheless in relation to these it involves something new. As far as the Eleusinian mysteries are concerned (as representing the Greek mysteric pattern), it would not be possible to claim that the initiate considered his soul as being divine by origin and essence, nor, apparently, that initiation brought about the 'divinisation' of his soul.[7] As we have already suggested, the Eleusinian type of initiation rather provided the initiate with 'good hope' of life after death, by establishing a relationship with the gods of the underworld by means of the rituals.

4 *Initiation*, ed. Bleeker (1965), pp. 154–71; and Bianchi, *op. cit.*, pp. 10–13 and 739*ff*. See also *Numen* XII, 3 (1965), pp. 161–78.

5 Empedocles, B 115 and 126 (Diels).

6 See 'Péché originel et péché "antécédent"', *Revue de l'histoire des religions* CLXX (1966), pp. 117–26.

7 See 'Saggezza olimpica e mistica eleusina nell'inno omerico a Demetra', *Studi e materiali di storia delle religioni* XXXV (1964), pp. 181–7.

Otherwise, there are reasons for believing that the very experience of the disappearing and reappearing mystery-god was able to favour unconsciously the idea of an analogy with the destiny of man (one may recall, for instance, the analogy established in the *pinakes* of Locres between the rape of Persephone and the departure of the deceased). Further, the vicissitudes of the mystery-god—once fulfilled by the new mysteriosophical experience, implying a more direct contact with the divine—was able to favour the idea of a divine soul, embodied as a result of some primordial incident, and involved in a process of mortification in the body and of final liberation. It goes without saying that the *cyclical* rhythm of the presence and absence of the fertility god is not identical, as Rohde pointed out so long ago, with the *linear* destiny of the soul, imprisoned and then liberated; but it is worth observing that the mysteriosophical destiny of the soul, also implying a metensomatosis, is partly cyclical, being linked with procreation. Thus the cyclical pattern and its cosmic fertility are beneficial in the mystery cults, as they were in the seasonal rituals of the fertility cults,[8] but in mysteriosophical experience, on the other hand, they are sources of evil and of suffering ('destiny')—a conflict of principle which nevertheless witnesses to a certain continuity of ideas, especially since the mystery cults of the Eleusinian type consisted of more than the element of seasonality and fecundity (which is the most visible element of the fertility rituals of the Near East).[9] On the contrary, they seem to have been essentially concerned with soteriology, not merely as a collective manifestation, but also involving the personal destiny of the individual, determined through initiation.

This being so, we may regard the *Totenpässe*, the Orphic tablets of Magna Graeca, as a remarkable example of this mysteriosophical reinterpretation of Eleusinian soteriology: in them the soul of the deceased, on passing into the other world, recognises its own divine origin and affirms that it has been oppressed in the world by the power of a sorrowful destiny but that it is now in process of being liberated from the sorrowful wheel of rebirth.[10] It affirms, it is true, that it has

8 It is well known that the seasonal rituals and myths of fertility in western Asia and Egypt in the period before Hellenism should not be regarded without more ado as 'mysteries', since there is no evidence that their character was esoteric, initiatory and soteriological with regard to the individual, as opposed to the land. It is, however, probable that here and there various characteristics of this kind could be manifested in one or other of these cults.

9 Cf. note 8.

10 Kern, *Orphicorum fragmenta* (1922), Nos. 32, 224 and 229. On the Orphic

become divine after having been human;[11] but this in no way excludes the idea, however vague and generic it may have been, of its divine origin ('I too am of your [divine] race').[12]

It is, however, clear that the situation is less simple than the alternatives posed by Tröger might lead one to believe.[13] It goes without saying that our series 'fertility rituals–mystery cults–mysteriosophy–gnosticism'[14] should not be regarded as an evolutionary series, since there are many other historical factors which need to be taken into consideration (beginning with the initiatory and 'mystery' trends of the religions of hunters and agriculturalists). But it must be stressed at the same time that our 'series' should not be understood as being purely phenomenological.[15] On the contrary, it has a concrete historical content, comprising numerous elements of continuity to which we have drawn attention on many occasions—for instance, between the seasonal fertility rituals and Eleusis, between the mystery cults and the Orphic mysteriosophy (the case of the *Totenposse*, the *kathodoi* of Kore, etc), and finally between the Orphic doctrine of *sōma–sēma* and the fallen *daimon* and the Gnostic teachings concerning the soul and its fall.

However, the terminology used in these matters is liable to give rise to misunderstandings. For example, the 'mystery cults' of oriental origin existing in the Hellenistic age should be considered, according to our terminology, rather as cults of the mysteriosophical type, granted the very probable presence in them of speculations concerning the soul and its liberation beyond the planetary spheres; this is certain in the case of Mithraism, on the evidence of formulae attested by Origen,[16] which are virtually identical to certain formulae of the Ophite Gnostics.

---

concept of liberation from 'cyclical' times, see Brandon, *History, Time and Deity* (1965), chapter IV, and *id.*, 'Time in some ancient initiatory rituals', in Bleeker, *Initiation*, p. 45.

11 Cf. Tröger, *op. cit.*, p. 23.

12 Empedocles also affirmed that it had passed through various forms of living existence before being restored to its divine quality.

13 It is true that Tröger himself introduces distinctions following different phases of development in Eleusinian religion.

14 See notes 4 and 8 above.

15 We may refer here to the criticisms of Drijvers, 'The origins of Gnosticism as a religious and historical problem', *Nederlands Theologisch Tijdschrift* XXII (1967–68), pp. 342*f.*, and Rudolph, 'Gnosis und Gnostizismus, ein Forschungsbericht II, *Theologische Rundschau* XXXVI, I (1971), pp. 42–4.

16 *Contra Celsum* VI, 31; see Bianchi, 'Protogonos', *Studi e materiali* XXVIII, 2 (1957), pp. 115–33.

Archaeological evidence from Mithraic sites, particularly at Ostia, tends in the same direction. On the other hand, it would be impossible to claim that the adepts of the Graeco-Roman mystery cults would always have accepted the doctrines of the divinity of the soul and of *sōma-sēma*. All in all, it is a matter of a highly detailed complex of instances, to which our quadripartite series might, we believe, supply a useful key.

We have already mentioned the doctrine which implies the concept of a certain instability (and hence ambiguity) of the soul. We propose now to elaborate this idea, with the help, on the one hand, of documents of mysteriosophical spirituality (which also survive in many Platonic and neo-Platonic formulae, in so far as they imply the *sōma-sēma* concept and the doctrine of the divinity of the soul) and, on the other, of documents of Gnostic spirituality.

It is well known that the essential question of Gnostic soteriology is practically identical with that of Gnostic metaphysics, anthropology and animology. In general, a distinction is drawn between two categories of Gnostic doctrines: those in which the subject of the destiny of fall and reintegration is the Anthropos, a divine (or para-divine) entity, masculine or androgynous; and those in which the subject is Sophia or Ennoia, also divine or para-divine, but feminine. In both cases it is a matter of a celestial hypostasis having to do with the *plērōma*—a hypostasis which stands in a problematical relationship to the soul,[17] or rather to the divine element of the soul, which in all forms of Gnosticism is somehow involved in a story of fall and reintegration. In general, this 'essential' or divine element of the soul of the Gnostic is an emanation or fragment of the fallen divine hypostasis. The latter remains for the most part at the centre of attention: so much so that one might be justified in defining Gnosticism as a doctrine of the instability of the divine, or rather of the 'para-divine', the peripheral

17 It is known that the problem is acute in respect of the Simonian doctrine attested by Irenaeus. Is the destiny of Ennoia–Helen to be understood as in some way or other linked with that of the soul, of every soul, or is her case unique, in which event the salvation of man depends solely on 'faith' in her and in Simon? In our opinion, the possibility of a link (and thus of an interpretation more fully Gnostic of Irenaeus' version of Simonianism) must be considered seriously. On this question, see Frickel, *Die 'Apophasis megale' in Hippolyts Refutatio* (1968), and Salles-Dabadie, *Recherches sur Simon le Mage* I (1969), in which the question is considered in the light of the entire corpus of evidence concerning Simon Magus.

divine' which is Sophia or Anthropos (in the cases in which it is considered to be fallen, and not as the quintessence of the supreme Being). But there are cases in which the centre of attention and of the drama is precisely the soul, although hypostasised in its turn as 'Soul'. In these cases Gnosticism stands out more clearly for what it always is —a doctrine, or better, an experience of the 'instability' and the ambivalence of the soul within the framework of its own anthropological dualism (*sōma-sēma*; 'divine' soul versus 'animal' soul).

The presence of this hypostasis, *psychē*, in the doctrinal panorama of Gnosticism is of the utmost religio-historical importance. In fact hypostases like Sophia and Anthropos underline the significance of the Jewish component in the Gnostic repertory (which otherwise remains entirely Greek in its fundamental doctrines of *sōma-sēma* and of the *kosmos* cave, and in what we have called the doctrine of the instability of the soul). But when it is a matter of the vicissitudes of the Psyche, Greek Orphic–Platonic references are no less *de rigueur* than in the case of other aspects of Gnostic animology.[18]

There are two Gnostic texts which mention the hypostasised soul, and which we propose to consider: the Naassene Hymn, and the treatise called *Exegesis on the Soul*. The Naassene Hymn[19] uses the ternary system proper to Ophite Gnostic speculation: there is Mind, and there is Chaos; and between the two, in an intermediary and unstable position, Psyche.[20] Psyche is henceforth fallen, oppressed by evils, wandering and lost in the 'labyrinth'[21]; Jesus comes to save her by showing her 'the secrets of the holy way'.

In the treatise[22] the situation of the Psyche is similar. The drama is not in any way concerned with legends about the multiplicity of hypostases or of aeons, but insists on the feminine (and therefore diminished) character of the soul in this world, since in her previous celestial condition she was androgynous. She will be rescued by the *monogenēs*, the 'only son' (neither divided nor diminished), who is her

18 We are referring, for example, to the Basilidian doctrine of the soul who is not *monomerēs*, and to the idea of the 'accretions' of the soul.

19 Hippolytus, *Ref.* v: 10, 2, pp. 102: 23–104: 3 (Wendland); Völker, *Quellen zur Gesch. d. Christl. Gnosis* (1934), p. 26*f.*

20 . . . *ποτὲ <μὲν> βασίλειον ἔχουσα βλέπει τὸ φῶς, ποτὲ δ᾽εἰς ἐλεεῖν᾽ ἐκριπτομένη κλάει* . . (v. 6*f.*).

21 *λαβύρινθον ἐσῆλθε πλανωμένη* (v. 13).

22 Krause and Labib, *Gnostische und hermetische Schriften aus Codex II und VI*, Abhandl. deutsch. archäol. Instituts Kairo, Koptische Reihe II (1971), pp. 68–87; Krause in *Die Gnosis* II, ed. Förster (1971), pp. 125–35.

masculine counterpart in the celestial realms, and who will, as her husband, reconcile her to the world of the Father.

In view of the evident links between this 'nuptial' anthropology and that of Plato's *Banquet* (189d *et seq.*), it is clear that the hypostasisation of the Psyche in the *Exegesis on the Soul* recalls Plotinus and his doctrine of the fall of the soul when separated from the Mind. Moreover, in both Plotinus and the treatise, it is not precisely a matter of a plurality of souls, involved (according to the Orphic–Platonic vision) in their individual destinies, but rather of a hypostasis, Soul, unique and real—though evidently conceived as the prototype of souls in the plural. We may reassure ourselves as to the Greek provenance of this speculation simply by recalling that Plato already knew of the general cosmic hypostasis called soul, although in another context (the world soul). And it is very probable that Middle Platonism would be able to explain the origin of the hypostasised and cosmically intermediary and unstable soul with which we are concerned.

Another document which may be added to the dossier on our question of the Soul hypostasis in its doctrinal contexts would appear to be the fable of Eros and Psyche, in books IV–VI of the *Metamorphoses* of Apuleius. The initiatory connections of this text have already been observed on a number of occasions.[23] Our intention here is rather to demonstrate the animological implications of this narrative and its characters. Two points in particular may be mentioned:

1 It may be observed that in the fable of Eros and Psyche the Soul hypostasis is presented as a personification, in an anthropomorphic and imaginative context. There are partial analogies in the novel *Baruch* of Justin the Gnostic,[24] and in the Simonian tale of Ennoia–Helen.[25] We know that Gnosticism, like the theology of mysteriosophical doctrines, was not beyond expressing itself in the literary genres of folkloristic fable and of the erotic novel.
2 Unlike what happens to the Soul in the *Exegesis on the Soul*, the girl Psyche in Apuleius' novel is not of a divine and celestial nature; nor does she fall into the world. She has a human nature (being the daughter of a 'king'), and rather falls back out of the superior state to which she had been raised by Love; only at the very end is she

23 See Merkelbach, *Roman und Mysterium in der Antike* (1962). A series of studies on this fable is collected in Binder and Merkelbach, *Amor und Psyche*, Wege der Forschung CXXVI (1968).

24 Hippol., *Ref.* V: 24, 2ff., p. 126: 2*ff.* (Wendland); Völker, *op. cit.*, pp. 27ff.

25 Irenaeus, *Adv. haer.* I: 23, 1–4; Völker, *op. cit.*, p. 2*f.*

received among the gods. But it is also worth noting that she is described from the beginning as an exceptional being, of 'divine' beauty, and otherwise incomparable. This is a clear reference to the superior status of the 'Soul', although lower than the genuinely divine level of Aphrodite and Eros. It might be said that she is the counterpart and the terrestrial image of Aphrodite herself.

These two facts suggest a twofold conclusion.

1 This type of reduplication of Aphrodite and Psyche in Apuleius' novel recalls the situation obtaining in the Gnostic treatise *The Hypostasis of the Archons*,[26] in which the celestial Eve, the feminine hypostasis of Deity, has her counterpart on earth, who is subject to a terrible degradation. These dual figures are the clearest possible expression of the intermediary and ambivalent character common to these feminine hypostases, however mutually different they may be in other respects.

2 More important: the vicissitudes of Psyche in Apuleius' novel bring us back to the intermediate, ambivalent and unstable (i.e. liable to fall) position of the Plotinian Psyche; but also of the souls treated in the Platonic myths of *Phaedrus*, the *Republic*, and elsewhere. The identical considerations apply to the question of the *cause* of the fall of Psyche in Apuleius. This cause, which has to do with mistrust and with the *curiositas sacrilega*, audacious and ruinous,[27] is not very different from *tolma*,[28] 'audacity', which causes the metaphysical fall of the Soul in Plotinus. Otherwise it is also found in the audacious indiscretion (again *tolmē*) of Sophia over against the Father in the Valentinism myth.[29] Now these three 'falls'—Psyche in Apuleius and Plotinus; Sophia in Valentinus; the fall of the souls in the Platonic myths—all indicate culpability; but all at the same time owe somewhat to fatality. That is to say, the fall of these entities is already inscribed in the cosmological and metaphysical sphere to which they belong,[30] a sphere which is typically 'intermediary' (though tending more towards the human in Apuleius and towards the divine in Valentinus) and thus 'unstable' and liable to what Jonas calls the 'devolution'[31] of these hypostases from the divine periphery. But it must

26 Leipoldt and Schenke, *Koptisch-gnostische Schriften aus . . . Nag Hamadi* (1960); Krause, in *Die Gnosis* II, ed. Förster, pp. 53*ff*., 170 (bibl.).

27 This *curiositas* corresponds to the *inprospera curiositas* which brings about the fall of Lucius (XI: 15, 1).

28 Ennead. III: 7, 11. Cf. Jonas, in *Le origini dello gnosticismo*, pp. 105, 213*f*.

29 Cf. Zandee, in *Le origini*, p. 205.

30 See note 6 above.

31 *Le origini dello gnosticismo*, pp. 90*ff*.; cf. *ibid*., p. xxvi.

be stressed that it is here a matter of an intermediary quality and an unstability which also applies to the souls of the Platonic cosmology, and which constitutes the real and fatal reason (a metaphysical reason) for their degradation and their fall into the material world. The primary source of this thought structure is, however, the Platonic dialectical dualism based ultimately on the metaphysical dualism of *idea* and *chōra*, and on the anthropological dualism between 'the soul of divine origin' and 'inferior human spheres'.[32] It goes without saying that Gnosticism has adapted this structure to its own dualism.

Returning to the fall of Psyche in the *Exegesis*, it must be observed that it is complicated by the introduction of a new element, foreign to Platonic and neo-Platonic speculation. What we there encounter is in fact a number of tyrannical beings, the *archontes*, who maltreat and contaminate Psyche, just as they maltreat and contaminate other more or less analogous feminine hypostases in other Gnostic treatises or doctrines (we are thinking above all of the terrestrial Eve in the *Hypostasis of the Archons*, and of the Simonian Ennoia-Helen). Evidently this aspect—the impurity of sexual intercourse between Psyche and the *archontes*—should be referred to the distinctive ethos of Gnosticism and its Jewish presuppositions; perhaps reference might be made at this point to the historically attested hostility of Hebraism to the fertility cults of Asia Minor (though one should not forget the mistrust with regard to the sexual theme which affects the Greek mysteriosophical tradition from 'Orpheus' to Empedocles,[33] down to Platonism. The condemnation of Aphrodite in the *Exegesis*[34] may finally indicate the Greek element in this context of the sexual misuse to which Psyche is subjected, though we prefer here to limit ourselves to observing the expression of a particular characteristic of Gnostic ideology).

However that may be, this is not the whole story, for the general concept of suffering inflicted on the soul by tyrannical demiurges is in fact genuinely Greek. While not forgetting the role which could have been played here by the Jewish concept of the angels of the nations, who oppress Israel and exercise a malevolent rule over the world,[35]

32 Bianchi, 'Anthropologie et conception du mal: les sources de l'exégèse gnostique', *Vigiliae Christianae* XXV (1971); cf. *id.*, 'La religione greca', in *Storia della religioni* II, ed. Castellani (1971), pp. 346–65.

33 See the last of the articles quoted above, note 4. Cf. also Heraclitus, B 20 D.

34 Förster, *op. cit.*, p. 135.

35 See Daniélou, 'Le mauvais gouvernement du monde', in *Le origini dello gnosticismo*, pp. 448–59.

it must be held that the idea of oppressive Titanic beings is essential to Orphic, and later to neo-Platonic speculation. It would not be necessary to worry too much about the actual date of these ideas (the myth of Zagreus interpreted anthropologically, etc), for a being of this type, hypostasised in Eris, Discord, is already envisaged in the Empedoclean myth of the fall of the soul *daimon*, who falls precisely because he 'believed' in the furious (i.e. cruel and ruinous) Discord. Otherwise, in the work of Empedocles of Agrigentum the metaphysical doctrine of the Sphairos assigns a demiurgic role to Discord, to the extent to which the Discord conspires in the existence of this world by provoking the separation of the primordial unity of the elements.[36] The Orphic funerary tablets of Magna Graeca attest to the same situation: it is precisely Moira, sorrowful Destiny, the ruler of this world of birth and death, who violently oppresses the souls before their liberation into the divine world. As for the Psyche of Apuleius' novel, she is oppressed by Fortuna *saeva et nefaria* before being set free by Love.

We may conclude by affirming that, all things considered, the drama of the Fall and the oppression of Psyche in the *Exegesis on the Soul* presupposes elements of Jewish origin, but that its basis and motivation are entirely Greek. This basis reveals—in differing circumstances—a common structure of dualism which, in the different versions which we have formulated elsewhere, inspires at one and the same time the soteriology, the anthropology and the animology both of Gnosticism and of the Greek religious current which we have called mysteriosophy.

Epilogue

We may add in conclusion one important qualification. We have mentioned in the preceding pages that the hypostasis Psyche is to be found in Gnostic texts and in texts of Platonic inspiration, but that the mention of souls in the plural, as subjects of particular soteriological destinies, is typical of the Orphic and Platonic texts, and also of the Gnostic texts. This fact prevents us from indulging in arbitrary generalisation. But it is also necessary to consider, by the same token, the Gnostic tendency to analyse the human being into three parts (*pneuma*, *psychē*, *sōma*), which complicates the framework. In this case the *psychē* is often regarded in fairly negative terms, in opposition to the concept

36 This demiurgic–'archontic' aspect of Eris was clearly seen by Hippolytus, who formulates it in a slightly anachronistic fashion according to the Gnostic style of expression (see *Ad Emped.*, B 115 D).

of the *pneuma* as the divine substance, corresponding to the *nous* of the 'philosophers'. This negative evaluation of *psychē* is clearly seen in the Valentinian category of the *psychikoi*, and in a Naassene text (Völker, p. 12), in which the *psychē* is the place and the means of the 'punishment' (*kolasis*) to which man is subject in this world. But it is also true that in the Gnostic texts the term *psychē* sometimes denotes precisely the divine part of man (i.e. it corresponds to the *pneuma* or to the *nous*),[37] and it is possible to quote texts (e.g. *Hypostasis o the Archons* 136: 4) in which the *psychē* is the vital element of man, infused by Deity into a body created by the *archontes*; this latter idea corresponds, *mutatis mutandis*, to the Greek idea attested in the literature and confirmed in the funerary art, according to which the *psychē*, a winged butterfly, is infused by Athena into the man fashioned by Prometheus.

It is well known that Jonas has surmounted the impasse created by this ambivalent use of *psychē* in the Gnostic texts by distinguishing a cosmic psyche, of archontic origin, and a supra-cosmic psyche, identical to the *pneuma*. This may well be so, particularly since reduplication is common in Gnostic systematics (the celestrial and terrestrial Eves in the *Hypostasis of the Archons*, the two Sophias of Valentinianism, and so on); but it is important that the principle on which this reduplication takes place should be properly understood. Now this principle consists precisely in the intermediary and 'unstable' character of the soul, following a long tradition which is expressed intensely in Plato, in the Platonic school and in the Gnostics. We may consider the trichotomy of the soul in Plato's *Republic* and *Timaeus*: only the first soul (or the highest of the three levels of the soul) is derived from Deity; the two others are derived only from inferior 'gods', those which have formed the human body—all this in order not to compromise Deity by associating it with 'malignity' (*kakia*) derived from matter. In the *Timaeus* these inferior demiurges act in harmony with Deity by obeying its explicit will; in the Gnostic systems it is precisely the opposite. At this point we have the entire difference between Gnostic dualism and Platonic dualism.

However, both the frequent ambivalence of the Gnostic term *psychē*

37 See now also *psychē* and her vicissitude (from being 'spiritual' she becomes 'material' in the body) as described in the *Authentikos logos* from Nag Hammadi (Krause and Labib, *Gnostische und hermetische Schriften, cit.*, pp. 133*ff.*) and other Nag Hammadi tractates quoted by Mac Rae in *Ex orbe religionum: studia G. Widengren* (1972) I, p. 479.

and the intermediary and unstable character of Psyche in the *Exegesis on the Soul* and the Naassene Hymn can be well understood by reference to the ternary scheme which is appropriate to Ophite gnosis, in which the intermediate role is played by another hypostasis, the *logos* serpent, subject to a *descensus* and *ascensus* entirely comparable to that of the *psychē*. But once more, it is precisely the ambivalent character—ambivalent because intermediary and 'unstable'—of Psyche and the *psychē*, which is the typical element (with the opposition between *pneuma* and body) of Gnostic spirituality and soteriology. And this characteristic, as we believe we have sufficiently demonstrated, is a legacy of Greece.

6

C. J. Bleeker

Man and his salvation in the ancient Egyptian religion

The subject of this volume—Man and his salvation—has rightly been called 'a primary focus of Professor Brandon's interest throughout his academic career'. Nobody who is familiar with the contents of his extensive study *Man and his destiny in the Great Religions* will question this. The work not only contains solid knowledge about a many-sided subject but also testifies to a personal interest in the problems of man's nature and lot. The last feature characterized the personality of Professor Brandon. Scholarly research into man's religious problems was combined with a vivid interest in man as a fellow creature. This was certainly the reason why for many years he sacrificed part of his time and energy to the work of the International Association for the History of Religions and of its British section. During this period he acquired such a high and universal esteem in the organisation, not only as a scholar but also as a friend, that during the congress of the Association in Stockholm in August 1970 he was elected its Secretary-General, a function hesitantly accepted but which he occupied with honour. The writer gladly offers his tribute to the memory of Professor Brandon, by treating a sub-section of the general theme, i.e. a segment of his special field of study, namely Egyptology.

To a certain extent Brandon has already paved my way. In his book mentioned above there is a paragraph on the ancient Egyptian conception concerning 'man and his destiny' which bears the title 'Immortality and the technique of its achievement'. It is quite understandable that Brandon in the general setting of his work dealt with the ancient Egyptian ideas about immortality. For this complex of concepts forces itself upon everyone who wonders how the ancient Egyptians conceived of the destiny of man. It is well known that they spared no trouble or expense to secure a happy after-life to their dead. It surely cannot be fully accidental that the major part of the remains of this remarkable civilisation and religion is of a funerary nature. The graves of the kings and of the noblemen—pyramids, mastabas, graves in the rocks—the funerary temples, the mummies, the papyri and articles of everyday use which are deposited in the graves along with the dead, not only testify to a strong belief in immortality but also yield information about the conception of the nature of man.

Yet it is easier to write about the ancient Egyptian conception of the destiny of man than about his salvation. The last word does not occur in the ancient Egyptian language. This fact evokes an interesting problem. S. Morenz has rightly remarked that the ancient Egyptian language does not possess words for 'religion', 'piety' or 'belief', words belonging to the constituents of modern religious terminology and also to the apparatus of the historian of religions.[1] On consulting the sixth volume of the well known *Wörterbuch der ægyptischen Sprache*, i.e. the *Deutsch–Ægyptisches Wörterverzeichnis in alphabetischer und sachlicher Ordnung*, one is surprised to discover how poor the ancient Egyptian language was in religious terms. There are certainly expressions for religious emotions. But the theological terminology is almost entirely missing. The sacral conceptions in use mainly refer to cult, both of the gods and of the dead. There are several words for (for example) the altar, the image of the deity, prayer, sacrifice, festivals, rooms of the temple, the priests and the ritual. But there is no trace of the notion of salvation.

An *argumentum e silentio* is not always cogent. Even if the notion is lacking, the matter may be present. The peoples of antiquity apparently had in some respects not yet reached the level of sophistication on which we are living and thinking. This certainly is the case with the ancient Egyptians. The problem of salvation had not yet appeared into the light of their clear consciousness. Therefore silence about this matter urges prudence. It is a sign of the incongruity between the structure of the ancient Egyptian religion on the one hand and the religious consciousness of the people of this age and the terminology of the historian of religions on the other side.

Moreover, *valent verba usu*. It is a common thing that religious and theological terms lose their original meaning in the course of time and are used in a figurative sense. This process can often be observed in our age of religious crisis. Therefore, it is possible for the term 'salvation' to be given a broader meaning, in the sense that man in some way or the other acquires spiritual happiness. There is no objection to using the notion in question in a general sense, but one should realise that it

1 Morenz, *Ägyptische Religion* (1960), p. 4.

thereby loses its original and pithy meaning. One has only to think of the religious verve and the theology of the organisation which calls itself by the characteristic name Salvation Army in order to understand what the author means. The salvation which this remarkable body offers to men has its clear presuppositions, i.e. the belief in a God who is holy but also gracious, so that he revealed himself in Jesus Christ in order to call sinful man to repentance, to pardon his guilt and to renew his heart. In this theology one recognises the main pattern of the type of religion to which Christianity belongs, i.e. the religions which are founded by a prophet, sent by God with a message to mankind.

The ancient Egyptian religion shows a totally different structure. It was not a religion that had been founded, but a belief which, so to speak, originated from the life of the people. The knowledge of the divinity was derived mainly from nature, from the cosmos, conceived of as a universe with an inherent world order. Thus the ancient Egyptians worshipped a plurality of gods, each of whom personified a facet of holy nature. There were no prophets to preach penance and conversion. Nor was there a canon of authoritative books, though there existed sacred books which contained hymns to the gods, spells for the dead and rituals.[2] The religion of the ancient Egyptians consisted in the worship of the gods in the hope of acquiring their favour, in the cult of the dead in order to assure them a happy after-life and in religious ethics of which the main principle was that both man's virtue and his happiness depended on his harmony with the world order.

This sketch of the religious climate of ancient Egypt makes it clear that the historian of religions should proceed carefully in handling the current words of his terminology, at peril of interpreting the facts in the wrong way.

This could actually happen with the notion of salvation. Man who experiences salvation is saved from a state of suffering, is liberated from some evil. This release can be of a twofold nature: man can be redeemed from his sin or he can be relieved from sufferings. The two great religions offering deliverance, Christianity and Buddhism, strike the two notes respectively: Christianity will deliver man from his guilt; Buddhism shows the path leading to freedom from suffering.

Thus the cardinal question arises: how did the ancient Egyptians understand sin and suffering? Did they possess a keen sense of sin and suffering? For an ardent longing for salvation in the strict sense of the

2 Bleeker, 'Religious tradition and sacred books in ancient Egypt', in *Holy Book and Holy Tradition*, ed. Bruce and Rupp (1968).

word can arise only when people experience sin and suffering so intensely that they are burdened by them and wish to be liberated from the burden.

As to the first point, the ancient Egyptian sense of sin, the first step to be taken is a linguistic inquiry into the Egyptian words which are used to indicate sin and guilt. It appears that the Egyptian language had at its disposal ten words which can be translated by sin[3] and possessed six words which express the idea of guilt.[4] On closer observation one detects that both groups of words have more than one significance, so that they do not render the pure concepts of sin and guilt. The words for sin can also cover the idea of all that is bad, both what one does and what one undergoes, and hence, crime, foolishness, injustice, calamity, suffering, damage. The words for guilt occasionally have to be translated by the terms 'mistake', defect', 'misfortune', 'offence', 'action for debt'. By themselves these shades of meaning are not surprising. In modern languages guilt can have a financial, a juridical, an ethical and a purely religious meaning. Yet a striking feature of the Egyptian language in this respect is that sin proves to be closely connected with the disagreeable, with foolishness, and that guilt is linked with the idea of error and with financial and juridical shortcomings. Therefore the question arises whether the ancient Egyptians ever used these words in their purely ethical and religious meaning. Second, the question looms whether the ancient Egyptians had a keen sense of sin and guilt, which is the presupposition of salvation.

Yet it is not difficult to quote a number of clear pronouncements of sin and guilt. They are not to be found in the documents of the State religion, i.e. in the texts which contain hymns, myths and rituals. The confessions of sin and guilt are utterances of what has been called 'the religion of the poor', which is known to us by a series of texts from the Theban necropolis, dating from the Nineteenth Dynasty. These texts have been published, translated and commented upon by A. Erman[5] and later by B. Gun.[6] The latter scholar rightly remarks that generally 'the Egyptian was little disposed to humble himself before the deity' and that 'the attitude of the "miserable sinner", so characteristic of the Christian and other Semitic religions, is unknown to the official writ-

3 ỉw, ỉwj.t, ỉsf.t, ʿw.t, wẖɜ, bwt, btɜ, ẖww, ẖɜb.t, ʿb.

4 wn, ẖbn.t, śẖf, gbɜw, ʿḏɜ, btɜ.

5 Erman, 'Denksteine aus der thebanischen Gräberwelt, *Sitzungsberichte der Berl. Ak. der Wiss.* (1911), pp. 1086*ff.*

6 Gun, 'The religion of the poor in ancient Egy pt', *I.E.A.* III, pp. 8*ff.*

ings'. However, through the texts on the memorial stones from the Theban necropolis there clearly runs a sincere feeling of sin and guilt. A few quotations will furnish sufficient proof.

Highly interesting is the stela which Nefer-'abu dedicated to the so-called 'Peak of the West', the mountain top on the west side of the Nile, in the neighbourhood of the Theban necropolis. This mountain top was supposed to be the home of a serpent goddess, Meretseger. Nefer-'abu makes the following confession:

> [I was] an ignorant man and foolish,
> Who knew neither good nor evil;
> I wrought transgression against the Peak,
> And she chastised me.

However, Meretseger showed mercy to Nefer-'abu. She cured the illness which befell him. Therefore he thankfully declares:

> She turned again to me in mercy;
> She caused me to forget the sickness that has been [upon me].

Another inscription tells that a man felt induced to glorify Ptah, who cured him from blindness, caused by the wrath of the god on account of perjury. We read:

> I am a man who swore falsely by Ptah, the Lord of Truth
> And he caused me to behold darkness by day.

These quotations testify to a remarkable type of religion, i.e. to a sincere sense of sin and to full confidence in the mercy and the forgiveness of the deity. Here one is tempted to use the word 'salvation'. But it is evident that this is exceptional in ancient Egypt. Both Erman and Gun have raised the question of how this unusual type of piety can be explained. Is it an undercurrent passed over in silence by the official documents and here coming to the surface? Or is this type of personal piety stimulated and favoured by the atmosphere of a larger freedom of the spirit, prevailing under the Eighteenth and Nineteenth Dynasties, of which the theology of Amenophis IV–Echnaton and the art of his age give striking testimonies?

However that may be, attention should be paid to the quality of this sense of sin. On closer observation it appears that it does not originate from a feeling of unholiness, but that it is roused by the fact that the persons in question are afflicted by calamity, more specially by illness and blindness, interpreted as a chastisement for sin. Only in a few cases does one meet persons who are really conscious of their sinful nature. Mostly people speak about the bad deeds which they have done.[7] Therefore the confessions of sin have a tang. The ancient Egyptian regrets that he has been foolish and therefore has behaved badly. This conclusion reinforces the linguistic analysis of the words for sin and guilt. Consequently the well known Egyptologist H. Frankfort has spoken of 'the absence of the concept of sin' in ancient Egypt. In his opinion, 'the Egyptian viewed his misdeeds not as sins but as aberrations . . . He who errs is not a sinner but a fool, and his conversion to a better way of life does not require repentance but a better understanding.'[8] Thus there is narrow room for salvation.

The sense of sin includes the fact that man is conscious of his insignificance against the deity. This feeling was foreign to the ancient Egyptians. This does not mean that they were lacking in awe of their gods. There is evidence to prove that the Egyptians now and then fell under the impression of the *mysterium tremendum* of their gods. The famous pillar hall in the temple of Amon at Karnak testifies, with its rows of colossal pillars, compared to which man dwindles into nothingness, to a sharp sense of the awe-inspiring nature of Amon. The Egyptians feared the wrath of their gods. The pyramid texts, for instance, sometimes picture the gods as beings who must be adored with the same feelings of fearful respect as the pharaoh before whom his subjects abase themselves in order to express their deep reverance. Yet there is, as W. B. Kristensen rightly remarked,[9] a characteristic difference between the Semitic and the Egyptian conceptions of the relation between the divinity and man. The Semites stressed the distance between God and man. God is a mighty lord, man is his slave; God is a living reality, man is the dust of the earth; God is holy, man is sinful. The Egyptians felt themselves akin to their gods. This is clearly seen from the spells for the dead. In these spells the dead repeat, with remarkable persistence, that through death they have become like the gods. Let me quote a couple of striking utterances. At the end of spell 147 of the *Book of the Dead* we read: 'Every blessed dead for whom this spell is recited will possess eternal life in the hereafter and will be of the same nature as Osiris.' In spell 153 the dead man declares 'I am Re, who appeared from Nun [the primordial ocean], my soul is a deity.' Thus the dead man identifies himself here with the creator god. It sounds

7 Bonnet, *Reallexicon der ägyptischen Religionsgeschichte* (1952), pp. 759*ff*.
8 Frankfort, *Ancient Egyptian Religion* (1948), pp. 73*ff*.
9 Kristensen, *Het leven unit de dood* (1949), pp. 8*ff*.

blasphemous, but that is not the intention. For the Egyptians knew and respected the distance between god and man. Even the pharaoh, a son of the sun god and the queen, was not the equal of the gods. He was called the good god. The gods were classified as the great gods. However, the quotations from the spells for the dead express the conviction that man is so closely related to the gods that he can participate in their nature. It is evident that the notion of salvation in the strict sense of the word does not fit into this religious context.

As has been remarked, salvation can also mean liberation from sufferings, as Buddhism preaches. Thus the question arises: were the Egyptians weighed down by the misery of life? The answer is: not at all. Naturally, one can quote well known texts which offer a pessimistic evaluation of life or ventilate loud complaints about its misfortunes and the corruption of society. Famous is the dispute over suicide, in which a man talks to his soul, being weary of life.[10] Well known is the song of the harper, who teaches that the glory of life passes, that even the sumptuous graves of people of renown disappear.[11] One could also mention the so-called *Protests of the Eloquent Peasant* who held nine appeals in which he complains of his laborious life and his many adversities.[12] These texts show that the Egyptians knew periods of anarchy which induced in them a gloomy look on life and society. Naturally the life of the great masses was not carefree. Yet this did not foster the pessimistic outlook which lies at the root of Buddhism. On the contrary; the ancient Egyptian lived, on the whole, in an optimistic mood, because he had confidence in life. Therefore there was no room for the longing for salvation from earthly suffering.

And yet it is possible to defend the thesis that the ancient Egyptians strove after salvation, if the latter is taken in a broader sense, meaning a state of happiness and bliss. Actually each belief is intended to make man's life more rich, more free, more intense. Every religion shows the path of salvation. The ancient Egyptian one was no exception. It is interesting to investigate what salvation may mean in this context.

When Frankfort says, in the passage quoted above, that according to the ancient Egyptian conception 'He who errs is not a sinner but a fool', the words give the impression that the Egyptians were motivated by a spirit of shallow utilitarianism. This is by no means Frankfort's intention. What he tries to clarify is the conception that only wisdom

10 *Ancient Near Eastern Texts relating to the Old Testament*, ed. Pritchard, second edition (1955).

11 *Ibid.*, p. 467.

12 *Ibid.*, p. 407.

can prevent man from both foolishness and sin. One can become acquainted with this wisdom by reading the many books of wisdom which apparently were popular in ancient Egypt, e.g. the sayings of Ptahhotep, of Kagemni or of Amenemope. These books do not contain profound philosophical speculations, but practical wisdom to be applied in ordinary life. The quintessence of this wisdom is that man should understand that the path of salvation consists in a life in accordance with Ma-a-t, the world order.

Ma-a-t is a curious deity.[13] The Helipolitan myth tells that the sun-god Re established Ma-a-t in primeval times. The world order has eternal value and is normative for all domains of the world and of life. Ma-a-t stands its ground, notwithstanding periods of social disorder and moral corruption. This conviction gave the ancient Egyptians confidence in the meaning of life and in the future. Ma-a-t is both a notion and a goddess. As a notion it represents certain social and ethical values, such as truth, righteousness, order in society. As a goddess Ma-a-t personifies the world order to which the gods also are bound. Ma-a-t gives expression to the typical world view of the people of antiquity, who conceived of the different departments of the world and human life as a whole, a unity. Analogous ideas are Tao in ancient China, Rita in ancient India, Asha in ancient Iran and in a certain sense Themis in ancient Greece.[14] These notions synthesize the different fields of life and culture, such as science, art, religion, ethics, State policy, which in modern times are fully autonomous and separate from one another. In regard to the present argument it should be stressed that according to the Egyptian conception, salvation—i.e. freedom from sin and suffering—is guaranteed only by harmony with Ma-a-t.

He who lives according to Ma-a-t is a *ma-atj*.[15] This means that he has no great vices. But it includes more. We realise this when we read the following inscription on a grave: 'One wishes water for the wise man, wind for the silent one; one wishes the West [the nether world] for the silent one, the realm of death for the *ma-atj*.' Here the *ma-atj* stands parallel to the wise man and to the silent one (*gr*). The last notion in particular deserves attention. It is not used only for the court official who is discreet and who does not talk unwisely, it also stands for an ideal which the Egyptian defined thus: 'Cool of mouth in the presence of the king, friendly and silent, quiet of heart, harmonious

13 Bleeker, *De beteekenis van de Egyptische godin Ma-a-t* (1929).
14 Bleeker, *Inleiding tot een phaenomenologie van den godsdienst* (1934), pp. *66ff.*
15 Bleeker, *Ma-a-t*, pp. 30–1.

of nature, free from passions.' Here arises the picture of the true aristocrat who shows generosity, wisdom and restrained dignity. Yet deeper, more religious tones ring through the notion of *gr*. In the Theban texts mentioned earlier we read: 'Thou, Amon, art the Lord of the silent who comes on the call of the abandoned one', i.e. the humble, the lonely. This significance of *gr* reminds us of the notion *anaw* in the Psalms and the terms πραυς, ταπεινος, πτωχος τῳ πνευματι in the New Testament. It is true that each of these notions stands in a different spiritual context, but together they represent a religious standard of life which in the relevant texts is described as follows: against the 'hot one', i.e. the passionate, the greedy, the quarrelsome, the proud, the impious, stands the 'silent one', i.e. the restrained, the modest, the humble, the patient, the obedient to God. In Egypt the 'silent one 'derives his spiritual quality from the fact that he is a *ma-atj*, i.e. that he lives according to Ma-a-t. He has acquired 'salvation'.

Christian doctrine teaches that on earth salvation can be realised only partly and provisionally. The true salvation happens first in, by and after death. That was also the conviction of the ancient Egyptians. One of the dominant ideas of the funeral texts is the fervent and endlessly repeated wish of the dead man that he might be 'justified', i.e. that he might be pure and unblemished in the face of Osiris, the god of the realm of the dead. He therewith refers to a mythical archetype: the well known legal action before the court of the gods in which Osiris—and Horus—were justified, with the aid of Thoth. In the case of the dead person the judgment is enacted by the weighing of his heart against a feather, the sign of Ma-a-t, in the presence of Osiris and the forty-two judges, whilst Thoth assists and records the result. The representation of this so-called psychostasis in the vignettes of the *Book of the Dead* and the judgment of the dead itself are so well known that they need no further explanation.

Attention should be paid to the term 'justified', in the Egyptian language *ma-a-cheru*. The last word consists of two parts: *ma-a*, true, and *cheru*, voice. The two parts could apparently be separated, as appears from the wish of the dead: 'May my *cheru* be *ma-a* in the hall [of the judgment], because I was *ma-a-cheru* on earth.' Also, in regard to Horus it is said, 'Horus was found *ma-a*, as to his *cheru*.' Certainly this means that the testimony of Horus and of the dead were truthful. But it has also a deeper meaning. In the case of the judgment of the dead, it is well known that the dead man recites a confession in which he declares that he has not committed certain sins. Now it is peculiar that he enumerates not only ethical sins (robbery, murder, adultery) and cultic transgressions (abusing the gods, sampling the offerings), but also encroachments on the cosmic order: damming up running water, stifling living creatures at birth. These cosmic sins lead back to the element *cheru* in *ma-a-cheru*. The people of antiquity ascribed magical force to the voice, to the spoken word. In the voice the life force is inherent. Thus *ma-a-cheru* is he whose spiritual quality corresponds to Ma-a-t. This can first be tested in the realm of the dead. According to the ancient Egyptian conception, the nether world was the seat of true divine life. For only that life is divine and creative which is able to arise from death. Thus the true 'salvation' takes place in the hereafter. There the judgment can be passed not only on the ethical quality of man but also on his cosmic, his truly religious value.

Finally it can be remarked that in the foregoing observations on 'salvation' in ancient Egypt, although they are not incorrect, the accent is somewhat misplaced, in so far as the subject is approached exclusively from the individual angle. In Christian theology salvation is mainly a personal affair. The Egyptians lived in collectivity. Their religion, as we know it from the surviving evidence, was primarily a religion of the State. Thus the question arises whether salvation had any significance in the common religious life of the people. It can be answered in the affirmative if salvation is again taken in a figurative sense. It cannot be doubted that the cult had a liberating influence on all people who attended it. By worship of the gods one was freed from the grip of evil forces. Theoretically, the pharaoh conducted all religious ceremonies. As son of the sun god he was the true high priest who could mediate between the gods and men. He acted in a certain sense as saviour. It is the festivals, the culminating points of the cult of the gods, which can be considered as the most significant means of salvation. For the festivals raised expectations of the religious renewal of man and society. I have dealt with this theme elsewhere, and reference to my *Egyptian Festivals as Enactments of Religious Renewal* will perhaps absolve me from the duty of enlarging on the subject here.

7

F. F. Bruce

Salvation history in the New Testament

I

In one of his earliest works—*Time and Mankind* (1951)—Professor Brandon described the distinctive Hebrew conception of history as 'the revelation of divine providence'[1] and discussed the part played in this conception by the motif of 'salvation history' (*Heilsgeschichte*), which (following Gerhard von Rad) he considered to have played a significant part in Israel's amphictyonic cultus, and then in the Yahwistic narrative, 'enshrining,' as he says, 'not only a brilliantly told story of the nation's past, but a veritable philosophy of history, in which is set forth in the clearest way the great doctrine which was ever after to dominate the Hebrew mind and to determine its peculiar destiny, namely, that of Israel's election by Yahweh to be his own people among the nations of the world.'[2] The Yahwist thus 'gave to the recollection of the past a new status and value' in a way which 'marks the passing from the intuitive stage of thought to that of the explanatory', thus 'bringing into history the teleological motif, from the influence of which history has never since been able completely to emancipate itself'.[3]

In the Pentateuch the outstanding instance of the cultic recital of Yahweh's mighty acts is the direction in Deut. 26: 5ff. that the Israelite settler in Canaan, presenting the first fruits of his harvest at the sanctuary, should recount the story of his father, the 'wandering Aramaean',[4] who

went down into Egypt and sojourned there, few in number; and there he became a nation, great, mighty and populous. And the Egyptians treated us

1 Brandon, *Time and Mankind* (1951), pp. 59*ff.*; cf. the chapter entitled 'History as the revelation of divine purpose' in his *History, Time and Deity* (1965), pp. 106*ff.* 2 *Time and Mankind*, p. 82. 3 *Ibid.*, pp. 83*f.*

4 Cf. von Rad, *Das formgeschichtliche Problem des Hexateuchs* (1938), pp. 3*ff.*, English translation in chapter 1 of *The Problem of the Hexateuch and Other Essays* (1966), pp. 1*ff.*, especially pp. 3*ff.*

harshly, and afflicted us, and laid upon us hard bondage. Then we cried to Yahweh, the God of our fathers, and Yahweh heard our voice, and saw our affliction, our toil and our oppression; and Yahweh brought us out of Egypt with a mighty hand and an outstretched arm, with great terrors and signs and wonders; and he brought us into this place and gave us this land, a land flowing with milk and honey . . .

This outline recurs, in amplified form, in a number of psalms (cf. Pss. 78; 105; 106) and in Ezra's prayer of confession recorded in Neh. 9:6*ff.* In Ps. 78:67 the recital continues on past the settlement in Canaan to Yahweh's establishment of the Davidic dynasty on Zion:[5]

He rejected the tent of Joseph,
    he did not choose the tribe of Ephraim;
but he chose the tribe of Judah,
    Mount Zion, which he loves.
He built his sanctuary like the high heavens,
    like the earth, which he has founded for ever.
He chose David his servant,
    and took him from the sheep folds;
from tending the ewes that had young he brought him
    to be the shepherd of Jacob his people,
    of Israel his inheritance.
With upright heart he tended them,
    and guided them with skilful hand.

This form of the tradition of salvation history persists into the New Testament, where it appears succinctly in Luke's account of Paul's speech in the synagogue of Pisidian Antioch (Acts 13:17*ff.*):

The God of this people Israel chose our fathers and made the people great during their stay in the land of Egypt, and with uplifted arm he led them out of it. And for about forty years he bore with them in the wilderness. And when he had destroyed seven nations in the land of Canaan, he gave them their land as an inheritance, for about four hundred and fifty years. And after that he gave them judges until Samuel the prophet. Then they asked for a king, and he gave them Saul the son of Kish, a man of the tribe of Benjamin, for forty years. And when he had removed him, he raised up David to be their king, of whom he testified and said, 'I have found in David the son of Jesse a man after my heart, who will do all my will.'[6]

5 This forms an exception to Professor von Rad's generalisation that Yahweh's guarantee of the continuance of David's dynasty, unlike his deliverance of Israel from Egypt, 'was never taken up into the series of these confessional statements' (*Old Testament Theology*, English translation, I [1962], p. 306).

6 A conflate quotation from Ps. 89: 20; 1 Sam. 13: 14; Isa. 44: 28.

But no longer do David's dynasty and Solomon's temple mark the climax of Yahweh's saving dealings with his people, as they did in Ps. 78; the mention of David now provides the cue for the superimposing of a Christian recital on that of ancient Israel. The promises made to David regarding the perpetuity of his house are now seen to be fulfilled in 'great David's greater Son', and from David we go straight to Christ:

> Of this man's posterity God has brought
> to Israel a Saviour, Jesus.

The story of Jesus, from John the Baptist's ministry to the resurrection appearances, is then summarised, and the relation of this new *kērygma* to that of earlier days is made plain:[7]

We bring you the good news that what God promised to the fathers he has fulfilled to us and to our children by raising Jesus, as indeed is written in the second psalm,

> 'Thou art my Son,
> today I have begotten thee.'[8]

And as for the fact that he raised him from the dead, no more to return to corruption, he spoke in this way,

> 'I will give you the holy and sure blessings
> of David.'[9]

Therefore he says also in another psalm,

> 'Thou wilt not let thy Holy One see
> corruption.'[10]

For David, after he had served the counsel of God in his own generation, fell asleep, and was laid with his fathers, and saw corruption; but he whom God raised up saw no corruption.

That is to say, the divine promises made to David were fulfilled neither in his own experience nor in that of his immediate successors, but in his definitive descendant, Jesus.

II

That such a presentation of salvation history is found in Luke's writings is all of a piece with his general perspective; of all the New Testament

7 On the relation of this New Testament *kērygma* to that of the Old Testament, cf. Wright, *God who acts* (1952), pp. 70, 81.

8 Quoted from Ps. 2: 7.

9 Quoted from Isa. 55: 3.

10 Quoted from Ps. 16: 10.

writers he has been called *par excellence* the 'theologian of redemptive history'.[11] According to one distinguished school of thought, that of Rudolf Bultmann and his disciples, this is a feature of the change of outlook occasioned by the delay of the *parousia* (a much overworked factor in the development of early Christian thought, in my judgment), an aspect of the 'incipient catholicism' (*Frühkatholizismus*)[12] which the work of Luke is held to share with other later New Testament documents (outstandingly the letter to the Ephesians).[13] No exposition of this theme has been more influential in recent years than Hans Conzelmann's *The Theology of Saint Luke*,[14] in which it is argued that Luke replaced the primitive perspective, in which the Christ event is itself the *eschaton*, by a new schema in which the Christ event marks the midpoint of time, preceded by 'the time of Israel' and followed by 'the time of the Church'.

The evidence that Luke breaks with the perspective (say) of Mark in envisaging a post-Easter period of rather lengthy duration is not unambiguous. In Mark's eschatological discourse it is stated that 'the gospel must first be preached to all the nations' (13: 10) before the end (*telos*) comes, and if, in Luke's version of that discourse, Jerusalem is to be 'trodden down by the Gentiles, until the times of the Gentiles are fulfilled' (Luke 21: 24), the period appointed for Gentile domination need not be greatly prolonged. This statement, though not paralleled in the Markan discourse, is not Luke's invention; it is a commonplace of prophetic expectation, with a counterpart in the Johannine Apocalypse, where the outer court of the temple, unlike the sanctuary itself, 'is given over to the Gentiles, and they will trample over the holy city

11 Cf. Lohse, 'Lukas als Theologe der Heilsgeschichte', *Evangelische Theologie* XIV (1954–5), pp. 254*ff.*; Flender, *St Luke: Theologian of Redemptive History*, (1967).

12 Cf. Bultmann, 'Heilsgeschichte und Geschichte', *Theologische Literaturzeitung* LXXIII (1948), pp. 659*ff.* (a critique of Cullmann, *Christus und die Zeit* [1946], translated as *Christ and Time* [1951]), English translation in *Existence and Faith* (1964), pp. 268*ff.*; Vielhauer, 'Zum "Paulinismus" der Apostelgeschichte', *Evangelische Theologie* X (1950–1), pp. 1*ff.*, English translation in *Studies in Luke–Acts*, ed. Keck and Martyn (1966), pp. 33*ff.* C. K. Barrett sums up the situation more accurately when he says that Luke 'may present us with some of the raw material of "primitive Catholicism", but hardly with the thing itself' (*The Signs of an Apostle* [1970], pp. 53*f.*).

13 Cf. Käsemann, 'Ephesians and Acts', in *Studies in Luke–Acts*, pp. 288*ff.*

14 English translation (1961) of *Die Mitte der Zeit* (1954); the German title indicates the thesis of the book much more precisely than does the English title.

for forty-two months' (Rev. 11: 2). This passage probably belonged to an independent 'little apocalypse' (the 'little scroll' of Rev. 10: 8–10 which the seer was commanded to eat) which has left traces also in Josephus;[15] in incorporating it into his own apocalypse John placed a new interpretation on it. Luke need not have limited the 'times of the Gentiles' to three and a half years, but he did not think of them as extended indefinitely. On the contrary, those who saw the fall and military occupation of Jerusalem were to take knowledge that the redemption of the saints and the manifestation of the kingdom of God were at hand (Luke 21: 28, 31).

III

Unfortunately the discussion of the presence or absence of a salvation-history pattern in New Testament document writings has not always been carried on dispassionately. Some members of the Bultmann school, for example, have treated its presence as a deviation from the primitive gospel as well as a symptom of 'incipient catholicism', and have expressed disapproval of it as an attempt to find an adventitious security[16] in place of that challenge to enter authentic existence which is, in their estimation, the heart of the gospel.[17] Much of their criticism is directed against the idea that history *per se* constitutes salvation, an idea which, in its secularised form of Nazi ideology, they had to resist a generation ago.[18] But 'salvation *in* history' is not open to the objections which can be levelled against 'salvation *as* history'.[19] However, the exegete's first question, with regard to this or any other pattern, is not 'Is it right or is it wrong?' but 'Is it there or is it not?'

That it is there in Luke ('wrong' though it may be) is agreed; any

15 In Josephus' moralising reflections on the assassination of the former high priests Ananus II and Jesus son of Gamala (*BJ* IV: 314–25); cf. Bruce, 'Josephus and Daniel', *Annual of the Swedish Theological Institute* IV (1965), pp. 154*f*.

16 Cf. such an independent disciple of Bultmann as Käsemann: 'To put it bluntly: with salvation history one is always on the safe side' (*Perspectives on Paul*, English translation [1971], p. 62).

17 For an extreme expression of this attitude cf. the title of an essay by Fuchs: 'Christus, das Ende der Geschichte', *Evangelische Theologie* VIII (1948–9), pp. 447*ff*.

18 Cf. Käsemann, *Perspectives on Paul*, pp. 52, 64.

19 Contrast the German title of Cullmann's *Heil als Geschichte* (1965) with that of the English translation, *Salvation in History* (1969); the change was the author's own decision. The thesis of this magisterial treatment of the subject is certainly not that history *per se* constitutes salvation or revelation.

suggestion that it is there in Paul—that is to say, in the genuine Pauline writings—tends to be resisted or minimised.[20] Good Lutherans as they are, they regard Paul's proclamation as the purest expression of the Christian gospel; but they are prone to recast Paul in an existential image which other students of his writings, approaching them with different presuppositions, do not always recognise as the real Paul.

In this there may be an inadvertent parallel between them and Marcion in the second century. Marcion had no time for salvation history; the gospel as he understood it, and as (in his eyes) Paul preached it, was a new beginning, devoid of all *praeparatio evangelica*, which was first heard on earth when, in the fifteenth year of Tiberius, Jesus 'came down [from heaven] to Capernaum, a city of Galilee', to reveal the unknown Father. He made Luke's record the basis of his *Euangelion*, indeed, but jettisoned the element of salvation history by beginning with the chronological note in Luke 3: 1, going straight on from there to the narrative of 4: 31*ff*., and omitting Acts from his canon.[21]

Hans Conzelmann, for his part—on quite un-Marcionite principles so far as concerns the Gospel of Luke, in which he finds salvation history expounded—treats Luke 3: 1–20 as the prologue to the Gospel and leaves the first two chapters as a whole out of the picture in expounding Luke's theology.[22] This may seem a little strange, in view of the place which these two chapters give to the history of salvation—salvation, too, in most comprehensive terms, embracing (as in the song of Zechariah) 'salvation from our enemies and from the hand of all who hate us' (in good Maccabaean tradition)[23] as well as the 'knowledge of

20 Käsemann freely recognises its presence in Paul: 'I would say that it is impossible to understand the bible in general or Paul in particular without the perspective of salvation history' (*Perspectives on Paul*, p. 63, in an essay on 'Justification and salvation history in the Epistle to the Romans'). But he insists that 'salvation history must not take precedence over justification. It is its sphere. But justification remains the centre, the beginning and the end of salvation history' (p. 76).

21 Tertullian, *Adv. Marcionem* IV: 7.

22 He points out that the opening sentence of Acts 'seems to fix the limits of the first book in such a way that the story of his [Jesus'] birth and childhood is not included' and relates the 'began' of Acts 1: 1 to that of Luke 3: 23 (*The Theology of Saint Luke*, p. 16). It is possible that the 'first book' of Acts 1: 1 was Proto-Luke (cf. Williams, 'The date of Luke–Acts', *Expository Times* LXIV [1952–3], pp. 283*f*.; *The Acts of the Apostles* [1957], pp. 12*f*.); but Professor Conzelmann's examination of the third Gospel is not limited to Proto-Luke.

23 Cf. Winter, 'Magnificat and Benedictus—Maccabaean psalms?' *Bulletin of the John Rylands Library* XXXVII (1954–5), pp. 328*ff*.

salvation in the forgiveness of sins' (Luke 1: 71, 77). Again, the song of Simeon practically supplies Luke's history with a title in the words 'Mine eyes have seen thy salvation'[24]—salvation, once more, in comprehensive terms, including 'a light for revelation to the Gentiles' as well as 'for glory to thy people Israel' (Luke 2: 30–2).

Outside the sphere of influence of the Bultmann school, the place of salvation history in Paul's thinking has been recognised by scholars of widely divergent viewpoints. We may think, on the one hand, of the late Johannes Munck's major work, *Paulus und die Heilsgeschichte* (1954),[25] and, on the other, of Professor Brandon's account of Paul's peculiar contribution to the Christian idea of history as 'a two-phased plan in a divine teleology'.[26] How far Professor Brandon's outlook differed from Professor Munck's is evident from his full-scale review of the English translation of *Paulus und die Heilsgeschichte*;[27] yet it was plain to both that Paul thought in terms of salvation history.

The Paul of Acts clearly thinks in such terms—not only in his synagogue speech at Pisidian Antioch, but also in his address to the Athenian Areopagus. This address, as Professor Conzelmann points out, 'takes world history as one of its themes', embracing 'the ideas of the Creation (the past), of God's dominion over the world (the present) and of the Judgement (the future)'.[28] The claim that the fact of Jesus marks the end of the time of ignorance and the irrevocable declaration of God's will, with the accompanying summons to repentance, is underlined by the framework of universal history in which it is set. It should be emphasised, indeed, that the interval preceding the future judgment is no long one: the summons to repentance is enforced by the certainty of the coming judgment day. A judgment in the indefinite future is a less pressing sanction than one which is fixed and imminent. But, for those who cannot see salvation history as a prominent motif in Paul's thought, the presence of this framework would in itself, apart

24 So, at the end of Luke's narrative, the gospel is summed up as 'this salvation' (Acts 28: 28; cf. 13: 26).

25 English translation, *Paul and the Salvation of Mankind* (1959). A preliminary study of Rom. 9–11, which formed part of the basis for this work, was published later as *Christus und Israel* (1956); *Christ and Israel* (1967).

26 Brandon, *History, Time and Deity*, pp. 148*ff*. (On pp. 148*f*. he makes some noteworthy observations on the senses in which Christianity may be called a 'historical religion'.)

27 Brandon, 'The perennial problem of Paul', *Hibbert Journal* LVIII (1960), pp. 378*ff*.

28 *The Theology of Saint Luke*, p. 168.

from any other consideration, be a sufficient argument that the Areopagus address is thoroughly Lukan and essentially non-Pauline.[29]

IV

But does the Paul of the epistles reveal a salvation-history pattern of thought? He does, in his earlier and later epistles alike, although his understanding of it is controlled by the centrality of justification by faith in his thought.[30] In writing to the Galatians, for example, he insists that it was in 'the fulness of time' that 'God sent his Son, born of woman, born under the law, to redeem those who were under the law, so that we might receive adoption as sons' (Gal. 4: 4*f.*). The 'fulness of time' means that the age of law had run its course, and was now about to be superseded by the age of the Spirit, inaugurated by the accomplishment of Christ's redemptive work. The age of law was the apron-string stage of the people of God, when they had to be subjected to rules and regulations; now they had come of age and were to exercise responsible freedom as God's free-born and fully grown sons: 'because you are sons, God has sent the Spirit of his Son into our hearts . . . so through God you are no longer a slave but a son' (Gal. 4: 6). As Paul viewed the course of sacred history, the age of law was a parenthesis in the record of God's dealings with his people[31]—a necessary parenthesis in the *praeparatio evangelica*, but one which broke into, although it did not suspend, the operation of God's saving grace.[32] For, centuries before the law was given, that saving grace was enshrined in the divine promise to Abraham and his offspring: 'In you shall all the nations be blessed.'[33] In making this promise, which (according to Paul) was to find its definitive fulfilment in Christ, himself descended from Abraham,

29 Cf. Haenchen, *The Acts of the Apostles*, English translation (1971), pp. 515*ff*. For a different point of view cf. Gärtner, *The Areopagus Speech and Natural Revelation* (1955).

30 Cf. Käsemann, *Perspectives on Paul*, pp. 70*ff*., where, in reference to the view that justification by faith is a polemical expedient and therefore a subsidiary factor in Paul's theology, he remarks that 'it is not without irony that it is left to radical historical criticism, as represented by the Bultmann school, to defend the Reformed heritage'.

31 Cf. Gal. 3: 19; Rom. 5: 20*f*.

32 The gospel line, in Paul's view, runs on from Abraham to Christ, and even after the giving of the law 'David pronounces a blessing upon the man to whom God reckons righteousness apart from works' (Rom. 4: 6–8, quoting Ps. 32: 1*f*.).

33 Gen. 12: 3, LXX (cf. Gen. 18: 18; 22: 18), quoted in Gal. 3: 8, 16.

God 'preached the gospel beforehand to Abraham' (Gal. 3: 8), and in making the response of faith to that promise Abraham became the prototype of all who thereafter, hearing the gospel, were to believe God and have that fact reckoned to them for righteousness. In Christ the patriarchal promise is realised, and in Christ believers receive the inheritance of which the promise spoke, and of which the present impartation of the Spirit is the initial pledge.[34]

Paul had probably been brought up to believe that the age in which he lived ('this age') would be separated from the resurrection age ('that age') by the 'days of the Messiah', and that in the days of the Messiah the law, as known in 'this age', would be abrogated. When he became a Christian this schema was not essentially altered, except for his assurance that, since Jesus was the Messiah, the 'days of the Messiah' had begun. The messianic throne, however, was set up not on earth but at the right hand of God, where the risen Lord would continue to reign until God had subdued all his enemies for him (1 Cor. 15: 24–8). The completion of the messianic reign would mark the inception of the resurrection age. For the people of Christ on earth the 'days of the Messiah' coincided with the 'age of the Spirit', who enabled them to maintain union with their exalted Lord, to experience in anticipation the heritage of glory into which they would enter fully at the resurrection, and to enjoy, as the free-born and adult sons of God, an inward liberty such as was unknown under the law. Paul's denunciation of those who tried to impose the law on his converts was due not only to his indignation at an attempt to deprive them of this liberty but also to the implication that, if the age of law was still in force, the days of the Messiah had not yet begun. If so, Jesus was not the Messiah—hence the vehemence of his anathema on those whose preaching led logically to that conclusion.[35]

The allegorical exposition in Gal. 4: 21*ff.* of the dispute between Sarah and Hagar over their respective sons (Isaac and Ishmael) is scarcely an instance of the salvation-history pattern as we find it in the treatment of Abraham's faith in the preceding chapter. True, Paul probably saw significance in the fact that the dispute broke out in Abraham's family, so that Isaac represented Abraham's spiritual

34 Gal. 4: 6; 5: 18; Rom. 8: 10*ff.*, 14*ff.*, 23; 2 Cor. 1: 22; 5: 5.

35 Gal. 1: 8*f.* Cf. Schweitzer, *The Mysticism of Paul the Apostle*, English translation (1931), p. 186; Baeck, 'The faith of Paul', *Journal of Jewish Studies* III (1952), pp. 93*ff.*; Schoeps, *Paul*, English translation (1961), pp. 168*ff.*; Davies, *The Setting of the Sermon on the Mount* (1964), pp. 180*ff.*, 446*ff.*

offspring, sharers by faith of the promise, while Ishmael represented his biological descendants, still held in legal bondage. But this allegorisation has very little to do with historical exegesis.

On the other hand, the 'typological' treatment of the exodus and wilderness narratives in 1 Cor. 10: 1–11, which is closely linked with the presentation of Christ as 'our passover' in 1 Cor. 5: 7*f.*, does exhibit the features of salvation history. The parallel drawn there between the early experiences of Israel and the New Testament phase of the existence of the people of God belongs to the tracing of a recurrent pattern of divine action and human response which was well established in primitive Christianity and appears independently in a number of New Testament writings.[36]

V

But nowhere does Paul expound salvation history more fully than in his classic exposition of the gospel as he understood and proclaimed it—the Letter to the Romans. The first sentence of the letter includes the statements (1) that 'the gospel of God', to the ministry of which Paul was set apart, was 'promised beforehand through his prophets in the holy scriptures' and (2) that Jesus 'was descended from David according to the flesh', while admittedly, and more important, he was 'designated Son of God in power according to the Spirit of holiness by his resurrection from the dead' (Rom. 1: 1–4).

Not once but in several ways this letter presents God's salvation in a historical setting. The outline in Rom. 1: 18*ff.* of the progressive unveiling of divine retribution against the sin of men—whether of gentiles without the special revelation of the law, or of Jews whose knowledge of that revelation renders them the more culpable—forms the background to the unfolding of divine grace in the gospel.

The portrayal of Abraham as the prototype of the man of faith and ancestor of the family of faith, which was sketched briefly in Gal. 3:6*ff.*, is elaborated in Rom. 4: 1–25.[37] The holy land which was promised to Abraham and his descendants is now expanded to comprise the whole world, which through the gospel is to accept the kingship of Christ. But the central blessing of the promise made to Abraham—justification by faith—is not postponed to the time of ultimate fulfil-

36 Cf. Heb. 3: 7*ff.*; Jude 5.

37 Käsemann, 'The faith of Abraham in Romans 4', in *Perspectives on Paul*, pp. 79*ff.*

ment: Abraham received it on the spot when he 'believed God, and it was counted to him for righteousness';[38] and the same blessing is enjoyed on the spot by those in any generation who similarly take God at his word.

When this is borne in mind, the defects which have been pointed out in a purely salvation-history approach to Paul are avoided. The challenge to decision can come, and the response of faith can be made, at any point along the line. Yet the Christ event has made a difference to the pointing of the challenge and the eliciting of the faith: the 'now' of 2 Cor. 6: 2 ('*now* is the acceptable time . . . *now* is the day of salvation') is the 'now' of Acts 17: 30*f.* ('God *now* commands all men everywhere to repent, because he has fixed a day on which he will judge the world in righteousness by a man whom he has appointed, and of this he has given assurance to all men by raising him from the dead').[39]

Another combination of salvation history with the existential challenge is presented in the Adam–Christ analogy of Rom. 5: 12–21. Adam is the solidarity of unregenerate mankind, a solidarity of sin and death, destined to be broken up and superseded by the regenerate solidarity of righteousness and life in Christ. But for Paul, Adam, representative man though he is, is as much a historical figure as Christ, the representative of the new humanity. He traces the time sequence from Adam to Moses, during which sin was present in latent form, as was shown by the prevalence of death, even in the absence of explicit law; from Moses to Christ, during which latent sin was brought into the light and caused to proliferate under the action of explicit law;[40] followed by the new age inaugurated by Christ, into which his followers have entered and in which grace reigns through righteousness to eternal life. But Adam and Christ, the two poles of this course of history, are nevertheless present realities, and the gospel confronts the man in Adam with the call to enter into authentic life as a man in Christ. The salvation history is presented in terms not of evolution from Adam to Christ but of antithesis between Adam and Christ; and also, though not in the same way, the relation between Moses and Christ is one of antithesis, not evolution.

38 Rom. 4: 3, quoting Gen. 15: 6.

39 Conzelmann (*The Theology of Saint Luke*, pp. 205*f.*) presses a distinction which I fail to see between the emphasis of Acts 17: 30*f.* and that of Paul's doctrine of resurrection and judgment.

40 This regime of law is represented as parenthetic (*nomos de pareisēlthen*, Rom. 5: 20), as in Gal. 3: 19.

VI

One of the most valuable contributions made by Professor Munck to this subject relates to Paul's understanding of his own role in the accomplishment of salvation history.[41] He knew himself called, from the hour of his conversion, to be Christ's apostle to the gentiles; indeed, in the light of that experience he knew himself to have been set apart even before his birth to fulfil that ministry.[42] In his letters and in the record of Acts his call is recorded in terms reminiscent of the call of Hebrew prophets: as Jeremiah was divinely consecrated and appointed, before he was born, to be 'a prophet to the nations' (Jer. 1: 5), as the Isaianic Servant was given to be 'a light to the nations', that Yahweh's salvation might reach 'to the end of the earth' (Isa. 49: 6), so Paul's commission was 'to proclaim the word fully, that all the gentiles might hear it' (2 Tim. 4: 17).[43]

The call of Israel was to make known the saving message of their God to the other nations, and the original apostles and other leaders of the Jerusalem Church regarded themselves as the believing remnant of Israel whose mission was first to bring their fellow Israelites to the acknowledgment of Jesus as the Messiah, so that through their witness the surrounding nations might in turn be brought into allegiance to the Son of David. Something of this outlook appears in the exegesis of Amos's oracle about the re-erection of David's fallen booth ascribed by Luke to James the Just at the Council of Jerusalem.[44] Paul deviated from this understanding of the redemptive plan in one particular which, while it was chronological, was nevertheless of the utmost moment to himself, for it involved his place in the working out of God's purpose. Despite the natural interpretation of those prophetic writings which spoke of Israel's mission to the world, God in his wisdom had so ordered it that the gentiles as a whole were to embrace his salvation, brought near in Christ, before the Jews as a whole did so. If the order of presentation was 'to the Jew first, and also to the Gentile' (Rom. 1: 16), the

41 Munck, *Paul and the Salvation of Mankind*, pp. 41*ff.*—although his clear insight into this self-understanding of Paul is unfortunately linked with an improbable interpretation of Paul as the 'restrainer' of 2 Thess. 2: 6*f.*, taken over from Cullmann, 'Le caractère eschatologique du devoir missionnaire et de la conscience apostolique de S. Paul', *Revue d'histoire et de philosophie religieuses* XVI (1936), pp. 210*ff.*

42 Gal. 1: 15; cf. Rom. 1: 1.

43 An authentic Pauline passage (*me iudice*).

44 Acts 15: 15–18, quoting Amos 9: 11*f.*

order of acceptance was 'by the gentile first, and only then by the Jew'. True, a small number of Jews (including Paul himself) had already believed the gospel, and this was an earnest of the full-scale conversion of Israel in due course; but for the present the majority of the people were afflicted by a temporary spiritual blindness, which prevented them from recognising in Jesus the true hope of Israel.[45] During this interval the gospel was being eagerly accepted by gentiles, not least as a result of Paul's apostolic energy. The day would come, however, when the people of Israel would recover their spiritual vision and, suddenly realising that the salvation into which the gentiles were entering through faith was their own ancestral heritage, would be stung to jealousy and claim their proper share in the blessings which were primarily theirs. As a son of Israel himself, Paul eagerly desired to speed this happy consummation, and saw in his own apostolate the means of doing so. For while the immediate effect of his ministry was the conversion of gentiles, its indirect effect would be the provoking of this revulsion of feeling in Israel. And Israel's embracing the gift of righteousness through faith in Christ instead of trying to establish their own righteousness by the works of the law would unleash for the world the greatest blessing it had ever known and be signalled by the *parousia*.[46] The course of salvation history would thus be complete. Well might Paul magnify his office, for if he discharged it faithfully and without intermission he would indeed be a figure of eschatological significance, the preparer of the way for Christ's manifestation in glory, as John the Baptist had been for his first appearing.

For Paul, the, salvation history was no mere theological schema, intellectually constructed as an object of admiration or a source of imagined security: it was the redemptive action of God in which he was personally and totally involved—first as its beneficiary when the risen Lord apprehended him and conscripted him as his messenger, and then as its herald among the gentiles. Paul, as much as Luke, presents us with salvation history, but Paul sets it in a perspective which is peculiarly his own.

VII

A brief mention must suffice for the salvation history perspective of Ephesians, in which the Church, God's masterpiece of reconciliation in

45 Rom. 11: 25; 2 Cor. 3: 14*ff*.
46 Rom. 11: 11–16, 26*f*.

which Jew and gentile become 'one new man' in Christ (2: 15), is also his pilot scheme for the reconciled universe of the future, to be manifested when his 'plan for the fulness of time' is complete (1: 9*f.*); of Hebrews, in which the age inaugurated by Christ is the age of unobstructed access to God, which the preceding age adumbrated by means of shadows or 'copies', serving as object lessons of the reality now experienced; of the Apocalypse, in which the ancient imagery of the woman, the child and the dragon, the war in heaven, and much else, is reborn to become the vehicle of a new rehearsal of the salvation history consummated in the final triumph of the slaughtered Lamb and his faithful followers.

VIII

Of all the questions relating to salvation history in the New Testament none is so important as that which concerns Jesus' own attitude. Here the primary fact is that the proclamation of the kingdom of God in itself implies a salvation-history perspective. This is true whether or not the kingdom of God is linked with the Son of Man and no matter how the timing of the kingdom in Jesus' proclamation is understood. It may be understood in terms of realised or futurist eschatology, or in terms of an existential summons. In fact, room must be found for both 'already' and 'not yet' in even the earliest gospel strata bearing upon this question. But no matter: the term itself cannot be understood apart from its Old Testament background, and in particular the announcement in the book of Daniel that, when gentile dominion has run its destined course, 'the God of heaven will set up a kingdom which shall never be destroyed . . . and it shall stand for ever' (Dan. 2: 44). This kingdom is to be bestowed, when the appointed time comes, on the 'saints of the Most High' (Dan. 7: 18, 22, 27). So when Jesus, on the morrow of John the Baptist's arrest, began to proclaim that the appointed time had fully come and the kingdom of God had drawn near, and called on his hearers to repent and believe the good news,[47] his words must inevitably have been taken to mean that the climax of history was at hand and that the eternal kingdom foreseen by Daniel was about to be established, whatever form that kingdom was to take. Similarly, when he assured his disciples that, 'little flock' as they might be in comparison with the big battalions of the day, it was the Father's good pleasure to give them the kingdom,[48] it was difficult to avoid the

47 Mark 1: 14*f.*

48 Luke 12: 32.

conclusion that they were the 'saints of the Most High' on whom, according to Daniel, that kingdom was to be conferred. Indeed, the whole process of Old Testament history led up to the situation in which these disciples were involved: 'Blessed are the eyes which see what you see! For I tell you that many prophets and kings desired to see what you see, and did not see it, and to hear what you hear, and did not hear it' (Luke 10: 23*f*.; cf. Matt. 13: 16*f*.).

The establishment of the kingdom would be attended by a crisis which would overwhelm with disaster those who were not prepared to meet it, as surely as the deluge of Noah's day and the destruction of Sodom overwhelmed those who refused to be warned in time.[49] Between the time of the ministry ('already') and the consummation of the kingdom ('not yet') Jesus saw an interval of indeterminate duration (even if it might not exceed the lifetime of 'this generation'), introduced by the rejection and passion of the Son of Man, apart from which there would be no advent of the kingdom 'with power'.[50] Those parables which presuppose a delay in the *parousia* are not necessarily the product of the historical delay; to suppose that this must be so is to assume in advance that the *parousia* in Jesus' teaching is invariably imminent. In any case, Jesus not only viewed the time of his ministry as inaugurating the consummation of the divine purpose for the world, towards which all past time had been moving forward, but he viewed himself as the key figure and agent in bringing about the culmination of salvation history. The preachers and theologians of the early post-Easter decades, according to their varying perspective as the sequel to Jesus' ministry unfolded itself, were concerned to develop and reinterpret an understanding of salvation history which came to expression in Jesus himself. But as in Paul salvation history is the 'sphere' of the justifying grace of God, so in Jesus it is the 'sphere' of the Father's pardoning love portrayed in his parables and in his personal friendship towards outcasts and sinners.

These reflections were intended to be offered as an inadequate tribute to a scholar whom I had come to appreciate as a colleague and friend for over twelve years, a scholar whose own contributions to New Testament study provided a stimulus and challenge to myself and to many fellow labourers in the same field. The original draft of the paper, completed only a few days before Professor Brandon's untimely death,

49 Luke 17: 22ff.
50 Cf. Mark 9: 1, 12; 13: 30; Luke 17: 25.

ended with an expression of hope that he would continue for many years to enrich us with further contributions to learning as he had so generously done in the past. This hope, alas, must now remain unfulfilled. But with gratitude for all that he was and did may be coupled the hope that his memory will inspire many more to follow his example and shed fresh light on the history of religion.

8

J. Duchesne-Guillemin

Jesus' trimorphism and the differentiation of the Magi

When Marco Polo visited Iran on his way to China he was told the following story about the Three Wise Men:[1] Jesus had appeared to them, as they separately entered the stable at Bethlehem, in three different forms corresponding to the age of each, namely, as a young man, an adult, and an old man.

In 1951 Leonardo Olschki[2] saw the source of this conception in the three- or fourfold manifestation of the Iranian god of time, Zurvan. He also adduced the Ismaïlite belief that the *imam* combines the three ages in his person, while his divine substance remains unchanged.

Olschki's article was cited by Monneret de Villard in his book *Le leggende orientali sui Magi evangelici*, published the following year, in which he also quoted from the Armenian *Gospel of the Infancy* about Jesus appearing in three forms corresponding to the three gifts. But he concluded as follows:[3] 'questo problema . . . attende chi saprà compiutamente risolverlo'.

Elsewhere[4] I have tried to show that the representation of the Magi themselves as a youth, an adult and an old man stemmed from the Hellenistic cult of Aion, no matter whether this cult had been influenced by the Zurvan belief or not.

Only in 1966–7 did H. Puech briefly take up this theme in his seminar of the École Pratique des Hautes-Études, Paris, and announce[5] his intention to seek an explanation of the threefold appearance

1 *Il Milione*, chapters 31 and 32.

2 'The Wise Men of the East in oriental traditions', *Semitic and Oriental Studies presented to W. Popper* (1951), pp. 381–6.

3 *Le leggende orientali sui Magi evangelici* (1952), p. 79.

4 'Die drei Weisen aus dem Morgenlande', *Antaios* (1965), pp. 234–52; 'Addenda et corrigenda', *Iranica Antiqua* (1967), pp. 1–3; 'Espace et Temps dans l'Iran ancien', *Revue de synthèse* LV–LVI (1969), pp. 259–80. Parts of these articles have been translated here.

5 *Annuaire de l'École Pratique des Hautes Études*, 5e section (Sciences religieuses) (1966–7), p. 130.

of Jesus in his assimilation to the personified Aion, 'cette sorte de réplique occidentale de Zurvan akarana'.

As a first stage in his research he gave two parallels to the Marco Polo testimony. The first is an illustrated ms. from the eleventh century in the Library of the Patriarchate in Jerusalem.[6] The three Magi, of different ages, see Jesus in the grotto in three different forms and later on exchange their impressions. 'The first said, I saw him as a little child, the second, I as a man of thirty, the third, I as an old man. And they wondered at this change in the appearance of the new-born.' This homily is attributed by Franz Dölger to John of Euboea.

The second text, cited by Puech (after Abbé Marcel Richard) in the following year, is an illustrated gospel book of the eleventh century in the Bibliothèque nationale:[7] Jesus is represented on a miniature in three forms and with three names, as an old man, *Παλαιὸς τῶν ἡμέρων*, as an adult, *Χριστὸς*, and as a youth, *'Εμμανυήλ*. The text is a homily of John of Damascus, in which the symbolism of the three ages is combined with that of the three gifts: to the first of the three kings, who offers Jesus gold, as to a king, he appears as a three-year-old child, like a son of God; to the second, who offers him frankincense as to a god, he appears as a man of thirty; to the third, who offers him myrrh as to a mortal man, he appears as an old man with white hair, looking like the 'Ancient of Days'.

If we survey the whole material, including the Marco Polo story, it becomes apparent that two different themes are here merged, which ought to be sorted out, namely: (1) the appearance of Jesus in different forms; (2) the differentiation of the Magi as a youth, an adult and an old man. Of the two themes, Puech has treated only the first, adducing a wealth of texts from the 'occidental' tradition,[8] in which Jesus appears in different forms:

1 In the Armenian *Gospel of the Infancy*, already cited by Monneret, Jesus appears in different forms according to the gifts offered, namely, as a child in the manger, as the son of an earthly king, and as Christ dead and resurrected. In another chapter of the same apocry-

6 Ms. 14, with illustration on folio 106v, a photograph of which was made available to me through the kindness of the Archbishop and of Professor R. J. Zwi Werblowsky of the Hebrew University.

7 Ms. gr. 74, f. 167, reproduced here, plate 8.1.

8 'Occidental' here means Mediterranean, as opposed to the Iranian tradition referred to by Olschki.

Plate 8.1 *Courtesy Bibliothèque nationale, Paris*

Plate 8.2 *Courtesy Princeton University Press*

Plate 8.3 *Courtesy Osvaldo Böhm, Venice*

phal gospel Jesus transforms himself into child, an adult and an old man, later to resume his former appearance.

2 According to Photius, Jesus appears to his disciples as a child, a youth and an old man.

3 In Peter–Acts 21 and chapter 29 of the *Vita Aberci* Jesus appears to three old women, or to two groups of old women, as an old man, a beardless youth and a little child. It is to be noted that the persons to whom he appears are not themselves of different ages, as will be the case with the Magi.

4 In John–Acts Jesus appears once as a 'handsome man', then as a bald old man, then, to James, as a child and as a youth.

5 In chapter 14 of the *Martyrdom of Peter* Simon the Magus (the first of the Gnostics) transforms himself successively into a child, an old man, a youth.

6 In the prologue to the *Apokryphon Johannis* Jesus appears to John in three different forms, two of which are specified, namely, as a child and as an old man.

Puech comments illuminatingly:[9]

> Autant deviner que Jésus est ici conçu sur le type de l' *'Αιὼν* en qui coexistent passé, présent, avenir, qui englobe et réunit en soi les trois dimensions du temps, les trois stades successifs d'une durée totale, correspondant, pour ce qui est de l'homme, aux trois âges de la vie: enfance ou jeunesse, maturité, vieillesse. Le sens et l'origine du thème de la 'trimorphie' appliqué à Jésus sont par là, nous a-t-il déjà semblé, susceptibles d' être découverts: Jésus doit être, en l'occurrence, une figure, une personnification de l' *'Αιὼν*.

I propose here to develop this point a little, then briefly to tackle again the second one, left aside by Puech, namely, the differentiation of the Magi.

I

In order to explain the role of Aion in the emergence of Jesus' trimorphism we must recall, however succinctly, the origin of the Epiphany.

The anniversary of Mithra's birth was celebrated on 25 December—on the very day, that is, which was later chosen, at Rome, for the date of Christmas. Until then the birth of Christ, the adoration of the Magi and the baptism of Christ had all been celebrated on 6 January. This

9 *Annuaire*, p. 130.

day had been, before Christianity, notably in Egypt, the birthday of Aion, the god of time, and it is probably from Egypt that the Christian festival on that day spread to the whole of Christendom, including the West. In a reverse movement, the 25 December Christmas festival spread from Rome into the whole orient. There were thenceforth the two successive feast days we know: Christmas on 25 December, Epiphany on 6 January.

Leaving the latter aside for the moment, we may first consider the 25 December festival before Christianity. It commemorated Mithra's birth, but, as its date implies, it regarded this birth as a periodic event, namely, the annual return of the solar brilliance after its greatest diminution at the winter solstice. That birth or its memory was therefore celebrated as a forthcoming event. However, the new-born Mithra is never represented as a suckling baby in swaddling clothes, but as a young boy, called *saxigenus* or *πετρογένης*.

What exactly did that epithet mean? To judge by all the figurations, it meant that Mithra had been born from the stone as fire from the flint, or rather, as the sun rises from behind mountains. On the other hand, we must not forget that this festival was celebrated in the Mithra temples, which had—in allusion to the vault of heaven—the shape of grottoes. From there to the conception of Mithra as born in a grotto was but a short step.

We may now put ourselves in the new perspective created by the birth of Jesus and the gospel story. We must first note that according to the canonical gospels Jesus was born in a crib: it is nowhere said that it was in a grotto. Thus three notions ran parallel to each other:

1 The infant Jesus born in a stable.
2 The boy Mithra springing from the stone.
3 Mithra's birth celebrated in grotto-shaped temples.

How did these three notions coalesce? A passage in Justin Martyr gives the impression that the similarity had been noticed. Hence it is that, from Justin onwards, with Origen and in the apocryphal *Gospel of James*, Jesus was deemed to have been born in a grotto.

There is little doubt that the three elements Virgil welded together in his fourth Eclogue, namely, the return of the golden age, the solar kingship and the infant saviour, already existed a long time before him, even if they had not yet been welded into a synthesis. The Babylonian doctrine of the Great Year and, earlier, the conception of a periodic renewal and an eternal return had spread the hope in a new era as far as Italy. This is proved by Roman coins at least since Caesar's death. The idea of a new era was attached, particularly in Egypt, to that of the emergence of a new king. Also in Egypt the king was expressly conceived of as solar. Moreover, we recall, each year on 25 December the return of the solar light was celebrated and on 6 January the renewal of Aion.

Finally—and this introduces the third theme—the return of the sun was represented as the birth of a child, Isis the virgin giving birth to the boy Horus, the solar child.

We may now pass to the 6 January festival. On this day, as we saw, the birth of Aion was celebrated. But Aion was conceived and represented now as a child (by Heraclitus, Euripides, etc), now as an adult in the prime of life (in the picture described by John of Gaza, under Justinian), now as an old man (by Claudian, in 400): he totalised in himself, like Jesus in his different appearances, the three ages of life.

The conception that human life was divided into three ages seems hoary and certainly reached back to classical antiquity. It was shared by authors like Aristotle. Admittedly, no pictorial representation of it has survived, earlier than the eighth century fresco in the bath of Quseir Amra[10] in Jordania, in which we see the old man, the adult and the youth. But although the painting is late, its motif, like that of all the others in this building, belongs to the old, classical style. The central figure, the adult with his vine grapes, might allude to Dionysos, who was identified with Aion . . .

But there is about Aion a perfectly clear document—which however, has not been adduced by Puech, and by myself only belatedly.[11] This is the Aion mosaic at Antioch, published by Doro Levi in 1944. It gives a nice transition, as we shall see, to our second theme, the differentiation of the Magi.

In front of a personage designated as Aion three others are seated, named the Chronoi—respectively Past, Present and Future—with features easily recognisable: a white beard, a black beard, no beard. I propose[12] to see in this mosaic the model of the differentiation of the Magi into an old man, an adult and a youth in front of God.

This presents no chronological or geographical difficulty, as is the case with a representation from Luristan dating back to the eighth century B.C.—and, moreover, suspect; I adduced it in my 1965 article

10 A reproduction is given in 'Addenda et corrigenda', plate 1.
11 'Espace et Temps', pp. 260*ff*. Here plate 8.2.
12 As I did in 'Espace et Temps', p. 261.

for no other reason than because the Antioch mosaic was then still unknown to me.[13] On the Luristan plaque, published in 1958 by Ghirshman,[14] there appear before a mythical figure three sets of worshippers: children, adults and old men. This distribution seems particularly suitable to the case of worshippers of a being otherwise characterised as a god of time, for he has wings as well as two faces—symbols of the bisexuality that is normal in a god of origins. An allusion has been recognised here to the god Zurvan, who had in Syriac the epithets *Ašoqar*, *Frašoqar*, *Zaroqar*, terms adapted from the Avestan and clearly designating him as god of youth, manhood and old age.

But to return to the Antioch mosaic. There are in this case, as I said, no further chronological or geographical difficulties. Antioch was the Asiatic metropolis where the word 'Christian' was first heard. And stylistic criteria allow the work to be dated to the middle of the third century, *viz.* about the time when Christianity was officially recognised by Constantine and Christian art came out from the Catacombs.

What may have been the purpose of the patron of this mosaic? Did he want an illustration of a philosophical debate on Time that flies and Eternity that remains? Did he simply want to see represented in picture form a hoary conception of human life, or to introduce a religious connotation (mark the incense-burner) into this conception? The three purposes are not mutually exclusive. And the scene, with its three times facing Eternity, seems very appropriate to account for the representation of the three wise men as a youth, an adult and an old man in the presence of God. For it is perhaps not by a mere chance that in the Christian world the three Magi do not merely present themselves before God but figure as worshippers of a god who manifests himself at the very time of year in which the year—hence time itself—is renewed, namely, on Aion's birthday.

II

In their most ancient figurations the Magi of Bethlehem were identical to each other and they all wore the Phrygian cap. This, by the way, did not characterise them as priests of Mithra but merely, as Franz Cumont has proved, as Iranians. We see them represented in this manner, for instance, on the fourth century sarcophagus relief in the

13 My wife Marcelle brought it to my notice.

14 Ghirshman, 'Le dieu Zurvan sur les bronzes du Luristan', *Artibus Asiae* (1958), pp. 37*ff*. Reproduced also in my *Antaios* article, plate XII.

Latran Museum, or on the wood relief of the Porta Sabina, about 400. They were distinguished from one another only by their gifts—gold, frankincense and myrrh—the number of which, undoubtedly, had determined that of the Magi themselves—in contradistinction to the twelve Magi who, according to another version of the legend, were destined to evangelise the East.

The differentiation of the Magi took place along two different lines. In the recently discovered Catacomb of the Via Latina in Rome, the three Magi are seen, two of whom have a beard, but it is not possible from the black-and-white picture in Mr Ferrua's book to distinguish the colour of their beards. I have had a look at the catacomb myself[15] and have been able to ascertain that one beard is brown, the other blond. No white one, then. This fresco therefore represents only some sort of attempt at varying the appearance of the Magi: it does not—or, to be more precise, does not yet—show the differentiation into the three ages which so often appears later on. When, in fact, is this new differentiation first attested?

We may leave aside the conception found in St Augustine, to whom the Magi represented the three world parts: *primitiae gentium*. Similarly in the Armenian *Gospel of the Infancy* cited above, Caspar comes from India, Balthasar from Persia and Melkoun from Arabia. And it is said in the Nestorian liturgy that the kings of Persia and India, with the one from China, prostrated themselves before the king from the house of David.

The other conception is not attested in writing until the eighth century, namely, in the Venerable Bede, who, however, must have found it elsewhere, for he is not generally suspected of inventing things. According to him, then, the three Magi represented the whole human race in its three ages. And they are described as follows in a text falsely attributed to him and entitled *Collectanea et flores:*

> primus fuisse dicitur Melchior, senex et canus,
> secundus nomine Caspar, iuuenis imberbis, rubicundus,
> tertius fuscus, integre barbatus, Balthasar nomine.

The *Manual of Painting* on Mount Athos enjoins that they should be so represented; and so do they appear in innumerable paintings and sculptures in the whole of Christendom. In fact, the first preserved images of this representation precede Bede's book by many centuries.

15 It is not yet open to the general public. Special admission was granted me through the good offices of Professor E. Cerulli.

Since it is difficult to see, from the photograph available to me, whether the Magi on the sarcophagus at Castiliscar, Spain, are of the same age or not, the earliest unequivocal representation of the three Magi in the three ages of man dates from the sixth century; it is to be found at Monza, near Milan, on the famous *ampullae* that were sold to pilgrims in the Holy Land as containers for the oil of the cross and probably reproduced monuments in Bethlehem.

Of approximately the same date is the relief of the San Marco architrave, in Venice,[16] on which it will be noted that the Magi, although clearly of different ages, still all wear the Phrygian cap.

16 West portal of the north façade, here plate 8.3.

9

Mircea Eliade

The dragon and the shaman

Notes on a South American mythology

The history of modern interpretations of myth, from Max Müller to Claude Lévi-Strauss, constitutes a fascinating subject for a monograph in the history of ideas. After being declared a disease of language (Max Müller), a naive animistic creation (E. B. Tylor), a playful and debasing fancy (Andrew Lang), a projection of astral phenomena (the German astral-mythological and pan-Babylonian schools), a verbalisation of ritual (W. Robertson Smith, Jane Harrison, and the British myth-and-ritual school), or a fantasy related to a primordial parricide (Freud) or to the collective unconscious (Jung)—myth has begun to be understood in a more positive way. That is, myth has come to be seen either as a sacred story, model and justification of a meaningful and creative human life; or as the expression of 'primitive', but no less valid, logical processes. The first group, in this more recent and positive form of interpretation, insists on the *religious values* of myth, while the second group, and particularly Lévi-Strauss's interpretation, emphasises the *logical structures* of mythical thought.[1] In general, the first group consists of historians of religions, the second group of anthropologists and folk-lorists.

I do not intend to summarise here my own understanding of mythical thinking and of the role of myth in religious life.[2] I shall content myself with a brief discussion of some relations between myth and 'history' in a particular archaic population, namely the Peruvian Campa. But, as I have argued elsewhere,[3] I do not think we can grasp the structure and function of mythical thinking in a society which has

1 I have discussed the theories of myth from Max Müller to Lévi-Strauss in an article to appear in *Dictionary of the History of Ideas*, ed. Wiener: 'Myth in the nineteenth and twentieth centuries'.

2 See especially *Myth and Reality* (1963).

3 See 'Cosmogonic myth and "sacred history"', in *The Quest* (1969), pp. 72–87.

myth as its foundation if we do not take into account the *mythology in its totality* and, at the same time, the *scale of values* which such mythology implicitly or explicitly proclaims. Now in every case where we have access to a still living tradition, and not to an acculturated one, one thing strikes us from the very beginning: the mythology not only constitutes, as it were, the 'sacred history' of the tribe; not only does it explain the total reality and justify its contradictions, but it equally reveals a hierarchy in the series of fabulous events that it reports. In general, one can say that any myth tells *how something came into being*—the world, or man, or an animal species, or a social institution, and so on. But by the very fact that the creation of the world precedes everything else, the cosmogony enjoys a special prestige. In fact, the cosmogonic myth furnishes the model for all myths of origin. The creation of animals, plants or man presupposes the existence of a world. Even in those religions where the cosmogonic myth *stricto sensu* is unknown (as is the case, for example, with many Australian religions) there is always a central myth which describes the *beginnings* of the world, that is, what happened before the world became as it is today. Thus there is always a *primordial history*, and this history has a *beginning*—a cosmogonic myth proper, or a myth that describes the first, germinal stage of the world. This beginning is always implied in the sequence of myths which recounts the fabulous events that took place after the creation or the coming into being of the universe, namely, in the myths of the origin of plants, animals and man, or of the origin of marriage, the family, death, etc. Taken all together, these myths of origin constitute a fairly coherent history.

Now this primordial, sacred history, brought together by the totality of significant myths, is fundamental because it explains, and by the same token justifies, the existence of the world, of man and of society. This is the reason why a mythology is considered at once a *true history*: it relates how things came into being, supplying the exemplary model and also the justification of man's activities.

Provided we take into consideration the central myth of a particular society, we are able to grasp its 'existential' value for the members of that community. Not only does the mythology constitute the model for all responsible human action, but it also provides an explanation for what the West terms 'history' and 'historical events'. As we shall presently see, the cosmogonic myth and its sequence, the myths of origin, help a 'primitive' population to find out the meanings of a series of tragic historical events; furthermore, such myths provide the means to resist the terror and the despair brought by the catastrophic historical events. In the last analysis the mythology gives us the key to understanding the recent history of an archaic society. Indeed, we discover that in some cases an archaic society does not collapse under the 'terror of history,' but, reinterpreting the central (i.e. the cosmogonic) myth, finds the strength to adapt to a critical situation and thus to survive in the new historical context. In other words, the 'sacred history' revealed in the traditional mythology enables an archaic society to *live historically* and even to 'make' history.

The South American tribe of the Campa admirably illustrate what I consider to be the fundamental meaning and function of the cosmogonic myth. As a matter of fact, I do not see what other interpretation can be brought forward that can better account for the exceptional role of the cosmogonic myth and the myths of origin.

The Campa, who belong to the Arawak linguistic family, are the largest tribe living in the Peruvian mountains. Although known from the sixteenth century, and investigated by such scholars as Otto Nordenskiöld and Günther Tessmann, only very recently, and thanks especially to the Peruvian ethnologist, Stefano Varese,[4] have we begun to understand their religious and cultural traditions. The great interest of this tribe for our theme resides in the fact that, having at our command a large number of written sources from the sixteenth to the eighteenth century, especially letters and memoirs from missionaries and colonial administrators, and now, in the last few years, beginning to know their traditions, we are able to judge how they reacted to the most tragic event in their history, namely, the encounter with the conquering Spaniards.

According to Campa mythology, in the beginning the god Oriátziri created the world, the animal species and lastly the Campa and the neighbouring tribes. But white men do not belong to this primordial creation. They came into being later on, and their appearance announces the imminent end of the world. The myth tells us that white men emerged from the subterranean aquatic darkness; consequently, they are assimilated to the monstrous dragon Nónkhi, i.e. to the principle of Evil, the author of disease and death. Indeed, the myth narrates how, immediately after his emergence, the white man exterminated the entire population of the Campa, with the exception of the primordial shaman, who, thanks to his spiritual powers, could not be

4 I am using especially his book *La Sal de los cerros: notas etnográficas e históricas sobre los Campa de la selva del Perù* (1968).

destroyed. But this primordial shaman will ultimately triumph over the white man, for, in the mythical beginning, the shaman defeated the dragon Nónkhi. In other words, the appearance of the white man has an eschatological significance: it proclaims the imminent end of the world and the creation of a new world, wholly regenerated, a world where white men will definitively return to their subterranean, larval pre-existence.[5]

The shaman, or the eschatological Hero, fights the powers of Evil in order to reinstall the primeval perfection. Such eschatological crises have taken place many times, the most recent being the rebellion of the national 'messiah', Juan Santos Atahualpa, in the second half of the eighteenth century.[6] This Atahualpa regained political, spiritual and economic autonomy for the Campa by defeating the Spanish colonial troops and driving out the Christian missionaries. For more than ten years the Campa lived in almost complete independence. Moreover, this messianic movement did not end in despair and nihilism, as is usually the case with modern millenaristic and messianic cults. Nothing is known of Atahualpa's death. Probably he died some ten years after the proclamation of the rebellion, but the Campa believe that he simply 'disappeared', being 'transformed into smoke'.

Thus a series of important and interrelated historical events—the appearance of the white man in the sixteenth century and Juan Santos Atahualpa's successful 'messianic' revolution against the Spanish colonial authority in the eighteenth century—were reinterpreted in the perspective of the tribal mythology, and specifically as the two most spectacular moments: the end of one cycle and the beginning of a new one, the terrifying yet exalted interval when the *Endzeit* is expected to merge into the *Urzeit*. Such transformation of historical events into mythical episodes does not imply an evasionistic ideology. The Campa did not withdraw from historical actuality in order to take refuge in a fabulous, supernatural universe. They lived in what we call the *historical present*, and tried to cope with the new situation created by the presence of the Spanish troops and mercenaries. The Campa did not proclaim from the very beginning the demonic nature of white men, but only when the Spaniards, by their own actions and behaviour, identified themselves with unknown and fatal diseases, with

5 Varese, *op. cit.*, pp. 129*ff.*
6 *Ibid.*, pp. 64*ff.* See also, by the same author, 'La rebelión de Juan Santos Atahualpa: un movimento mesiánico del siglo XVIII en la selva peruana', *Actas y Trabajos, XXXVI Congresso Internacional de Americanistas* (1966).

violence and death. The cosmogonic myth helped the Campa to understand the nature of the invaders and to find out their origin: they could only be a new epiphany of the primordial dragon and, consequently, their birthplace must have been the underworld. Once the Campa understood the real identity of the *conquistadores*, they knew what was going to happen in the near future—the end of the world, but also the victory of the primordial shaman against the dragon's new manifestation, the white man. The pre-existent myth gave sense and meaning to the tragic historical moment, and also reassured the Campa that this tragedy would be followed by a splendid restoration of the traditional order.

The central element of this eschatological myth, i.e. the possibility of understanding history and of overcoming it, consists of the presence of the shaman, the charismatic hero, and of the certainty that so long as the traditional science and spiritual power are still with the Campa, there is hope for a better future. The *real* tragedy begins when this element of continuity, represented by the shaman's traditional science, is menaced. Another significant myth illustrates such a danger.

A long time ago, say the Campa, they were poor. They did not have many things, but they could obtain what they needed through bartering with neighbouring tribes, and also by going to ask for them from a divine being, Pachakamáite. This Pachakamáite was neither a Creator nor a demiurge, but he was the author and owner of all the foods and tools possessed by the missionaries and the colonists, including the salt which could no longer be obtained, as it had been formerly, through traditional barter. Pachakamáite lived very far away, and to reach him was tantamount to an initiatory ordeal. One had to enter into dark caves and to conquer the monster which defended the goods. For this reason, before departing the voyagers painted their faces and clothes. Once in the presence of Pachakamáite other initiatory trials were in store for the voyager: he could not sit down, and after receiving the gifts, he had to run away, pursued by a demonic female being.[7]

The return of the hero was a beneficial event for the entire community because every member of the tribe partook of the divine gifts brought by the traditional commerce. (One can understand from this episode the drama of a traditional society when Westerners negate its original cultural activity as well as its sacramental life and its sacred

7 See the mythological text translated and interpreted by Varese, *La Sal de los cerros*, pp. 138*ff*.

commerce.) Pachakamáite lives very far away, and in our days the road is blocked by the white man's barricades. In the old times the traditional traders and the shamans could reach Pachakamáite, but now traders as well as shamans are all dead. Today the Campa have lost the 'saving science' and are decadent. Their material and spiritual poverty is explained by the loss of contact with divine life, and thus the loss of the traditional free exchange of goods. As in so many other messianic 'cargo cults', the Campa likewise consider the goods of Western origin as gifts of one of their own supernatural beings (in this case, Pachakamáite). These divine gifts are supposed to have been intercepted and confiscated by the white man, who refuses to distribute them freely. Instead he sells them for money.

In such a situation of total despair and spiritual disorientation, the only hope of the Campa is in the shamans; only they can save the traditional, primeval order.[8] Thus, waiting for the restoration of the primordial order is not an illusory idealisation of the past, nor a negation of the future, but such waiting proclaims the will to live in harmony with the fundamental principles of the traditional Campa civilisation.

Even from this summary presentation of the cosmogonic myth and the complementary myths of origin, we can judge their 'existential' and 'historical' (ultimately political) function. The tragic encounter of the Campa with the white man, *conquistadores*, missionaries and administrators alike, finds a meaning and a justification in the myth of the dragon, Nónkhi. A historical event is thus integrated into the sacred tribal history. Consequently, the event is not only passively 'accepted' but also brings forth a real 'historical' reaction (e.g. Atahualpa's rebellion), because the myth proclaimed from the beginning the final defeat of the dragon by the primordial shaman. Thus the myth both provides 'meaning' for historical events and supplies the framework for further historical actions: the 'messiah' Atahualpa could arise and triumph against the Spaniards because in mythical times the primordial shaman conquered the dragon, Nónkhi, *fons et origo* of the white man. Likewise, in spite of the fact that in our days the white man has blocked the road to Pachakamáite, with the result that the Campa now live in poverty, there is always the hope in a new epiphany of the primordial shaman, who will restore the traditional order and civilisation.

In sum, the example of the Campa[9] illustrate once more the central

8 See *ibid.*, pp. 133*ff.*: 'El Chamanismo Heroico'.

9 It is hardly necessary to add that the Campa are not an exception. We have

role of the cosmogonic myth and of the myths of origin in a 'primitive' culture. Such myths ought not to be considered of the same status as other, secondary or aetiological, myths and fairy-tales, although all these types of traditional narrative present an analogous structure. They are 'sacred stories', and as such they inform the entire religious, cultural and 'historical' life of the society.

---

quoted other examples in several previous works, from *The Myth of the Eternal Return* (1949) to 'Cosmogonic myth and "sacred history"' (1967).

10

James M. Fennelly

The primitive Christian values of salvation and patterns of conversion

The history-of-religions method for the understanding of Christian origins is interdisciplinary. It requires the exploration of fields of study transcending conventional schemes which oft-times restrain the creative and discourage clarity.[1] One of the highest honours we may present to the late Professor S. G. F. Brandon is the acknowledgment that he pioneered the search for the roots of early Christian growth with such foresight that future generations will perceive greater value from his work than even present acclaim might suggest.

The topic of man and his salvation in Christian origins might be disposed of in very simple terms by applying Paul's definition of salvation and Luke–Acts' understanding of the beginnings of Christianity, with the assurance of Ignatius of Antioch that this is the correct procedure. The Pauline concept of salvation emphasised a deep emotional experience in which the individual participated in a death–resurrection pathos in harmony with Christ, which manifested itself in a new life. Obviously Paul's own conversion acted as the pattern for his personal understanding of the nature of salvation, even though it was not the normative one for the Church Fathers (aside from Ignatius), who conceived of the saving work of Christ as providing the believer with a share in a future earthly kingdom.[2] The integrated rendition of the growth of the Church in Luke–Acts is a personal reconstruction of Christian origins moulded out of earlier Greek and Aramaic documents which were at times contrary to the interests of the author, who desired to establish a concept of an harmonious development of the religion

1 Bleeker, 'Comparing the religio-historical and the theological method', *Numen* XVIII (1971), pp. 9–29. A similar attitude is recommended for the use of psychology as a tool equal in importance to form criticism! Grant, 'Psychological study of the Bible', in *Religions in Antiquity* (1968).

2 McGiffert, 'Apostolic age', in *Encyclopaedia of Religion and Ethics*, ed. Hastings, I (1908), p. 620.

centred around the supreme authority of the Apostles and suggesting one definitive theological source.[3] These two highly individual interpretations, Paul on salvation and the author of Luke–Acts on the beginnings of Christianity, cannot be combined to create an objective evaluation of the subject. The opposite may be substantiated by simply reversing the equation and utilising Christian origins as in Paul and Salvation as derived from Luke–Acts.

There is also a wide separation among scholars because of theological and ecclesiastical presuppositions. W. D. Davies, in a comprehensive review of these positions, concluded with a description of how Protestant and Roman Catholic preconceptions relating to the supernatural nature of the founding of the Church predetermine the individual's judgment.[4] Protestants regard the establishment of the Church as a social necessity, while Roman Catholics view it as a divine ordinance. In so far as possible we must approximate a form of nominalism, current in the history-of-religions methodology, as the most promising route.

The *filum labyrinthi* (if such can be said to exist) will be found only with an expansion of materials, methods and assumptions.

> With regard to New Testament theology, this means that the major focus for the next generation lies neither in a return to the effort to recover the lost threads of continuity in the history of ideas from author to author nor in the unrelated juxtaposition of converging or diverging understandings of existence (although ongoing research in both dimensions will play a part in any future synthesis of significance), but in the tracing of word as it comes into language. For in this movement one can trace the historical trajectory to which understandings of existence can be meaningfully related and hence historically interpreted.[5]

To achieve this, the enormous collection of heterodox material can no longer be ignored. Apocryphal and non-canonical writings must be given full value as genuine examples of one part of the total picture of primitive Christianity.[6] The assumption that orthodox preceded heterodox was seriously disputed by W. Bauer and has been substantiated by the Nag Hammadi manuscripts.[7] Finally, if additional

3 Lake, 'The preface to Acts and the composition of Acts', *Beginnings of Christianity* v (1933), p. 4.
4 Davies, *Christian Origins and Judaism* (1962), pp. 220*ff.*
5 Robinson, 'Word in theology', *Soli Deo Gloria* (1968), p. 104.
6 Hennecke, *The New Testament Apocrypha* I (1963), p. ii.
7 Bauer, *Orthodoxy and Heresy in Earliest Christianity* (1971).

light is to be shed on the subject, it will be necessary to use the findings of archaeology, sociology, economics, psychology, etc, to add insight to the evidence on hand. Thus one must expand the field of interpretation and revise the old presuppositions as the sole avenue to a more creditable conclusion.

The mystical experience of individualised salvation was certainly not new to Paul nor to other religions. A. D. Nock has gathered several illustrations from the claims of conversion in his book on early Christianity in its cultural setting.[8] While Paul appears to have had a traumatic ecstasy, of a type fitting E. H. Erikson's category for such an ineffable encounter,[9] he represents a small minority of his generation.[10] Paul manifested a desire to escape from what he thought to be an intolerable reality, and he exuded the preconditions associated with sudden conversion. In psychological terms the metamorphosis of Acts 9: 1–19, 22: 4–16 and 26: 9–18, while abundant with textual variants and specifically ignored in the body of the Epistles, is solidly substantiated in the essence of Pauline theology. Linn and Schwarz give a criterion describing the psychological nature of a mystical experience (religious or non-religious) which is suggestive of much that we know about Paul.

> According to the mystic it [the experience] is inexpressible and indescribable; it is never possible to convey what it is like to one who has not had the experience.[11]

There is no reason why such an event must be connected with epilepsy, as was done by Klausner.[12] For the mystic the universe has been plumbed (2 Cor. 12: 1–10); it is accompanied by a sense of authority (1 Cor. 4: 14–20), and the subject is in the grip of a higher power (Phil. 3: 12). In the mystical state one has the capacity to reconcile opposites (Rom. 6: 5–11), and it always involves a retreat from reality and a withdrawal from one's fellow men (Gal. 1: 17). Deissmann suggested that such psychological events were the 'starting point for the first Jesus cult in Palestine, and the genuine precondition for the rise of the Christian cult-community which now began to organise itself.'[13] But it is diffi-

8 Nock, *Conversion* (1933).
9 Erikson, *The Young Man Luther* (1958), pp. 173–5.
10 Knox, *Chapters in a Life of Paul* (1950), p. 17; Brandon, *The Fall of Jerusalem* (1957), p. 153.
11 Linn and Schwarz, *Psychiatry and Religious Experience* (1958), p. 196.
12 Klausner, *From Jesus to Paul* (1943), pp. 328–9.
13 Deissmann, *Paul* (1926), p. 123.

cult to find a similar conversion experience for other members of the early Church, and it is impossible to provide theological substantiation for such mysticism outside Paul and perhaps 1 Peter, John and 1 John.[14] The limited appeal of an ecstasy forces one to doubt whether it is at the heart of the earliest message of salvation. The vast majority of traumatic raptures are retrogressive, obliging the individual to retreat to a childhood synthesis of faith. Paul's conversion had the qualities of a second encounter, conveying the impression that his childhood religion had been that of a *diaspora* Hellenistic Judaism, a mysticism similar to that described by E. R. Goodenough.[15] His experience of Christianity was a return–release from the radicalism of Hillel's school to his childhood Judaism. Such a conversion was the antithesis of the Disciples' encounter. Jesus must be considered as a leader whose basic evaluation of reality reflected the critical needs of his generation. Men saw in him their aspirations, and he became the objectification of their longing for salvation. The essence of the vocation of Saviour may not be limited to a sensation of an ineffable metamorphosis. Converts who experience a crisis of religious awakening and transfer from one religion to another represent only a minute fraction of the membership of any sect. The rapid expansion of Christianity infers that it was an *old* religion at its inception. In his study of adolescent religious awakenings G. W. Allport noted that 14 per cent had a definite crisis reaction, 15 per cent had emotional stimulus, with the individual able to point to a particular moment or time of religious reorientation, while 71 per cent had a gradual awakening.[16] Without specific evidence to contradict this pattern we must propose a wider scope to the interpretation of salvation than the profound but limited view manifest in Paul.

The New Testament (apart from Paul's own dominant figure) is predisposed towards groups acknowledging salvation corporately (Acts 2: 41, 4: 14, 6: 1, 8: 14; Rom. 11: 25; 1 Cor. 1: 16, etc). The Gospels show only a limited concern for particular individuals but they describe people in accord with social conditions. There were beggars, rich men, tax collectors, scribes, fishermen and slaves as well as Greeks, Jews, Romans and the *'Am-Ha'arez*. Characters are catalogued according to a theological, political and socio-economic pattern. The new religion had a *kērygma* for the benefit of every rank and class in society. Christianity spread so rapidly and in such diverse directions that it was

14 McGiffert, *loc. cit.*
15 Goodenough, *By Light, Light* (1935), pp. 259–64.
16 Allport, *The Individual and his Religion* (1960), p. 37.

not co-ordinated, and a variety of theological interpretations were simultaneously in vogue among the divergent groups. At a date long before A.D. 70 a multitude of predispositions about salvation and numerous views concerning the meaning and purpose of the life and work of Jesus were extant. Each estimate had a claim to authority founded upon the Jesus myth, and each was convinced of the absolute validity of its own exegesis. Men interpreted the acts of Jesus in response to their problems. This may be illustrated through the following early Christian precepts of salvation.

1. There was a salvation through warfare known by Christian zealots who fought for the kingdom, anticipating divine assistance by a Lord who would return to lead them in final battle. This would include Judas Iscariot and the Zealots described by Brandon.[17] They would be similar to those of Qumran who anticipated an actual war between the Sons of Light and the Sons of Darkness.[18] The highest honour would be to usher in the messianic kingdom, and if it were at the cost of one's mortal life it would be to the benefit of one's eternal glory. The enemy was Rome, and the Kingdom of God was a free Palestine. Emotional needs were satisfied in military–political action.

2. There was an encratitic salvation which rejected marriage and emphasised sexual continence. No need to abandon the world or to go into isolation to escape the fates, for chastity would preserve the virgin and prepare him/her for the reception with the Bridegroom. Tatian understood that salvation required sexual abstinence, and so did the author of the *Gospel to the Egyptians*, as well as those of the Acts of John, Acts of Peter and others.[19] Encratitic sympathies are in Paul (1 Cor. 7) and Matthew (Matt. 19: 10–12) and may be associated in all traditions with the personal life of Jesus himself. This interpretation remained popular in Eastern Christianity for the next 400 years and was defended by Bishop Aphraates as the highest form of morality.[20] It created an exclusive religious elite of pure souls.

17 Brandon, *The Trial of Jesus of Nazareth* (1968), p. 33; also of great importance, by the same author, 'The effect of the destruction of Jerusalem in A.D. 70 on primitive Christian soteriology', *Sacral Kingship* (1959), pp. 471*ff*.

18 Atkinson, 'The historical setting of the "war of the Sons of Light and the Sons of Darkness" ', *Bulletin of the John Rylands Library* XL (1958), pp. 373*ff*.

19 Hennecke, *op. cit.*, I, p. 166. Clement of Alexandria, while writing against encratism, implicitly acknowledges its validity in terms of early roots. Cf. Simon, 'The apostolic decree', *Bulletin of the John Rylands Library* LII (1970), pp. 456*ff*.

20 Burkitt, *Early Eastern Christianity* (1904), pp. 120*ff*.

3. There was a proto-gnostic salvation attached to the story of the redemption of fallen wisdom. This was associated by the Church Fathers with the arch-heretic Simon Magus. This Simon from Samaria sought to imitate the life of Jesus, convinced that the definitive event in the myth was an episode parallel to the redemption of the woman at the well (John 4: 7*ff.*). The figure of the fallen Helen was first to be raised and released from bondage, after which all men who understood would gain salvation.[21] Those who suffered from disabling pain caused by the separation of body and soul (identity crisis) found relief in the re-establishment of wisdom (super-ego) to its commanding role, regaining for humanity the proper dominance of reason over flesh. Those predisposed to Jewish wisdom literature and certain forms of Greek philosophy found satisfaction in this type of pronouncement of Christian revelation.

4. Proto-gnostic salvation manifested a variety of forms, one of which was ascetic. The trend which separated man from an evil society by inducting him into a pure community had been present in many earlier periods and in the Jewish Essenes, Pharisees and Therapeutae.[22] This ascetic estimate of salvation was later combined in some localities with Encratism, etc, to form additional schools of doctrine.

Asceticism required the initiate to abandon the physical dissipation evident in the corrupt and evil age in which he was bound as a prisoner. The ascetic discipline re-established the primacy of knowledge and pledged a freedom from the tyranny of cosmic *heimarmenē*. It created an athletic rigour which gave assurance to the troubled soul. It provided salvation from the relativity of a life void of assurance by the application of discipline and rigid physical control as the means to enlightenment.

5. A second form of wisdom salvation was demonstrably libertine. In Paul's first letter to Corinth pure knowledge had given birth to moral freedom (1 Cor. 5: 1). Members had been released from the guilt of the flesh and from conventional morality. Those overcome by this knowledge defied virtue and felt an obligation to perform every imaginable deed of concupiscence so as 'to exhaust the physical powers of nature'.[23] Previously they had lived under a restrictive legalism and they put forth arguments for a concept of salvation which abhorred all forms of control or conventional social practice. It was the opposite of the ascetic life but constructed on the same premise.

21 Jonas, *The Gnostic Religion* (1963), p. 108.
22 Jeremias, *Jerusalem in the Time of Jesus* (1967), p. 248.
23 Jonas, *op. cit.*, p. 273.

6. In 1 Cor. 12 and 14 there is the description of a charismatic salvation visible as a traumatic enthusiasm. It was not Paul's own choice of activity, but a regressive manifestation of glossolalia, with its roots deep in pre-Christian mysticism.[24] It was pre-eminently a group experience which demanded repetition at regular intervals in the company of similarly motivated associates. The pre-verbal state of ecstasy allowed an escape from the frustrations of an insoluble socio-economic condition.

7. Earliest Alexandrian Christianity was a sophisticated Hellenistic-Jewish salvation. The re-enactment of the Exodus from Egypt's flesh-pots through the Red Sea into a new life, was symbolic for those strangely elite Therapeutae of Philo's contemplation.[25] All the evidence indicates a Christian community in Alexandria composed of Jews of social prestige and economic standing who found in the new cult a life-unifying myth. Similarities between Philo and the New Testament cannot properly be explained apart from the theory that men in harmony with the Alexandrian Jew's philosophy became Christians. H. Chadwick proposed that there is 'food for thought' in the apocryphal legends of the conversion of Philo in Rome by Peter as well as the meeting of the Alexandrian with St John.[26] These Hellenists were joined by a cell of politically dissatisfied and economically persecuted Greeks to form the core of the adherents.[27] Apollos had probably been part of this group, who were distinguished by the author of Acts as those who 'knew only the baptism of John' (Acts 18: 26). Salvation was a social movement healing an old animosity in the presence of a new adversary.

8. The Jewish society of the ancient world (both in Palestine and *diaspora*) was the prime recipient of the *kērygma*. A concept of salvation by works may be found affirmatively in the Epistle of James and negatively throughout the Pauline corpus. Those associated with a works-salvation theology have been described as 'Judaisers'. In early studies there was an attempt to polarise Jewish Christians, with gentile Christians seeking to discover the reason for Christianity's growth along

24 Beare, 'Speaking with tongues', *Journal of Biblical Literature* LXXXIII (1964), p. 229; Behm, *Theologisches Wörterbuch zum Neuen Testament* I, pp. 722–7.

25 Philo, *De vita contemplativa*, 85–6.

26 Chadwick, 'St Paul and Philo of Alexandria', *Bulletin of the John Rylands Library* XLVIII (1966), p. 306.

27 Fennelly, 'Origins of Alexandrian Christianity' (unpublished Ph.D. thesis, 1967); Bruce, 'Christianity under Claudius', *Bulletin of the John Rylands Library* XLIV (1962), pp. 312*ff*.

Hegelian lines.[28] One aspect of salvation was to simplify 'good works' so that they could be reasonably understood by the people of the land.

9. Other Judaisers found the source of their salvation in the maintenance of the sacrificial Temple cult. In Acts 3 and 4 Peter and James were still attached to Temple worship. The chronology of Luke–Acts should not lead one to assume that the period of Temple-centred devotion was short-lived. It is wiser to propose that some believers worshipped at the shrine until its destruction in A.D. 70. Afterwards, for a number of generations, perhaps in another guise, they continued in some small city.[29] This Christian caliphate was very Semitic in its response to religious innovation by a charismatic leader.

10. The controversies over the original nature of the eucharist demonstrate the variety of interpretations active in the primitive Church, and provide a clue to separating different theological positions. Jewish Christians celebrated a sabbath supper, while there are enough aspects of the mystery cult in the sacrament to establish at least a core who believed that they supped with the God at the Lord's table.[30] Through sacrifice and ritual the members became conscious of salvation as a physically objective event. Ritual provided a mechanism of introversion which, during emotional stress or critical periods, supplied assurance of complete protection and ineffable trust. Regular repetition in times of ease was essential to ritual efficacy under duress. In primitive religions ritual affords the means by which individuality is formed out of the collective conscience.[31]

11. Most significantly, the message of salvation permeated national groups. These nations were of three configurations. (*a*) There were the regional peoples, once autonomous but now discriminated against by Rome and her allies, who sought through a common religious confession to regain their dignity and preserve their culture within the *koinonia*. The Samaritans were an example of this. The injunction of Matt. 10: 5 forbidding evangelisation among gentiles and Samaritans only serves to prove how early and earnestly they embraced the new religion.[32] (*b*) There were also nations of people defined as Greeks,

28 Canney, 'F. C. Baur', *Encyclopaedia Biblica* XI (1916), 3: pp. 540–1.

29 See Professor Brandon's protest over Pella in *The Fall of Jerusalem*, p. 169. Eusebius, *Eccl. Hist.* III: v, 3–4.

30 Bultmann, *Theology of the New Testament* I (1952), pp. 148*ff.*; Nock, *Conversion* (1933), p. 234; Lietzmann, *Mass and Lord's Supper* (1953), fasc. 6, pp. 318–29.

31 Wach, *Sociology of Religion* (144), pp. 40*ff.*

32 Jeremias, *op. cit.*, pp. 352*ff.*; on the Shephelah see Smith, *Historical Geography*

Persians, Macedonians, Egyptians, freedmen, slaves, etc, by the Roman government for the purposes of taxation and political supervision.[33] These 'nations' were no longer viable units of economic–political function and were more native to the locality than the 'foreign' name might imply. Philo, for example, was a Jew with Roman citizenship who was classified as a Greek Alexandrian.[34] This multifarious Roman nationality scheme, with its rigid socio-economic limitations and tax responsibilities, led many to seek in religion a community which might save them from an intolerable level of personality and culture group diffusion. This was exhibited in the later Coptic Church, where the classical Egyptian gods and goddesses were 'baptised' and, phoenix-like, arose from the ashes of Roman domination, reconstituted as Christian saints.[35] (*c*) Third, there were economic 'nations' composed of associations engaged in similar or interdependent trades. These were once centred on particular nationalities and cities, but the ethnological quality was no longer relevant and the merchants formed trade guilds. The clothing industry and its companion leather crafts created such a sodality, which was pre-eminent as a nucleus for the spreading of Christianity in the east Mediterranean.[36]

These eleven categories (and the list is not exhaustive but suggestive) affirm doctrines of salvation considered by the adherents as original and primary. Salvation in the Lord resolved individual and corporate tensions and brought relief to a wide range of psychological and socio-economic perplexities.

What were these issues? From what did people need to be saved? Once again we must catalogue the major available features.

1. People required salvation from *themselves* through a mystical adventure in which the tensions of an intolerable separation of mental authority (super-ego) from bodily drives (libido) was resolved in an ineffable theophany. This is a crisis of the late adolescent manifest in a

---

of the Holy Land (1931), pp. 167–71; Neusner, 'Christianity in Adiabene', in *A History of the Jews in Babylonia* III (1968), pp. 354*ff*.

33 *BGU* V: 1–1210; Rostovtzeff, *Social and Economic History of the Roman Empire* I (1957), pp. 185–91. Sadly, Rostovtzeff does not list the classes. P. Oxy. 255 of A.D. 48 gives a partial list in the form of a census return in lines 20–2.

34 Philo, *In Flaccum*, 54, 74, 78–85, etc.

35 Bell, *Egypt* (1948), pp. 113*ff*.; MacMullen, *Aegyptus* (1964), p. 196.

36 Broneer, 'The Apostle Paul and the Isthmian Games', *Biblical Archaeologist* XXV (1962), pp. 2*ff*.; Neusner, *Jews in Babylonia* I (1969), p. 95; Heichelheim, 'Roman Syria', in *An Economic Survey of Ancient Rome* (1959), pp. 208–11.

variety of religious systems in the Hellenistic world. The tension was exaggerated to create conversion in the Adonis–Cybele cult with the activities of the *galli* priests as well as among the devotees of Isis.[37] It is a sign of the extremity to which men were driven in the desire to achieve true personal identity, and it had numerous forms of expression in Christianity (Matt. 19: 12). In an age of frustrating perplexity old systems of security were being destroyed, as is evident in the eschatological foreboding of the period. One form of resolution was found in a personal mystical salvation apocalyptically perceived.

2. From Augustus to Antoninus Pius the overwhelming issue of the era was sidereal astrology. Men received assurance and certitude from the stars, which was quickly transmuted into fatalism and despondency.[38] The saviour gods (both lords and ladies) were entreated to release the unfortunate from a fixed astral destiny.[39] Tatian was aware that astrology was an invention of demons who enslaved men through the stars. Renunciation of worldliness and the acceptance of Christ freed men from bondage to the heavens.[40]

3. The centralising authority of the Roman State, which had unified the Mediterranean world, was also the source of a social disintegration associated with the loss of local political autonomy. Constantly reinforced throughout the empire, imperial rule was a recurring cause of riot and revolution. Ardent devotion to the ideals of the city State was the higher allegiance which inspired the *pagan* martyrs of Alexandria to defy Claudius.[41] The *polis* had been understood throughout Greek history to be 'one big family' or 'an all-in-all partnership'. This was in direct contrast with the Roman *res publica*, which must always be considered in conjunction with the *res privata*. Both these rights rested upon the presupposition of direct Roman control of all real property.

> With all the fervour of a true Roman, Cicero believed that the mission of his country was to make the world safe for property.[42]

Subjugation of the individual to property rights (particularly land), along with the destruction of the pre-Roman local political freedom,

37 Lucian, *The Syrian Goddess*, 51; Apuleius, *Metamorphoses* XI: 50.

38 Cumont, *Astrology and Religion Among the Greeks and Romans* (1912), p. 50; but it is Jonas, *op. cit.* pp. 254*ff.*, who is most emphatic.

39 Nock, *op. cit.*, pp. 101*ff.*; Bultmann, *Primitive Christianity* (1956), p. 147. It was very dangerous politically for a man to have an imperial destiny in his stars, and yet essential if he aspired to reach the highest office.

40 Tatian, *The Discourse to the Greeks*, 8–11.

41 Rostovtzeff, *op. cit.*, II, p. 560, note 11; p. 587, note 19; Bell, *Egypt*, p. 89.

42 Cochrane, *Christianity and Classical Culture* (1944), p. 45.

had a major impact on the dismantling of the Graeco-oriental culture. It gave rise to a myriad of unsuccessful revolutions and massive demonstrations as well as innumerable successful religious sects and mystical revelations. Christianity codified the Hellenistic reactions to the totalitarian demands of the Roman State, which, while explicitly humane, were implicitly degrading and debasing. Paul, oft-times considered a defender of Roman authority, recognised the transitoriness of its dominion and emphasised its ultimate limits, distinctly recommending Christians to construct an independent system of jurisprudence separate from that of the State.[43]

4. Co-ordinate with the rise of Roman power which created a loss of human dignity was the decline of the religious and social functions of the Hellenistic city. Bultmann wrote about the crisis of the city State:

> Thus there was a very real danger of the gods losing their authority, of the city state and its laws passing increasingly into human control and being subordinated to their private and collective interests.[44]

A utilitarian relationship between the city and the individual had arisen, with Roman law replacing the suzerainty of the gods.[45] Men had found personal worth in the city State as direct participants in its worship, work and political activity. Human wills were merged in corporate action, with tangible reward and punishment. The citizen and the pariah workman both observed the performance of the government use of wealth in public spending and *they*, often in the name of the local gods, provided the necessary control to restrain flagrant abuses. Riots and strikes supplied a common means of popular redress. The worship of the emperor gave neither citizen nor sojourner the feeling of loyalty once so worshipfully dedicated to the gods of the city. The common man had limited participation in the imperial cult, and a rejection of government policy by the populace did not affect Roman rule. Strikes and protests which had once had an impact on

43 Cullmann, *The State in the New Testament* (1957), p. 61. The Jews had their own very complete and sophisticated system of law, which was used both in and out of the Roman empire: Neusner, *Jews in Babylon* (1969). For the important concept of Christianity as a State within a State, see Erhardt, 'The adoption of Christianity in the Roman empire', *Bulletin of the John Rylands Library* XLV (1962), 97–114.

44 Bultmann, *Primitive Christianity*, p. 109.

45 J. Fennelly, 'Roman involvement in the affairs of the Egyptian shrine', *Bulletin of the John Rylands Library* L (1968), pp. 317*ff*.

the god and his immediate representatives (the liturgy-providing aristocracy) were repressed without effecting change. The loss of basic popular opposition which, through religious terminology, appealed to the higher authority of the god, marked a forfeiture of dignity which would in time demand alternative avenues of expression. Neither the rioting nor the quieting parties at Ephesus were consciously aware that Paul (Acts 19: 23–41) was presenting a viable alternative to their religious, urban and economic frustrations, which they erroneously attributed to him and not to broader causes.

5. The people sought salvation from Roman economic determinism. Whereas trade had increased during the early Roman period, and the average peasant lived in a bartering society immune to monetary crisis, efficient Roman methods of tax collection, a conservative policy towards gold and the development of the Mediterranean as an imperial farm created massive restraint of trade which affected everyone. The urban workers were the first to suffer privation. Food riots were a regular feature in all cities during times of depression, such as when Tiberius hoarded gold.[46] The rural population felt a similar crisis with the approach of drought, or when little revision was made of their annual tax quota in response to seasonal fluctuations. The historical records abound only in the enumeration of the generous exceptions which were granted in times of unusual disaster. The sole oriental temple bank left inviolate was in Jerusalem, where Rome's Eastern ally had received a favoured position, as well as being allotted the privilege of transporting gold to and from the Temple across international frontiers. Pilate jealously coveted this wealth, and Vespasian re-financed his empty coffers when the Temple treasure was finally confiscated. The Romans had captured the ancient temples of the orient, emptied them, and then attempted to employ them as means of collecting revenue. Only a few sectors of the economy were free from government interference, and these provided the financial resources for the religious movements which would undermine Roman authority.

6. For the purposes of order and taxation, a rigid social structure had been established which was carefully maintained by government officials. The *Gnomon* of the *Idios Logos* (*BGU* v:1) explicitly delineated laws for marriage, property, inheritance, adoption and education as determined by specific national–racial groups.

46 Rostovtzeff, *op. cit.*, i, pp. 144–99; ii, p. 623, note 49; Tacitus, *Annals* vi: 13–17.

Those who style themselves improperly (in public and private documents) and those who knowingly concur therein are fined a fourth of their estates.[47]

People sought to change categories which were no longer functional. There was more variety of wealth, education and status within the designated groups than between them, causing considerable friction. Both *In Flaccum* and *De legatione ad Gaium* are treatises seeking to prove that the Alexandrian Jews had originally been assigned to a higher status than was currently being accorded to them.[48] A drastic revision of the classification of citizenship was imperative, but the *constitutio Antoniniana* of Caracalla (A.D. 212) was too late and too limited to affect the social revolution, which had surpassed the intended reform.[49] Both before and after the *constitutio* the traditional Roman technique for dealing with similar social issues was a 'temporary measure of relief and a further extension of compulsion'.[50]

7. The decay of popular confidence in the Graeco-Roman pantheon created a severe pressure on the mythological resources of society. The incalculable family of gods had furnished the basic psychic symbols enabling men to speculate (within culturally accepted patterns) on the nature of government, ethical responsibility, life and eschatology. The ancient religious myths, deprived of their respectability, were transformed by a multitude of new and old sects which sought to fill the vacuum. Each attempted to present a unifying theology which was totally oriental and yet fully acceptable to the Hellenised mentality. Plutarch sought to achieve this in his discourse on *Isis and Osiris*, dedicated to the well informed priestess Clea of Delphi.[51] The loss of essential confidence in the ancient pantheon, which no longer provided for the unity of classes to the benefit of the city State or the ethnic shrine, gave occasion to a personality fragmentation and a religious dissociation. Men sought salvation from this condition.

8. Finally, there was the usurpation of philosophy by astrological mathematics. The rule of the stars was such that speculative thought became irrelevant, since the process of history had been predetermined. The conversion of Justin illustrates the turmoil of one young Hellenist from Palestine who had sought meaning in philosophy, and found the roots of philosophy in Semitic Christianity.[52] Discredited, philosophy

47 *BGU* I: 42.

48 Josephus, *The Jewish Wars* II, 487–93, for an expansion of this same problem.

49 Bell, *Egypt*, pp. 92–4.

50 *Ibid.*, p. 48.

51 Plutarch, *Isis and Osiris* I, I.

52 Justin, *Dialogue with Trypho*, 2, 3, 7, 8.

was unable to defend itself on its own intellectual terms and fell victim to the argument that the Old Testament prophets and Moses were the forerunners of all Greek philosophy. The descendants of those who invented the alphabet claimed primacy over all thoughtful endeavour. This pre-Christian argument had its anticipated reaction in Justin the Palestinian, whose change of mind gave him the longed-for respect he needed from his own tradition. Similar thought underlies the symbol of the redemption of the fallen Sophia, which was also a part of the primitive *kērygma*. The age was ripe for a philosophy which would allow for the genuine re-emergence of the intellectual culture of the East.[53] In so far as star calculations held sway, rational contemplation was in disrepute.

These eight essential categories, brought into focus by the Roman empire, were subcutaneously active long before imperial suzerainty. The Romans brought the issues to the foreground owing to their efficient government, even though they too suffered under the same stress.

There are four general conclusions which may be propounded, upon a definition of salvation as: that human experience which met the needs and interests of people so that it resolved cultural dissociation and displeasure, thereby providing a reorientation to life, displacing and transforming prior intellectual and emotional affiliations.

1. Men discovered salvation as an economic freedom to expand independent of Roman commercial domination. An alternative economic system had become necessary to replace the vulnerable ancient temple as co-ordinator of workshops and supplier of investment capital. The synagogue performed this function on a limited racial scale and provided the model for Christianity.[54] Businessmen heard the *kērygma* in the two languages of trade: Koine and Syriac Aramaic. Paul travelled the commercial routes and timed his visit to Corinth to coincide with the great market created by the Isthmian games.[55] It was in the *agora* that the *kērgyma* was exchanged as a letter of salvation. The garment industry (with the leather workers) was particularly receptive to Christianity, as represented by Dorcas, Aquila, Prisca, Lydia, Simon

53 Jonas, *op. cit.*, pp. 23–7.

54 The synagogue at Sardis was in the centre of such a business complex. Certain economic functions appear to have taken place inside the building during the normal weekdays: Hanfmann, *Bulletin of the American School of Oriental Research* CLXXXVII (1967), pp. 25*ff*.

55 Broneer, *op. cit.*, pp. 5*ff*.

the tanner, perhaps Phoebe, and, of course, Paul. Early house-churches were found in places famous for weaving and sewing. The Mediterranean mercantile navy was also intimately involved in the transmission of the religion. The first messengers of the faith headed straight to the coastal port cities. Shipping remained one of the few sectors in which an individual was able to amass a personal fortune. Marcion's great wealth, which he so generously used to support his religious activities, may have come from shipping; if not, early tradition assigned it to that most prosperous business.[56] Among the first genuine Christian letters extant from the Egyptian papyri is a note of credit from a Fayyum bishop to the bishop at Rome in connection with a shipment of corn.[57] The need for an alternative economic system circumventing imperial control and reduplicating the oriental concept of shrine and workshop at the junction of the trade routes was fulfilled in the development of Christianity. Religion in the orient today, among Eastern Christians and the major forms of Islam, is built on this same economic foundation. The sects, meanwhile, still preserve themselves in certain trades, e.g. Mandean silversmiths in Ahwaz and Basra.

2. Men found salvation to be a form of class mobility and group acceptance apart from the rigid Roman social policy. The cult of Asklepius was a major innovator of social revolution. It was the first large Hellenistic religion to invite the sick, lame and blind of all nationalities and races (all classes and social ranks) into the one shrine. For A. Harnack this universal healing cult was the precursor of the Christian syncretism.[58] But only Sidon could boast a shrine along the Levantine coast. All other centres were on remote islands or at the edge of the city, independent of political and economic affairs. There can be no question that the saviour was also considered a healer, but of equal importance was the fact that men anticipated a realignment of the class structure. It was the body social which was most urgently in need of surgery. Slaves and free, Jew and Greek sought harmony in the same *oikoumene*. Old laws of diet and rules of intermarriage, such as persisted among the Jews, were terminated and replaced by new regulations.[59] The Kingdom of God became a new world wherein the changed

56 Tertullian, *De praescriptione haereticorum*, 30; Justin, *Apology* I: 26.

57 Bell, 'Evidences of Christianity in Egypt in the Roman period', *Harvard Theological Review* XXXVII (1944), pp. 185*ff*.

58 Harnack, *Mission and Expansion of Christianity* I (1908), pp. 101*ff*.

59 Jeremias, *op. cit.*, pp. 271*ff*.; Grant, 'The Kingdom of God in the New Testament', in *Sacral Kingship* (1959), p. 443.

relationships were accepted as valid currency. In Jerusalem a Christian community of mixed classes attempted to live a communal life within the city walls. At first they maintained their association with the Temple, but soon found that the Church was the true successor to the Temple. Care of widows and orphans, long attached to the religious ordinances in various cultures, became the concern of the Christian society which sought to replace the older shrines and may well have operated in opposition to Roman law (*BGU* 1: 18, 41, etc). The disintegration of social structures accompanying the destruction of the city State was compensated for by the development of a new *civitas dei* where social rank had been realistically reassigned.

3. Men encountered salvation as a renewed and creditable mythology which was old and oriental (Jewish monotheism being a survival of the ancient ethnic religions) and yet new and unique (Jesus of Nazareth had lived—or existed in some form—until *c.* A.D. 33). Christianity re-established the authority of God over law, which was the primary religious loss suffered at the disintegration of the independent city State. Within the new theology man found a means to reassert the existent spiritual superiority of the East over the West. A single universal mythology including both realisable and future eschatology had been created.[60] During the earliest Christian history one section of the Church attached the culture myth of the death–resurrection–enthronement of the king to the events in the life of Jesus of Nazareth. It was this significant act which stimulated the Christian restructuring of oriental thought. The correlation was always suggestive, providing for adaptations in accordance with the diversity of enthronement myths in vogue. Only the canonical gospels put forth this interpretation. They too had a 'sayings' tradition as source, allowing the speculation that the connection with the Jewish form of the Mesopotamian myth was not conceived of immediately.[61] This adaptation may well be the key to Christian growth. The simile of M. P. Nilsson is apt at this point:

> Religion is like a grove with tall and stately trees, which reach the sky and strike the eye from afar, and with an undergrowth of brushwood and grass. It is easy to fell the trees, and, like the pines in the proverb which King Croesus referred to when he threatened to eradicate the Milesians like a pine, they do

---

60 Cullmann, *Salvation as History* (1967).

61 Every bit of material gathered so masterfully by Lindars could be interpreted to fit this proposition, which he too casually dismissed. See Lindars, *The New Testament Apologetic* (1961), pp. 75–138.

not put forth new shoots, although new trees can be planted instead of old ones. But the undergrowth persists. The brushwood and the grass may be cut down or even burned off, it springs up again. Every year the undergrowth brings forth the simple leaves and blossoms. It changes only if the mother soil is changed. This took place in ancient Greece, as it does today, through the rise of new conditions of life, industry, commerce, democracy, and intercourse between peoples and classes. Popular religion changed accordingly.[62]

4. Men experienced salvation as a new community, with the Church functioning as the co-ordinating unit. There was a gradual re-investiture of municipal rights. The imperial spirit of religious toleration was destroyed by the Kingdom of God. Christian martyrs died with the same devotion and commitment as the Alexandrian martyrs. Nations and cities which had been dissolved, or integrated with their natural enemies in a common administrative district, reaffirmed their independent identity. Natural enemies accepted the same religion but were careful to establish differences of interpretation and disparate sources of authority. Early Samaritan Christianity generated its own characteristics, as is observed in the Gospel of John.[63] Before the end of the first century Jewish Christians and Samaritan Christians were able to hurl anathemas at each other (Matt. 10: 5, John 8: 39, 48, etc). The Samaritans are a good example of a disfranchised people placed under the partial supervision of their natural enemies who appear to have joined Christianity in large groups (John 4: 39–42). A similar response came from other border peoples.[64] The Adiabenes became Christians almost as suddenly as they had become Jews a century and a half before.[65] Edessa, Armenia, Antioch, Egypt and North Africa developed local theology and tradition which fostered an emerging regional identity. The presupposition that Christianity spread from a central point with a single message which was later syncretised by paganism is not tenable. There were a number of true primary gospels. It was the Roman government which viewed all the varieties of Christianity as one community.[66]

62 Nilsson, *Greek Folk Religion* (1961), p. 139.
63 Buchanan, 'The Samaritan origin of the Gospel of John', *Religions in Antiquity*, ed. Neusner (1968), pp. 158*ff*.
64 Eusebius, *Eccl. Hist.* 1: 1.
65 Neusner, *Jews in Babylonia*, p. 356.
66 Ehrhardt, *op. cit.*, pp. 102–3.

11

John R. Hinnells

The Zoroastrian doctrine of salvation in the Roman world

A study of the oracle of Hystaspes

Salvation is of the essence of religion. Belief in God or gods is not a central part of a number of traditions, but salvation is the mainspring of much if not all religious experience (if by that term we mean release from the bonds which the believer is convinced ultimately oppress him, be those bonds the disintegration of tribal society, loneliness, suffering or death). The understanding of the nature of those bonds and therefore of how release can be obtained varies not only from community to community but even within a single group or tradition. Despite the glories of the Roman empire and the enormous benefits it bestowed on its citizens, the search of the individual for salvation was as fervent then as at any other period or in any other region of the Western world. Equally, the varieties of salvation and of paths to it were as great then as at any other time. Scholarly attention has generally been concentrated on two particular approaches, those of the mystery cults and those of the State cults. Important though these undoubtedly were, they are not the sum total of the approaches to salvation in that empire. Generally the mystery cults offered salvation from the burdens of life by the promise of a better hereafter or by denying the importance of material life compared with the spiritual union with God. The oppressions of life were dealt with by directing vision elsewhere. But in view of the way in which the State cults were used to justify and uphold the existing social order it was inevitable that some religious movements should seek a religious salvation which had important political implications. The implications of this fact for the study of Christianity were, of course, an area of study in which Professor Brandon was particularly interested. To many rulers, both local and imperial, the great problem posed by Christianity was simply that its followers refused to participate in the State cults, a refusal viewed with political rather than theological concern.[1] Ultimately the Christian

1 It would not, however, be true to imply that purely religious attitudes were

answer was to attempt the marriage of Christian faith and Roman cultural (including political) ideals. The conversion of Constantine to Christianity could not have occurred had it not been preceded by the conversion of Christianity to Roman culture. The Church's answer to the political–soteriological conflict was marriage, but not all religious revolutionaries, within or without the Christian fold, could accept such an answer. The purpose of this paper is to examine what was evidently an extremely popular oracle which looked for a form of salvation that involved the overthrow of the Roman empire.

The oracle of Hystaspes is referred to by Justin Martyr, Clement of Alexandria, Lydus de Mensibus, Aristokritos and Lactantius but is not otherwise extant. It is said by these early writers to be a Persian text foretelling the overthrow of evil and of the Roman empire, the return of rule to the East and the coming of a saviour. Although the text was so popular and important in the second century that Justin ranked it with the Sibyl and the prophets, it has hardly been studied by modern scholars and virtually never in English.[2]

---

not important in the opposition to Christianity. See T. D. Barnes, 'Legislation against the Christians', *Journal of Roman Studies* LVIII (1968), pp. 32–50. I am indebted to Mr R. Gordon for drawing my attention to this article, for reading my paper and offering many helpful criticisms. I also wish to express my thanks, as ever, to my 'guide and stay', Professor M. Boyce, for her unfailing help, guidance and inspiration.

2 Previous studies of the oracle are, in chronological order: Wagenmann, 'Hystaspes', in Herzog and Plitt, *Realencyclopädie für protestantische Theologie und Kirche* VI (1879), pp. 413–15; Kuhn, 'Eine zoroastrische Weissagung in Christlichen Gewande', in *Festgruss an Rudolph von Roth* (1893), pp. 217–21; Kruger, 'Hystaspes', in Hauck, *Realencyclopädie für protestantische Theologie und Kirche* VIII (1900), pp. 507–9; Böklen, *Dir Verwandtschaft der judisch-christlichen mit der persischen Eschatologie* (1902), pp. 95*f*.; Schürer, *Geschichte des jüdischen Volkes im Zeitalter Jesu Christi* III (1909), pp. 450–3; Harnack, *Geschichte der altchristlichen Literatur* I (1893), p. 863; Bousset, *Pauly–Wissowa Realencyclopädie* (1894) IX, I, cols. 541*f*.; Reitzenstein and Schaeder, *Studien zum antiken Synkretismus aus Iran und Greichenland* (1926, reprinted 1965), pp. 50*f*.; Windisch, *Die Orakel des Hystaspes* (1929); Cumont, 'La fin du monde selon les mages occidentaux', *Revue de l'histoire des religions* (1931), pp. 64–96; Benveniste, 'Une Apocalypse pehlevie: le *Zamasp Namak*', *ibid.* (1932), pp. 337–80; Messina, *I Magi a Betlemme e una predizione di Zoroastro* (1933), pp. 74–82, 136*f*.; Bidez and Cumont, *Les Mages Hellénisés* (1938), I, pp. 215–22, II, pp. 359–76; Fuchs, *Geistige Widerstand gegen Rom*, second edition (1938); Monneret de Villard, *Le leggende orientali sui Magi evangelici* (1952), chapter I; Duchesne-Guillemin, *The Western Response to Zoroaster* (1958), pp. 90*f*.; Widengren, *Iranische-semitische Kulturbewegung in parthischer*

There are four problems which will be tackled here. First, an attempt will be made to reconstruct a picture of the oracle, its nature and its theme, by collecting all the relevant texts. Second, the question 'Did the oracle emanate from Jewish,[3] Christian,[4] Mithraic,[5] Chaldaeo-magian syncretic[6] or Zoroastrian[7] circles?' Third, attention will be paid to the doctrine of the saviour in the oracle: was it part of the original oracle, and, if so, what was the identity of the saviour? Finally the question of the oracle's date will be considered.

I *Texts concerning the oracle of Hystaspes*

The first task is to collect all the relevant texts. The quotations will be numbered in roman numerals and the lines in arabic numerals for ease of reference. They are presented in three categories: texts explicitly referring to Hystaspes, texts illustrating the method of Lactantius—an author whose outstanding importance for this subject will soon emerge—and finally texts from Lactantius which do not explicitly refer to Hystaspes but which for reasons given below are thought to contain ideas taken from that oracle.

(a) *Texts explicitly referring to the oracle of Hystaspes*

I *Justin Martyr*

> The Sibyl and Hystaspes have given out that this whole system of incorruptibles shall be destroyed by fire.[8]

II *Justin Martyr*

> But through the agency of evil demons, death was proclaimed against those who read the books of Hystaspes, or the Sibyl, or the Prophets, that they [i.e. the demons] might through fear turn their readers from receiving the knowledge of the good, and keep them

---

Zeit (1960), chapter 8; Eddy, *The King is Dead* (1961), pp. 32–6; Duchesne-Guillemin, *La Religion de l'Iran ancien* (1962), p. 263; Widengren, *Die Religionen Irans* (1965), pp. 199–207; Duchesne-Guillemin, 'The religion of ancient Iran', in *Historia Religionum*, ed. Bleeker and Widengren, I (1969), p. 347.

3 So Schürer and Harnack.

4 So Arendzen, Kuhn, Kruger, Messina.

5 Cumont and Widengren, for example, though the *Roman* mysteries are not necessarily implied.

6 Windisch, *op. cit.*

7 So Eddy.

8 *Apologia* I: 20, 1; translation that of J. Kaye (1821).

slaves to themselves; which in the event they were not able to accomplish.[9]

III *Clement of Alexandria*

He [i.e. God] distinguished the most excellent of the Greeks from the common herd; in addition to *Peter's Preaching* the apostle Paul will show, saying, 'Take also the Hellenic books, read the Sibyl, how it is shown that God is one, and how the future is indicated. And taking Hystaspes, read, and you will find much more luminously and distinctly the Son of God described, and how many kings shall draw up their forces against Christ, hating Him, and those that bear His name, and His faithful ones, and His patience, and His coming.'[10]

IV *Lydus de Mensibus*

That the Chaldeans of the school of Zoroaster and Hystaspes, and the Egyptians, took the days of the week from the number of the planets.[11]

V *Aristokritos, 'Theosophy'*

In the fourth place . . . he adduces the oracles of a certain Hystaspes, king of the Persians or Chaldeans, a man of most distinguished birth (he says) and hence a receiver of a revelation of divine mysteries concerning the Saviour's incarnation; at the end of the book he set down a very abbreviated chronology from Adam until the days of Zeno, in which he asserts that the fulfilment would take place after the completion of 6,000 years; for, he says, it is written (*Ps.* 89: 4) that a thousand years are with the Lord as one day; in six days God made the universe and rested on the seventh. After the passing of 6,000 years, which are counted as equivalent to six, everything ought to come to a halt.[12]

---

9 *Apologia* I: 44. I am heavily indebted to Miss M. Elliott (MME) of King's College, London, Dr J. P. Kane (JPK) and Mr P. Martin (PM) of Manchester University for their counsel, guidance and translations of various Greek and Latin texts. The prescription referred to by Justin may be that cited by Iulius Paulus and quoted by Otto in his edition of Justin: 'He who consults astronomers concerning the welfare of the emperor of the higher interests of the State, or he who consults soothsayers, omen readers or prophets, is punishable by death, together with the one he consults . . .' (Paulus, *Sentent* V: 21, 3–4 = FIRA II, second edition (1968), pp. 406*f*., trans. JPK).

10 *The Miscellanies* VI: 5. Written between A.D. 190 and 200; translation that of W. Wilson in The Ante-Nicene Christian Library series, XII, p. 328.

11 II: 4 (MME).

12 C. fifth century A.D. The translation (MME) is from the text in Bidez and Cumont, II, p. 363. This passage is a summary of the fourth of a series of

VI *Lactantius*

Hystaspes also, who was a very ancient king of the Medes, from whom the river which is now called Hydaspes received its name, handed down to the memory of posterity a wonderful dream upon the interpretation of a boy who uttered divinations, announcing, long before the Trojan nation, that the Roman empire and name would be taken from the world.[13]

VII *Lactantius*

For Hystaspes, whom I have named above, having described the iniquity of this last age, says that the pious and faithful, being separated from the wicked, will stretch forth their hands to heaven with weeping and mourning, and will implore the protection of Jupiter; that Jupiter will look down to the earth, and hear the voices of men, and will destroy the wicked. All these things are true except one, that he attributed to Jupiter those things which God will do. This in fact was suppressed by the deceit of the demons, viz. that at that time the Son of God would be sent by the Father, to destroy all the wicked and set free the pious.[14]

VIII *Lactantius*

Wherefore since all these things are true and certain, being foretold by the unanimous annunciation of all the prophets, since Trismegistus, Hystaspes, and the Sibyls have all foretold the same things, it cannot be doubted that all hope of life and salvation rests solely in the worship of God.[15]

(b) *Texts illustrating the method of Lactantius*

IX But the voices also of prophets of the world, agreeing with the heavenly, announce the end and overthrow of all things after a short time, describing, as it were, the last old age of the wearied and wasting world. But the things which are said by prophets and seers to be about to happen before that last ending comes upon the world I will subjoin, being collected and accumulated from all quarters.[16]

---

books in which the author tries to show the concord between pagan and Christian writers.

13 *Divine Institutions* VII: 15. Translations from this source are those of Mr P. Martin, based on Fletcher, *The Works of Lactantius*, Ante-Nicene Library (1871).

14 *Ibid.*, 18.

15 *Epitome of the Divine Institutions*, 73.

16 *Divine Institutions* VII: 14.

x These are the things which are spoken of by the prophets as about to happen hereafter: but I have not considered it necessary to bring forward their testimonies and words, since it would be an endless task: nor would the limits of my book receive so great a multitude of subjects, since so many with one breath speak similar things.[17]

(c) *Texts (from Lactantius) in which Hystaspes is not referred to but appears to be used*

XI *[On the signs of the end]* For righteousness will so decrease, and impiety, avarice, lust will so greatly increase, that if there shall then happen to be any good men, they will be a prey to the wicked, and will be harassed on all sides by the unrighteous; while the wicked alone will be in opulence, but the good will be afflicted in all calumnies and in want. All justice will be confounded, and the laws will be destroyed. No one will then have anything except that which has been gained or defended by violence: boldness and violence will possess all things. There will be no faith among men, nor peace, nor kindness, nor shame, nor truth; and thus also there will be neither security, nor government, nor any rest from evils. For all the earth will be in a state of tumult; wars will everywhere rage; all nations will be in arms, and will oppose one another; neighbouring States will carry on conflicts with each other; and first of all Egypt will pay the penalties of her foolish superstitions, and will be covered with blood as if with a river. Then the sword will traverse the world, mowing down everything, and laying low all things as a crop. And the cause of this desolation and confusion will be this, because the Roman name, by which the world is now ruled (my mind dreads to relate it, but I will relate it, because it is about to happen), will be taken away from the earth, and the government return to Asia; and the East will again bear rule, and the West be reduced to servitude.[18]

XII First, the kingdom will be enlarged, and the chief power, dispersed among many and divided, will be diminished. Then civil discords will perpetually be sown, nor will there be any rest from deadly wars, until ten kings arise at the same time, who will divide the world, not to govern, but to consume it. These having increased their armies to an immense extent, and having deserted the cultivation of the fields, which is the beginning and overthrow of disaster, will lay waste and break in pieces and consume all things. Then a most powerful enemy will suddenly arise against them from the extreme boundaries of the northern region, who, having destroyed three of that number

17 *Divine Institutions* VII: 15.
18 *Ibid.*, 15.

who shall then be in possession of Asia, shall be admitted into the alliance by the others, and shall be constituted prince of all. He shall harass the world with an intolerable rule; shall mingle things divine and human; shall contrive things impious to relate . . . And at length, the name being changed and the seat of government being transferred, confusion and the disturbance of mankind will follow. Then, in truth, a detestable and abominable time shall come, in which life shall be pleasant to none of men.

Cities shall be utterly overthrown, and shall perish; not only by fire and the sword, but also by continual earthquakes and overflowings of waters, and by frequent diseases and repeated famines. For the atmosphere will be tainted, and become corrupt and pestilential—at one time by unseasonable rains, at another by barren drought, now by cold, and now by excessive heat. Nor will the earth give its fruit to man: no field, or tree, or vine, will produce anything; but after they have given the greatest hope in the blossom, they will fail in the fruit. Fountains also shall be dried up, together with the rivers; so that there shall not be sufficient supply for drinking; and waters shall be changed into blood or bitterness. On account of these things, beasts shall fail on the land, and birds in the air, and fishes in the sea. Wonderful prodigies also in heaven shall confound the minds of men with the greatest terrors, and the trains of comets, and the darkness of the sun, and the colour of the moon, and the gliding of the falling stars. Nor, however, will these things take place in the accustomed manner; but there will suddenly appear stars unknown and unseen by the eyes; the sun will be perpetually darkened, so that there will be scarcely any distinction between the night and the day; the moon will now fail, not for three hours only, but, overspread with perpetual blood, will go through extraordinary movements, so that it will not be easy for man to ascertain the courses of the heavenly bodies or the system of the times; for there will either be summer in the winter, or winter in the summer. Then the year will be shortened, and the month diminished, and the day contracted into a short space; and stars shall fall in great numbers, so that all the heavens will appear dark without any lights. The loftiest mountains also will fall, and be levelled with the plains; the sea will be rendered unnavigable.[19]

XIII For the human race will be so consumed, that scarcely the tenth part of men will be left; and from whence a thousand had gone forth, scarcely a hundred will go forth. Of the worshippers of God also, two parts will perish; and the third part, which shall have been proved, will remain.[20]

19 *Ibid.*, 16.

20 *Ibid.*, 16.

XIV (There will be a time of forty-two months when power will be given to a king 'out of Syria', born from an evil spirit):

That will be the time in which righteousness shall be cast out, and innocence be hated; in which the wicked shall prey upon the good as enemies; neither law, nor order, nor military discipline shall be preserved; no one shall reverence hoary locks, nor recognise the duty of piety, nor pity sex or infancy; all things shall be confounded and mixed together against right, and against the laws of nature. Thus the whole earth shall be laid waste, as though by one universal robbery. When these things shall so happen, then the righteous and the followers of truth shall separate themselves from the wicked, and flee into solitude. And when he hears of this, the impious king, inflamed with anger, will come with a great army, and, bringing up all his forces, will surround all the mountain in which the righteous shall be situated, that he may seize them. But they, when they shall see themselves to be shut in on all sides and besieged, will call upon God with a loud voice, and implore the aid of heaven; and God shall hear them, and send from heaven a great king to rescue and free them, and destroy all the wicked with fire, and sword.[21]

XV Then the middle of the heaven shall be laid open in the dead and darkness of the night, that the light of the descending God may be manifest in all the world as lightning. [After describing this event in terms taken from the Sibyl and the New Testament, Lactantius goes on . . .] There shall suddenly fall from heaven a sword, that the righteous may know that the leader of the sacred warfare is about to descend; and He shall descend with a company of angels to the middle of the earth, and there shall go before Him an unquenchable fire, and the power of the angels shall deliver into the hands of the just that multitude which has surrounded the mountain, and they shall be slain from the third hour until the evening, and blood shall flow like a torrent; and all his forces being destroyed, the wicked one alone shall escape, and his power shall perish from him.[22]

XVI Therefore they who have known God shall be judged, and their deeds, that is, their evil works, shall be compared and weighed against their good ones; so that if those which are good and just are more and weighty, they may be driven to a life of blessedness; but if the evil exceed, they may be condemned to punishment.[23]

XVII . . . when He shall have judged the righteous, He will also try them with fire. Then they whose sins shall exceed either in weight or in number shall be scorched by the fire and burnt; but they whom full

21 *Divine Institutions* VII: 17. 22 *Ibid.*, 19. 23 *Ibid.*, 20.

justice and maturity of virtue have imbued will not perceive that fire.[24] [5]

2 *The 'origins' of the oracle of Hystaspes*

Three problems inherent in the discussion need to be made explicit. What impressed the Christian writers who referred to the oracle was its resemblance to Christian doctrine, and their use of it is not likely to have lessened that resemblance. Allowance must therefore be made for a view of the oracle seen through 'Christian-tinted spectacles'. The second problem is the nature of 'the oracle'. Aristokritos (text v, line 1) refers to the oracle*s* (plural) of Hystaspes, and Lydus (text iv) refers to the school of Zoroaster and Hystaspes. Was there one oracle, several, or an amorphous collection of traditions of various dates and divergent theologies circulating under the name Hystaspes? Clearly, it is dangerous to presuppose, even if we may conclude, that 'the oracle' of Hystaspes was a unified whole. The third problem relates to Lactantius, our best source for Hystaspes. He explicitly states (texts ix and x) that he utilises various sources without making specific reference to them. Hence we may assume that in *Divine Institutions* and *The Epitome*, he sometimes uses Hystaspes without saying so. Any attempt to trace such a passage without ourselves knowing Hystaspes is clearly hazardous, yet the nature of scholarly curiosity is such that the attempt has been and will continue to be made; nor is it without justification. Since Hystaspes was either an imitation of an Iranian text or genuine Iranian material (texts iv, v and vi), the criteria which will here be deployed in such circumstances are that, first, the relevant passage must contain ideas not found either in the Bible or in the Sibyl—Lactantius' two other main sources—and, second, that the idea must be found in the mainstream of Iranian thought. Then, but only then, may it be held that Lactantius is using Hystaspes. Such rigid criteria may exclude some passages from Hystaspes where the oracle's theology overlapped with the other sources, but they may also exclude extravagant theories.

The actual form of the oracle, a political dream vision (text v, lines 1–2; vi, lines 4–6; xi, lines 18–22) resembles *Dan.* 2, the vision of Nebuchadnezzar, a political dream vision the last part of which (*Dan.* 2: 34*ff*.; cf. text vi, line 5, xi, line 19) refers to the fall of Rome, and is interpreted by a prophet described as a youth (*Dan.* 1: 1–7; cf. text vi). It is, however, premature to conclude from this, as some have

24 *Ibid.*, 21.

done, that the oracle was therefore composed by Jews or Christians. There are Persian, specifically Achaemenid, models. Thus Herodotus[25] and Cicero[26] attribute such visions to Cyrus, the former referring to both Hystaspes and the rule of Asia. Libanius attributes such a dream to Cambyses, where Mithra directs the monarch in his westerly campaigns.[27] The model of Hystaspes need not therefore be Jewish; the question of provenance can be determined only on questions of content.

Two features of the apocalyptic scheme outlined by Lactantius do not accord with traditional Christian belief, but do agree with the Iranian apocalyptic tradition as evidenced by the Middle Persian texts, chiefly the *Bundahišn*, *Zand ī Wahman Yašt*, the *Jāmāsp Nāmag* and the *Dēnkard*.[28] The first concerns the idea of judgment. In text XVI, lines 2–3, men's deeds are weighed in the balance: those whose good deeds predominate pass to blessedness, the others to hell. All men (text XIX) have to pass through the eschatological fire which will burn the wicked but leave the righteous unharmed. Mechanistic ideas of judgment and a fire which all men must pass through, wicked *and righteous*, do not form part of the Christian tradition but are part of the normative Iranian apocalyptic tradition.[29]

25 *Histories* I: 208 (Penguin Books edition), p. 98.

26 *De divinat.* I: 23, 46, referring to D(e)inon's *Persica*.

27 *Oratio* XI: R. 293, lines 6–15.

28 Which I abbreviate, as usual, *G. Bd.* (Greater or Iranian recension), *ZW*,

28 Abbreviated here as *G. Bd.* (Greater or Iranian recension), *ZW*, *JN* and *Dk* respectively. A preliminary note on the date, nature and value of literature here cited dates from the ninth century A.D. and later. This late date does not, however, necessarily proscribe its use in this context. The *Bundahišn* represents a priestly compilation, in translation, of ancient and scriptural passages on various themes (including apocalyptic ones). The *Zand ī Wahman Yašt* and *Jāmāsp Nāmag* represent different descendants of a lost scriptural apocalyptic text and the *Dēnkard* is an encyclopaedic work embodying a great deal of ancient material; books 7–9 are largely collections and summaries of old and scriptural passages. On the nature of these books see, above all, Boyce, 'Middle Persian literature', in *Handbuch der Orientalistik* (1968) IV, I, section 2, *Literatur*, No. I, pp. 31–66.

29 Something of the concept was known in the time of the Prophet: *Ys.* 48: 8, 51: 13. But see, above all, *G. Bd.* 30 (on the individual judgment and weighing of the actions) and 34: 17*ff.* on the general judgment and the fire. References to the *Bundahišn* in this paper will be to the Greater (or Iranian) *Bundahišn* in the edition of B. T. Anklesaria, *Zand-Ākāsīh* (1956). As this is not widely available, reference is given afterwards in square brackets to the Indian version translated in *Sacred Books of the East* v, ed. West. If no such reference is given this implies that the shorter Indian version does not contain

The second feature of the apocalyptic scheme in Lactantius which accords with Iranian thought are the signs of the end. Text XII, lines 19–21, refers to cities perishing by fire, the sword, overflowing waters, disease and famine. Cumont saw in the 'overflowing waters' a reference to the apocalyptic floods indicated in *G. Bd.* 33: 30, 'the terrific rain which they call "*malkūšān*" for three years', one of the outbursts of evil prior to the coming of the saviour (Sōšyant) when fire will sweep the world.[30] Although fire and flood are linked in a number of Jewish and Christian writings, the flood is always the primeval flood and the fire always apocalyptic.[31] Disease as an apocalyptic sign is not found in the Bible in the same sense as it is found here. The plagues of *Zech.* 14: 12 and *Rev.* 11: 6 are rather different, not least because they are sent by God and are not outbursts of the destructive spirit. It is, however, fundamental to Zoroastrian theology that all disease and illness is the manifestation of evil; suffering cannot be due to God.[32] The combination of the evils of fire, flood and disease in one short passage does, therefore, strongly suggest an Iranian background.

Cumont also noted a number of striking parallels between passages in Lactantius and *ZW* with regard both to the apocalyptic signs of the end in nature and to the cosmic apocalyptic signs.[33] Here we are deal-

the reference. Similarly, the *Zand ī Wahman Yašt* will be quoted in the edition of B. T. Anklesaria, *Zand-ī Vohûman Yasn* (1957); the *Sacred Books of the East* reference is given afterwards in square brackets for readers unable to consult Anklesaria.

30 'La fin du monde'. On the rain of *malkūšān* see *Dēnkard* VII: 9, 3*f.*; *Dādistān ī Mēnōg ī Xrad* 27: 27–31; *Dādistān ī dēnīg* 37: 95. The primary source is the Pahlavi gloss on *Vd.* II: 22; see Anklesaria, *Pahlavi Vd.*, p. 27, discussed by Darmesteter, *Études iraniennes* II (1883), pp. 203*f.* I owe this reference to M. Boyce.

31 Josephus, *Antiquities* I: 70; *Life of Adam and Eve*, 49; 2 *Pet.* 3: 5–12. Mr Gordon has drawn my attention to the association of fire and flood in Greek tradition, for example in Plato's account of the destruction of Atlantis. He kindly supplied the following reference: H. von Arnim, *Stoic vet. Frag.* II, No. 5, pp. 596–632; also Plato, *Timaeus*, 22c–23c; Philo, *De actem mundi*, 146–7. In view of the influence of Greek thought on the Judaeo-Christian tradition it is perhaps all the more remarkable that the latter did not associate the two catastrophes. As the association of the two in Lactantius is made alongside a number of other features paralleled in Iranian thought, it is reasonable to assume that we are here dealing with an Iranian rather than a Greek source.

32 For a convenient exposition and collection of texts on this subject see Zaehner, *The Teaching of the Magi* (1956), especially chapter 4.

33 'La fin du monde', pp. 76*ff.*

ing with a passage from our category (*c*) above, wherein Lactantius does not name his source but follows his practice, related in category (*b*), of simply outlining his sources' teachings. The parallels here with Iranian apocalyptic symbolism are outstanding and can best be set forth in tabular form. In table 11.1 there are no biblical or Sibylline

Table 11.1
Apocalyptic signs in nature

Subject	*Lactantius, text* XII	*Zand ī Wahman Yašt*
Unreliability of the rains	'at one time by unseasonable rains, at another by barren drought.'	'The rain, too, will not rain at the proper season.' (4: 45 [2: 41])
Alternate heat and cold	'now by cold, now by excessive heats.'	'The hot wind and the cold wind arrive.' (4: 44 [2: 42])
Plants apparently flourish but bear no fruit	'No field, or tree, or vine will produce anything; but after they have given the greatest hope in the blossom they will fail in the fruit.'	'[and] that which thrives will not become ripe . . . those which thrive will not be wholesome and tasteful.' (4: 18*f.* [2: 31])
Drought	'Fountains [or springs] also shall be dried up, together with the rivers.'	'the waters of rivers and springs will diminish.' (4: 46 [2: 42])

parallels; thus the criteria we imposed for acceptance of an Iranian source are undoubtedly fulfilled. With table 11.2 there is more doubt, since biblical or Sibylline parallels can be seen. But it is only in the Iranian text that the various signs include the reference to the shortening of the day, month and year, so that this too appears to derive from an Iranian source. Since Lactantius refers to no other Iranian source than Hystaspes, we may reasonably identify his source here as Hystaspes also.

Benveniste has adduced good reasons for believing that Hystaspes is a direct descendant of the Avestan source behind *ZW*.[34] In a study of

34 'Une Apocalypse pehlevie', pp. 372–80.

Table 11.2
Cosmic apocalyptic signs

Subject Lactantius, from text XII	*Biblical text*	*Sibylline text*	*Iranian apocalyptic text*
Sun darkened	*Mark* 13: 24 *Rev.* 6: 12ff.	VIII: 190*ff.*; 342*ff.*	'the Sun's rays will be very level and much concealed; the Sun will show a melancholy sign.' (*ZW* 4: 16 [2:31], 6: 4 [3: 4])
Moon darkened	*Mark* 13: 24 *Rev.* 6: 12*ff.*	VIII: 190*ff.*; 342*ff.*	'the Moon will change [her] colour, and [there] will be melancholy, darkness and gloom on earth.' (*ZW* 6:4 [3: 4])
Stars falling	*Mark* 13: 15 *Rev.* 6: 12*ff.* *Isa.* 34: 4	VIII: 190*ff.*; 342*ff.*	'On the night the prince will be born, a token will come to the earth, stars will rain from the sky.' (*ZW* 7: 6 [3: 15])
Mountains lowered	*Isa.* 40		'This earth will become [a] plain . . . [there] will be no hill nor summit.' (G. *Bd.* 34: 33 [30: 33])
Sea unnavigable		VIII: 236	'the water of rivers and springs will diminish and it will have no increase.' (*ZW* 4: 46)
Shortening of year, etc			'the year, month and day [will be] shorter.' (*ZW* 4: 16 [2: 31])

the apocalyptic Pahlavi text *JN* he established that, contrary to earlier opinion, that text is not merely a later adaptation of *ZW* but is rather an independent, perhaps even more reliable, descendant of the now lost common parent, the Avestan *Wahman Yašt*. Hystaspes may well be part of this family. It not only embodies features in common with *ZW*, as we have seen, and with both *ZW* and *JN*,[35] but also with *JN* alone. The oracle is not, therefore, a copy of any one known Iranian text but is a representative—like other extant Iranian works—of a group of texts embodying the teaching of an Avestan apocalyptic book. There are five features in Lactantius which have no parallel in *ZW* but are found in *JN*. They are: the wars between neighbouring cities;[36] the overthrow of three kings by a powerful enemy from the north;[37] the eschatological earthquakes;[38] the survival of the apocalyptic terrors by one-third of the worshippers of God;[39] and the prophecy of the transference of power to the East.[40]

To the arguments of Cumont and Benveniste a further point may be added. Underlying certain passages of Lactantius concerned with the signs of the end (texts XI, XII, XIV, XV) there is a theology which has no logical place in Christian thought but which is fundamental to orthodox Zoroastrianism. The basic point of the biblical tradition concerning the apocalyptic woes is that they represent signs of the end. This is true of the Iranian tradition, but it also has a deeper understanding of them. The woes represent the ultimate assault of the disruptive and chaotic forces of evil on good, or *aša* (Vedic *ṛta*): the apocalyptic parallel to that shattering of cosmic order at creation by the assault of the demonic forces which produced such cosmic effects as earthquakes, the growth of mountains and the movement of the sun, and in the human sphere producing illness, pain and death in what was before the assault a world of perfect harmony, order, peace and health.[41] The signs of the end represent the ultimate assault of these very same forces of chaos, destruction and disorder. The events which typify this final period are not, therefore, isolated phenomena but the various symptoms of the one malaise. Thus the point behind *ZW* 4: 26 [2: 36], 'the basest slaves will advance forward to the mastery of the Iranian

35 E.g. hot and cold winds, *JN* 26; unseasonable rains, *JN* 29.
36 Text XI, lines 13*f*.; cf. *JN* vv. 42*f*.
37 Text XII, lines 10*f*.; cf. *JN* 95.
38 Text XII, line 10; cf. *JN* 28.
39 Text XIII, lines 3–5; cf. *JN* 72.
40 Text VI, line 5, XI, lines 19–22; cf. *JN* 5–13.
41 See *G. Bd.* 4 [3].

villages', or 4: 35 [2: 38], 'the inferiors shall take the daughters of patricians, nobles and sages to wife', describe what is, theologically speaking, the same phenomenon as *Dēnkard* VII; 8, 4, 'shame at the truth of the religion, and at the praise, peace and liberality and other goodness', or *ZW* 4: 16 [2: 31], 'the year, month and day will be shorter', for all are manifestations of disorder, that force which is ultimately opposed to Ohrmazd's creation and will. It is precisely this theological presupposition which lies behind text XI, lines 1–11, XII, lines 21–30,41*ff*, and XIV, lines 1–7. Indeed, the last passage reads like an assessment of the Zoroastrian apocalyptic woes: 'all things shall be confounded and mixed together against right, and against the laws of nature'. The degree of theological unity, and at times the remarkable correspondence of detail, can best be illustrated in tabular form (see table 11.3).

The few passages which are omitted from text XII in this table (for example, 'righteousness will be cast out and innocence hated'), although having no explicit parallel in the known Iranian texts, summarise very well the fundamental spirit of Zoroastrian apocalyptic. The significance of this argument, like that of Benveniste, is not merely that another block of material in Lactantius is added to the oracle of Hystaspes, but much more that the oracle is seen to represent accurately the typical and traditional—both in general spirit and in detail—Zoroastrian apocalyptic theology as evidenced by the main representatives of that tradition—*Zand ī Wahman Yašt*, *Jāmāsp Nāmag*, *Bundahišn* and *Dēnkard*.[42]

Widengren and others, while noting the Iranian elements of the oracle, allow for the possibility that it was composed by a Hellenist with a knowledge of Iranian religion.[43] Although this possibility cannot be completely excluded, it may be thought most unlikely, for analysis has shown that it emanated from a person, or circles, with a deep understanding of the very heart of Zoroastrian theology. It does not seem to me to bear the stamp of an onlooker summarising or

42 The tabular form may be slightly misleading in this instance, for the blank spaces do not necessarily indicate the absence of a similar idea. In a number of instances a Zoroastrian text presupposes the matter explicitly mentioned in Lactantius but does not refer to it. Thus the idea of the destruction of law is presupposed throughout the *ZW*, but it is not referred to in the relevant space because the precise wording does not occur. This fact underlines rather than detracts from the argument concerning the parallel character of the texts.

43 *Die Religionen*, p. 200.

collecting ideas, for if that were the case one might reasonably expect a superficial or garbled account which failed to appreciate the subtleties of the total Zoroastrian theology. Rather, the oracle of Hystaspes seems to me to reflect the convictions of a believer. Further, this analysis suggests that the oracle was a theological unity (see our second problem in section 2, page 133). This can be said at least for the form of the oracle known to Lactantius; other writers provide insufficient material for us to pass judgment on the nature of the oracle with which they were acquainted.

3 *The figure of the saviour in the oracle*

Windisch believed that the original oracle did not contain a reference to the coming of a saviour.[44] He interpreted text VII, lines 7–10, as meaning that in the version which lay before Lactantius there was no reference to the Son of God. He therefore took the reference to a saviour in the version which lay before Clement (text III, lines 4–8) as a Christianised version of the oracle, believing it easier to assume the addition of references to the coming of a saviour than their omission. Cumont objected to this that it would require that in the original Iranian version it was Ohrmazd himself who intervened on behalf of the righteous, a belief for which there is no Iranian evidence. To judge from the extant Zoroastrian texts, it would be odd if an Iranian text did not include a reference to a coming saviour.

A careful reading of Lactantius, however, suggests that the early Father was not trying to say that Hystaspes did not refer to the Son of God, but rather that he did not report that the saviour would destroy the wicked and set the rightous at liberty. For the passage following our text VII continues: 'which, however, Hermes did not conceal', and then refers not to the coming of the Son of God but to the fact that 'God brought His world to its ancient state and restored it'. After this reference to the final state, Lactantius turns to a passage from the Sibyl on the saviour to supplement Hermes, a passage stating that 'God shall send a king from the sun, who shall cause all the earth to cease from disastrous war'. To return to Lactantius' comment on Hystaspes, it is worth noting that the Latin construction used throws emphasis on the purpose for which the Son of God came. Lactantius' comment is: 'it has also been withdrawn [from this oracle] through the deception of the evil spirits, how the Son of God would be sent by the Father *in*

44 *Op. cit.*, pp. 35*f.*, 39, 74*f.* See also Cumont, 'La fin du monde', pp. 68, 84*f.*

order to destroy the impious and set free the faithful'.[45] Lactantius therefore objects not to the omission of the Son of God but to the failure to spell out the particular consequences of the saviour's coming. This omission may have been due to one of two reasons. Perhaps Hystaspes, like *ZW*, *JN* and *Dk* VII: 8 (and their ancient source?), dwelt on the signs of the end and the coming of the saviour rather than on the consequences. Alternatively, it may be that Hystaspes, like the Middle Persian texts, but unlike Lactantius and the Christian tradition, did not teach the ultimate separation of all men into righteous and wicked; rather, that all men, after temporary reward or punishment in heaven or hell, would eventually be one. Lactantius may therefore be objecting to an orthodox Zoroastrian doctrine which he believed was inspired by the evil spirits. It is interesting that there appears to be little or no Iranian content to the picture of the renewed world in *Divine Institutions* VII: 24, a fact consistent with either of these explanations. Both solutions do justice to the total context of the passage from Lactantius, but whichever is adopted it follows that the original text *did* contain a reference to the saviour.

Who, then, lies behind the figure of the Son of God (Clement), the saviour (*Theosophy*), the leader of the sacred warfare, the great king (Lactantius)? Cumont and Widengren conclude that it was Mithra.[46] The fact that the oracle is evidenced only in the West and during Roman times, but not in Iran, must inevitably incline one to the position that we have here the god of the 'Persian' mysteries. Such a soteriological role for the god would be in harmony with what I have argued elsewhere.[47] The reference to the saviour as the leader of the sacred warfare (text XV, line 6) would accord well with the picture of the warrior god of the ancient *Mithra Yašt*.[48] The solar imagery, too, would fit in with the picture of the god we gain from Western sources. There are, however, difficulties. Some of the reasons advanced by Cumont are not strong. He states, for example, that the oracle of Hystaspes included a belief in a world week and the rule of the planets over world

45 Italics mine. The text reads: 'et illud non sine daemonum fraude subtractum, missum iri a patre tunc filium dei, qui deletis omnibus malis pios liberet, (from Bidez and Cumont, *op. cit.*, II, p. 370). The *qui* clause with the subjunctive is, of course, equivalent to *ut* plus the subjunctive and denotes purpose. I owe this observation to my friend and colleague Dr J. P. Kane.

46 'La fin du monde', pp. 70*ff.*, and *Die Religionen*, pp. 199*ff.* respectively.

47 'Reflections on the bull-slaying relief' in *Mithraic Studies*, ed. Hinnells (Manchester, 1973).

48 See stanzas 8, 10*f.*, 20, 25, 35, 36, 39*f.*, 76, 96, 102. 140.

periods which in some systems culminated in the rule of the sun—here Mithras, the king from the sun.[49] Unfortunately, the chief passage in Lactantius referring to the world week, *Divine Institutions* VII: 14, does not mention Hystaspes, nor is there any indication of an Iranian source in that section, nor is there mention of the rule of the sun. Lydus (text IV) does state that those of the school of Hystaspes took the days of the week from the number of the planets, but that does not support the much larger theory, including the rule of the sun. Nor is it really the case, *pace* Cumont,[50] that *rex magnus* must indicate a sun god. Indeed, it is not absolutely certain that the expression *rex magnus* was in fact derived from Hystaspes. The fact that Zoroastrian theology has been seen to underlie Hystaspes also makes a Mithraic background questionable. If, with Cumont, one accepts that Zoroastrian theology (as opposed, for example, to non-Zoroastrian Iranian theology) lies behind Roman Mithraism, then the identification with Mithras may be acceptable, but such an assumption is being questioned more and more. It may not be possible to give a confident affirmative answer to the identification with Mithras until a fundamental re-examination of Mithraism has taken place.

Perhaps a more likely candidate for identification with the saviour is the Zoroastrian saviour, the Sōšyant. In the Zoroastrian tradition with which we have been concerned (i.e. those texts which appear to derive from the lost Avestan archetype) he is generally presented in priestly terms,[51] but that may be due to the fact that they are priestly compilations. It is quite plausible that in a text produced in a political context as a part of subversive propaganda, the Sōšyant could be presented in more kingly terms, for it was a Zoroastrian belief that religion and kingship were brothers.[52] The solar imagery is a little more difficult to explain. If it could be shown that the planetary speculation and the rule of the sun were basic to Hystaspes, this would be difficult to reconcile with the Sōšyant for he has no such connections in any extant texts. Yet such a development in the Sōšyant imagery is by no means impossible in a pantheon of merging functions, especially under Western

49 'La fin du monde', p. 73. Cumont's thesis concerning the apocalyptic schema of planetary rule in Mithraism has been seriously questioned by Gordon, 'Franz Cumont and the doctrines of Mithraism', in *Mithraic Studies*.

50 *Ibid.*, p. 86.

51 See for example *G. Bd.* 34: 23 [30: 25], where he performs the final *Hōm* sacrifice.

52 See Zaehner, *The Dawn and Twilight of Zoroastrianism* (1962), chapter 14.

(Anatolian?) influence. We have seen, however, that such a point is not proven. Perhaps one of the strongest arguments for the Sōšyant is one against Mithras. Roman Mithraism appears to have been anything but subversive. It was never persecuted, but rather received imperial patronage. In an interesting article Gordon argues that Mithraism in fact was a stabilising factor in Roman society. He rightly points out that the ideal Mithraist is generally represented as the image of social conformity; that within the structured religious hierarchy of the cult, promotion came only by acceptance of and submission to authority; the cult's aim was the escape of the soul from the world—not (unlike Zoroastrianism) the transformation of the world.[53] In short, Mithraism does not appear to have been the sort of cult likely to produce the politically revolutionary concept of salvation found in the oracle of Hystaspes (texts VI and XI). Thus there are three facts which suggest that the figure was the Sōšyant: the thoroughly Zoroastrian nature of the apocalyptic imagery; the plausibility of the idea of Zoroastrian texts or oracles containing anti-Roman sentiment; and the fact that the person and work of the Sōšyant were known to the West.[54] It would therefore seem that in the present state of our knowledge the figure most likely to lie behind the Son of God in Hystaspes is the Zoroastrian Sōšyant.

4 *The date of the oracle of Hystaspes*

Windisch and Cumont argued for a date in the first century B.C. or A.D., a date qualified by Cumont as not earlier than Pompey's invasion of Syria, though he gives no reason for this and it is difficult to see one.[55] Windisch notes that Mithradates Eupator was the chief representative of anti-Roman sentiment in the occidental world in the first century B.C., a point taken further by Widengren, who asserts not only that Eupator used the oracle for propaganda in his battles against Rome but also that he represented himself as the fulfilment of the oracle; for Widengren that means the incarnation of Mithra.[56] That Eupator used the oracle in his struggles is by no means implausible, but it cannot be argued that because a particular setting is suitable it must *therefore* have evoked it. In support of Eupator's use of the

53 'The social function of Mithraism', *Religion* II, 2 (1972).
54 The texts are largely Syriac. See Bidez and Cumont, *op. cit.*, II, pp. 126–35.
55 Cumont, 'La fin du monde', p. 65; Windisch, *op. cit.*, p. 70.
56 *Die Religionen*, p. 200.

oracle it might be pointed out that oracles concerning him are said to have been popular:

Every city agrees to superhuman honours for him and invokes the god-king (or calls him to their aid): on every side oracles and prophecy rule over the inhabited world.[57]

Eddy suggests a date of *c.* 190 B.C., on the grounds that anti-Western propaganda and talk of a return of rule to the East would be natural in the Persian reaction to the Hellenism which followed in the wake of Alexander's invasions. Text VI, line 5, would originally, on this interpretation, have been applied to the Macedonians and have been re-applied to the Romans in a later situation.[58] Text XI, lines 21*f.*, referring to the return of rule to the East and Asia, together with the Zoroastrian theology exhibited by the text, does give plausibility to this as the original date of the oracle, though that by no means excludes the possibility of the oracle having been used later by Mithridates. Since plausibility does not amount to proof, the date of the oracle cannot be said to have been established. For a text to gain international renown and rank alongside the Sibyl and the prophets in the mind of a second century Christian, a date some time in advance of the first century A.D. must be allowed. Again, the fact that Clement knew Hystaspes as among the Hellenic books (text III, line 3) must push the Iranian original back in time. If the arguments of Reitzenstein, Cumont and Benveniste concerning the Iranian origin of the Oracle of the Potter are accepted,[59] then the transportation of another apocalyptic text from Iran referring to a saviour king from the sun in the mid-second century B.C. would make a similar date for Hystaspes likely. The date at which the oracle of Hystaspes was composed would therefore appear to be not later than the first century B.C., with hints, but no more, that it may have been the second century B.C.; the possibility of later (Hellenistic?) redactions must also be allowed for.

The conclusion of this paper is, therefore, that the oracle of Hystaspes is a genuine Iranian—specifically, Zoroastrian—work; and that, in accord with the orthodox Zoroastrian theology which the oracle reflects, behind the saviour figure is the Zoroastrian Sōšyant. The composition of the oracle should be dated to the first century B.C. if not earlier.

57 Poseidonius 87 (Jacoby, p. 246, 4–6, fr. 36) = Athenaeus 5: 50. 213B (PM).
58 *The King is Dead*, p. 34.
59 Reitzenstein and Schaeder, *Studien zum antiken Synkretismus*, pp. 38–52; Benveniste, *op. cit.*, pp. 372*f.*; Bidez and Cumont, *op. cit.*, II, p. 372.

If the conclusion of a Zoroastrian origin for the oracle is accepted, there are important implications for certain other studies. One of the perennial problems of studies of Zoroastrian apocalyptic is dating its development and establishing the antiquity of its component parts or episodes. If the oracle of Hystaspes was Zoroastrian, it provides detailed support for the brief reports of classical authors and literary critical work on the Pahlavi texts. This support is particularly valuable in the case of the apocalyptic 'woes'. Whereas the doctrines of the saviour and of fire can be traced in the Gathas and the extant Avesta,[60] the only early evidence for the 'woes' is the testimony of Plutarch, *Isis and Osiris* 46 and his source, Theopompus.[61] This testifies to the antiquity of the general pattern of plague and famine, wars, successive ages and the idyllic pattern of the final state, but does not give the corroborative support to the general theological structure or the particular detail which is given by the oracle of Hystaspes.

The second implication is for studies of Zoroastrian influence on the Judaeo-Christian apocalyptic traditions. If such theories of influence are to have credibility, then the historical aspect of the question must be faced—was Zoroastrian eschatology known to people in the West? The studies of Widengren and Neusner have established that there was contact between the Parthians and the West, specifically with the Jews.[62] A Zoroastrian origin for the oracle of Hystaspes would show that historical contacts brought to the West some Zoroastrian apocalyptic as well.

The third implication is for Mithraic studies. Although the Mithraic origins of the oracle have been rejected, again the fact that Zoroastrian apocalyptic traditions expressing pure Zoroastrian theology were well known in the Roman empire at what was the formative period of

60 See Hinnells, 'Zoroastrian saviour imagery and its influence on the New Testament', *Numen* XVI (1969), pp. 163–73.

61 '. . . evil things have been mingled with the good. But there will come a determined period when Areimanios bringing plague and famine must be utterly destroyed by these, and made to vanish away; and the earth having become flat and level, men shall have one life and one commonwealth, all being blessed and speaking one tongue. And Theopompus says that, according to the Magi, for three thousand years in succession the one of these gods rules and the other is ruled; for the next three thousand they fight and war and break up one another's domains; but finally Hades is to fail, and men will become happy, neither needing food nor casting shadows.' (Trans. Moulton, *Early Zoroastrianism* [1913], pp. 403–5).

62 Widengren, *Iranisch-semitische Kulturbewegung, passim*; Neusner, *A History of the Jews in Babylonia* (1965), vol. I, *The Parthian Period.*

Roman Mithraism is something which Mithraic scholars should not ignore. Indeed, for all who are interested in the Roman empire it is interesting to note that before and after the time of Justin Martyr there were not a few who turned away from the mystery and State cults in their search for salvation and looked to the teaching of the prophet of ancient Iran, awaiting the coming of a saviour who would overthrow all that was evil, including the Roman empire, in order to establish the apocalyptic kingdom of God on earth.

12

Hywel D. Lewis

Sin and salvation

It is not easy to give one comprehensive definition of 'sin'. This is because the term has been used in so many different ways at different times and places. Even within the same general context the nuances and associations of the use of this word are so many and so subtle as to defeat any attempt to iron them out in one rigid analysis. In some popular uses it stands for anything which we find in some way offensive, even natural calamities. But in the more serious use of the word we may find two elements which are fairly persistent and present together. One of these is the notion of moral evil, the other is the idea of some offence against God. Much in the further use of the word depends on how these ideas in turn are themselves understood.

Few would use the word 'sin' today except in a context where something is to be denounced, to be avoided or guarded against. If a practice is sinful this means that one should not indulge in it; preachers may thunder against it with the implication, as a rule, that people should forswear it. But the likelihood of the word 'sin' being used in such a context depends largely on whether the main concern remains a religious one. Where religion has declined, the likelihood is that some other words—'wrong', 'foul', 'rotten', 'abominable' and their obscene or blasphemous equivalents will be used. Even 'wicked' tends to pass out when the religious element is weak.

This is reflected also in scholarly and sophisticated writings on moral or religious questions, and in many cases carries with it radical differences of approach to what are substantially similar problems. In times past this happened less extensively, but there are differences in the way ethical problems have been treated in the past which are due mainly to variations in the strength of the religious factor involved. We thus find ethical problems treated more explicitly on their own account by Greek writers than by Hebrew ones. But generally, in the past, ethical problems have presented themselves in a context which is also religious, although this does not mean that ethical ideas have been wholly absorbed into religious ones.

On its ethical side the idea of sin will depend largely on the way moral evil is understood. But at many times the distinction we draw today between moral and non-moral evil is not very clearly recognised. There is thus a tendency to equate all forms of evil with sin. Whatever is bad in the universe would thus be sinful, including ignorance, suffering, and even some blight or malfunctioning in the order of nature. But a more sophisticated view would temper this, at least to the extent of regarding such natural evils as consequences or indications of sin rather than as explicit manifestations of it. In some cases natural evil might also be thought to be the cause of sin, as when men are said to sin through ignorance—without, however, being always thought less culpable on that account.

This conflation of moral and non-moral evil comes about more readily when the religious element in the idea of sin predominates. Any sort of blight or imperfection must be thought offensive to God; a challenge to his perfection or goodness, or inherently offensive to his holiness. In less theistic religions all forms of evil will be thought to be some kind of marring or rupturing of some ultimately perfect wholeness of things and not to be countenanced in any ultimate reckoning. Indeed, natural evil tends in this way sometimes to determine the main character of sin, as when sin is thought of primarily as uncleanness. This is helped further when, as often happens in early times, there is no clear distinction between physical and spiritual being. But even in these contexts the element of culpability remains. In some ways it is even intensified in the idea of offence against God, adding a new dimension to what is already thought vile or improper. On the other hand, the more the idea of culpability predominates the harder it is to avoid some distinction between moral evil and natural or non-moral evil. As we shall see, there are some ways in which religion, while on the one hand deepening this distinction, tends also, rather paradoxically, to obscure it. To understand how this comes about is one of the main clues we have to some very perplexing features in more profound and formative elements in various accounts of sin.

For enlightened thought the distinction between moral and non-moral evil seems quite fundamental, and, in as much as the idea of sin involves a fundamental ethical ingredient of moral evil, a grasp of this distinction is essential for a sound examination of the subject.

Moral evil is that for which one may be properly blamed or held to account. If someone says 'How horrible!', thinking of some grievous wound I have suffered in an accident, then I take this quite differently from the way I would take it if the same words were used of my personal conduct. As a rule we use very different sets of words in these cases—'bad', 'unfortunate', 'appalling', 'distressing' and so on, on the one side, 'wicked', 'brutal', 'vicious', 'guilty', 'sinful', on the other; and, although we extend the use of these words beyond the strict boundaries, we also understand generally that we are doing so metaphorically, e.g. a vicious illness, a vile wind, a wicked bend in the road, or even as a term of affection: 'the old sinner'. If I am ill, or if I fail an examination, or if I have no ear for music, no one seriously blames me—unless it can be shown that these conditions are due to some neglect on my own part in the past. Even then the real blame would attach to my earlier neglect. Normally we just commiserate with the sick, with those who are ill-endowed in some respect or fail a test. We do not say that they are vicious, bounders, rotters or sinners. Such terms of condemnation would be singularly out of place. It would be equally absurd to suppose that ills and privations of the sort indicated are invariably due to sin or moral misdemeanour on the part of the person concerned. Some parts of the Bible do suggest that the ills men suffer are a retribution for their own wickedness, and the same idea may be found in features of some non-Christian religions. But the Bible also provides firm correctives to this, for example in the Book of Job or in the words of Jesus about the man born blind—'Neither hath this man sinned, nor his parents.' He would be a bold man who would maintain today that men's afflictions were a direct reflection of their sinful state.

We have thus to draw a sharp distinction between moral and non-moral good or evil. Non-moral goods are health, happiness, physical enjoyment and skills, intellectual and artistic attainment, happy personal relationships and so forth. These seem to have nothing directly to do with sin, though men, as we shall see, have sometimes thought otherwise. Sin falls more to the side of moral evil, and the distinctive feature of this is that blame and condemnation (and perhaps punishment) are appropriate. This in turn implies accountability; I can be blamed only for something I have brought about and which is in some way within my control. If I can convincingly say 'I could not help it' I seem free from all censure. It seems absurd to find fault with me for what I could not avoid. If sin goes with moral evil and guilt, then it seems to be confined to what an agent directs or controls himself, to deliberate or voluntary undertaking.

At the heart of the problem of sin is, therefore, the problem of freedom. What sort of freedom does accountability involve? Many answers have been given to this question, and we cannot enter here exhaustively into so large a topic. But, on the face of it, certain things are ruled out. We cannot be held accountable for merely physical failings or limitations. I am not to be blamed for failing to save a drowning man whom I could not reach in time. Nor, if I am overcome by fumes in a burning building, is the death of the other victims to be laid at my door. If I did my best no one can complain, even when a more robust or skilful person might have done better. If I am tied in a chair no one blames me for failing to sound the burglar alarm.

These are very clear cases of moral excusability. Closely allied is the excuse of ignorance. We may say, in some sense, that the motorist has run over the child in the road. This is our rough description of the tragedy. But many things have to be settled before blame is apportioned. There can be no blame if the child dashed into the road at the last minute, or if the brakes unexpectedly failed, or if the driver had a sudden blackout. This does not mean that the accident may not prove tragic for the driver as well as the child; it could be peculiarly so if the child were his own. But, however terrible the circumstances, no enlightened person would begin to think in terms of blame or guilt in this situation. For that, it must be suspected that the driver had in some other way contrived the accident or been at least negligent. If it is known that he had taken reasonable care of his car, was driving at a normal speed etc, then we must say that he had no reason to suspect that the brakes were faulty or that the child would run out into the road; and, 'if he could not have known', he could not be blamed. Ignorance therefore exempts entirely.

In this context theological writers have made much use of the phrase 'invincible ignorance'. This is perfectly proper. I may be ignorant of some things, which it is important for me to know, through neglect in the past. I have not taken reasonable pains when there was time. In this case we would still be disposed to say that it was for my neglect that I was to blame, not for the present exceptional and disastrous consequences, which may cause me the deepest anguish. But, subject to the qualification 'invincible' or 'unavoidable', however this be thought to apply, it seems plain that one cannot properly incur blame or be guilty through ignorance. If sin involves moral evil it thus seems impossible to 'sin in ignorance'. This has, however, been extensively questioned in theological writings, and not all religious thinkers would agree that invincible ignorance exempts. We shall return to this later.

A further distinction is worth noting here, that between ignorance of fact and ignorance of principle. Oliver Twist knew what he was doing in point of fact in picking pockets, but, as instructed by Fagin, thought it a fine thing to do. More seriously, men have sacrificed their first-born, have burnt the martyr at the stake, have launched and perpetuated avoidable wars, have held slaves in bondage, in the full confidence that it was their duty. Where the line is to be drawn in these cases between ignorance of fact and ignorance of principle is not always clear, the main differences in men's ethical judgments seeming to turn more on questions of fact (what ensues in the long run, etc) than on radical differences of principle. But there must clearly be evaluation at some stage, and it is possible to err in assessing the facts as well as in determining what they are. The way this is thought to happen will depend on our view of the nature of moral judgments. But few would doubt that it is possible to err on a strictly moral issue as well as on questions of fact. If ignorance exempts in the one case will it not do so in the other?

To admit that all ignorance exempts may lead to what seem to be very paradoxical results. But before we note these, reference must be made to yet another dimension of the question of accountability. For even when it is established that we ought to act in a certain way, the question arises whether we are truly free to do so. There may be no outward hindrances or mental limitations. But if I intensely dislike what is expected of me can I still do it? Is my will free, and in what sense? Am I not perhaps determined by heredity, by environment, or by the will of God? This is the central ethical problem of freedom, and no discussion of sin can afford to disregard it.

Among the attitudes adopted to this problem the ones most relevant to our topic are these. First there is the view of those who take up an uncompromisingly determinist position. For them there can be no proper question of choice or responsibility. Hobbes said that he did not accuse any man by his words any more than he would accuse the beast for devouring its prey. Men act as their nature prompts them, and our proper course is to accept this and reckon with it without any ultimate recrimination. Praise and blame and punishment are still meaningful, but only as devices to affect people's future conduct. But even that is questioned in some recent work, the idea of responsibility being superseded entirely by the notions of social maladjustment or disease, for which society must provide the right treatment in the interest of its own members. This view finds considerable support in recent work on social science and social pathology, and Barbara Wootton[1] refers with obvious sympathy to the views of thinkers who regard the concepts of responsibility and guilt as 'theological and metaphysical anachronisms' best relegated to 'the amusement of the religious and others'.

It is understandable that social workers and students of social pathology should be impatient with certain muddled religious ideas which seem to frustrate them in their work; and more will be said on this shortly. In their zest to put social work and social studies on a stricter scientific basis and bring it into line with advances in other subjects, they also pass easily to the notion that an exhaustively scientific account can be given of all human conduct—in all its aspects. Inclining to determinism, they also see clearly that the ideas of guilt and kindred ingredients of the traditional doctrine of sin have no place. In this they have an admirable consistency. They are mistaken, however, in supposing that their work presupposes an exhaustively determinist account of human conduct. There may be areas of conduct which are free in a way that does not upset the patterns and continuities which the student of social science must assume. It is also risky to allow one's preoccupation with extreme and abnormal situations to affect unduly one's general conspectus on the situation of men and their environment. But if much which influential social scientists assume is sound there can be no room for the concept of sin or any religious implications of it.

Another much canvassed approach to the ideas of choice and responsibility is that which restricts freedom to our abilities to carry out whatever we decide or choose to do. But this, although widely current in recent ethics, hardly gets to the core of the problem. The real issue is whether the choice or decision is itself free. If it is not, then again it is hard to retain the notion of accountable conduct in the way usually presupposed in the notions of culpability and sin.

Others have recourse to the notion of self-determination. Our conduct is, in the last resort, bound to be what it is, but this comes about through the ways various elements in our environment are taken up into our own natures and modified thereby—we are not subject to mechanical determination from without. The complexities of this process and the fact that it continues to the very moment of action

1 See especially her *Social Science and Social Pathology* (1959), chapter VIII.

make any rigid prediction of individual conduct impossible. Our actions may thus be said to be in a very profound sense our own and free; they express our own personalities, and we may thus be held to account for what we do. These ideas have a long history, going back to prominent features of Greek philosophy, and they became central themes in the writings of notable idealists in the nineteenth century.[2] Some outstanding ethical writers of today[3] endorse the account of freedom as self-determination.

If these doctrines are adequate it seems possible to retain the idea of sin, as involving genuine culpability, within the framework of some kind of determinism. We are not determined fatalistically by forces external to ourselves but through what we ourselves are or become. There is thus opened a way of escape out of many acute ethical and theological difficulties which have perplexed men down the ages. The idea of sin being transmitted, or being pervasive in the so-called human situation, is made easier of acceptance and we also find it easier to come to terms with the notions of God's omniscience and omnipotence. For we can say that, while the course of one's life is somehow preappointed and known to God, it is at the same time the life we elect to lead. If the seeming opposition of freedom and determinism can be overcome we have a considerable easement of some of the more perplexing features of widely held religious doctrines.

For many thinkers, however, this move is proscribed. They hold that if there is any sense in which our conduct is inevitable or preappointed, however flexible in other respects, we cannot be held accountable for it in the way required by the ideas of sin and guilt. Two courses, then, seem open. One—adopted, as we have seen, by some social scientists—is to dispense with the notion of inherently reprehensible conduct and all attendant moral and religious ideas of sin and condemnation. This does not mean that all intrinsic evaluation of conduct is at an end. There are still distinctions to be drawn, but they will fall into the class of the non-moral goods listed earlier. To be concerned about people in distress, to forgo one's own gain for the good of others, to be of an affectionate and agreeable disposition, to be patient and considerate, these will be admirable traits of character and conduct (and their opposites bad), not merely in the sense of social usefulness, but in themselves. We shall admire and praise them as we admire an athlete or a poet or a mathematician. No one can

2 See especially Bradley, *Ethical Studies* (1876), chapter 1.

3 For example, Ross, *Foundations of Ethics* (1939), chapter x.

help it if he cannot excel in these ways. We think it a pity if a man has no aptitude for music but we do not think of blaming him. We do not find fault with a person who cannot do mathematics however hard he tries. All the same, we deem it an excellent thing to be intelligent or artistic, and consider aesthetic enjoyment to be extremely worthwhile in itself. It is to these that distinctions of worth in conduct and character must be assimilated on the present view.

There are cultures in which this attitude rests more easily than in others. In Greek philosophy, though by no means in Greek mythology or Greek life and literature generally, the ideas of sin and blame and guilty violation of law have little prominence, and no sharp distinction is drawn between various aspects of the good life. Morals and aesthetics go hand in hand. To live well is to fulfil all that is latent in us, and, while this involves our intelligent involvement in what we do, the main conditions—as in the case of poetry, for example—are latent aptitude and appropriate stimulus and guidance in our environment; education and training are the all-important sources of the good life. We thus have the famous Socratic maxim that 'virtue is knowledge'. We are inevitably drawn to the good; it is indeed the true fulfilment of our own aspirations, and no one therefore 'sins'—if the word is now appropriate—except in ignorance. Even when the conditions of voluntary actions are specifically examined, to show how we seem to do wrong deliberately, the discussion tends to stay at the level of some of our understanding being blunted for a time or of a disposition being just latent.

On such views there are no inherently evil traits in our nature, nor any radical corruption. There can only be good out of its place or developed out of proportion to other aptitudes or not properly nourished and directed. There is no ultimately willing choice of an evil way. But it is also doubtful whether this does justice to the widespread sense of the enormity of sin, in our sense of being at fault, of having transgressed. What of remorse and condemnation? Must these be rejected as improper and wrong-headed frames of mind? That seems to go against basic convictions and to violate what many consider to be the main condition of our dignity as human beings. There remains, thus, only one course for those who are unable to reconcile freedom and determinism.

That is to accept a frankly indeterminist choice such that, granted all the situation involves and our own character as formed at the time, our action could still be different. But clearly this cannot extend to all our conduct. Otherwise life would be chaotic and the stock objection would be unanswerable: that the libertarian, by implying that any action could come from any man at any time, violates the obvious continuity of character and conduct. We do count on one another, we plan ahead privately and publicly, and life would not be possible otherwise. What the libertarian must hold is that there are some choices which are free in an absolute way, and as a rule the choices are confined to cases of a conflict between what we most want to do at some time and what we think we ought to do. Apart from this, conduct is predictable —though not, of course, unfailingly—in the normal way. It is possible in principle to anticipate what I shall feel like and want at some time and what I shall think it right to do. A grasp of this limitation on the claim proper for a libertarian to make, and refinements in the further presentation of it, mark a major advance in ethical theory in our day and a great clarification of the ethical issues that bear most closely on religious ones.[4]

Should we now say that sin, as involving moral evil, is confined to cases of wholly undetermined choice? If so, we run into difficulties over much that has been traditionally held and which, in some respects, has a ring of truth.

It has been held, for example, that sin is transmitted. It is thus basically a sinful state, though apt to issue in sinful acts. Our sin, on the simplest version of this doctrine, is the sin of Adam, the medium of the transmission, so it was also supposed, being the body. As the heirs of Adam, we are thus unavoidably corrupt, and, as a corollary, there is something peculiarly evil about the body, and especially concupiscence. This lent particular enormity to sexual sins, and it often meant also that all sexual activity, though some is unavoidable for procreation, is inherently bad; and the same condemnation was often extended to all other physical indulgence. This led to severely repressive attitudes from time to time and to extreme self-denying practices; it was one element in the determination of some hermits and members of monastic regimes to mortify the flesh by severe privations and keep themselves as unspotted by the world as possible. This would be a very different motivation for extreme puritanical existence from that recommended by Plato, who merely thought that physical indulgence was trivial and apt to hinder the development of the higher intellectual propensities of men—at least, of men destined otherwise to reach

4 For example, see especially Hartmann, *Ethics* III (1967), and Campbell, *In Defence of Free Will*.

great intellectual heights and exercise grave responsibilities. When the body was thought to be not just a nuisance but bad, it was also sometimes held that death had come about as the proper penalty for all for their part in the sin of Adam.

Other versions of these views laid less exclusive emphasis on bodily corruption and stressed the unavoidably self-seeking character of all human aims. With the slackening of the sense of a literal beginning of life with Adam and the demythologising of stories of creation and the Fall, attention was centred more on the allegedly corrupt state of man as an essentially self-seeking being. In this form the doctrine has been affirmed as fervently today as at any time in its history. For Karl Barth the nature of man is thought to be totally corrupt; Emil Brunner holds that the divine image in man has not been wholly lost and that, for this reason, we know good and evil, though we can never do it. In a peculiarly bold paradox he declares that 'if I feel I ought to do right, it is a sign that I cannot do it'.[5] Reinhold Niebuhr argues that, while there can be more or less in the outward consequences of sin, there is not properly a big sin and a little sin but only the universal sin of anything whatever that we do. This position is in no way confined to this school of 'Continental theologians': the doctrine of universal sin or the mass unavoidable sinfulness of 'man' has been a major theme in much other influential theological thought of our day.

The first comment to make here is that the notion of transmitted sin has very little biblical foundation. Although it has sometimes been ascribed to Gen. 3, scholars as notable as F. R. Tennant have pointed out that the passage does not yield the required doctrine except by special interpretation. The sin of Cain, in the subsequent story, is not connected with the sin of Adam. There are other parts of the Old Testament which suggest that sin is inherent in man from his birth, though this is not connected with the story of the Fall. But it is in apocalyptic and Rabbinic literature that we find the scriptural suggestions crystallised into a fairly firm notion of original sin derived from Adam. This must be presumed to have affected much in the teaching of St Paul, out of which doctrines of original sin were subsequently shaped (e.g. Rom. 5: 21–21). But it is only in isolated passages that we find this in St Paul, and these have not the precision of an explicit doctrine. At other times (see especially Acts 23: 1) his attitude seems very different, an ambivalence of great importance for a sound understanding of religion.

5 *The Divine Imperative* (1937), p. 74.

The same doctrines appear only in very qualified forms in the teaching of the early Christian Fathers, the main names here being Irenaeus, Origen and Tertullian. Influenced much by Philo, the main figure in Hellenistic Judaism, the most they seemed to have entertained was the thought that the power of men to resist evil was weakened, not wholly atrophied, by the Fall. It is in the teaching of St Augustine, vigorously opposed in this regard by Pelagius, that we find firm expression of the view that the depravity introduced by the Fall is complete, so that no one is able to will what is good. In the teaching of Aquinas and in the Scholastic period as a whole we return to a position nearer that of the pre-Augustinian Fathers, Duns Scotus and especially Abelard anticipating much in the course of subsequent liberal thought. But the doctrines of total depravity and of the essential sinfulness of concupiscence were reaffirmed in the Protestant teaching of Luther and Calvin in vigorous and at times extravagant language which lent much of its colour to the revival of Augustinian doctrines in Continental theology in our own day.

Our next comment must be on the way ethical and religious ideas are shaped at early and formative stages of culture. In primitive societies the sense of the distinctness of persons is weak, and the unit, for practical purposes, tends to be the group: a family or a tribe. Property is largely owned in a communal way and responsibility is corporate. A family as a whole is held to account for the transgressions of any of its members, this leading to protracted feuds and the start of early wars. This accounts for practices and judgments which seem to us savage and barbarous, as in the biblical story of the sin of Achan and the punishment by stoning meted out to him and his entire family, even his animals. To complicate things further the distinction between intention and actual accomplishment is not sharply drawn, and men are thus held to account for occurrences which they did not anticipate and which may have come about in an accidental way, quite independent of anyone's purpose. Owing to the very close association of religion and morality in early times, this would have affected the development of religion as well as morals; and in these ways men's ideas and attitudes on morals and religion will have settled into fairly rigid corporate forms which it took a long time to correct and discard, especially when they affected authoritative statements in sacred scriptures.

Even when the tendencies in question were corrected in more sensitive and enlightened thought, as in Jer. 31: 29, 30 and Ezek. 18: 18, yet it tends to persist in subtle ways and to be revived in times of distress and confusion, as in Nazi Germany, where entire communities and races were held permanently responsible for the alleged misdeeds of some. The famous German confession of guilt after World War II reflects the same attitude.[6]

A reinforcement of these tendencies, at the more intellectual level, comes about through the widespread tendency to hypostatise abstractions, the family, society, the State coming thus to be treated as entities on their own account. In religion, and especially theology, this takes a further acute form when the general or corporate use of 'men', proper enough when used with due understanding, is loosely extended to cover the notion of man as a super-entity, inclusive in some way of all men, which has had a history, a fall, a redemption, a destiny, etc. Strictly speaking, there are only individual men and women.

In addition, there are complications concerning the way we may do wrong in ignorance. Our ethical judgments are fallible. Some writers have concluded from this that we are sometimes bound to do wrong—indeed, that we can never be wholly certain that we have done what we should, as we are never wholly free from error. This is sometimes erected into a full and vigorous defence of the doctrine that sin is inevitable for all, since we are commanded to will 'what can neither be willed nor known'.[7] Such procedures depend, however, on a deep confusion between various senses of doing right. In medieval times the distinction was drawn between 'formal' and 'material' sin. In recent ethics much prominence has been given to the distinction between the subjectively right act and what is objectively right.[8] There is something we ought to do in some situation, but we may not be agreed about it. Integrity does not make us infallible. But while we are bound in some measure to do wrong objectively, this may be through no fault of our own, and we cannot thus be morally accountable or guilty in respect to it, however regrettable it is. If we are said to sin in such cases it can be only in a very subordinate and trivial use of the term. On the whole, as 'sin' is hard to dissociate from moral evil and guilt, it is unwise to extend it to 'material' or outward wrongdoing. We can thus, by holding the appropriate distinctions clearly in mind, continue to hold that no one sins in ignorance and that, however horrible the deed may be outwardly, everyone must be finally judged according

6 Cf. chapter VII of my *Morals and the New Theology* (1947).
7 De Burgh, *From Morality to Religion* (1938).
8 See Ross, *op. cit.*, chapter VII.

to his lights—this, of course, presupposing that every effort is made to come by as sound an understanding of our obligations as is possible for us. Not every fanatic can be excused on grounds of ignorance; there is much he might have done to restrain his own unreason.

This is one of the points where distinctive advances in recent ethics can help materially to clarify our thinking on religious and theological topics. It is, alas, also an area where many eminent theological writers of today have been most averse to welcome the helping hand of the philosopher.

A closely related area of theological controversy concerns the way we may have to come to terms with ideas and practices other than those which seem to us proper. We may deem one course to be strictly the ideal one but we may not be able to pursue it fully in an unsympathetic or hostile environment. What compromises of this kind are in order is a hard question with vast ramifications, but clearly some concession must be made to the views and situations of those on whose co-operation we depend. In Christian theology this has been handled largely in terms of a distinction between an absolute law (or a law of perfection) and a relative law, the formulation of the latter being affected in turn by the idea of a natural law and the fusion of this with the Roman notion of a law of nations (*ius gentium*). These distinctions have been helpful, though they have also been made the excuse for reluctance to conform to standards which could have been observed as professed. In this context also there arises the idea of a demand being genuine and properly required of us although not capable in fact of fulfilment. This should not lead to the ascription of guilt or sinfulness for non-compliance with an ideal which could not be fully implemented in certain situations or which, alternatively, was thought incapable of proper embodiment. We can be held to account only for failure to do what the circumstances in their fullness require. It is thus most regrettable that many religious thinkers, today as in the past, have held men under grim condemnation for non-compliance with ideals which they themselves affirm to be 'impossible'.[9] This is a further way in which the idea of inevitable sin has been given a new lease of life.

Moral attainment is also thought to be impossible by some because all are by nature bound to seek their own good. But we have seen earlier that the proper course to take here is to surrender the idea of accountability and guilt in any properly moral or religious sense. It is only by confusion (widespread, alas, in much theology) that we can

9 See Niebuhr, *Moral Man and Immoral Society* (1933).

be held under the condemnation of standards which we are constitutionally incapable of observing.

A further use of 'sin' in a weak sense should be noticed. It is sometimes used to designate weakness of character or inclinations to evil in our natures. No one can altogether avoid sin in this sense. There are bound to be ways in which even the most saintly will find it irksome to do what is right, and for most people, almost certainly for all, there will be some positively evil traits of character to be resisted and overcome—envy and dislike of other persons, bitterness and even fierce hatred. In conceding this we must not, however, go to the extreme of supposing that all our natural propensities are tainted or deprived of worth by the presence in our characters of worthless or evil traits. We must admit ingredients which are good in an unqualified sense in themselves—pity, compassion, benevolence, a genuine sharing in the gladness of others. Some religious thinkers have argued that these and similar estimable traits of character, and their embodiment on particular occasions, have an invariably selfish component, usually pride, which distorts them and takes away their inherent worth altogether: the great social concern of a Gandhi or the self-sacrifice of a Father Damien is no better in itself than the cruel impulses of a Nero or the machinations of a ruthless racketeer. This seems quite mistaken. We must acknowledge the genuinely estimable qualities of men's characters and not suppose that they are deprived of their quality of objective concern and nobility by any baser factors which may complicate our natures as a whole. Nor must it be overlooked that the mixture of good and evil in our natures varies a great deal from one person to another and from one situation to the next in the lives of various persons. What matters most at the moment, however, is the admission that there are elements in our natures which are positively bad, in themselves and not merely in their effect.

It is not altogether inappropriate to use the word 'sin' of these weak or bad traits of character; and many have seized on this as a way of retaining some form of the doctrine of original sin. There can be no serious objection to this, and the issue could turn out to be largely verbal. But on the whole it does not seem to be a procedure we should commend. In the first place, as Abelard stressed, we have no reason to connect those faults of nature with some initial transgression. They simply indicate what heredity and circumstance have made us, and although genuine moral wrongdoing—our own and those of others in the past as well as in the present—will have entered into this, that will be only as one factor among many. All this may be overlooked or distorted if we enclose it within the associations and rigidities of the language of original sin. In addition, and more important, it is doubtful whether the word 'sin' should be applied at all in this context. For it is too strongly associated already with the ideas of condemnation, blame, guilt, remorse, etc, to be applied without ambiguity to faults or failings of character which we do not directly control. No one should accept such failings with equanimity. We can do much to improve our own characters or those of others in the course of time, and it is one of our main duties to do so. But it is for this and for our other reactions to the situations that confront us, including our own feelings and desires, that we are properly accountable. No one can be blamed for being tempted, even when the main factor in the temptation comes from inferior elements in one's own nature, but only for yielding to temptation. It is here that the word 'sin' is strictly appropriate. Some writers reserve the words 'virtue' and 'vice' for good and bad elements of character, but there is some possibility of confusion here also.

We have now to relate this more closely to the religious ingredient in the idea of sin. The latter is often regarded as rebelliousness or some kind of offence against God. This is quite in order. For whenever the idea of God is present a new dimension is added to the heinousness of moral transgression. It is not merely the moral law which is violated and conscience which is outraged, there is also opposition to the will of a supreme and holy Being and resistance to his love where that is made manifest. But all this can be best understood when it is seen in the light of the general ways in which religious existence may be impaired. Religion depends on some consciousness of a supreme or transcendent Being, though the latter is not always thought of in explicitly theistic or personal terms. There is a case to be made for the view that even in the seemingly atheistic forms of religion, as in some types of Buddhism or Confucianism, there is some reference to a supreme transcendent reality. This is subtly present also in various kinds of polytheistic and primitive religions. But the relationships of men to the supreme reality they apprehend and worship in this way may be confused and distorted in many ways.

One of these comes about in the overwhelming character of the sense of the presence of God, the sense of awe and majesty, of holiness too terrible to be borne, so splendidly described by Otto in his classic *The Idea of the Holy*. In this situation, especially when God is felt to be vividly present, the worshipper is overcome by a sense of his own unworthiness, his littleness before God; he becomes 'as dust, as nothing'. Nothing about him is better than 'dirty rags', and this tends to be expressed, in the white heat and rhetoric of prophetic utterance, in words of general self-abhorrence. The propensity is intensified where there is also a profound sense of properly moral guilt, and this leads to a conflation of the attitude of finite abasement in the presence of God and the sense of moral unworthiness. As the situation tends to be described in colourful terms of self-condemnation, this comes to be solidified more expressly later into a distinctive belief in a general moral inadequacy divorced from the consciousness of any particular evil conduct. Such conflation of a religious shortcoming, or of the sense of it, with properly ethical aspects of our existence, is one of the major explanations of passages in the scriptures and elsewhere which seem to reflect a sense of pervasive and unavoidable debasement.

This is intensified when the same process affects our inability to respond as fully as we should to the splendour of the divine presence in experience, to match up to its opportunities and challenge and worthily cultivate it in the whole of our lives. We fail as a lover might fail or as a poet or scientist fails, however hard he tries, to match up to the splendour of his vision. When psalmists and prophets express this, they do not do so in the cautious and considered language of the philosopher, or with measured heed to the limits of its application, but as a total experience. It is for us in due course to reflect on what they have said, to disentangle the various strands in it and note the various ways in which prophetic utterance has application. This is one of the main contributions of philosophy to religion; failure to carry it out effectively and consistently has been one of the main reasons for the perpetuation of religious doctrines which violate our basic ethical convictions and present avoidable obstacles to many who are otherwise drawn to religion. Some forms of the doctrine of original sin—the belief in the inevitably corrupt or tainted nature of unbaptised infants, for example, and the doom that awaits them—have made religion very repellent for many thoughtful and sensitive persons.

The confusion to which I have alluded takes place more easily because of our proneness to suppress a great deal in experience which imposes a strain upon us. Recent psychologists, in noting this, have stressed especially our sense of guilt. But when guilt and the sense of religious shortcomings are trodden down into some subconscious level of our existence, then the conflation of them, and the ensuing confusion in our thoughts and attitudes, is greater and more pervasive than when such frames of mind are to be viewed in the clearer light of reflective conscious experience.

A further form of religious shortcoming is idolatry. This rarely appears at the crude level of merely bowing before graven images or supposedly supernatural beings. It has within it as a rule an element of genuine worship which is also perverted. This comes about in the following way. We have seen that the sense of the living presence of God imposes a strain: it is 'tremendous' and not to be endured, and men thus tend, in scriptural language, to flee from the presence of God. But they are also drawn to God, they thirst after him; and to cope with this situation, they attempt to reduce the impact of the divine upon them by incapsulating it within the finite media by which it is transmitted. Such media, including not only instruments of worship and holy places but our own roles and religious offices, become in this way the centres of a certain religious perversion which, as affecting our own inner attitudes especially, can again be easily confused and conflated with the sense of distinctively moral shortcomings in a way that parallels the confusions already noted and merges with them, thus disposing us further to the same general misunderstanding and regrettable reactions.

The main clue to the paradoxical situation whereby we find ourselves attracted in some fashion to pronouncements which seem also to be ruled out by our moral convictions is this. Moral wrongdoing has various effects besides the evil intended by the doer of it; there are repercussions on the state of mind of the agent as well as the harm to the victim. Prominent among these is the way evil-doing drives us back on the unavoidable inner aspect of finite consciousness. We do not know other persons as we know ourselves. Even in the most intimate relationships there is some element of mediation; we depend on what we see and generally observe, but we know our thoughts and feelings in having them, though of course we do not know our permanent dispositions in the same way. The inwardness of present experience does not preclude its also being objective, but it does mean that we are subject to some kind of privacy at all times. There is some tendency to resist this and to break away from it by getting to know other persons strictly as we know ourselves. This is inherently impossible, but failure to realise that and attempts to bring the inner existence of other persons within our own account for many perversions of aim and the inflaming of passions beyond their proper place in a rounded existence. This is not without relevance to our theme, but the point of most importance now is that, instead of there being a healthy balance between the inner aspect of experience and our genuine contact with the world around us, wrongdoing causes the inwardness to have undue prominence, even in circumstances where, for ordinary purposes, we continue our normal round and reasonable dealings with other persons. As this becomes acute, there is a sense of being cut off, of becoming subject to what Bertrand Russell described as 'sombre solitude' which causes the profoundest distress and eventually a disintegration of personality. A spiritual debility sets in with the loosening of our hold on the world around us and with this comes a sense of destitution, fear, lostness. We desperately need to be involved with others and our material environment but find ourselves increasingly unable to attain such involvement. The fulfilment of our existence in healthy relationships with other persons is defeated and we find ourselves wholly unable to survive on our own resources, however rich in themselves these may be.

The situation has its most grave and disturbing form in the case of our consciousness of God. For persons who have become profoundly conscious of God and understand the ultimate purpose of their existence in fellowship with him (and with others within the bond of such consciousness), the sense of being cut away from this rich source of their own spiritual existence leads to the agony and the distressing situation, to the desperate and despairing cries from the depth, which have been so vividly described in various religious works and scriptures. It is what hell and the penalty of sin, the sense of impending doom and damnation, really mean; and this is what they have meant down the ages, however obscured and confused by wider notions and superstitions which affect even the profoundest expression of them.

The situation to which allusion has been made, and which would need much greater space to present properly, develops, moreover, in a cumulative way. Although we cannot, strictly, be guilty of the sins of others or be evil in a way divorced from what we intend, we can be caught in circumstances where the effect of wrongdoing on its perpetrators has affected the general setting and character of our personal relations and in this way perpetuated and extended the sense of isolation and lostness brought about by moral evil. This in turn is aggravated by our being aware that, in seeking our own good or comfort at the expense of the greater claims of others, we are opposing not merely an objective moral demand but also what God has increasingly made known to us as the supreme concern of the love he has for us. We find it generally hard to have a sincere relationship with people we have misled and wronged, however we try to maintain the appearances of it, and until deep repentance sets in there is no genuine restoration. This is peculiarly so in the case of God, and as we are the heirs of a situation in which the effect of the resultant isolation has established itself, it is hard to avoid a sense of lostness and alienation which is not strictly relative to our own shortcomings or turpitude. It is here that we find our main clue to what has traditionally been said about sin and especially about the bondage of sin and the doom it implies.

It is in this context that the idea of salvation, in any theistic form, has its proper place. In the Christian religion the means of salvation is pre-eminently found in the way God makes his presence increasingly known to men and discloses the depth of his love in special interventions in history, not primarily in the outward course of events, but in the modification of these through profound personal experience of God and the patterning of this to uncover, in finite forms we can apprehend, his concern and purpose for us. This has its climax in the alleged coming of God in the form of a man, that is, taking on fully human limitations, to enter himself, not in transcendent knowledge, but in actual being, into the extreme limit of men's lostness and destitution. By encounter with this, as made known in scriptural records and subsequent testimony, a means of abiding restoration and renewal is opened up. How it operates, and how the paradox of a God—not merely taking the appearance of a man, but being human—is to be further understood, are acute central problems of Christian theology which cannot be treated further here.

It must be added, however, that the clue suggested to central religious themes in these ways, making our normal personal relationship our guide, finds extensive support and exemplification in general literature, and not least in impressive fiction of the present day, however little expressly concerned with religion.

The modes of experience in question now, however, are usually expressed, in live religious awareness, in colourful figurative terms; and some element of symbolism is unavoidable in religious discourse. But this can also be a prime source of misunderstanding, especially as figurative language tends to be perpetuated on its own account and divorced from the distinctive and live situation which gave it birth. This is one of the main sources of the travesty and distortion of religious truth, and in combination with other factors it has led to the proliferation of vicious dogmas which have been a major hindrance to the true life of religion. This may be seen very clearly in various doctrines of sin and salvation where juristic metaphors are taken out of their context and crudely interpreted to yield various notions of a cruel God sentencing the sinner to appalling torment as retribution for a sinful state which is not even due to the transgression of the individual himself. This is one of the main points where sensitivity to the true purport of religious utterance is essential.

At the opposite extreme we have those who would empty religious utterances of any truly transcendent reference. In doctrines of sin and salvation this often takes the form of reinterpreting what is religiously affirmed in terms of various complexes and deviations of aims which profound psychology has been able to set out more clearly for us today. We owe much to psychology, and its help in unravelling complexities of our nature can be inestimable in religious study. But this is also a subject where narrowness and brashness can be disastrous. The psychologist needs to cultivate a careful understanding of the basic purport of notions of sin and salvation as they appear in genuine religious experience and to penetrate beneath their surface appearance and their conventional expressions if he is not to confuse his own subject with undigested alien matter and at the same time deprive us of the substantial service he can render the student of religion and the practitioner alike.

In religions which are not explicitly theistic the idea of salvation is addressed more to the general condition of men and not so directly to a situation brought about by moral transgression. It is directed less to the bondage of sin than to a bondage or limitation under which we generally suffer in all aspects of finite existence. The main idea is still that of liberation, but the interpretation of it is much more general. On some views the world as we now encounter it is an illusory one; the true reality of the world, and above all of ourselves, is some supreme, transcendent or all-encompassing being in which the true being of all is found. Salvation thus lies in breaking away from this world of illusion, or alternatively realising that it is an illusion, and uniting ourselves or becoming lost in the one true reality, the One which is all in all. Various disciplines are commended as ways of achieving this liberation from the bondage of finite illusion, ranging from high moral endeavour and intellectual discipline and meditation to extreme ascetism and mortification of the flesh. The extent to which the ultimate release involves the extinction of individual personality varies, but the general aim is to pass beyond finite particularity and its attendant ills and limitations. This is the usual aim of Hinduism, but powerful voices, like those of Sri Aurobindo, have been raised from time to time, and specially recently, in protest against a too other-worldly concept of salvation. Present existence is thus given greater place as the sphere of divine activity.

Other forms of an overall notion of salvation are directed especially to the idea of a principle in the order of our existence which prescribes, from one existence to another in a round of rebirth, what our lot in justice is to be. Suffering is here given a pre-eminent place in the ills we endure, but the ultimate aim is not just escape from suffering as such but from the process of *karma* and the round of rebirth itself. By illumination a distinctive insight is obtained into the conditions, including especially a certain kind of ignorance, which bind us to our present state. By such illumination, obtained again through various disciplines, a state of *nirvāṇa* is reached which snuffs out desire and the pains of deprivation. This has also been thought of as a total eclipse of our being, but scholars are reluctant to understand *nirvāṇa* in this way today, and as there is much in Buddhist scriptures which suggests a subtle grasp of a transcendent order of being, there is more inclination to understand the alleged release and illumination in terms of some relation to a reality beyond finite being which is not to be comprehended except in terms of the way to its attainment.

It must not be thought, however, that the idea of culpable action and of accountability is absent from the contexts where the idea of salvation has its more general application. There are in any case many varieties and modifications within various relatively distinctive religious attitudes and cultures. It has not been impossible for deterministic conceptions of human existence to carry within them, paradoxical though it may seem, a sense of personal accountability. There has also come about of late a profounder grasp of the elusiveness of human personality which precludes any particularisation of it in quasi-material terms but which establishes it also as the most irreducible form of particular existence.[10] With insights of this kind, and a subtler grasp of the true implications of transcendent being, we may find ourselves in various religions converging more on the notion of ourselves as distinct and fully accountable beings finding a way of salvation in the fulfilment of ourselves in right fellowship with a transcendent Reality which does indeed transform the whole of our existence, including

10 See my *The Elusive Mind* (1969).

the attainment of a richer mode of being than the present one and its involvement in the grosser forms of physical limitations, but which also has at its centre a distinctive and costing way in which the divine comes to terms with and overcomes the infirmities due especially to the waywardness of our own wills and deliberate evil actions.

13

Trevor Ling

Buddhism in Bengal

A changing concept of salvation?

It is in connection with the later period of the history of Indian Buddhism—that is, from about the eighth to the twelfth century C.E. —that Bengal is more frequently mentioned in general histories of Buddhism. The tendency would be justifiable if Buddhism had entered Bengal later than any other part of India, or if there was something exceptional about the nature of Buddhism as it developed in early medieval Bengal. It is the latter assumption which is often made. Sir Charles Eliot, for instance, in a chapter entitled 'The decadence of Buddhism in India', after noticing that it was in north-eastern India that Buddhism survived when it had disappeared from north-western, central and southern India,[1] comments that 'Bengal, especially western Bengal and Bihar, was the stronghold of decadent Buddhism'.[2] He describes it in the Pāla kingdom as 'corrupt', although, he adds, it 'was flourishing so far as the number of its adherents and royal favour were concerned'. He observes that from 700 to 1197 'local superstitions were infecting and stifling decadent Buddhism'.[3] The source of the corruption he identified as Tantrism, whose influence was, in Eliot's view, 'powerful and disastrous'.[4]

Eliot has not been singled out because he is the special representative of this point of view with regard to later Buddhism but because his work has been fairly widely known and influential, and because in writing in this way he was reflecting the judgment of a number of scholars on this period of Indian Buddhist history. Broadly, the assumption has been that it was in Bengal that Indian Buddhism came to the end of its 1,700-years career, somewhere around 1200 C.E.; that 'late' Buddhism was Tantric, that is to say, it employed what have been called 'sexo-yogic practices'; that this 'Tantric' Buddhism was 'degenerate'; that Bengal is therefore to be remembered as the home

1 Eliot, *Hinduism and Buddhism* II (1921), p. 108.
2 *Op. cit.*, p. 109. 3 *Op. cit.*, p. 127. 4 *Ibid.*

of a form of Buddhism which was late and degenerate, and that largely for these reasons it was the place where Indian Buddhism died. Concerning the final stage in this story of senility there are differences of opinion; in the view of some, Buddhism expired and was absorbed into the eternally patient, waiting arms of Hindu theism,[5] or died 'to be born again in a refined Brahmanism'.[6] In the view of others, it lived on enfeebled and almost unrecognisable in the village cult of the god called Dharma, which is still widely practised in the western districts of West Bengal.[7]

All this might be taken to suggest that there was something in the Buddhism of Bengal that was somehow significantly more 'Bengali' than Buddhist, especially if the view is held that Tantric beliefs and practices had originated in Bengal.[8] It might be supposed that in Bengal Buddhism was subject to local cultural influences of a significantly different kind, which caused it to develop a new and unhealthy strain. Against this idea—that Bengal had some special modifying effect on Buddhism—certain considerations need to be emphasised. They are (1) that the Buddhist presence in Bengal was not confined to the later period, but was represented there at least from the time of Ashoka; and (2) that the original ideas, structure and emphases of early Buddhism were in essence preserved faithfully down to the time when the Afghan Muslim invasion changed the scene drastically. It is with these two points that this paper is mainly concerned.

It was in association with the rule of the emperor Ashoka in the third century B.C. that the full implications of Buddhism, as a civilisation rather than a religion, were seen.[9] Whether the Buddhism of the Pali canon can all be attributed to Gautama the Buddha may be questioned, but what does appear to be more certain is that the system of belief and practice reflected in those texts is the Buddhism which flourished in the Ashokan period. Its principal point of distinction from other philosophies and ideologies of the time was its denial of any permanent, unchanging, individual self or soul, and its insistence that it was this false notion that lay at the root of human ills. Connected with this

5 Mitra, 'The decline of Buddhism in India', *Viśva-Bhārati Annals* VI (1954), pp. 161–4.

6 Radhakrishnan, *Indian Philosophy* I, p. 609.

7 Śāstri, *Discovery of Living Buddhism in Bengal* (1897).

8 This view has been challenged most recently by Lalmani Joshi in his *Studies in the Buddhistic Culture of India* (1967), pp. 324–9.

9 This analysis of early Buddhism is worked out at greater length in the present writer's *The Buddha* (forthcoming).

analysis of the human condition was another feature unique (in the first instance at any rate) to Buddhism, and that was the community called the *sangha*. The *sangha* both provided the necessary environment in which the correction of the false, unwholesome idea of the individual self could take place, and also was the new, restructured area of human society and consciousness which resulted from the breaking down of this false notion of self. The name *sangha* had formerly been applied to the old tribal republics which were, in the Buddha's day, fast disappearing in the Gangetic plain before the onward march of the great monarchies, Koshala and Magadha. In one of these tribal republics, that of the Shakyas, Gautama had been brought up; his father was one of the leading citizens of this small State, which was, in political structure, somewhere in between a tribal republic and a monarchy.[10] Closely associated with the growth of towns, the diversification of the economy and the spread of monarchical government was the emergence of a marked spirit of individualism. It is significant that the vast majority of the discourses of the Buddha in the Pali canon are represented as having been delivered in one or other of the two great royal cities of the time, Shravasti and Rajagriha.[11] In the face of the growing malaise or *anomie* of the time, associated as it was with the growth of individualism, the Buddhist solution was the rejection of the notion of the individual self; not merely in theory, however, but in practice. In the life of the new *sangha* human existence was to be reconstituted and the one weakness which had undermined the old tribal *sanghas* and led to their downfall, namely the growth of selfish dissension and personal ambition, was to be eliminated. Thus in early Buddhism the arena of salvation was the *sangha*.

While this was happening, however, there remained the problem of the vast majority of men still outside the *sangha*, the *puthujjana* or common man. It is quite clear from the many references in the Pali canon to the *puthujjana* that the masses are regarded as constituting, on the one hand, the potential area into which the life of the *sangha* would expand (or, in other words, its source of recruits) and, on the other, a potential threat to the life of the *sangha* because of the blindness, quarrelsomeness, covetousness and violence which characterise the *puthujjana*.[12]

10 See Sharma, *Republics in Ancient India* (1968), chapter VIII, and Ghoshal, *A History of Indian Public Life* II (1966), chapter X.

11 See Malalasekera, *Dictionary of Pali Proper Names* II (1938), p. 1127.

12 *Aṅguttara Nikāya* I: 27; II: 216; *Saṃyutta-Nikāya* IV: 201 and Pali Text Society, *Pali–English Dictionary*, under *puthujjana*.

The solution which is envisaged in early Buddhism is one which acknowledges the necessity of a strong king. But it was also desirable that he should be not a tyrant, acting arbitrarily, but a wise monarch, ruling with moral justice and benevolence. It was therefore important that a close link should be established between the king and the Buddhist *sangha*. During the Buddha's lifetime just such a link had existed between him and the kings of Koshala and Magadha, namely, Pasenadi and Bimbisara, who were his close friends and supporters, and who frequently sought his advice. After the Buddha's *parinibbāna* it was not until the reign of the emperor Ashoka, however, that this ideal structure of society really came into being.

In what we may call the classical pattern of Buddhism there is a clear three-cornered relationship, which may be represented as in the diagram. Each of the relationships (a), (b) and (c) is a two-way or

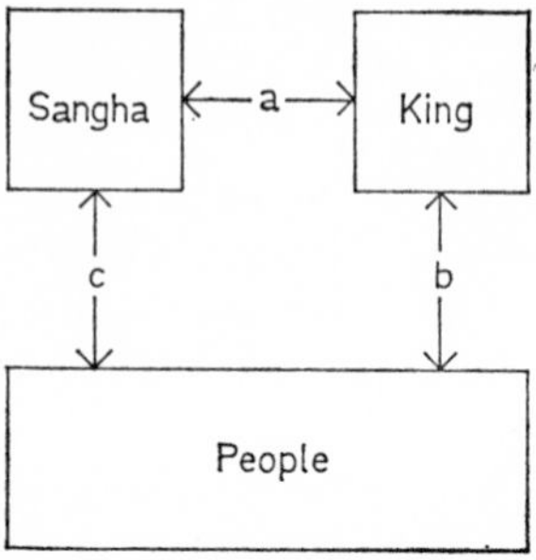

reciprocal relationship: (a) is the relationship between *sangha* and king, in which the king accepts the moral guidance of the *sangha*, and in particular of the Dharma which the *sangha* guards and transmits; in return he protects the *sangha* and promotes its interests; (b) is the relationship between king and people, one in which the king, acting justly and benevolently, is given in return the loyalty of his subjects and the due observance of his laws; (c) is the relationship between the mass of the people and the *sangha*, in which the latter provides an inspiring moral example which helps the people to keep their own moral goals high (an illustration of the principle enunciated by Durkheim: 'It is necessary that an elite put the [moral] end too high, if the crowd is not to put it too low'[13]), while in recognition of their highly honourable role in society the *sangha* receive from the mass of the people the material necessities of life.

13 Durkheim, *Elementary Forms of the Religious Life* (Doubleday Anchor edition, 1961), p. 356.

It will be observed that the role of the *sangha* in a Buddhist society *vis-à-vis* the people is mainly moral: to provide a practical example of moral integrity, and to instruct the people in the Buddhist ethic. Even for the 'specialist' lay follower, the *upāsaka*, it is largely moral inspiration that he derives from the Buddhist *arahant*, as the text of the *Aṅguttara Nikāya* I: 211*ff*. makes clear.[14] So far as other beliefs and practices are concerned, the monk, like the Buddha himself, shows an unusual tolerance. The householder may continue to believe in demons and spirits, in the local gods, or in some supreme god such as Brahma or Sakka; when he is ready to pass beyond such beliefs he will; until he is ready to do so it is foolish to attempt to force him or persuade him. Theological or credal orthodoxy is not a feature of the classical pattern of Buddhist culture. From the very beginning of Buddhist history the lay people who surrounded and supported the *sangha* entertained a host of beliefs in non-human, celestial beings of various kinds. The Pali canon abounds with references to them; the *Mahā Samaya Suttanta* provides a good example; this is, however, only one among many which could be quoted.[15] Beliefs of this kind have no bearing on the Buddhist scheme of salvation, except that their prominence in the tradition and literature at any given time suggests that the *sangha*, far from being cut off from the world in its own private search for salvation, is on the contrary in lively contact with the common people. This is how the Buddhist scheme for total salvation, if it is to work at all, will work best. There is a frontier between the *prototype* society of those who have overcome the false notion of self, with all its consequences, or are seriously engaged in doing so, and the much larger area of *existing* society which has as yet not experienced even the beginnings of this *Visuddhi* or purification, and it is this frontier which has to be kept open so that there can be free intercourse back and forth. In other words, the prominence of popular beliefs within the Buddhist tradition at any given period will be an indication that the scheme is working well, rather than the reverse.

It is with these considerations in mind that we can re-approach the history of Buddhism in Bengal. What will then be discovered is that the question of decadence has been wrongly defined by Eliot and those others who have regarded medieval Buddhism in Bengal as decadent. The implication is that in belief and practice the Buddhism of Bengal

14 See Pali Text Society, *Gradual Sayings* VIII, pp. 190*ff*.

15 *Dīgha-Nikāya* II. See Rhys Davids, *Dialogues of the Buddha* II, fifth edition (1966), pp. 284*ff*.

in the later part of the Pāla period had fallen away from the purity of the earlier, presumably Magadhan, forms. This is not what the available evidence suggests.

Before we embark upon a brief outline history of Bengal Buddhism it may be necessary to remind the reader of the shape of the territory. The name 'Bengal' has been used to denote various different expanses of territory at different times in history; as it is used here the word will be taken to mean the territory which went by the name of Bengal on the eve of partition in 1947, and which is approximately conterminous with the area where Bengali is the major language. On the western side of Bengal is the Chotanagpur plateau, part of the central Indian upland, and from this plateau an arm stretches out north-eastwards into the plains, an arm which is called the Rajmahal hills. The Ganges river, flowing south-eastwards, passes the northern extremity of these hills, and thereupon sends a large channel (originally the river's main channel) due south, to flow through Calcutta and so into the Bay of Bengal. This is the Hooghly or Bhagirati river, which forms the western side of the delta; to the west of it, running up to the edge of the Chotanagpur plateau, are the westernmost districts of Bengal.[16] The main channel of the Ganges, however, after the Bhagirati has left it, continues in a south-easterly direction towards its outlet to the sea on the eastern side of the delta, below the Chittagong hills. Half-way in this journey across the Bengal plain the Ganges is joined from the north first by the Brahmaputra, flowing southwards from the end of the Assam valley, and then by the Meghna, flowing south from the Shillong hills. The triangle formed by the Bhagirati on the west, the Ganges on the north and the southern edge of the delta (the Sundarbans) is relatively recently deposited land, and bears little historical evidence from ancient times.[17] It is along the northern side of the Ganges, as it flows through central Bengal, that most of the ancient sites of Buddhism are to be found. It is here that most of the kingdoms which existed in this region in the ancient and medieval periods had their capitals: Gaudha (or Gaur), Mahāsthān, Vikrāpur and Paṭṭikera. There is, however, one important Buddhist site to the west of the Bhagirati–Hooghly river, and that is the ancient port of Tamralipti.

16 Namely the modern administrative Districts of Birbhum, Burdwan, Hooghly, Howrah, Bankura, Purulia and Midnapore.

17 See Chatterji, *The Origin and Development of the Bengali Language* I (1926), p. 74. The area referred to comprises the modern Districts of Kushtia, Jessore, Khulna, Faridpur and Barisal.

The port of Tamralipti (modern Tamluk, approximately thirty-five metres south-west of Calcutta) provides us with a clear link with the Ashokan period. It was from this port in Bengal, according to the *Mahāvaṃsa*, that the Buddhist mission from Ashoka's capital city, Pāṭaliputra, sailed for Ceylon to establish the *sangha* in that island. It is an ancient city, mentioned in a number of early Sanskrit sources,[18] and was fairly certainly within the territory of Ashoka's empire. There is other, epigraphic, evidence which points to the conclusion expressed in 1958 by G. M. Bongard-Levin that 'the fact that Bengal was part of the Maurya empire has been finally established'.[19] Similarly, Barrie M. Morrison has recently recorded that 'during the third century B.C. the Mauryan empire exercised political control [in the delta] as is evidenced by the Brāhmi inscription of Pundranagora'.[20] He adds that from excavations at that site in central Bengal, north of the Ganges (known also as Mahāsthān) 'many Mauryan coins and other artifacts datable in the fourth and third centuries B.C. have been recovered' and that this, with textual evidence of various kinds, confirms the view that the delta 'was under the control of the Mauryan empire'.[21] It is known that Jainism found its way into Bengal at an early period, and was certainly 'able to entrench itself in Bengal as early as the third century B.C.'.[22] In the view of W. W. Hunter the people of western Bengal were familiar with Buddhism long before they came under the influence of Brahmanism. 'Buddhism', he wrote, 'was the first form of an elaborated religious belief which the Bengali people received.'[23] Hunter's view is wholly in keeping with the evidence which has accumulated since then, some of which has just been noted, that Bengal was part of the Mauryan empire. With the officers and administrators from Ashoka's court there went, as we know, the members of the Buddhist *sangha* into every corner of the Mauryan empire, to make known the *dharma* and establish the *sangha*. It could hardly have been otherwise in Mauryan Bengal.

The Buddhism which Bengal first received would, therefore, have been the kind whose basic structure we have noted. Under the political

18 See Law, *Indological Studies* III (1954), p. 62.

19 Bongard-Levin, 'Epigraphic document of the Mauryas from Bengal', *Journal of the Asiatic Society of Bengal* XXIV (1958), p. 83.

20 Morrison, *Political Centres and Culture Regions in Early Bengal* (1970), pp. 13*f.*

21 *Op. cit.*, p. 14.

22 West Bengal District gazetteers: Banerji, *Bankura* (1968), p. 70.

23 Hunter, *Annals of Rural Bengal* (1897), p. 99.

rule of one who was himself a Buddhist sympathiser and supporter and who conformed as closely as any ruler could to the ideal king of the Pali texts, the *sangha* in Bengal would have been free to play its proper role as adviser and moral guide to the ruler and his officers, and also to expand steadily and unhindered, a process which would have been facilitated by the favourable climate provided by a just and benevolent government. For in many respects Ashoka's kingdom was more nearly a welfare State than anything India has experienced since, until modern times.

The mass of the people outside the *sangha* would have continued to adhere to their local forms of belief and mythology, which at this period in Bengal were probably as yet un-Aryanised and of a generally Dravidian character. But from contact with the members of the *sangha* which was now established among them they would have gained glimpses of a different view of life which would in the course of time, as it has in other countries with a living Buddhist tradition, have modified their outlook on life and gradually influenced their moral conduct. It would, moreover, have led a certain proportion of them into membership of the *sangha* itself. At the end of the fourth century C.E. the Chinese pilgrim Fa Hsien visited Bengal in the course of his travels in India. Then, as in Ashoka's time, the principal port seems to have been Tamralipti (Tamluk).

> From Champa [now eastern Bihar], journeying east about fifty *yojanas*, Fa-hsien arrived at the country of Tamluk, where there is a seaport. In this country [i.e. region] there are twenty-four monasteries, all with resident *bhikkhus*, and the Buddhist faith is very flourishing. Fa-hsien stayed here for two years, copying out sutras and drawing pictures of images.

At the end of his stay he took passage on a large merchant vessel and after fourteen days reached Ceylon.[24]

It is clear that Buddhism had expanded throughout Bengal by this time. Out of a considerable body of evidence one example may be given. This is a copper plate inscription found at Guṇaighar in Tipperah (modern Tripura, on the extreme eastern edge of Bengal, north of Chittagong). The inscription dates from 507 C.E. and from the references to the monastery it is evident that there had been time for the place to have become old and in need of repair. A gift of land was being made by Vainya Gupta

24 *The Travels of Fa-hsien (399–414* A.D.*), or, Record of the Buddhistic Kingdoms*, retrans. Giles (1927), pp. 65*f*.

To Ācārya Śāntideva, the Buddhist monk of Mahāyāna school, in order that perfume, flowers, lights, incense, etc, for [the worship of] Lord Buddha thrice a day may be provided perpetually in the abode of the Buddhist monks of Vaivarttika sect of Mahāyāna school, constructed by him [Śāntideva] in the Vihāra, dedicated to Avalokiteśvara, and garments, food, beds, seats, and medicines for diseases may be supplied to the host of monks, and also in order that breaks and cracks in the monastery may be repaired.[25]

From this and other evidence it is clear that by the fifth century of the Christian era Buddhism, both of the Hīnayāna and of the Mahāyāna modes, was known in Bengal from the extreme western to the extreme eastern borders. We are not concerned here to consider the respective claims of each of these two modes to represent more faithfully than the other the essence of the Buddhist way. Only an extremely bigoted Theravadin could seriously accuse the great classical Mahāyāna schools of being corrupt or decadent forms of Buddhism. The allegation we are concerned with concerns only Tantric Buddhism, and the view that this was corrupt Buddhism, specially characteristic of Bengal. Since it does not come on to the Buddhist scene in Bengal in any recognisable way until the time of the Pāla kings (eighth to twelfth centuries) it is clear that Buddhism existed a long time in Bengal before it became 'corrupt'. This is not to say that forms of belief and practice of a Tantric or sexo-yogic kind cannot be found before the Pāla period; indeed, some scholars have seen the roots of such practices in the Indus Valley civilisation of the third and second millennia B.C.[26] So far as the adoption of Tantric practices by Buddhists is concerned, L. Joshi has shown, after a careful examination of the views of Winternitz, B. Bhattacharya, Tucci and others, that 'the historical beginnings of Buddhist esoterism [Tantrism] go back at least to the first century B.C., when the Vaitulyakas flourished . . . ' He adds that Tantrism seems to have influenced certain sections of the Buddhist *sangha* some centuries before Asaṇga composed the *Prajñāpāramitā sādhana*.[27] Asaṇga, it will be remembered, was from Gandhāra in the north-west of India. It is clear that the weight of the evidence regarding the areas in which Tantric Buddhism first emerged shows that the north-west and the south of India share this distinction. No places in Bengal are referred to in so many and diverse ancient and medieval texts as centres of esoteric Buddhism as are Śrīparvata, Dhànyakaṭaka and Potalaka in South India.[28]

25 Maity and Mukherjee, *Corpus of Bengal Inscriptions* (1967), No. 10, p. 68.
26 Joshi, *op. cit.*, p. 304. 27 *Ibid.*, p. 318. 28 *Ibid.*, p. 326.

It is not that we are deficient in information about Buddhism in Bengal in the period before the rise of the Pāla kings. The Chinese pilgrims Hiuen Tsiang and I-Tsing both visited Bengal in the course of their travels in the seventh century C.E., and both commented fairly fully on the state of Buddhism there at that time. By the time Hiuen Tsiang made his journey, in the second quarter of the seventh century, Buddhism was declining in many areas of India outside Bengal—declining, that is to say, in the number of monasteries and in the degree of support and approval it was receiving from rulers. This was especially true of parts of north-west India, such as Gandhāra (whose monasteries, as described by Hiuen Tsiang, were ruined and deserted) and the south of India.

In what is now known as Bengal, Hiuen Tsiang visited four 'countries' and reported on the state of Buddhism in each of them. The first place he visited was the kingdom of Puṇḍravaharddhana, in central Bengal, to the north of the Ganges and to the west of the Meghna river.[29] Its capital is better known by the later name of Mahāsthān.[30] The country around the capital was densely populated, wrote Hiuen Tsiang, its rich soil producing all kinds of grain and good supplies of fruit. The people were said to 'esteem learning'. There were about twenty monasteries, with a total of about 3,000 *bhikkhus*, who adhered to both Hīnayāna and Mahāyāna. In addition he found about a hundred temples belonging to various religious groups, of whom the Jains were the largest. A few miles to the west of the capital was the great monastery called the Bhasu Vihāra, a splendid place with courts 'light and roomy' and well furnished with lofty towers and pavilions. About 700 *bhikkhus* of the Mahāyāna lived there, including some whose names were famous throughout eastern India. There was also a *stupa* which Hiuen Tsiang says was built by the emperor Ashoka. Another monastery near this place contained a statue of the Bodhisattva Avalokiteśvara, and this was an object of great veneration among the local people.[31]

29 Beal, *Buddhist Records of the Western World* II (1884), p. 194. Puṇḍravaharddhana corresponded to the modern Districts of West Dinajpur, Dinajpur, Bogra, Rajshai, Pabna, Mymensingh and Dacca.

30 The site of Mahāsthān is about seven metres north-north-west of the town of Bogra.

31 The ruins of these places were identified in 1879–80 by Major-General A. Cunningham, Director-General of the Archaeological Survey of India. See 'Report of a tour in Bihar and Bengal in 1879–80', *Archaeological Survey of India* XV (reprinted 1969), p. 102*f*.

After visiting what is now Assam, Hiuen Tsiang came to the country of Samataṭa, that is, the part of Bengal which lies to the east of the Meghna river, down to the borders of Burma. The land was low-lying and rich in crops; 'the flowers and fruits grow everywhere'. The climate was mild, and the manners of the people agreeable. The men were hardy, of small height and dark complexion; 'they are fond of learning and exercise themselves diligently in acquiring it'. He found there thirty or more monasteries, all of the Theravādin school. There were also many temples of other cults, the Jains again forming the majority. Near the capital was a *stupa*, also said to have been built by Ashoka. A nearby monastery contained a *Buddha-rupa* of green jade, 8 ft in height; like the image of Avalokiteśvara at Mahāsthān this too was venerated by the local people for its mystical power.[32]

Going westward from Samataṭa (possibly by sea) the pilgrim came to Tāmralipti, the port of western Bengal. Here too he found a fertile and bountiful land, whose people he describes as 'quick and hasty . . . hardy and brave'. There were about ten monasteries and about a thousand *bhikkhus*. Again he found a *stupa* built by Ashoka.[33] The last place he visited in Bengal was Karṇasuvarṇa, on the Bhagirati river, a little south of the modern Berhampore. Here also the area of the capital city was thickly populated and the people were very prosperous. There were ten or so monasteries, and about 2,000 *bhikkhus* of the Hīnayāna. There were about fifty other temples, and non-Buddhists were numerous. There was also, however, a large monastery just outside the city in which congregated 'all the most distinguished, learned and celebrated men of the kingdom'. They strove, writes Hiuen Tsiang, 'to promote each other's advancement by exhortations, and to perfect their character' or, to take the literal meaning of his words, 'to promote their mutual perfection by shaping and smoothing [in the sense of polishing] their reason and virtue'.[34] This provides a very interesting piece of evidence to show that the function of the *sangha* as it appears in early Buddhism and as it is outlined above ('the necessary environment in which the correction of the false, unwholesome idea of the individual self could take place') was still being maintained in Bengal in the seventh century.

In the middle of the seventh century, soon after the time of Hiuen Tsiang's visit, a period of political chaos occurred when Bengal was the scene of political rivalry and struggle among local rulers. This

32 See Beal, *op. cit.*, pp. 199*f.*

33 *Ibid.*, p. 200*f.*

34 *Ibid.*, p. 202.

came to an end around the year 750 with the election of Gopāla as king, and the founding of the Pāla dynasty which was to rule Bengal for about four centuries. The Pāla kings were supporters of the *sangha*, both in Bengal and in Bihar, where their territory also extended.[35] They describe themselves as 'chief worshippers of the Buddha'.[36] The Pāla period was one of considerable building of Buddhist monasteries; for instance, the large monastic complex at Pāhāṛpur[37] does not appear to have been in existence at the time when Hiuen Tsiang was travelling in this part of Bengal. It has been identified[38] as the great Somapura *vihāra* founded by the second of the Pāla kings, Dharmapāla (c. 770–810). It was well maintained throughout the succeeding three centuries and recent archaeological evidence indicates that it was a flourishing, prosperous and influential Buddhist centre in the twelve century.[39] It is, observes Dr Hussain, 'the largest single monastic building so far discovered in the whole Indian sub-continent'.[40] The memory of its prosperity is preserved in references to Somapura which are found in Tibetan Buddhist writings of the early seventeenth century.

During the period of Pāla rule in northern, central and western Bengal the life of the common people appears to have been simple but comfortable. The evidence of copper plate inscriptions of this period suggests, however, that it was in the south-east of Bengal, in the kingdom of Samataṭa, that the Buddhist *sangha* found even stronger support than in the Bengal of the Pālas. This south-eastern region was ruled by the Chandras, a dynasty of five generations which lasted from the beginning of the tenth century to the middle of the eleventh. One of these, at least, Laḍaha Chandra, is known to have been a Buddhist, since he also, like the Pālas, describes himself as *Paramasaugata* or chief worshipper of the Buddha. His reign (1000–1020), which was devoted 'entirely to peaceful religious acts', was recorded also as having been a time when the kingdom enjoyed 'general prosperity and secure conditions'.[41] Some of the other Chandras appear to have inclined

35 Hussain, *Everyday Life in the Pāla Empire*, Asiatic Society of Pakistan, publication No. 23 (1968), pp. 23*ff.*

36 Hussain, *op. cit.*, p. 192.

37 About eleven metres north of the modern Santahar. Excavated by the Archaeological Survey Department in 1923–34. See A. Cuningham, *loc. cit.*, pp. 117–20.

38 Hussain, *op. cit.*, p. 45.

39 *Ibid.*, pp. 46*f.*

40 *Ibid.*, p. 47.

41 Chowdhury, *Dynastic History of Bengal, 750–1200* A.D., Asiatic Society of Pakistan, publication No. 21 (1967), p. 182.

more towards Vaishnavism or Shaivism; Laḍaha Chandra, too, seems to have been a patron of Vaishnavism. However, the *sangha* was certainly well represented in this part of Bengal during these centuries, much more strongly than in any other part. The very extensive inscriptional evidence shows that donations of land, etc, to Buddhist monasteries were much more frequent and numerous in this part of Bengal than elsewhere.[42] Morrison's survey of the evidence for the whole period between 433 and 1283 C.E. leads him to the conclusion that 'Vaishnavism was strong in the north, central and eastern parts [of Bengal], while Buddhism was well patronised in the east'.[43] The large number of monasteries in eastern Bengal at this time suggests there must have been strong local support from the people of this densely populated region.

So far as the Pāla kingdom is concerned, Dr Hussain's examination of the plaques, sculpture, architecture, bronze images, coins and copper plates found at Pāhārpur and Mahāsthān leads her to conclude that the worship of Hindu gods was widely prevalent. Among the images found are those of Śiva, Sūrya, Viṣṇu, Brahmā, Gaṇeśa and Kuvera, the god of wealth. Images of Śiva in close embrace with Durgā or with Pārvatī were also popular, and may be taken as evidence of Tantric or sexo-yogic beliefs. Many of these were found in Buddhist *vihāras*.[44]

It was during the Pāla period that the Tantric literature began to be produced within the Buddhist milieu in Bengal.[45] The Buddhist iconography of the period also bears witness to the fact that during this period Vajrayāna, the Buddhist form of Tantrism, had begun to develop.

> The icons of the various Buddhist gods and goddesses of the period and also the representation of some of the gods (including the Lord Supreme as Hevajra or Vajreśvara, or Vajrasattva, as he was variously called in esoteric Buddhism (with their respective female consorts in a state of union (*yuganaddha*)) will indicate the introduction of the female element in the Buddhist religion of the time.[46]

The significance of these developments in the Pāla period needs to be considered very carefully. It would be easy to reach superficial and

42 Morrison, *op. cit.*, p. 153.
43 *Ibid.*, p. 154.
44 Hussain, *op. cit.*, p. 193.
45 Das Gupta, *Obscure Religious Cults*, third edition (1969), pp. 11–13.
46 *Ibid.*, p. 13.

incorrect conclusions. First there is the significant fact that Buddhism existed in Bengal from the Ashokan period to the time of the Pālas, and throughout this period of about a thousand years it was, on the evidence we have considered, the Buddhism of the Hīnayāna and Mahāyāna which was practised in the monasteries, not the Tantric or Vajrayāna. If the cultural life of Bengal was to blame for the emergence of a 'corrupt' and 'decadent' Buddhism in this part of India, then it is very strange that it seems to have had no such effect for about a thousand years.

For it is quite clear that the structure of Buddhism under the Pāla dynasty, and especially in the earlier period, was as good a representative example of the classical pattern as can be found in any period of Buddhist history or in any country. When it is alleged that Buddhism in Bengal was 'in decline' in the centuries immediately prior to the Muslim invasions of about 1200 C.E., one must question what concept of 'decline' is being used. By using the criteria of an exclusivist and intolerant Semitic theistic religion one might make out a case for saying that Buddhism, in so far as it had an open frontier with popular beliefs and practices, was (and always had been) in decline; only, these criteria happen not to be relevant to the psycho-socio-political philosophy which was Buddhism. For classical Buddhism to have been in a state of decadence or decline would mean that the triangular pattern of relationships between *sangha*, king and people was no longer functioning in the traditional way. This cannot be said with any truth to have been the case. There is good evidence that the period of Pāla rule in Bengal was, in Morrison's words, a 'cultural high point in the pre-Muslim history of eastern India'.[47] The Pāla kings exercised a lively patronage of art and literature. The period of their rule was one 'which witnessed the highest political and intellectual achievements of the people of Bengal' ever reached until then.[48] The monasteries of Bengal became famous for their learning, and 'an extensive Buddhistic religious and philosophical literature was produced'.[49] Sanskrit scholarship in general flourished in Bengal during this period, and a recently published anthology of Sanskrit poetry, compiled by a Buddhist scholar of the latter half of the eleventh century, indicates the extent to which the Pālas and Chandras by their patronage encouraged Bengali poets of court and monastery.[50] According to the Tibetan writer Tāranātha,

47 Morrison, *op. cit.*, p. 16. 48 Chatterji, *op. cit.*, I, p. 80. 49 *Ibid.*
50 Ingalls, *An Anthology of Sanskrit Court Poetry, from Vidyākara's Treasury* (1965 and 1968).

a new and vigorous movement in sculpture began in north central Bengal in the ninth century. The fame of Bengal's Buddhist culture attracted the attention of the Tibetan kings and after repeated invitations the famous scholar Atiśa eventually arrived in Tibet in the year 1042. Atiśa's prestige and the authority are said to have been unparalleled, and to have given a new direction to the practice of Buddhism in Tibet. It is significant that one of the main reasons why the Tibetan kings were anxious to invite the Bengali Buddhist Atiśa[51] was in order 'to combat the freer and coarser interpretations of tantric theories to which the Tibetans seem to have been particularly drawn'.[52] In collaboration with an older contemporary, Lūyī-pāda or Lui, Atiśa had prepared a Buddhist Tantric work, and his collaborator Lui was also the composer of some of the earliest Bengali *Caryā-pada* poems. These poems 'embody the religious tenets of Sahajiyā Buddhism, which was a later offshoot of Tantric Buddhism'.[53]

S. K. Chatterji has pointed out, however, that the language of these *Caryā* poems is very clearly that of the western districts of Bengal, as distinct from east Bengal, or Samataṭa, the realm of the Chandra kings. Some uncomplimentary references to the people of eastern Bengal also suggest a west Bengal origin for this corpus of literature.[54]

It is thus clear that Tantric ideas and practices had become a matter of serious interest in the Buddhism of some parts of Bengal by the end of the tenth century. The context in which this is properly seen is that of classical Buddhism's open-frontier policy, with popular contemporary religious beliefs and practices. This was not peculiar to Bengal, but characteristic of the Buddhist *sangha*'s policy throughout its history, from ancient Magadha to modern Burma. The particular form of popular religious ideas which goes by the name of Tantra was also widespread throughout India. The Bengali *Caryā-pada* poems were part of a tradition common throughout various regions of India[55] which centred around what may be described briefly as the mysticism of sexual love, or the transcendence of individuality through the experience of conjugal union. Religious ideas and practices of this sort would appear to have had a special appropriateness for Buddhism,

51 Born *c.* 982 at Vikramapura (near the modern city of Dacca) in eastern Bengal.

52 Snellgrove and Richardson, *A Cultural History of Tibet* (1968), p. 129.

53 Das Gupta, *op. cit.*, p. 5.

54 Chatterji, *op. cit.*, I, p. 117.

55 Das Gupta, *op. cit.*, p. 5.

whose central concern was the transcending of the notion of individual self and the widening of the area of consciousness. But a Buddhism that was out of touch with the people would have remained out of touch with these ideas. It is a measure of the liveliness of the contacts between *sangha* and people in the Pāla period that Tantric ideas were coming within the province of Buddhism, there to be adapted and expressed in ways that could serve the continuing central concerns of the Buddhist system, and, as we have noted briefly with regard to Atiśa, to be purified of their coarser features.

The final question remains, however, whether the substitution of Tantric practices for the earlier methods of Buddhist meditation and community life and discipline did not entail also in fact a major shift of emphasis with regard to the goal of the *sangha* life. The experience of a wider consciousness than that of the individual was in this case extended only to two people, or what were originally two separate, individual centres of consciousness. In the case of the older forms of *sangha* life and meditation the expansion of consciousness was within an infinite field, potentially the whole of human society.

However, the adoption of these Tantric popular beliefs and practices was particularly characteristic of the Mahāyāna schools; among these it was perhaps the school of Vijñāna-vāda which was most favourably disposed to receive and develop such ideas. The history of Buddhist thought and practice displays a certain dialectical character, as T. R. V. Murti, for example, has noted.[56] Murti, however, considered that it was one simple process of thesis–antithesis–synthesis, the synthesis in his view being the Mādhyamika school. But the dialectical model does not cease to be applicable to Buddhist thought at that point. The Mādhyamika, as the new thesis, produced as its antithesis, the Vijñāna-vadā and Vajrayāna. It is conceivable—and, in view of Buddhist history until that stage, likely—that another synthesis would have been reached had Buddhist history been allowed to continue. The Hīnayanā schools were, as we have noted, well represented in Bengal during the Pāla period. It is an interesting fact that Hīnayāna and Mahāyāna have interacted upon each other at many points in Buddhist history, not least in the countries which are now thought of as predominantly either one or the other.

The central concept of salvation can therefore in certain quarters of Bengal Buddhism be said to have shifted when Tantric practices were

56 *The Central Philosophy of Buddhism* (1955).

adopted. But counterbalancing, or what would have been dialectically acting, elements were not absent. Buddhism in Pāla-ruled Bengal had not declined to some low point of vitality where it had almost ceased to be Buddhism. The *sangha* was strong, well supported by the people and esteemed by the kings. Its strength and vigour, its open frontier with the life of the people, were the reasons for the appearance of the Vajrayāna. The idea that it had all but run out into the anonymity of a village cult, the worship of a villagers' god called Dharma, as was suggested by H. P. Sastri, has been effectively disposed of by scholars since his time.[57] There is, in fact, no reason to suppose that, but for the Turkish invasion, the later history of Buddhism in Bengal, and especially in east Bengal, which was more remote from the traditional areas of strength of Brahmanism, would have been significantly less 'Buddhist' than that of neighbouring Burma, where Mahāyāna and Hīnayāna schools continued to interact, and where Buddhism, spared the Islamic invasion which Bengal suffered, survived in its classical form to modern times.

57 See, for example Bhattacharya, 'Dharma and serpent worship in Bankura District', West Bengal District gazetteers: Bankura, *cit. supra*, pp. 207–22, and Das Gupta, *op. cit.*, part IV.

14

Geoffrey Parrinder
The salvation of other men

The search for salvation is recorded in the very dynamism of the human mind, indeed it appears as the fundamental and the universal aspect of it . . . Whatever else a religion may or may not be, it is essentially a reaching forward to the ideal of salvation.

This and similar statements on the centrality of salvation occur in a recent Vatican publication.[1] They indicate the central and universal nature of doctrines of salvation for religious thought and life, and also suggest the problems of the coexistence of different schemes of salvation.

In the study of soteriology there soon appear claims for the absolute truth and validity of the salvation offered, and the superior or universal nature of the saviour. Christian doctrines have plainly expressed such beliefs, but they have not been alone in so doing. A useful biblical summary, which may reflect a baptismal catechism, states that 'the grace of God has appeared for the salvation of all men' in Jesus Christ, 'who gave himself for us to redeem us from all iniquity and to purify for himself a people of his own' (Titus 2: 11*f*., RSV). Here the universal scope of salvation is expressed, its method of action and its aim of forming a special company of people. Yet 'all men' are the objects of this salvation, and this imposed a missionary task upon the agents; in such proselytising work Christianity followed Buddhism and was in turn followed by Islam, each with its claim to dispense saving truth for all who would hear.

The mission of the Church in offering salvation to all men is often criticised, and attack has at least been right where it has revealed both unworthy methods and ignorance of the teachings of other religions. Further, because of their exclusive salvation, missions have been regarded as imperialistic or even militaristic, though such aspects of

1 *Religions; Fundamental Themes for a Dialogistic Understanding* (1970), pp. 87 and 175.

their activity have been particularly characteristic of medieval and modern times, in which social and racial factors have played as large a part as religious ones. Despite the Old Testament background of tribal religion and national wars, the first Christians conducted their mission peaceably and underwent considerable sufferings. The New Testament breaks with the Old in speaking only of struggle against fleshly lusts and spiritual evil, 'for though we live in the world we are not carrying on a worldly war' (2 Cor. 10: 3). Paul exhorted Timothy to 'fight the good fight of faith' but this, like the Christian armour and the race to obtain the crown, served as illustration for purity and perseverance. J. S. Trimingham has demonstrated the complete break between Old and New Testaments in religious aggressiveness.[2]

Long after biblical times, when persecution ceased and the dubious accession of Constantine brought first of all imperial protection and later help in propagating its message to the Church, it was too easy for those who had once been persecuted to persecute deviant heretics and, under Charlemagne, even to indulge in 'holy war' against the heathen. Runciman has shown how much the early Fathers and the Eastern Churches were opposed to any warfare, and many Christian writers in both East and West regarded 'holy war' as blasphemous. Although the Arab armies from the seventh century occupied much of the Persian, Byzantine and Roman empires, and there was pressure against Christianity within their realms, yet Christians, as 'people of the Book', were not strictly the object of Islamic *jihād*; they received a recognized place as religious communities (*dhimmīs*), and there was considerable tolerance on both sides. In the great days of the twin Christian and Islamic empires centred at Constantinople and Baghdad, says Runciman,

> a Byzantine felt far more at home at Cairo or Baghdad than he would feel at Paris or Goslar, or even at Rome. Except in rare times of crisis and reprisals the authorities in the Empire and Caliphate agreed not to force conversions on either side and to allow the free worship of the other religion.[3]

Things were different in the West, where men were 'uneasily aware that in most respects Moslem civilisation was higher'; the military society, with its ideals of chivalry that emerged out of European barbarism, influenced the Papacy, and from the ninth century Popes began to justify wars on behalf of the Church. The disastrous and ill-

2 Trimingham, *Two worlds are ours* (1971), pp. 8*ff*., 27*ff*.

3 Runciman, *History of the Crusades* (1951), p. 88*f*.

named Crusades which followed devastated the Orthodox lands almost as much as the Islamic ones, ultimately failing in their purpose of holding Jerusalem and contributing directly to the decline of Constantinople.

In modern times commercial overseas exploitation and aggressive imperialism not only accompanied Christian missions but added their taint to missionary methods and propaganda. Militarism and imperialism are still too common in hymnology, and it is instructive to compare the bellicose 'Onward, Christian soldiers' (dishonest as well—'one in doctrine'!), by an Anglican parson whose life spanned most of the British imperial era (1834–1924), with the pre-imperial 'Soldiers of Christ, arise', which simply paraphrased Paul's imagery of defence against spiritual evils. Criticism of Western European aggressiveness, then, is not a product of squeamish modern suburban Christianity but a recovery of New Testament attitudes to which non-suburban Tolstoy, Gandhi, Luthuli and others have directed us. Western European Crusades, Inquisitions, imperialism and racialism can be seen today as indefensible and obstacles rather than aids to the progress of good news about universal salvation.

To return to the New Testament, Christ was said to have been sent as Saviour of the world (1 John 4: 14), and there is no doubt that first century Christians came to regard him as having a unique and universal role. Faith in the uniqueness of Christ, rather than in another teacher like Paul, no doubt grew out of very early devotion to the risen Lord, the belief that he was the one Messiah and the final Word of God who would appear again in the *parousia*. Less attention has been paid to the development of devotion than to the intricacies of doctrinal formulas and the controversies associated with them, but popular adoration of Christ gave Christianity great appeal and remained its motive force. For devotion and doctrine Christ is the Saviour of the Christian and, potentially at least, of all men. But how this salvation is effected and whether theories of sacrifice, expiation, substitution, intercession, moral influence and so on, are still valid and indispensable to soteriology are matters that need fuller consideration elsewhere. Our concern here is with the fact of faith in the Saviour, and the attitudes of those who hold this faith towards other religions and their saving figures.

Belief in the centrality of Christ has been essential to Christian soteriology. For the moment words like 'supremacy', and perhaps even 'uniqueness', may be avoided, as having possibly imperialistic overtones. But it is difficult to imagine how Christianity could survive without Christ at its centre; it would lose its special significance and conviction; even worse, its devotional life would wither away. The small and fading appeal of Unitarianism and other movements of reductionism in doctrinal and devotional content, as well as a general decline in Church membership, can be largely attributed to a weakening of faith and to indifferentist attitudes which affect devotion. This explains orthodox Christian uneasiness in taking part in united services with people of different religions if the emphasis is syncretistic and reductionist, even to the extent of removing references to the divinity of Christ or the Trinity from what are otherwise Christian hymns and prayers. Fr Klostermaier, after sharing in Hindu devotions and processions, with their passionate attachment to Krishna and stirring plays, said, 'I asked myself whether we did not render Christ very doubtful service by simplifying his message—when we make of him a teller of stories, a moralizing schoolmaster, a less-than-serious dreamer. By remaining on the surface of an outward religiosity, do we really preach Christ?'[4] It would seem much better to share in the distinctive devotions of other people, where they permit and wish it, and welcome them to our own specific worship, rather than unite in worship set at the lowest common denominator.

Yet it must be recognised that, if Christ is held to be central for Christian soteriology, similar claims are made for the founders or principal figures of other religions in the context of their doctrines and worship. The Jew or Muslim who may feel that Christians could abandon faith in the divinity or centrality of Christ, and follow Jesus simply as a human and fallible teacher, may fail to recognise that a similar process of devotion has been at work in his own religion. The indispensable role of Muḥammad for Islamic devotion is much under-estimated in the West because of concentration upon 'critical' history which sees the Prophet 'warts and all' but feels nothing of his numinous appeal as the very Light of God, pre-existent and sinless.

The orthodox Jew believes that Moses, 'peace be to him', was 'the chief of the prophets, both of those that preceded and those that followed him', as declared in the thirteen principles of the faith formulated by Maimonides and set out in the Daily Prayer Book. Even more, the Torah 'constitutes the ultimate uniqueness of the religion of Israel',[5] and to the mystic the Torah alone is the beautiful maiden who dis-

4 Klostermaier, *Hindu and Christian in Vrindaban* (1969), p. 118.
5 Epstein, *Judaism* (1959), p. 30.

closes herself in love to her lovers. Similarly, Theravāda Buddhism is not comprehensible without the sole Buddha of this present long era, 'the god beyond the gods', all-knowing, all-seeing, the fountainhead of *dharma*. In Mahāyāna Buddhism the Buddhas and *bodhisattvas* are in turn essential to devotion, and in Hindu Vaishnavism and Śaivism no amount of knowledge or works could displace the central role played by devotion to Vishnu and his avatars or to Śiva.

Faith not only in the centrality but in the supremacy or uniqueness of the saviour seems to be a characteristic of many if not all religions, a fundamental and recurring feature of religious phenomenology, from Yahweh to Mao. This may be illustrated from Hinduism, which is often regarded as the home of polytheism and therefore of tolerance, as if that meant indifference to which god was supreme. No doubt the luxuriant multiplicity of gods in the early Vedas slowly produced a 'henotheism' among the thoughtful—'that which is One the seers speak of in various terms'—though, to worshippers of Indra, Varuna and the like, no doubt each god was all-demanding. In due course monism and monotheism become dogmatic, fitting everything to their own pattern, either reducing the 3,306 deities to the one impersonal Brahman or regarding the other gods as subordinate to the one true God.

The *Bhagavad-Gītā*, in which religion comes again to dominate over philosophy, has no doubt of the supremacy and uniqueness of Krishna. While it follows and quotes the Śvetāśvatara *upanishad* it is remarkable that it never mentions Śiva by this name. Those who worship other gods desire the success of their ritual actions, but it is really 'in my path' (Krishna's) that all men go (*Gītā* 4: 11–12). Nothing higher exists than Krishna, who is the supreme Brahman, the primal deity, and the chief of all classes of gods, among whom even Vishnu receives only passing mention (7: 7; 10: 12; 10: 21*f.*). Moreover, those who worship other gods do so in ignorance, constrained by the desires of their own natures. Truly, worshippers of the gods go to them, but whatever faith they have comes from Krishna himself, though he is not revealed to everyone and the deluded world does not recognise him (9: 20–6 is most instructive). But for all who cast their works on the Blessed Lord he quickly becomes their saviour from the ocean of the round of deaths, and he will make them dwell in himself for ever (12: 7). This salvation is offered to both sexes and all classes (9: 26 and 32). Such teaching is not henotheism but the first appearance of uncompromising monotheism, and it is accompanied by injunctions not to tell the secret to the undevout and warnings of eternal exclusion for the wicked (18: 67; 16: 19*f*.).

The Vishnu *purāna* goes further, to warn of the sin of conversing with heretics, Buddhists and Jains: they must not even be given civil speech, since this destroys religious merit; they should not be sheltered and those who merely talk to shaven ascetics fall into hell (3: 18). The Agni, the Matsya and the Bhāgavata *purānas* speak of the Buddha as an avatar of 'illusion and infatuation', whose followers committed sinful deeds capable of taking them to hell. But more kindly later poets, like Tulsī Dās, spoke of the God of pure intelligence and the abode of virtues who became an avatar in 'compassionate Buddha'.

Down the ages devotional Hinduism has continued to emphasise the supremacy of the god worshipped, and this has been well illustrated by Gonda in his Jordan lectures on the mutual relationships of Vaishnavism and Śaivism. Exclusive Vaishnavas, following the *Gītā*, do not like to call the rival Śiva by his principal name but prefer to speak of Rudra or Śaṁkara. A true Vaishnava is 'devoted to one God or goal' (*ekāntin*) and this 'exclusivism' (*ekāntibhāva*) leads such a devotee to avoid direct contact with Śaivas and to purify himself if he has to receive a non-Vaishnava priest as a guest. Indeed, if a Vaishnava recites a text given by a teacher of another sect he is threatened with millions of years in hell, while on their side Śaivas sometimes promise hell to those who refuse to honour Śiva. The famous Trimūrti, proclaimed as the threefold unity of Brahmā, Vishnu and Rudra, is taken by Śaivas as showing the diverse manifestations of Śiva, but Vaishnavas regard it as revealing the manifold Vishnu.[6]

Not simply communal quarrels between Hindus and Muslims, or political and social disputes, but religious prejudice also has marred Indian efforts towards tolerance. In the nineteenth century Fr Dubois in Pondicherry spoke of Vaishnava contempt for the linga-worshippers, while Śaivas promised hell to those who wore the *nāman* of Vishnu. He described bands of holy men provoking each other with obscene abuse, though admitting that their conflict rarely entailed bloodshed. Gonda says that nowadays Vaishnavism tends to be 'passively intolerant' and that its aversion to the other cult is reflected back in Śaivism. Even the prevalent tendency to 'inclusivism', recognising the divinity of the other cult, which is not the same as adaptation or syncretism, has qualifications. There are some who admit that followers of other

6 Gonda, *Viṣṇuism and Śivaism* (1970), pp. 92*ff*.

religions and doctrines have more or less of the truth, but they prefer their own religion. The ordinary man may not combat or reject different opinions, but he feels and perhaps says that they are not so good or efficacious as the doctrine of his own religion. Other ways may be valid for people at a lower level of spiritual life, but they are regarded as inadequate and not leading far enough on the road to the final goal of salvation.[7] Similarly, Dhavamony has shown that Śaivism teaches that one's own mental and spiritual abilities are not enough to achieve concentration, which is bestowed only by the grace of Śiva. And it is thought that Śiva is worshipped in all other religions, even if they do not call him by that name.[8]

An amusing illustration of a similar attitude appears in a review by S. Dindayal.[9] Annoyed by Raymond Panikkar's attempt to reveal *The Unknown Christ of Hinduism*, this writer misquotes and accuses Panikkar of twisting verses from the *upanishads* to suit his own purpose. Then he declares that it is Hindu principles which are forcing Christianity to change its dogmatic stand. 'One may rightly assume that it is the unknown presence of Krishna and his liberal teachings that are working among a small minority in the Church, causing rebellion against authority and seeking more freedom.'

It is not only devotional cults which tend to stress uniqueness and thereby become exclusive. Readers of Radhakrishnan may feel that his catholicity only thinly veils a monism, or negative syncretism, which motivates his constant attempts to fit all manner of diverse writers into the same pattern. In an early book he already pressed the theme that 'the fundamental truths of a spiritual religion are that our real self is the supreme being, which it is our business to discover and consciously become, and this being is one in all'.[10] Philosophers and theologians who might question this dogma would be regarded as insufficiently enlightened and their doctrines inadequate, and similar themes appear in his very later works.

Such considerations are not intended to cast any slur upon the claims of Christianity or Hinduism or any other religion to the uniqueness of its soteriology, but simply to look at the facts which demonstrate a strong tendency in religious life. It would indeed be strange if a religious

7 *Ibid.*, p. 95*f*.
8 Dhavamony, *Love of God according to Śaiva Siddhānta* (1971), p. 190.
9 Dindayal, 'All truths in Hinduism come from Christianity!' *The Bookshelf*, November 1970, p. 25.
10 Radhakrishnan, *Eastern Religions and Western Thought* (1939), p. 32.

faith, firmly held, were to consider the object of its devotion and author of its salvation as inferior to others, or even on the same level as them. This kind of indifferentism belongs to ages of unbelief like our own, not to passionate conviction, whether Christian or Hindu, Islamic or Marxist. And whether academic study has any convictions or not, it is important that basic elements of religious life, however unpalatable, should be given due attention.

The claim to the universality of the salvation offered by a religion may lead it not only to emphasise the supremacy or uniqueness of the saviour but also to encourage an exclusive attitude towards followers of other religions. This may conflict with universalism, and 'salvation for all' is usually taken to mean 'only if they believe in the approved fashion'. Christian students of comparative religion are well aware that if they expound the principles of another religion to a Western audience they are liable to be challenged with biblical texts such as, 'there is no other name under heaven given among men by which we must be saved' (Acts 4: 12) or 'no one comes to the Father, but by me' (John 14: 6). It is hardly agreeable to one's listeners to suggest that such verses are unauthentic, even if they are, and little more convincing to explain them away in the light of more universal texts. The need, so apparent today, for a Christian theology of other religions, and of other saviours, has been prevented for centuries by a dogmatic exclusiveness which logically defeats the universal purpose of salvation. Yet not only are there many who reject the offer of a particular salvation, and may understandably, if not fairly, be excluded from its goal, but there are many more who are ignorant of it and countless multitudes who follow other ways to salvation.

The ancient problem of the lot of pagan ancestors of Christians is still left untouched by most theologians, along with the fate of millions still living who do not accept the faith. Apart from consigning them all to hell, there have only been few and generally unsatisfactory attempts at dealing with these problems, which are great obstacles to popular belief. Bede Griffiths remarks that today, not only in the East, 'the problem of the salvation of the unbeliever is something which is continually before one's eyes . . . It seems to me that it is one of the most urgent problems, if not *the* most urgent problem which faces a Christian everywhere today'.[11]

The problem of the salvation of the Jews was vital to Paul, and

11 Griffiths, *Christian Ashram* (1966), p. 191.

he gave it more careful attention than the wider problem has received from most later theologians. After asserting that both Jews and Gentiles were in error, for 'all have sinned and fall short of the glory of God', he then declared that the righteousness of God had come in Christ 'for all who believe' (Rom. 3: 22*f*.). Later he struggled with the more difficult question of unbelieving Israelites who, as people sometimes say now about other non-Christians, were 'ignorant of the righteousness that comes from God and seeking to establish their own' (Rom. 10: 3). But Paul thought that the unbelief of Israel was only temporary, as a means whereby salvation might be fully offered to others, 'until the full number of the Gentiles comes in, and so all Israel will be saved'. Then perhaps even more universally, 'God has consigned all men to disobedience, that he may have mercy upon all' (Rom. 11: 25*f*. and 32).

The New Testament says little of other religions beyond Judaism, apart from dislike of their many gods and idolatry. The Roman and Greek gods are not mentioned in the Gospels and little elsewhere. It is true that, as conservative theologians tend to say, Jesus did not confront 'religions', but he did encounter people of other religions and praised the faith of the Roman centurion and the charity of the heretic Samaritan. Not much is known of Paul's meetings with Epicurean and Stoic philosophers in Athens, though according to Acts he quoted from their poets and told them to seek God, since he is not far from each one of us (Acts 17: 18*ff*.). Elsewhere he said that some of the Gentiles had the law written on their hearts, witnessed by their conscience, and they did by nature what the law required (Rom. 2: 14*f*.). According to Acts also, Peter told Cornelius that in every nation anyone who fears God and does what is right is acceptable to him (10: 35). Universal salvation seems to be guaranteed by Paul's words to the Corinthians: 'As in Adam all die, so also in Christ shall all be made alive . . . God has put all things in subjection under his feet . . . that God may be everything to every one' (1 Cor. 15: 22*ff*.). Paul seems to have taken for granted that there was some knowledge and service of God outside Judaism, and also that both Jews and Gentiles would all be saved. But in many later centuries Christians seem to have forgotten that truth, wherever it is found, must come from God. Only now has the second Vatican Council declared that 'the Catholic Church rejects nothing which is true and holy in these religions'.[12]

Once again there is a direct link between the New Testament and

12 *The Documents of Vatican* II (1966), p. 662.

modern times, and a great deal of unfair and condemnatory missionary propaganda needs to be forgotten or lived down. Better than even the New Testament teachers we are now aware of the extent and riches of the world's religions, and if Israel must be saved, then so must other communities. The symposium *Religions* touches briefly on Christian failings and sketches the Roman Catholic attitude. It mentions devotions to the saints as persons of particular significance for the history of salvation and criticises 'the exaggerations of the Protestants regarding the exclusiveness of Christ's work'. The Church 'brings salvation to all men, who may, if they live uprightly, though they do not know the Church, participate in the salvation of God and of Christ even outside the visible membership of the Church', but not without her, for the Church is 'the universal sacrament of salvation'.[13]

Such concessions to the idea of the salvation of men outside the visible Church have long been accepted by Rome through devices such as the baptism of desire or the presence of implicit faith, rather like the 'uncovenanted mercies' which some Churches have admitted for others with which they disagreed. But these are applied to individual and exceptional cases, and religions as social entities and theologies have hardly been considered hitherto. The Vatican Council, however, in its *Declaration on the Relation of the Church to Non-Christian Religions*, did hand a few bouquets round. These religions 'often reflect' a brightness of the truth; Muslims are regarded 'with esteem', Buddhists recognise the inadequacy of the world, and Hindus 'probe the mystery of God and express it with a rich fund of myths and a penetrating philosophy'. The significance of the myths of avatars like Krishna and Rāma, and possible links with doctrines of the Incarnation, may be hinted at but were not explored.

The possibilities, but also the dangers, of exploiting such apparent similarities between religious doctrines continue to receive attention. Klostermaier insists that Christian preachers have been wrong to present Christ in India as an avatar, even as the sole and exclusive avatar. Such a presentation does not make sense, he says, because in Indian theology there are many avatars and a unique one is a contradiction in terms, as missionaries would have known if only they did not 'always consider studies a superfluous waste of time'. But Klostermaier claims that Bhakti theology does have a category to express 'the uniqueness and exclusiveness of Christ'; this is in the Pañcharātra teach-

13 *Religions* (1970), p. 102*f.*

ing of an 'issue' from Brahman which could be adapted to express the uniqueness of Christ. But since other manifestations of Brahman are envisaged in this philosophy, the value of such doctrine may be limited.[14]

It seems that Christian theology cannot escape affirming the supremacy of Christ (Klostermaier calls it 'uniqueness and exclusiveness', despite his tolerant attitude) not only within Christianity but also in relation to other religions. This seems to go along with a general 'fulfilment' doctrine such as that propounded sixty years ago in Farquhar's *Crown of Hinduism*. Generally this is taken to regard all other religions as Old Testaments, at best, preparing the way for Christ but now being abolished. A similar but less 'abolitionist' attitude, stressing fulfilment and growth, seems to be assumed by Panikkar's *Unknown Christ of Hinduism*. Both approaches are disliked by the Hindu Dindayal, who criticises the notion that the Indian gods and avatars 'can all be seen as finding fulfilment in Christianity', though he fails to note the clear distinction that is now made between Christianity and Christ. Yet a comparable process is at work in other religions, since Hindus apply their avatar concept and Muslims their prophetic category to Christ. It is a valid activity to study the adequacy or otherwise of such interpretations, both within the general theories of avatars and prophets and within the context of Christian or other religious commitment.

At the Bombay Roman Catholic conference which produced *Christian Revelation and World Religions* there emerged a recognition of the place of other religions in the divine plan of salvation, not only in the past but now. Against the Barthians it was affirmed that other religions are 'not just natural theology, natural piety, natural morality', but 'what truth they teach is from God'. Men can be saved 'in their own non-Christian religions', which are 'the historical way to God for their followers'.[15]

In a more recent publication the ex-Jesuit Charles Davis declares that the presence of God in other religions has not been recognised hitherto because of 'the fixation of Christians upon dogmatic belief', which was 'a long-lived but none the less temporary distortion'.[16] The claim, made by conservative theologians, that because Christ is the universal Saviour therefore other religions are abolished, is not only against the plain facts but makes the questionable assumption that the work of God is being

14 Klostermaier, *op. cit.*, p. 115, and see Parrinder, *Avatar and Incarnation* (1970), p. 59.

15 *Christian Revelation and World Religions*, ed. Neuner (1967), pp. 13*ff*.

16 Davis, *Christ and the World Religions* (1970), pp. 104, 121*f*.

carried on exclusively by the Church. But if other religions really are vehicles of faith, then they must be ordained by God and have their plan for the world, and who is to say that their role is now finished? There must be no denial of genuine religious faith, no assertion that Christians have nothing to learn from others, and no declaration that other religions have no function now in the order of divine providence.

In the early years of this century there was a campaign for 'the world for Christ in this generation', and people talked expectantly of the collapse of Islam and other religions. Not only did this attitude show an appalling lack of understanding of Islam, let alone sympathy with it, but time has shown that Islam or Marxism might become the world religion instead of Christianity. For a religion that claims to be universal can be fatally weakened by colour prejudice in its own ranks. But what was really meant was perhaps 'the world for Christianity', and though the campaign has been forgotten its theme is continued in much of the talk about the world Church. Yet Davis very seriously questions whether a world Church is a biblical doctrine and whether it is a desirable goal. The ecumenical movement among the different Churches if it ever unites them, could be promoted in the wider field of various religions; but it may be doubted whether one monolithic Church is desirable for Christianity and whether one sole religion would benefit mankind. In any case, religious pluralism is now a fact of life, acceptable as providential, and likely to continue for a very long time, if not for ever. The role of the Church is rather one of 'representation', says Davis, for it is elected to its special role and may exercise direct and indirect influence on others, rather like the function attributed to the 'saving remnant' in ancient Israel.

Other practical problems were faced, and not altogether solved, by the Bombay conference. Such were whether non-Christian students in Christian schools should be encouraged to worship according to their own religion, and, further, whether religious instruction in these religions should be given by Christian teachers or even by leaders of those faiths brought in for the purpose. Then there were questions of taking part in Hindu worship, and whether a Christian might accept *prasāda*, the food which has first been offered to a god and is his gift to the community of worshippers. But other problems loom behind these practical concerns.

The salvation of other men outside the visible Church and with no conscious knowledge of Christian soteriology can now be taken as accepted by eminent Roman Catholic and many Protestant teachers, developing the teachings of Paul. The concept of the unknown Christ is similar to belief in the Holy Spirit, God himself, at work before or beyond the Incarnation in Jesus. Other religions are now regarded as means by which God has brought salvation to men at many times and places, for salvation is the gift of God and not the property of any Church. It is evident that such considerations demand a radical re-assessment of the place and service of missions in the modern world.

But there are not only religions, which are ill-defined entities, but religious figures who are regarded as saviours. They are revered by their followers as agents of salvation, but how can they be regarded from the outside? It is important always to make clear what audience is being addressed. It may make sense to a Christian to speak of the unknown Christ of Hinduism, but in a purely Hindu context this might be taken amiss, as criticisms of the concept from Hindus have shown. And the Western critical evaluations may go contrary to the attitudes of faith. W. Montgomery Watt, in a careful assessment of Muḥammad, emphasises the Prophet's greatness, defends him against calumny, and speaks of his creative imagination and perhaps prophetic revelation. No doubt this is as far as an academic assessment can go, and it is compelled to add that 'not all the ideas he proclaimed are true and sound' and that some of the Qur'anic ideas are unsound. To a Muslim this would be quite unacceptable, but in view of the Qur'anic denial of the death of Jesus on the cross it is clear that a dilemma remains between Muslim and Christian teachings which is very difficult, if not impossible, of solution.[17]

Raymond Panikkar, in a review, has asked whether there could be an orthodox Christian theology of the avatar in Krishna which would be acceptable to his followers. It seems doubtful, but some points may be suggested. Christians may learn from the teachings attributed to Krishna in the *Bhagavad-Gītā*, and not only for instruction but for inspiration. W. Cantwell Smith has asked the unusual but important question 'Is the Qur'ān the Word of God?'. He develops this to mean not only is the Qur'ān the Word of God to Muslims, but can it speak from God to Christians? Similarly a Christian may hear God speaking through many lines of the *Gītā*, so that it is a revelation to him, out of another tradition but from the one God.[18]

17 Watt, *Muhammad, Prophet and Statesman* (1961), p. 239*f*.

18 Panikkar, review of *Avatar and Incarnation*, *Journal of Theological Studies* XXII (1971), p. 321*f*.; Smith, *Questions of Religious Truth* (1967), pp. 37*ff*.

Similarly, Christian recognition may be given to the importance and value of belief in the Krishna avatar. Christians may learn from the Krishna story, not simply in its detail but also in its symbolism, with its passion and submission, dark night of the soul and rapturous reunion with God. This can be done whether the avatar is held to be a real incarnation or is distinguished clearly from it. Yet such concessions, and other generous acknowledgments, would hardly go far enough for a devout Vaishnava, either in expressing his devotion or giving a theology of the avatar which he could accept.

The reason is to be found in Panikkar's second question, whether there may be a Vaishnava interpretation of the Incarnation of Christ acceptable to Christians. Such has not yet appeared, for all interpretations seem to be inadequate, both regarding the Jesus of history and the Christ of faith. And for both Vaishnavism and Christianity this is because of the point made earlier in this paper, that it is a fundamental feature of belief in the Saviour that he is supreme and even unique.

We are faced, then, with the continued coexistence of different schemes of salvation and different saviours, worshipped under their particular names, though it may be recognised that God, or Christ, who is the Saviour of all and in all is at work in each one of them in varying degrees. Faith demands attachment, passionate even, to the revelation that comes personally within one's own tradition. Individuals may change to another allegiance, often at great cost, but most men will not change, and their faith should not be depreciated.

Does this mean that what Christians, or Hindus and Muslims and others, say from their denominational viewpoint will often appear not meaningful to those who do not share their particular presuppositions? Inevitably, to some extent, but there is better understanding now of what other religions teach and how their followers worship, and in the sympathy which looks for the truth everywhere there is hope that men may get the 'feel' of other religions, by recognising their validity and their comparability with one's own religious life.

Although the study of doctrines of salvation in different religions is a valid academic exercise, in dealing with religion there are deeper levels which are beyond criticism but in which religions are closer together than may appear on the surface. Indeed, to recognise the fervour and sincerity of belief in salvation within a particular religion, and in its object of devotion, may bring a better appreciation of religion in general than is obtainable by assuming that all schemes of salvation are illusory. Evans-Pritchard has shown how unsatisfactory are many accounts of primitive religion, because they are influenced by 'assumptions that the souls and spirits and gods of religions have no reality'.[19] So the unbeliever looks for some theory to explain away the religious illusion, psychological, social or economic. But one who accepts the reality of spiritual being, while he may find some concepts of God and the soul to be inadequate by his own standards, yet does not regard them as mere illusion. Rather than explain things away, he is deeply concerned to understand the manner in which people conceive of reality and their relations to it. Similarly, one who believes in salvation for himself ought to be able most easily to accept that other people also find it essential, and the task of religious understanding is to discover the different ways in which salvation and the saviour are conceived. Within each religion there are doctrines which have been heavily marked by local concepts of theology, philosophy, law and sacrifice, but beneath them are wider concepts which express the essence of religion itself. Therefore the salvation of other men can be recognised as a universal, operating within particular contexts, and understood as not exceptional but normal.

19 Evans-Pritchard, *Theories of Primitive Religion* (1965), p. 121.

15

James Robson

Aspects of the Qur'anic doctrine of salvation

Sūra 40: 44[1] is the only Qur'anic verse where the word for 'salvation' (*najāt*) occurs: 'O my people, how is it with me that I call you to salvation and you call me to the Fire?' explained by the next verse, 'You call me to disbelieve in God, and to associate with him that whereof I have no knowledge, while I call you to the Mighty, the Forgiver'; cf. 2: 221. Disbelief and polytheism are to be punished by the Fire, in contrast to which Muḥammad calls the people to a forgiving God, somewhat reminiscent of Paul's distinction between the wages of sin and the gift of God (Rom. 6: 23).

Although *najāt* occurs only once, the root from which it comes occurs often, expressing deliverance from calamities and occasionally in connection with eternal salvation. 39: 62 speaks of God at the Resurrection delivering the god-fearing, who will be unaffected by evil or grief. 19: 73 assures the god-fearing of deliverance from Jahannam. 61: 10–12 speak of merchandise which will deliver believers from a painful punishment, *viz.* belief in God and striving with one's goods and person in God's way. The result will be forgiveness of sins and fine dwellings in the Gardens of Eden.

26: 169 speaks of Lot and 66: 11 of Pharaoh's wife praying for deliverance from the evil practices of those among whom they live. In the latter instance the prayer is preceded by a request that God will build her a house in the Garden. Prophets and others are delivered in this life from physical or moral calamities; believers are delivered from eternal punishment.

It has often been felt that the Qur'anic idea of salvation is deliverance not so much from the power of sin as from eternal punishment. 2: 197 contains a prayer for good in this world and the next, and for protection from the punishment of the Fire. 3: 14 says, 'O our Lord, we have

1 The verse numbering is that of Flügel's Qur'ān text, followed by a number of English translations.

believed, so forgive us our sins and protect us from the punishment of the Fire.' Belief and forgiveness are recognised as necessary for deliverance.

Believers

The root *āmana* ('to believe') is, naturally, frequent. 4: 151 speaks of reward for those who believe in all God's messengers without distinction, and 4: 174 says God will admit to his mercy and grace and guide in a straight path to himself those who believe and seek their protection in him. 14: 32 speaks of giving believers and wrongdoers appropriate treatment. 72: 13 says that those who believe in their Lord fear neither loss nor injustice. But normally, besides belief, good works are necessary for final salvation. 2: 59 says, 'Believers, Jews, Christians, Ṣābi'ans, whoever believe in God and the Last Day and act uprightly, will have their reward with God and experience neither fear nor grief'; cf. 5: 73. 34: 36 specifies a double reward for those who believe and act uprightly, adding that they will be secure in lofty mansions. 19: 61 says that God, who always fulfils his promise, will admit those who repent, believe and act uprightly to Gardens of Eden. 25: 70–6 say God will substitute good deeds for the evil deeds of those who repent, believe and act uprightly. Other characteristics of such people are that they never give false witness; when they come upon anything vain they pass with dignity; when reminded of God's signs they do not act like deaf and blind people; they pray that they may have comfort in their spouses and offspring and be models to the god-fearing. They will be rewarded with the upper room for their endurance and will be welcomed there with greetings and salutations of peace. In that excellent resort and dwelling place they will remain for ever. The common reward for those who believe and act uprightly is Gardens with rivers, more details sometimes being given; cf. 2: 23, 76; 4: 60, 121; 7: 40; 10: 9; 11: 25; 18: 30, 107; 22: 14, 23; 30: 14; 31: 7*f*.; 32: 19; 42: 21; 47: 13; 64: 9; 65: 11; 85: 11; 98: 7, etc.

The prosperous

The fourth form of *falaḥa* occurs frequently for those who prosper. 23: 1–11 describe the believers, whose prosperity is the inheritance of an eternal abode in Paradise, as having the following characteristics: humility in prayer, avoidance of vain talk, payment of *zakāt*,[2] main-

2 Legal alms, levied on property exceeding a certain minimum possessed for a year; *A Dictionary of Comparative Religion*, ed. Brandon (1970), p. 407.

tenance of sexual morality, faithfulness regarding pledges and covenants, and careful observance of the prayers. It is sometimes difficult to decide whether the prosperity is material or spiritual, in this life or in the next. 3: 100 calls for a community which urges people to what is good and forbids what is unworthy, saying they are the prosperous ones, meaning material or spiritual prosperity in this life, or final prosperity in the hereafter. 7: 7 certainly has this last meaning, for, speaking of Judgment Day, it says that those whose scales are heavy will be the prosperous ones. 59: 9, which speaks of the Medinans who welcomed the Emigrants and treated them well even when suffering want themselves, says, 'Those who are protected from niggardliness of soul are the prosperous', referring most probably to a development of character in this world and reward in the next. 64: 16 ends with exactly the same words following on a warning against being led astray by one's family, and assurance that God has a great reward, so exhortation is given to fear God as much as possible and be generous.

The triumphant

Another root used of those who attain salvation is *fāza*, having the idea of victory, success or triumph. 9: 20 says that those who have believed, migrated, striven in God's cause with their goods and persons, have the highest rank in God's sight and are the triumphant. This verse seems to speak particularly of Muḥammad's own times and perhaps refers as much to this world as to the next. But 23: 112*f.* tell of God speaking at the Judgment about believers who had borne ridicule patiently, saying they are the triumphant ones.

The phrase 'the great triumph' (*al-fawz al-ʿaẓīm*) occurs a number of times. 4: 17 applies it to those who obey God and his messenger and will be brought to abide in Gardens through which rivers flow; cf. 9: 90. 9: 112 says God has bought the believers' persons and goods, in return for which he promises them the Garden, because they fight in God's name and kill the enemy or are killed. God has made this promise incumbent on himself in the Torah, the Injīl[3] and the Qur'ān, and no one fulfils his promise more faithfully than he. This bargain which merits rejoicing is the great triumph.

'The manifest triumph' (*al-fawz al-mubīn*) occurs twice. 6: 16 uses it,

3 Name given to a scripture believed to have been revealed to Jesus. Clearly derived from εὐαγγέλιον (Evangel); cf. Bell, *Introduction to the Qur'ān* (1953), p. 152; Parrinder, *Jesus in the Qur'ān* (1965), chapter 15.

referring to those who have received God's mercy at the Judgment through the punishment being averted, and 45: 29, referring to believers who have wrought good works and so are admitted by God to his mercy.

There are a few other uses of the root. 3: 182 says those who are kept away from the Fire and admitted to the Garden have achieved triumph. 78: 31 says there is a place of triumph (or a refuge—*mafāz*) for the god-fearing, and following verses describe the joys of Paradise. 3: 185 uses the same word, obviously in the sense of refuge, warning people who delight in being praised for things they have not done against imagining they are secure from punishment. It seems that the idea of triumph refers particularly to final salvation in the hereafter.

Forgiveness

The root *ghafara* ('to forgive') naturally appears often, as has been indicated in verses quoted already. 39: 54 indicates the magnitude of God's forgiveness, exhorting excessive sinners not to despair of God's mercy, for he is forgiving and compassionate, forgiving sins altogether. Lists of people for whom God has prepared forgiveness and a mighty reward are given in 4: 97*f*., 33: 35, and 48: 29.

Recompense

The blessings waiting in the hereafter are often mentioned in terms of a recompense, or hire, or wage (*ajr*, pl. *ujūr*), e.g. 3: 130 (excellent *ajr* for those who work); 29: 58 (upper rooms of the Garden); 39: 74; 9: 21*f*. These all refer to the Garden. 12: 56 and 90, referring particularly to Joseph, add that God does not allow the *ajr* of those who do well to perish. For similar language regarding faithful Muslims, cf. 3: 165, 7: 169, 9: 121, 11: 117 and 18: 29. 16: 43 guarantees a lodging in this world for the persecuted who have emigrated, but reminds them that the *ajr* of the hereafter is better. 5: 12 says God has promised those who believe and act uprightly forgiveness and a mighty *ajr*; cf. 4: 44, 76, 97, 114, 145, 160; 11: 14; 48: 10.

41: 7 says that believers who act uprightly will have a never-ending *ajr*: cf. 68: 3 (addressed to Muḥammad); 84: 25, 95: 6. 47: 48 says God will give *ujūr* to believers who act uprightly without asking them for their goods. 57: 11 asks who will lend God a good loan, saying that it will be doubled and that he will have a noble *ajr*: cf. 57: 17 and

73: 20 (which speaks of one's good deeds being with God in the next world; he is the one who gives the greatest *ajr*). 35: 8 promises forgiveness and a great *ajr* to those who believe and act uprightly; cf. 17: 10; 57: 7 (the good work here being contribution to *jihād*). 48: 29 and 33: 35 use *'aẓīm* ('mighty') of the *ajr*. 18:2 uses *ḥasan* ('fine') of the *ajr* for belief and upright deeds, and 48: 16 for obedience in fighting unbelievers.

God gives *ajr* to People of the Book (2: 59; 3: 199); cf. 5:73, which says they will have no fear or grief, a common phrase used of those who attain bliss in the hereafter but not so commonly applied, as here, to Jews and Christians. 57: 18 combines light with *ajr* for believers in God and his messengers, such believers being called the faithful and the witnesses in God's sight. 29: 26 tells of Abraham, to whom God gave Isaac and Jacob and in whose posterity God appointed the prophetic office and the Book, adding, 'We gave him his *ajr* in this world and in the hereafter he will certainly be among the righteous.' The *ajr* in this world presumably refers to the matters mentioned earlier in the verse. 33: 29 tells Muḥammad's wives that if they desire God, his messenger and the future abode, God has prepared a mighty *ajr* for those of them who do well. Verse 31 says God will give her *ajr* twice over to such as is obedient to God and his messenger and acts uprightly. For her God has prepared a noble provision. 39: 13 exhorts believers to be god-fearing. Those who endure will get an *ajr* without reckoning. 3: 182 says *ujūr* will be paid in full on the Day of Resurrection.

The *ajr* is commonly admission to the Garden, with all its bliss, which is the hope promised in other connections, but the manner in which it is expressed sounds rather like a business transaction. For so much uprightness there is an *ajr* which may even be paid twofold. But it is still payment for services received, which makes it difficult to treat it in relation to any deep understanding of salvation.

The pure

The root *zakā*, which refers to purity or alms-giving, is common. 4: 52 speaks of people who consider themselves pure, adding that God is the one who can declare those whom he pleases pure, and they will not be wronged a straw. 53: 33 says, 'Do not ascribe purity to yourselves; God knows best who is god-fearing.' 2: 123 speaks of a prayer of Abraham asking God to send the people a messenger of their own number to recite God's signs, teach the Book and the Wisdom and purify them. Verse 146 repeats these details as already accomplished, i.e. in Muḥammad's coming. But it is not clear whether 'purify' is the correct translation, or whether it should be 'impose the *zakāt*'. 92: 17*f*. say that the most god-fearing who gives of his property, seeking purification, will escape the Fire, purification here meaning clearly the payment of *zakāt*.

20: 78 says that Gardens of Eden through which rivers flow will be an eternal abode for those who have become pure. 35: 19 insists on each one's personal responsibility for his future. One cannot bear another's burden, and he who keeps himself pure does so for himself alone. Is there a suggestion here that maintaining purity is the result of one's own effort rather than something accomplished by God's help? Or is God's help naturally assumed? 87: 14*f*. say that he who becomes pure, mentions God's name and prays is the prosperous one.

Uncertainty

Some verses which speak of the prosperous use the word *la'alla*, about which translators differ. Muhammad 'Ali[4] has 'that you may be successful', A. Yusuf Ali[5] and Muhammad Zafrulla Khan[6] 'that ye may prosper'. The word normally means 'perhaps'. Sale[7] has 'peradventure', Palmer,[8] Bell[9] and Arberry[10] use 'haply', Blachère[11] and Masson[12] use *peut-être*, and Paret[13] uses *vielleicht*. It seems best to keep to 'perhaps'.

3: 200 says, 'Show endurance, believers, encourage one another to endurance, be on your guard, fear God. Perhaps you may prosper.' It is difficult to decide whether this applies to material or spiritual prosperity, or both. 3: 125 may refer to either where it says, 'Believers, do not devour interest doubled and redoubled, but fear God. Perhaps

4 *The Holy Qur'ān*, fifth edition (1963).
5 *The Holy Qur-an*, two volumes, third edition (1938).
6 *The Quran* (1970).
7 Wherry, *A comprehensive commentary on the Qurán, comprising Sale's translation and Preliminary Discourse*, four volumes (1896).
8 *The Koran*, World's Classics edition.
9 *The Qur'ān, translated with a critical arrangement of the Surahs*, two volumes (1937, 1939).
10 *The Koran Interpreted*, two volumes (1955).
11 *Le Coran*, two volumes (1949, 1950); one-volume, shorter edition (1957).
12 *Le Coran* (1967).
13 *Der Koran* (1963–6).

you may prosper.' 22: 76 exhorts believers to bow, do obeisance, serve God and do what is good, with the prospect that they may perhaps prosper, which may mean either material or spiritual prosperity. 5: 92 says that by avoiding wine, the game of *al-maisir*,[14] sacred stones, divining arrows, all of which are an abomination arising from Satan's work, people may perhaps prosper. As all these practices are considered sinful, the reference here is most probably to eternal salvation. 7: 67, which says that by remembering God's gifts people may perhaps prosper, is not clear as to whether it refers to this world, the next, or both. 24: 31 exhorts women to be modest and all believers to turn in penitence to God, for perhaps they may prosper. 27: 47 is addressed by Ṣāliḥ to Thamūd.[15] He asks why they seek to hasten evil before good, adding that if only they would ask God for forgiveness they might perhaps be shown mercy. 62: 10, telling the people they may resume their business after the prayers, for they may prosper, seems to refer chiefly to mundane affairs.

28: 67, in a passage connected with the Last Judgment, says that one who has repented, believed and done what is good may possibly be among those who prosper. Here *'asā* is used. Muhammad Ali uses 'maybe', but Muhammad Zafrulla Khan has 'will surely be among the prosperous'. A. Yusuf Ali has 'will have hopes to be among those who achieve salvation', leaving an element of uncertainty. This passage deals with eternal salvation.

Is God arbitrary in his dealings?

It has been commonly held in the West that the Qur'ān teaches that God's will is arbitrary in its choice of the saved and the damned, and many Muslims have thought the same. Some verses seem to provide good reason for this belief, but the language must be considered to see whether it is justified. The phrase 'God does what he wills' is common, e.g. 16: 95 says, 'God leads astray and guides whom he wills. You will certainly be asked about what you were doing.' 14: 4 says, 'God leads astray and guides whom he wills.' 13: 27 says, 'God sends astray whom he wills and guides to himself those who turn to him devoutly.' 2: 274 says categorically, 'God guides those whom he wills'; cf. 22: 16.

14 A gambling game in pre-islamic Arabia for parts of a slaughtered camel by drawing lots with arrows. See Montgomery Watt, *Muhammad at Medina* (1956), p. 299.

15 Ṣāliḥ is frequently mentioned in the Qur'ān as a prophet to Thamūd, an ancient people in North Arabia.

'Leading (or sending) astray' translates the Arabic literally, but Muslim translators prefer to tone this down. A. Yusuf Ali in his excellent translation uses 'leaves straying' or 'rejects from his guidance'. Muhammad Ali and M. Zafrulla Khan, who represent the two sections of the Aḥmadiyya movement,[16] also make the phrase sound milder, the former using 'leaves in error' and the latter 'adjudges astray' or 'lets go astray'. They feel that too literal a translation attributes injustice to God. But Daud Rahbar, in his penetrating work *God of Justice* (1960), has no hesitation in translating 'leads astray'.

If one takes some verses literally they do suggest that God chooses the saved and the damned without any obvious reason. There are, however, other verses which qualify the bald statement and give reason to question the accusation of arbitrariness. 6: 125 says that if God wishes to guide anyone he 'enlarges his breast' to Islam (i.e. makes him ready to accept it), but if he wishes to lead anyone astray he 'makes his breast narrow'. That, however, is not the end of the verse. It concludes with the words 'Thus God brings punishment on those who disbelieve.' Surely the point is that persistent unbelief has led to such a person being left without God's guidance. It may even involve leading him astray, or simply letting him remain in his evil courses. 14: 32 says that believers are established and wrongdoers are led astray. 2: 24 says, 'God sends many astray and guides many, but he sends astray only the profligates.' 74: 31–4 make it clear that those who believe in the Book are increased in belief, while the diseased in heart and unbelievers raise questions. This is followed by 'Thus God sends astray those he wills and guides those he wills,' which means that God guides people who believe but leaves those who insist in raising difficulties to their unbelief. 45: 22 says that God sends astray the one who takes his desire as his god. Such passages suggest that God's leading astray is due to persistent doubt or self-will.

Some verses show that guidance or leading astray are due to the behaviour of the people concerned. 38: 25, addressed to David, says, 'For those who go astray from God's way a severe punishment is in store because they forgot the day of reckoning.' People are here blamed for their straying. 76: 29–31 say, 'He who wills chooses a way to God, but you can will only if God wills. He makes those he wills

16 A movement, generally considered by Muslims to be heretical, established by Mīrzā Ghulām Aḥmad (d. 1908) in the Panjab; cf. *Encyclopaedia of Islām* I, second edition, pp. 301–3; *Religion in the Middle East* II, ed. Arberry (1969), pp. 349*ff*.

enter his mercy and has prepared a painful punishment for the wrongdoers.' The damned are clearly wrongdoers; the saved have chosen to seek God, who has confirmed their choice. 35: 9 says, 'God leads astray and guides those he wills,' preceded by a reference to those who think their evil conduct good. Muḥammad is told not to be sorry for them. 47: 1 says that God sends astray the works of unbelievers who have turned others from God's way.

Some other verses make the point even clearer. 'God assists to ease him who is generous, god-fearing, and acknowledges what is best, but to difficulty him who is niggardly, self-sufficient and denies what is best' (92: 5*ff.*). 'God chooses for the religion those he pleases and guides to it those who turn to him penitently' (42: 12). Those here said to be guided have evidently shown a desire for guidance. 4: 174 makes a direct promise of future well-being to those who hold fast to God, and 3: 96 says that those who hold fast to God have been guided to a straight path. On the other hand, 40: 36 says God leads astray every extravagant doubter.

But while God leads believers, there are verses warning that they may fall away. 6: 88 says, 'God guides those servants he wills; but if they associate other gods with him what they have been doing will not avail them.' Yet 9: 116 says, 'God does not lead people astray after guiding them till he makes clear to them what they should guard against.' 4: 136 gives stern warning: 'Those who believe, then disbelieve, then again believe, then disbelieve, and then increase in unbelief, God will not forgive or guide,' but 3: 80–3 modify the sternness, saying, 'How will God guide a people who disbelieve after believing? Their reward is that the curse of God, the angels and all people will be upon them, dwelling therein for ever, their punishment not being lightened, and they will not be respited.' Then follows verse 83, which says, 'Except those who have later repented and acted uprightly. God is indeed forgiving and compassionate'—thus, in spite of the earlier strong language, still making allowance for exceptions.

It seems reasonable to conclude from a study of relevant passages that, while some seem to say that final salvation or damnation is a matter of God's inscrutable choice, the many verses which are more explicit should rather be taken as a standard for the doctrine. While God is said to guide or lead astray those whom he pleases, we may modify this by reference to the verses which speak of him guiding those who turn to him and leading astray (or leaving in their false ways) those who are transgressors, or unbelievers or ungrateful.

Assurance

The mention of the assurance of ultimate salvation presents a problem. Sometimes it sounds as if God does not care but leaves the matter to man. 10: 99f. say that, if God willed, everyone in the land would believe, but no restraint must be imposed. No one can believe without God's permission. God lays the abomination on those who do not show understanding. These verses suggest, first, that God does not impose his will on man, then that his permission is necessary for belief, and finally that those who do not show understanding suffer. While the first and third parts treat man as responsible for belief or unbelief, the second might be interpreted as meaning that God has chosen certain people for belief, or, alternatively, that everything depends on God's grace. 18: 28 says categorically, 'Let him who wills believe and him who wills disbelieve,' laying the responsibility on man. Such verses suggest that man has it within his own power to assure himself of eternal salvation. 57: 21 exhorts people to strive to attain forgiveness and a Garden prepared for those who believe in God and his messengers. That is God's bounty, which he bestows on whomsoever he wills. If one takes the exhortation to strive along with the statement that God gives his bounty to whomsoever he wills, it may be argued, on the basis of our earlier discussion, that this means he wills to give it to those who have deserved it; cf. also the idea of recompense earlier considered.

Some verses which use the root *ghafara* ('to forgive') provide reason to feel assurance of ultimate salvation. For 39: 54, exhorting excessive sinners not to despair of God's mercy, see p. 208. 2: 215 says that believers, emigrants and those who have striven in God's way hope for his mercy, he being forgiving and compassionate. Bell and Arberry say, 'have hope in his mercy'. Blachère has 'ceux-là peuvent espérer . . .' Paret has 'dürfen . . . hoffen'. Masson has 'voilà ceux qui espèrent . . .' Muhammad Ali has 'These surely hope . . .', A. Yusuf Ali, 'They have the hope of the mercy of God', and Muhammad Zafrulla Khan has 'are those who hope . . .' Of those quoted, Masson and M. Zafrulla Khan keep most closely to the Arabic. But the reference to God being forgiving and compassionate surely suggests that this is not a bare statement that such people hope for God's mercy, for the context suggests there is assurance in their hope. But if one still has an element of hesitation about the quality of this hope, there can be no doubt about the assurance expressed in 17: 20, which says, 'If one who is a believer desires the hereafter and strives properly for it, the striving of such people is thankfully accepted.' 6: 82 also gives a guarantee, saying, 'Those who believe and do not mix their faith with wrong-doing will have security and will be guided.' 3: 61 says, 'God is the Friend (Patron) of the believers,' and 38: 27 asks rhetorically, 'Shall we treat those who believe and act uprightly like those who act corruptly in the earth, or shall we treat the god-fearing like the wicked?' Here is assurance for upright believers, as also in 4: 146 and 19: 61. But while belief is important for those who are to enter Paradise, believing only on the Day of Judgment is too late; cf. 6: 159.

Guidance

The root *hadā* ('to guide') is an important word in connection with our subject. It indicates that the process of salvation is not just an effort on man's part to live a good life which will merit reward in the next world; it is under divine guidance which is offered to all who will accept it. Man is not left to himself. One must therefore consider what the Qur'ān says about God's guidance. 64: 11 says, 'God will guide the heart of everyone who believes in him'; cf. 2: 209; 22: 53. 4: 174 first promises those who believe and take a firm hold of God an entrance into mercy and grace from God, then promises to guide them to him by a straight path. 3: 96 says that those who hold fast to God have been guided to a straight path. Some verses speak of classes of people who receive God's guidance. He guides those who strive in his cause (29: 69). Those who repent of idolatry, listen to God's word and follow the best of it are the ones whom God guides and who are endowed with minds (39: 19; cf. 42: 12). Those who believe and do what is right will praise God for guiding them to Paradise. They recognise their guidance as coming from God, whose messengers brought the truth (7: 40*f.*). 47: 5–7 say, 'God will not send astray the works of those who are killed in his way. He will guide them and reform their condition, and cause them to enter the garden.' As the verse stands, it suggests that this guidance is different from that mentioned above in other verses, as it is given after the death of the warriors. But there is another reading involving no change in the consonants: 'fight' instead of 'are killed'. Bell and Blachère prefer it in their translations, but the standard edition of the Qur'ān issued in Egypt gives the reading of Hafs, 'are killed', and translators usually keep to this.

God's guidance is spoken of as coming through the Qur'ān. 2: 1–4 call it guidance for the god-fearing who believe in the unseen, observe the prayer, give generously, believe in the revelation sent to Muḥammad and in earlier revelation, and are convinced about the hereafter. The Qur'ān, being God's word, is a fundamental part of his guidance to mankind, and therefore it is sufficient to mention some of the passages concerned: 2: 181; 5: 18 (addressed to the People of the Book); 6: 156; 16: 66, 91; 17: 9; 31: 1–4; 42: 52; 72: 1*f.*, etc.

Guidance is also through the medium of prophets. 6: 83–90 speak of a number whom God guided, giving them the Book, judgment and prophecy. Verse 90 says, 'These are they whom God has guided, so be led by their guidance.' The pronoun is singular and so is addressed to Muḥammad, who is exhorted to follow the guidance of his predecessors. Abraham was guided (16: 122; 26: 77*f.*). 21: 72*f.* say that God made Isaac and Jacob leaders to guide men, and inspired them to do good, establish prayer and the payment of the *zakāt*. Some prophets were given books. God wrote for Moses on tablets for the guidance of the people (7: 142). God gave Jesus the Injīl, containing guidance and light (5: 50). The Torah and Injīl were sent down in earlier times as a guidance for the people (3: 2). The Book God gave Moses was a light and a guidance for the people (6: 91). 28: 43 calls it a guidance and a mercy, adding, 'perhaps they may reflect'. 40: 56 calls it a guidance and a reminder to those endowed with minds, and 17: 2 a guidance.

Guidance may therefore come through the Qur'ān and earlier scriptures, and through prophets, but this is not always on the same level as the guidance given to those who believe and act uprightly, for it is made clear that acceptance of the guidance is a different matter. 76: 3 says that God has guided man as to the way, man being grateful or ungrateful. The word translated 'ungrateful' may also mean 'unbelieving'. Muhammad Zafrulla Khan combines both meanings in his translation: 'We showed him the way. He is either appreciative and follows it, or is ungrateful and rejects it.' 90: 10 says, 'We have guided him to the two highways.' Here a better translation would be 'We have pointed out to him . . .', following Muhammad Ali and Muhammad Zafrulla Khan, and also Blachère, Masson and Paret in French and German. It is not the same as the guidance promised to believers, who obviously accept God's guidance (direction) and follow the right path. 7: 192 and 197 say that people are unwilling to follow the guidance (direction) even if called to do so; cf. 18: 56.

Present salvation

A question touched on already in the preceding section is whether salvation applies purely to the life after death, or whether it applies to this life also. Sweetman[17] holds that 'to import Christian ideas of a present salvation into Islam only results in confusion'. Sell[18] had earlier said, with reference to the Qur'ān, 'We read much of guidance and instruction, but little or nothing of redemption. The Qur'ān nowhere teaches that the sinner must be regenerated.' Islam and Christianity differ in their outlook, but although we have seen, in the section on recompense, that the language of the Qur'ān sometimes seems to use the terms of the business world, we must recognise that fundamentally its doctrine depends on a sense of God's guidance and help to sinful man. And in Christianity, although people can in this life have an experience of redemption, only too often there are those who later fall away. In Christianity salvation is never complete in this world, but there should be gradual development. Within the body of Islam there is also ground for growth, and here too people may experience development. We must consider what the Qur'ān says.

20: 84 promises forgiveness to those who repent, believe, act uprightly and follow the guidance. This verse, in a story about Moses, must refer to this present life, but it still seems to suggest that man must make the effort by his own power. 14: 32 says, 'God establishes those who have believed by the word, which is firmly fixed, in this life and the next.' 2: 257 speaks of help in this world, saying, 'Those who disbelieve in Ṭāghūt[19] and believe in God take hold of the strongest handle, which will not break.' The following verse says, 'God is the Patron (Friend) of the believers [cf. 3: 61], who brings them out of darkness into light.' 48: 4*f*. say that it is God 'who has sent down the *sakīna*[20] in the hearts of the believers, that they may add faith to their faith, that he may cause them to enter Gardens through which rivers flow' (cf. verse 26). The increase of faith obviously refers

17 Sweetman, *Islam and Christian Theology* II, part I (1947), p. 210.

18 Sell, 'Salvation (Muslim)' in *Encyclopaedia of Religion and Ethics*, ed. Hastings, XI (1920), p. 149.

19 Probably means idols, or rebellious demons.

20 As an original Arabic word it suggests 'tranquillity', but it may be a borrowing from the Hebrew *Shechina*. In the Qur'ān it may mean 'Help'. Bell translates 'assurance'. In 2: 249 it suggests an idol in an ark said to be a sign of Saul's kingship. Cf. Jeffery, *The Foreign Vocabulary of the Qur'ān* (1938), p. 174.

to a development in this life, leading to a final consummation. 42: 24*f.* speak of God's acceptance of repentance and his pardon. He responds to those who believe and do good and gives them abundant blessing from his grace (bounty). 57: 28 clearly speaks of help received in this life, saying that the god-fearing who believe in God's messenger will be given a double portion of God's mercy, that he will appoint for them a light by which to walk, and will forgive them. 58: 22, after saying that those who believe in God and the Last Day will not be found in friendly relations with those who obstruct God and his messenger, says that God has inscribed faith in their hearts and supported them with a spirit from himself. They will eventually abide in Gardens where rivers flow. 47:8 says, 'If you believers help God, He will help you and make your steps firm', speaking of his help in the present. 40: 54 gives a promise including this life by saying, 'We shall certainly assist our messengers and those who believe, in this present life and on the day when the witnesses arise'. 41: 30*f.* tell of angels descending on those who acknowledge God as Lord and act straightforwardly. They assure them of the promise of the Garden and tell them not to fear or grieve, adding that they are their friends in this life and the next. The idea of angelic assistance is not quite clear here, but the angels are said to encourage righteous believers. 16: 99 says that male and female believers who act uprightly will be caused by God to live a good life for which they will eventually be rewarded.

Such verses give clear promise of divine aid in living the life demanded of believers, and deserve to be stressed. If, as we have seen, there are verses which seem to suggest that God's treatment of mankind is arbitrary, though such verses are often qualified, it should also be noted that the Qur'ān is full of assurance of God's forgiveness and help to penitent believers, which is not confined to the Day of Judgment and the hereafter, but is also offered in this world.

Salvation of women

Whether women can have salvation hardly requires mention nowadays, since most people seem at last to have realised the error of those who, even in fairly recent times, held that Islam offers them none. The Qur'ān is quite explicit. 16: 99, just quoted, is a verse in point. 33: 35 says that God has prepared forgiveness and a mighty reward for Muslim men and women who are believing, obedient, truthful, enduring, submissive, givers of alms, fasting, continent, always mindful of God. The point is emphasised by the repetition of 'men and women' along with each characteristic (cf. verses 29 and 31). In 3: 193 God says, 'I shall not let the work of any of you, male or female, go to waste.' 57: 12 speaks of the day when male and female believers will be seen, their light running before them and at their right hands, when welcomed to their abiding place in the Gardens through which rivers flow. See also 9: 73; 48: 5; 40: 43; 4: 125.

A Muslim's views

It may be fitting to conclude by quoting words of A. Yusuf Ali in appendix XII to his translation of the Qur'ān. On rewards he says,

> Is the 'Reward' apportioned to the merits or the deserts of the receiver? Not at all. At best our merits or deserts can amount to very little. But God's Mercy and Grace are vast and all-embracing . . . His justice is strict but in favour of man; but His Grace is beyond calculation. [p. 1465]

Later he says,

> There is no vicarious atonement: for there is individual responsibility. And yet it is not a doctrine of 'justification by deeds': for the best of our actions fall short of the 'heaven' which we hope for. Nor is it the same as the doctrine of *Karma* . . . For we have a lively faith in God's Grace and Mercy: it can and does intervene for us and accepts our repentance and amendment, and gives us fresh chances at every stage of our probationary life. But our will is an important factor. [p. 1466]

He holds that the Muslim idea of salvation

> consists not in being saved from the consequences of our sins by the sufferings or the merits of others, nor in *Nirvana*, or annihilation or absorption, but in the achievement of a perfected Personality, a Bliss that grows up within us, and does not depend on external circumstances. It may require the utmost effort or striving (*Jihād*) of a lifetime or more. But it is the Supreme Achievement, the attainment of all desires, the Felicity *in excelsis*. [p. 1469]

He teaches that salvation is dependent on repentance and amendment of our ways, that God provides help in our struggle, but that our will is an important element in the process. He naturally speaks also of the consummation in the hereafter, but it seemed enough to quote here passages connected with this life, a subject we have noted in our earlier discussion, but one often forgotten by Western writers.

16

Annemarie Schimmel

A 'sincere Muhammadan's' way to salvation

... and I was brought out of this exciting state by special grace and particular protection and peculiar blessing to the station of perfect unveiling and to the Reality of Islam, and was granted special proximity to the plane of the Pure Essence Most Exalted and Holy, and became honoured by the honour of the perfection of Prophethood and pure Muhammadanism, and was brought forth from the subjective views (*iʿtibārāt*) of unity, unification and identity toward complete annihilation, and was gratified by the ending of individuality and (outward) traces, and was exalted to 'remaining in God'; and after the ascent I was sent toward the descent, and the door of Divine Law was opened to me ... [*K* 400]

Thus writes Ḫwāǧā Mīr Dard of Delhi (1721–85), describing the mystical way which led him from his former state of intoxication and poetical exuberance to the quiet and sober attitude of a 'sincere Muhammadan' (*muḥammadī-yi ḫāliṣ*).[1] Mīr Dard—a contemporary of the great Nakšbandī saint Maẓhar Ǧānǧānān (d. 1781)[2] and of the religious reformer Šāh Walīullāh of Delhi (d. 1763)[3]—was the son of

1 Abbreviations: *K*, *ʿilm ul-kitāb* (1310 h); *N*, *Nāle-yi Dard*; *A*, *Āh-i sard*; *D*, *Dard-i dil*; *Š*, *Šamʿ—i maḥfil*, printed in one volume called *čahār risāla* (1310 h); *P*, *Persian Dīwān* (1309 h); *U*, *Urdu Dīwān*, ed. Dā'ūdī (1962). *NA*: *Nāle-yi ʿAndalīb* (1310). Every history of Urdu literature deals with Dard's Urdu poetry, thus de Tassy (1872), I: 408; Saksena (1927), pp. 55–9, Bailey (1932), Bausani (1958), Sadiq (1964), but none of them discusses the theological aspects or his Persian writings in detail. Cf. *Encyclopedia of Islam*, second edition, s.c. Dard; Schimmel, 'Khwājā Mīr Dard; in *German Scholars on India* (1973), and *id.*, 'Mir Dards Gedanken über das Verhältnis von Mystik und Wort', in *Festgabe deutscher Iranisten zur 2500-Jahrfeier Irans*, ed. Eilers (1971). The most detailed biography is that written by a descendant of Dard, Firāḳ, *Maiḫāne-yi Dard* (1344 h).

2 De Tassy, II: 297; Saksena, pp. 49–51; Bailey, No. 102; Bausani, p. 131; Sadiq, p. 81*f.*

3 *A History of Freedom Movement* I (1957), 492*ff.*; Qureshi, *The Muslim Community of the Indo-Pakistan Subcontinent* (1962), chapter IX; Bausani, 'Note su Shāh Walīullāh di Dehli', *Ann. dell Ist. Univ. Orientaie di Napoli*, new series (1961).

Muḥammad Nāṣir ʿAndalīb (1697–1758), whose family, Sayyids from Turkestan, had close relations with the Mughal court. Muḥammad Nāṣir's *pīr-i ṣoḥbat* was Šāh Saʿdullāh Gulšan (d. 1728),[4] a member of the Nakšbandīya, but more famous as a poet than as a mystic; he had been instrumental in the early development of Urdu poetry in Delhi. His love of music, contrary to the stern Nakšbandī attitude, was inherited by both Nāṣir ʿAndalīb and his son Mīr Dard. ʿAndalib's second mystical master was Pīr Muḥammad Zubair, the fourth and last *kayyūm* from the family of Aḥmad Sirhindī, the great Nakšbandī reformer of India and defender of phenomenological monism (*waḥdat aš-šuhūd*) (d. 1624).[5] Traces of Aḥmad Sirhindī's *kayyūmīya* doctrine can be found in some of Mīr Dard's statements about his own exalted rank in the hierarchy of the faithful (cf. *K* 426).[6] When Pīr Zubair died in February 1740 (a few months after Nādir Šāh's merciless plundering of Delhi), Nāṣir ʿAndalīb composed a vast Persian work, *nāle-yi ʿAndalīb, The Lamentation of the Nightingale*, which consists of a conglomerate of mystical allegories and theological, legal and philosophical discourses, often abstrusely connected, and interspersed with charming stories and verses. Mīr Dard considered this book (which his father had dictated to him) the highest expression of mystical wisdom, the source book for the teachings of the 'Muhammadan path'.[7]

For Muḥammad Nāṣir had been blessed—*c.* 1734—by a vision of the Prophet's grandson Ḥasan ibn ʿAlī, who had introduced him into the secrets of the true Muhammadan path (*aṭ-ṭarīka al-Muḥammadīya*, *K* 85). Young Dard—at that time about thirteen years old—became his first disciple and spent the rest of his life propagating the doctrine of

4 Saʿdullāh Gulšan had attracted the Urdu poet Walī Dekkanī to Delhi; through his work Urdu poetry was introduced to the north of India. Dard mentions (*A* 257) that Gulšan had composed 200,000 verses in Persian. Cf. Aṣlaḥ, *taḏkira-yi šuʿarā-yi Kašmīr*, ed. Rashdi (1346 š), *A*, No. 220.

5 Faruqi, *The Mujaddid's Conception of tauḥīd, id* (1940); *The Mujaddid's Conception of God* (1952); Ahmad, 'Religious and political ideas of Shaikh Aḥmad Sirhindī', *Rivista degli studi orientali* XXXVI (1961).

6 About the *kayyūm*, cf. Subhan, *Sufism: its Saints and Shrines* (1960), chapter xx. Discussed in detail by Ikrām, *Rūd-i kauṯar* (1969), based on Abū'l-Faiḍ Ḫwāǧā Kamāluddīn's Persian *rauḍat al-qayyūmiya* (unpublished). Cf. *Maiḫāne*, p. 42.

7 Cf. the *rubāʿī, P* 113: 'I do not read the *ʿawārif* [*al-maʿārif* by Abū Ḥafṣ Suhrawardī] nor the *futūḥat* or *fuṣūṣ* [*al-ḥikam*, by Ibn ʿArabī]—the *Nāle-yi ʿAndalīb* became my special litany'. Cf. *K* 38, 88, 90, and often *N* 65, 103; *D* 216.

'sincere Muhammadanism'. He succeeded his father in 1758, and never left Delhi despite the unending tribulations which befell the unlucky capital of the crumbling Mughal empire during the later eighteenth century. Besides instructing a considerable number of poets in Urdu poetry,[8] Dard was a prolific writer in Persian. His main work, the voluminous *ʿilm ul-kitāb* (1770), gives a detailed account both of his religious teachings and of his mystical experiences. The similarity of his religious views, as well as of his 'spiritual autobiography', with the viewpoints of the Egyptian Šādilī mystic aš-Šaʿrānī (d. 1565), as given in the latter's *laṭāʾif al-minan*,[9] is amazing. Essentially, Dard's *ʿilm ul-kitāb* was conceived as a commentary on the 111 *wāridāt* (short poems and prose pieces which 'descended' upon him during the 1750s),[10] but it has grown into an independent work of 111 chapters, each of them headed by the words *Yā Nāṣir*—thus alluding to his father's name as well as to a title of the Prophet and to one of God's Most Beautiful Names. Between 1775 and 1785 Dard composed the 'Four *risālas*', stylistically beautiful spiritual diaries; each of them comprises 341 aphorisms, again in reverence to his father, the numerical value of whose name, *Nāṣir*, is 341. Dard's Persian verses are scattered throughout his work, and have been collected in a little *dīwān*; his best known work, the small collection of Urdu poetry, is of exquisite beauty.

Dard was extremely proud of his rank as 'first of the Muhammadans', and his main aim was to draw as many people as possible into the Muhammadan path; once he relates how he succeeded in bringing his whole family under the protection of the Prophet and of his father (*K* 418).[11] The *ṭarīḳa Muḥammadīya* was, for him, the 'sect that is saved', whereas the seventy-two other sects are doomed to damnation (*K* 589);[12] and just as logic is the servant of all kinds of sciences, thus

8 Among Dard's disciples in poetry we may mention his brother and successor *Aṯar* (cf. Sadiq, pp. 107*ff*.) and his son *Alam*. Muslims and Hindus alike are found among his students; his friendship with the greatest Urdu love poet, Mīr Taqī Mīr, is well known (cf. Russell and Islam, *Three Mughal Poets* [1967], p. 56).

9 About Šaʿrānī, cf. Trimingham, *The Sufi Orders in Islam* (1971), p. 220; Brockelmann, *Geschichte der arabischen Literatur* II: 335 and supplements.

10 About the *wāridat*, cf. Schimmel, 'Yunus Emre', *Numen* VIII (1961), and *id*, '*Mir Dard's Gedanken . . .*'

11 The ideals of this *tarīḳa* are often described in detail, cf. *K* 90, 597, 578 (in Arabic).

12 About the seventy-two sects, proverbial in Persian poetry, cf. Watt, 'The great community and the sects', in *Theology and Law in Islam*, ed. von Grunebaum (1971), p. 26.

kalām, philosophy and mystical knowledge are merely servants of the *tarīḳa Muḥammadīya*, which is higher and subtler than anything else (*K* 157). For—as Dard says, with an allusion to the classical tripartition *šarīʿa–ṭarīḳa–ḥaḳīḳa*,[13] the *ḥaḳīḳa Muḥammadīya* (the pre-eternal reality of Muḥammad as the first individuation) is higher than all the other individuations; therefore the *šarīʿa Muḥammadīya* supersedes every other law, and the *ṭarīḳa Muḥammadīya* is, logically, the best and most comprehensive path leading to salvation (*K* 64; cf. 376, 380). To be sure, a number of religious leaders in the later eighteenth and early nineteenth centuries—like the Idrīsīya–Sanūsīya affiliations in North Africa[14] and especially Aḥmad Brēlwī in India[15]—had called their *ṭarīḳas* 'Muḥammadīya', and the veneration of the Prophet was their central aim; however it will be difficult to find a statement like Dard's words:

Humanity consists of Muhammadanism,

so that someone who is not a Muhammadan remains outside the fold of the faithful; he is, so to speak, not a human being at all, but intrinsically worse than an animal, as is proved by the Ḳur'ānic word 'They are like beasts' (*sūra* 7: 178; 25: 46) (*K* 432).

The 'sincere Muhammadan' will be qualified by the qualifications of the four caliphs, as Dard's father says (*NA* I: 430, 435), and the Prophet himself grants his companions, friends and disciples all the degrees of the stages of proximity, like the 'proximity to the perfections of Prophethood', of vicegerency, of wisdom, etc, according to the degree of their annihilation in him, their association with him, their dependence upon him etc (*NA* II: 335).

But how to become a 'sincere Muhammadan' and thus reach salvation? Dard, following his father's fundamentalism, sees in the *ṭarīḳā Muḥammadīya* nothing but the perfect reliance upon Ḳur'ānic and Prophetic traditions. He stresses, thus, the importance of the five pillars

13 Nicholson, *Commentary to the Maṯnawī of Ǧalāluddīn Rūmī*, VIII, 225, quotes the alleged *ḥadīṯ*: 'the *šarīʿa* are my words (*aḳwālī*) and the *ṭarīḳa* my actions (*aʿmālī*) and the *ḥaḳīḳa* my state (*ḥālī*)'. This *ḥadīṯ* forms the basis of the seventeenth century Malay mystic Ḥamza Fanṣūrī's *šarāb al-ʿašiqīn*: see al-Attas, *The Mysticism of Ḥamza Fanṣurī* (1970), pp. 416*ff.*

14 Cf. Trimingham, *op. cit.*, pp. 116*ff.*

15 Cf. *A History of Freedom Movement* I, pp. 556*ff.*; Ahmad, *Studies in Islamic Culture in the Indian Environment* (1964), pp. 210*ff.*; Qureshi, *op. cit.*, p. 196; Trimingham, *op. cit.*, p. 129. The comprehensive Urdu biography is Mehr, *Sayyid Aḥmad Šahīd*, two volumes (s.d.).

of faith; among them, prayer and fasting play, as for most mystics, the greatest role. Even though later accounts of his permanent fasting and the strict observance of supererogatory fasting practices may be slightly exaggerated Dard's whole attitude is, basically, ascetic.[16] But even more important than fasting is, for him, the ritual prayer; since, according to the Prophet's saying, 'ritual prayer is the ascension of the faithful'.[17] It is worth remembering that Dard wrote his first book, at the age of fifteen, about the *Secrets of Prayer*.[18]

Throughout his work, Mīr Dard has many allusions to the classical ways of education of the adept in the Nakšbandī tradition. There are, of course, differences in the mystical ways: some schools begin with the education of the lower soul—the 'greater holy war' (*K* 533); others with the purification of the heart; but since the mystical path is considered a cyclical movement, either way is useful (*K* 534). The disciple has to know that

Evil is what the religious law declares as evil. [*K* 432]

and that this world is the seed-bed for the other world (*K* 526):[19]

Each of our actions is like a rose or a thorn which we plant for ourselves. [*K* 98]

Eating, drinking, dressing are subject to detailed rules (*K* 521*ff.*; cf. the classical handbooks on Ṣūfī education).[20] Perfect trust in God, *tawakkul*, is basic for the disciple,[21] but if he experiences mental discomfort

16 Regarding Dard's ascetic practices, such as fasting for twenty-one days and nights without interruption, cf. *Maiḫāne*, p. 121.

17 Cf. Hug̃wīrī, *kašf al-maḥg̃ūb*, trans. Nicholson (1959), p. 302.

18 Lithographed together with Ahmad Sirhindī's *mabda' ū ma'ād*, on pp. 69–92 (s.d.).

19 This well known *ḥadīṯ* is elaborated by Gazzali, *Iḥyā' 'ulūm ad-dīn* IV, 123. Cf. McKane, *Al-Ghazali's Book of Fear and Hope* (1962); Furūzānfar, *Aḥādīṯ-i maṯnawī* (1334 s), p. 112, No. 338. Rumi says, more poetically, 'Sugar-cane will never grow when someone plants coloquints.' (*Dīwān-i kabīr*, ed. Furūzānfar (1336 š), No. 1337.)

20 Cf. Hujwīrī, *ed. cit.*, p. 42: 'Sufism consists entirely of behaviour . . .' (*Abū* Ḥafṣ Ḥaddād), and the relevant rules, *id.*, chapter XXIII. Every handbook of Sufism contains such rules. Among the independent works the most famous examples are: Abū Nag̃īb as-Suhrawardī, *ādāb al-murīdīn*; Abū'l-Mafāḫir Yaḥya al-Baḫarzī al-Kubrāwī, *aurād al-aḥbāb wa fuṣūṣ al-ādāb*, ed. Afšar (1347 s). Cf. Meier, 'Ein Knigge für Sufis' in *Scritti in onore di Giuseppe Furlani* (1957).

21 Cf. Reinert, *Die Lehre vom tawakkul in der klassischen Sufik* (1968).

during his attempt to rely absolutely upon God's gifts, he had better earn his livelihood and follow the advice:

Bind your camel's knees notwithstanding your trust in God. [*K* 241, 243][22]

Dard knowns the importance of *ḳabḍ*, the state of constraint, since

the stronger the compression the larger the expansion [*basṭ*]. [*K* 124]

Former masters had regarded the complete surrender to God in the state of *ḳabḍ* as preferable to the joyful expansion of the self in *basṭ*.[23] Over and over again patience is recommended:

Complaint and lament are calamities, patience and constancy are blessings and causes of salvation. [*K* 552].

As to the dichotomy of the states of *ṣabr*, patience, and *šukr*, gratitude, so often discussed by the early Ṣūfīs,[24] Dard links them exclusively with their primary cause, not with the world:

The sincere Muhammadans keep the antimony of 'The sight did not rove' (*sūra* 53: 17) before their eyes and do not care so much for the benefits and afflictions of this world as to connect their gratitude and patience with them. [*K* 346]

One of the requirements of the path, especially among the Naḳšbandīs, is *ṣoḥbat*, the conversation with the master, which guarantees not only a perpetual control of the disciple's progress but the constant flow of spiritual energy from the *šaiḫ* to the *murīd*. For, according to the *ḥadīṯ*, 'Religion consists in giving good advice'.[25] In rare cases the perusal of the master's books can be substitued for oral *ṣoḥbat*[26] (*K* 499; cf. 431).

The result of the whole 'journey', of devotions and recollections, is that the heart becomes free from all besides God, and is made ready for constant pre-

22 Quotation from Rūmī, *Maṯnawī* I: 912; cf. *Aḥādīṯ-i māṯnawī*, p. 10, No. 20.

23 The positive value of *ḳabḍ* is particularly stressed in the mystical theories of Ibn ʿAbbād of Ronda (cf. Nwyia, *Ibn ʿAbbad of Ronda* [1961]) since *ḳabḍ* means to be completely passive in God's hands.

24 For the different attitudes of early Sufis in the question of patience and gratitude, see Massignon, *La Passion d'al-Ḥallāj* (1922), p. 777; and almost every manual of Sufism.

25 *Aḥādīṯ-i maṯnawī*, p. No. 282.

26 Cf. Baqlī, *Sharḥ ash-shaṭḥīyāt*, ed. Corbin (1966), Section 159: 'The company [*ṣuḥbat*] of the gnostic is the spring-time of the Other World.' The rest of the sentence is not completely clear; the meaning amounts to: for the cool breeze from the highest realm manifests itself in his [?] breath.

sence and vision,[27] so that it keeps in its hand the thread of patience in affliction through contentment with fate, [the thread] of enduring distasteful events, and that of the strength to refrain from carnal desires. [*K* 307]

On the path different kinds of revelation (*kašf*) can be experienced. (1) *kašf kaunī*, as a result of asceticism, pious actions and purification of the lower soul; it becomes manifest in dreams and clairvoyance (2) *kašf ilāhī*, a fruit of constant worship and polishing of the heart, which results in the knowledge of the world of spirits and cardiognosy. (3) *kašf ʿaḳlī*, which can be reached by polishing the moral faculties, and can be experienced by the philosophers as well.[28] (4) *kašf īmānī* is the fruit of perfect faith, after man's acquiring proximity to the perfections of prophethood; then he is blessed by direct divine addresses; he talks with the angels, meets the spirits of the prophets, sees the Night of Might and the blessings of Ramaḍān in human form in the *ʿālam al-miṯāl* . . . (*K* 443).[29]

Miracles will occur to the wayfarer; they are real and true, but

miracles are the menstruation of men [*K* 449][30]

---

27 *K* 113: 'Presence is general, vision is special. When the traveller feels at every moment God's presence, he eventually reaches the "general" or "smaller" sanctity, and the illuminations of the actions come into his heart. When he, then, lives constantly in proximity to God and speaks with him without mediator, the stage of special sanctity can be granted to him, and the illuminations of the attributes dwell in his heart; he then loses himself in constant contemplation, like the angels. Here is the state of the sincere Muhammadan.' Cf. *K* 565. For the different illuminations, cf. the examples given by Nicholson, *Studies in Islamic Mysticism* (1921), p. 85.

28 *Kasf ʿaḳlī*, 'intellectual intuition', is reached through 'polishing of the moral faculties', *tahḏīb al-aḫlāḳ*—one wonders whether the title of Sir Sayyid Aḥmad Khan's (d. 1898) famous modernist journal, *tahḏīb ul-aḫlāḳ*, should have been chosen as an allusion to this 'intellectual illumination'.

29 Cf. Corbin, *Terre céleste et corps de résurrection* (1961); Rahman, 'Dream, imagination, and "*ālam al-mitāl*"', in *The Dream and Human Society*, ed. von Grunebaum and Caillois (1966). The vision of the *lailat ul-ḳadr*, the 'night of might' (*sūra* 97), as filled with light is often described in early hagiography. Cf. Šīrāzī, *Sīrat-i Ibn-i Ḫafīf-i Širāzī*, ed. Schimmel (1955), chapter x, §§ 12, 13.

30 This rather coarse statement is probably a corollary to a classical Sufi saying: *ṭālib-i maulā muḏakkar* . . . 'He who seeks the Lord is male, he who seeks the other world is a eunuch, and he who seeks this world is female': those who display their miracles are still dependent upon the applause of this world and are thus 'females', with all their impurities. Al-Attas *op. cit.*, p. 414, explains this saying, which is quoted in Ḥamza Fanṣūri's *asrār al-ʿarifīn*, that God avoids mystical union with those who perform miracles just as men avoid

for the friends of a king will never divulge the secrets he entrusts to them. Dervishdom does not consist of astrology and geomancy (*K* 447), but many of the contemporary *šaiḫs* are nothing but 'religious shopkeepers' (K 445).

Dard often attacks those who remain in the state of *sukr*, intoxication; overwhelmed by their mystical states, they

sing tunes which ought not to be sung. [*K* 284] [31]

For in the state of *sukr* the mystic experiences not a complete annihilation but only the *ḳurb an-nawāfil* (*K* 250) which is expressed in the famous *ḥadīṯ*:

... My servant doth not cease to draw nigh unto Me by voluntary works of devotion [*nawāfil*] until I love him, and when I love him, I am his ear, so that he hears by Me, and his eye, so that he sees by Me, and his tongue, so that he speaks by Me, and his hand, so that he takes by Me.[32]

Much higher is the state reached by the *ḳurb al-farā'iḍ*, the proximity of the legally prescribed actions, for this is the state of the Prophet, which is higher than that of the saints (*NA* 1: 272).

Dard knows from experience that the 'children of the Path' usually go through a period of intoxication when they reach 'adolescence', i.e. the middle stages of the path, and then they want to talk without restraint about love and union; but when they mature, i.e. come down

---

intercourse with a menstruating woman. The saying *Ṭalib-al-maulā* is known to me only from Indo-Muslim sources, although the classification of people interested in anything besides God among the 'effeminate' (who serve as male prostitutes) goes back to classical Sufism (cf. the stories about Shiblī in ʿAṭṭār's work, see Ritter, *Das Meer der Seele* [1955], p. 140). The mystical poet of Delhi in the late thirteenth century, Jamāl Hānswī, used to say:

He who seeks the world is ignorant [*jāhil*].
He who seeks the other world is intelligent [*ʿāḳil*].
He who seeks the Lord is perfect [*kāmil*].

the same with the rhyming attributes 'rejected' (*mardūd*) 'happy' (*masʿūd*) and 'praiseworthy' (*maḥmūd*), and with the attributes 'in perdition' (*hālik*), 'true wayfarer' (*sālik*), 'ruling' (*mālik*). Ahmad, *India's Contribution to Arabic Literature* [1968], p. 82.)

31 This is the expression used by ʿAbdulḳādir Gīlānī about Ḥallāǧ; cf. al-Ḥallāǧ, *kitāb aṭ-ṭawāsīn*, ed. Massignon (1914), p. 180.

32 The *ḥadīt* about the *ḳurb an-nawāfil* was very popular since early Sufism, cf. as-Sarrāǧ, *kitāb al-lumaʿ fi't-taṣawwuf*, ed. Nicholson (1914), p. 383; *Aḥādīṯ-i maṯnawī*, p. 18, No. 42.

in the circle of the path, they become moderate, and in old age, when the circle is completed, they prefer silence (*K* 127).

Dard often speaks of the cyclic movement of the mystic:

> Commencement and termination are one in our circle,
> We are the line of the compasses—our end is our beginning. [P 27]

This movement is connected, in his theological view, with the figure of the *šaiḫ*, not, as we would imagine, with a return to the primordial source of life in God.[33]

The Ṣūfī orders have always stressed the importance of the mystical leader without whom a steady progress on the path is impossible, and who exerts complete power over the *murīd*, who was in his hands like the corpse in the washerman's hand. *Fanā' fī'š-šaiḫ*, annihilation in the mystical guide, was, therefore, considered necessary for the *murīd*.[34] Dard underlines the importance of the *pīr* more than his predecessors:

> God's custom is to bring spiritual bounty from the living to the living.[35]

and even Uways al-Ḳaranī,[36] known as 'Ṣūfī without *šaiḫ*', was spiritually connected with the Prophet and received his initiation into the

33 Cf. *NA* I: 520: 'The end is the return to the beginning; the prophets have completed the circles of ascent and descent and rest in their natural centre.' The idea is often expressed in classical Sufism, but there 'the circle of existence begins and ends in God, is traversed by the soul in its downward journey through the intelligences, the spheres and the elements and then upward again, stage by stage—mineral, vegetable, animal and man—like as Perfect man, it completes its whole evolution and is reunited with the divine Soul of the world.' (Nicholson, *Commentary on Rūmī's Maṯnawī* VII, p. 10; cf. *ibid., pp.* 118, 220; *ibid.*, p. 140—another statement closer to that of Dard:
'The mystic . . . must rise from self negation to positive and active consciousness of life in God, return to the world and make God manifest by his words.')
Still closer to Dard's position is that of a late Turkish Naḳšbandī mystic: 'Our lowest way is the ascent from creation towards God, our highest way is the descent from God to creation.' (Şuşud, *Islam tasavvufunda Hacegân Hânedani* [1958], p. 161.)

34 The praise of the *šaiḫ* is commonplace in mystical literature; Rūmī goes so far as to declare, 'Infidel [*kāfir*] is he who has no faith in the *šaiḫ*.' (*Maṯnawī* II: 3325.) According to the alleged *ḥadīṯ*, 'He who has no *šaiḫ* is Satan.' (*Aḥādīṯ-i maṯnawī*, p. 30, No. 73.)

35 Early Sufis explain this word differently: knowledge must be received from 'the One who dieth not' (*Commentary on Rūmī's Maṯnawī* VIII, 56), not from a human master who is bound to die.

36 Uwais al-Ḳaranī, a contemporary of the Prophet in Yaman, never met him but was attracted to Islam and is, for most of the Sufis, the prototype of the

path through him; direct illumination is impossible—either it happens after the initiation or the mystic, after his first experience, seeks a master to guide him further (*K* 638).

The *šaiḫ* is in his group like the prophet in his people [*K* 60][37]

and the office of the *šaiḫ* is vicegerency of the prophecy, and thus not available to every saint (*K* 451). In Dard's case the association with the *šaiḫ* was even closer than usual. In general, the *šaiḫ* was considered the spiritual father of the disciple[38]—for Dard, his own father was at the same time his *šaiḫ*, and, as true Sayyid and 'Prince of the Muhammadans', blessed with the closest possible relation with the Prophet, with hereditary charisma. That leads him to develop his theory of ascent and descent in a form which was, as he complains, not accepted by his fellow mystics. He begins, naturally, with the *fanā' fī'š-šaiḫ*, which leads to the *fanā' fī'r-rasūl*, the annihilation in the Prophet, and culminates in the *fanā' fī Allāh*, annihilation in God, which, then, may turn into *baqā' billāh*, 'remaining in God', i.e. constant life in God. This *baqā'* is, however, also the first step on the way down:

anā' in God is directed toward God, and *baqā'* in God is directed toward creation, and one calls the most perfect wayfarer him who comes down more than others, and then again gets firmly established in the *baqā'* in the Prophet, and he who is on this descendant rank is called higher and more exalted than he who is still in ascent, for the end is the return to the beginning . . . But higher than he who has reached this stage is he who has found *baqā'* in his *šaiḫ*, for he has completed the whole circle. This is the terminating rank which God Almighty has kept for the pure Muhammadans whereas the others with all their power cannot be honoured by it . . . [*K* 115–16]

This experience was, of course, born out of Dard's extremely close relation with his own father, and could not be shared by anybody else; nevertheless, even if it were acceptable outside his own mystical path, we would prefer to see here not a cyclical but a spiral movement, since the disciple's relation with the *šaiḫ* in the first and last stages is experienced on completely different levels.

---

mystic who has not formally been initiated. Dard underlines, with his statement, that Islamic mysticism is based upon initiation. Cf. Meier, *Vom Wesen der islamischen Mystik* (1943): 'Die islamische Ordensmystik ist eine Initiation' (p. 16).

37 *Aḥādīṯ- maṯnawī*, p. 82, No. 224.

38 Cf. Ibn 'Arabī: 'The *murīd* is the son of the *šaiḫ*' (quoted in Andrae, *Die Person Muhammads in Glaube und Lehre seiner Gemeinde* [1917], pp. 371*f.*).

In his theories of ascent and descent Dard does not explicitly describe —as his father and many others had done—the 'journey towards God' as man's ascension to the rank of that divine name which is his Lord, *rabb* (*NA* I: 271), since every creature is *marbūb*, the passive correlation of one of the active divine names (the Prophet Muḥammad being the *marbūb* of the name Allāh, *K* 110).[39] Dard discusses God's Most Beautiful Names in a longish chapter (*K* 196*ff.*);[40] he first explains, in Arabic, their essence, then, in Persian, their relation to the creation, for

It is the light of the Names which illuminates creation. [*P* 76]

In the true Ṣūfī tradition, the sincere Muhammadans should recite the divine names every morning and evening, meditate upon their meanings, and, in case of need, invoke that name which is fitting for that peculiar occasion (*K* 201).[41] All the manifold names, however, point to the divine unity (*K* 217).

Meditation of the divine names is not the only method of *ḏikr* taught by Dard (cf. *K* 161*ff.*). In fact, constant *ḏikr* is, for him, the very centre of religious life (cf. *K* 624*f.*), the safest way that leads to Presence and vision.

And when one says *lā ilāha illā Allāh*—There is no deity save God—one should think in one's heart *lā maʿbūd illā Allāh*—There is no object of worship save Him—and *lā maqṣūd illā Allāh*—There is no object of desire save Him [*K* 624]

and

the most innermost of the innermost is *lā mauǧūd illā Allāh*—There is nothing existent save God

as he adds once (*K* 132), uttering thus the profession of faith of the monists whom he otherwise attacks so mercilessly.

39 Cf. Corbin, *Creative Imagination in the Sufism of Ibn ʿArabi* (1969), about the problem of *rabb* and *marbūb*, and the divine names, p. 120*ff.*

40 A good introduction into the importance of the ninety-nine Most Beautiful Divine Names, so central in Sufism, is Nicholson, *Studies in Islamic Mysticism*, p. 93.

41 The permanent recollection of the divine names is mentioned also by Dard's father, *NA* II: 108. About the importance of the letter *h*, *cf. Meier*, *Vom Wesen der islamischen Mystik*, p. 30, notes 16 and 17. A useful booklet about the qualities of the divine names as to be used in *ḏikr* is Ibn ʿAṭāʾullāh, *miftāḥ al-falāḥ wa miṣbāḥ al-arwāḥ* (1961). Dard even explains the well known *ḥadīṯ taḫallaqū bi'aḫlāq Allāh* ('Acquire the qualities of God') as 'Acquire the divine names' (*K* 217), name and attribute being for him interchangeable.

Dard teaches, in the Nakšbandī tradition, the *ḏikr* of the five *laṭā'if* (*K* 112), the spiritual centres of man, and develops, in the 110th *wārid* (*K* 637), his theories in a detailed Arabic description. He discerns the *ḏikr ḳalbī*, located in the heart, at the left side of the breast, pronounced in love and longing, the *ḏikr rūḥī*, performed at the right side of the breast in quietude and tranquillity; the *ḏikr sirrī*, pronounced in intimacy, close to the left side of the breast, the *ḏikr ḫafawī*, performed close to the right corner of the breast and connected with absence and extinction of the self, and the *ḏikr aḫfawī*, in the centre of the breast, which is the sign of annihilation and consummation. The *ḏikr* is, then, extended to the brain in perfect contentment (*ḏikr nafsī*, connected with the *nafs ḳaddīsa*, the sanctified soul)[42] and eventually permeates the whole being (*ḥaḳīḳa insānīya*), body and soul, when man reaches perfect recollectedness and peace—this is the *ḏikr sulṭānī*. The source of all recollection is love (*K* 637);[43] but, as Dard states (*K* 132), constant practice is required to attain the highest stage of *ḏikr*, which is a medicine for the soul—the physician, too, does not learn from books alone but has to practise his art. (Medical terminology is often applied to the mystics' psychological progress in Ṣūfī literature.)[44]

A peculiar description of *ḏikr* and meditation as given by Dard's father is worth quoting here (*NA* 1: 270):

He sees the blessed figure of the word *Allāh* الله in the colour of light written on the tablet of his heart and the mirror of his imagination . . . Then he will understand himself opposite to this form or beneath it or at its right or left side, and he should strive to bring himself towards this light . . . And whenever he finds himself in the middle of the rank of *alif* and *lām*, he must proceed and take his place between the two *lāms*, and then walk away from there, and bring himself between the *lām* and the *hā'*; and with high ambition he leaves this place too and sees himself in the middle of the ringlet of the *hā'*. At the beginning

42 The *nafs ḳaddīsa*, 'sanctified soul', is added to the classical stages of the *nafs* as built upon the *Kur'ānic* expressions *nafs ammāra* (*sūra* 12: 53), the lower soul, which incites evil, the *nafs lawwāma* (*sūra* 72: 5), the 'blaming soul', and the *nafs muṭma'inna* (*sūra* 89: 27), the soul at peace.

43 The close connection between recollection and love has always been highlighted by the Sufis, for 'man likes to mention the object of his love' (Sarrāǧ, *kitāb al-luma'*, p. 58; cf. *sūra* 33: 41). For Dard, love includes love of the Prophet and his family; cf. the last chapter of *K*, 637*ff*.

44 Cf., for example, Ibn Ḳayyim al-Gauziyya, *aṭ-ṭibb an-nabawī*: Muḥammad as physician of the heart. Rūmī often uses the image of love as physician, as Galen or speaks of the Universal Reason as embodied in the perfect mystical guide in terms of a physician of souls.

of his journeying will he find his head in this ringlet; but eventually he will find that his whole self has found repose in this house and will rest there free from all affliction and perilous calamities, and will find God as the Surrounding, and himself as the surrounded one.

This is a perfect interpretation of the highest goal of the Naḳšbandī mystic: not an intoxicated immersion in the godhead, but vision, contemplation of the eternal Light, surrounded by this Light but not lost in it, just as the pearl is in the ocean and yet distinct from it (*U* 52). This true confession of unity (*at-tauḥīd al-Muḥammadī*), according to Dard,

is immersion in the contemplation of God along with preservation of the stages of servantship [*ʿabdiyat*]. [*K* 609]

Dard frequently attacks those 'imperfect Ṣūfīs' who claim 'in their immature minds' to be confessors of Unity, but are in fact entangled in a sort of heresy, believing in *waḥdat al-wuǧūd*, ontological monism. Real *tauḥīd*, as he sees it,

is the essence of faith, and without it salvation from the punishments of the other world is as impossible as escape from worldly concerns. One has to accept everything as coming from God, and should exclaim in words and by one's whole attitude 'There is no power and strength save in God'. [*K* 595]

Faithful to the Naḳšbandī tradition, Dard repeatedly stresses the fact that 'man is man, God is God' (cf. *U* 143); for no state nobler than that of servantship (*ʿabdiyat*) is conceivable, nor any delight greater than the contemplation of one's Lord—union or unification on the level of divinity is impossible and purely imaginative (*K* 62*f.*). Was not the Prophet himself proud of being called *ʿabduhū*, 'His servant', during the exalted experience of his ascension (*sūra* 17: 1)?[45]

Vision of the all-penetrating divine Light in which all human faculties become united—that is Dard's whole hope and goal:

This place is the state of seeing, not of understanding; for the Prophet has said, 'O God, show me the reality of things as they are'[46] and not 'Make me undertand things . . .' [*K* 118]

---

45 This traditional Naḳšbandi viewpoint has found its most poetical expression in Muḥammad Iḳbal's *Ǧāvidnāme* (1932), 'Sphere of Jupiter', where the question of prophetology is discussed; cf. the translation by Arberry (1966), p. 99, and Schimmel, *Gabriel's Wing* (1963), p. 157.

46 *Aḥādīṯ-i Maṯnawī*, p. 45, No. 116.

Here lies also the difference between Moses, who was denied vision, and Muḥammad, who was blessed with vision (*K* 229), as the mystics had said so often.[47] And Dard prays accordingly (*D* 29):

. . . as much as here the act of 'Verily God created Adam in His image' is permanently the mirror-bearer of manifestation, yet the putting on of the veil of 'Sight does not reach Him' (*sūra* 6: 103) is likewise necessary for the Beloved's coquetry . . . Thou must not give these Muhammadans the blunt answer 'Thou shalt not see me' (*sūra* 7: 139) but put before the members of the community of Thy beloved the table of the royal food 'And he saw what he saw' . . .

To see Thee was the object of life—
When Thou art not found—then, what is life? [*U* 120]

O God, since Thou hast given an eye, show us Reality, for the object of the eye is seeing, and since Thou hast opened the door of seeking, open also the gate of arriving, for the goal of searching is reaching, and an eye which is not honoured by the vision on Unity is like a squinting eye . . . [*D* 117]

To be sure, God is the 'Beyond the Beyond', as Dard often calls him. He is the Necessary and Absolute who reflects his attributes in the contingent existences, thus endowing them with existence, so that creation can be compared to a broken mirror:

Just as in the particles of a broken mirror the One form is reflected, thus the beauty of the real Unity of existence is reflected in the different apparent ranks of beings [*K* 217]

i.e. the one divine Light is reflected in the different colours of created beings (*K* 170). Dard feels that the best way of describing this Absolute Existence at all is to apply to him a Ḳur'ānic name—not to call him *wuǧūd*, 'existence', a term invented by later generations, but 'Light', *nūr* (cf. *sūra* 24: 35).[48] It is this name under which God has revealed Himself to the Muhammadans, for

God brings you from the darknesses to the Light, e.g. brings you who are contingent quiddities [*māhiyāt*] from non-existence into existence. [*K* 107][49]

47 *NA* II: 129 explains that *īmān šuhūdī*, 'faith in vision', is the prerogative of the saints, whereas the normal faithful practice is *īmān bi'l-ġaib*, faith in the unseen.

48 Cf. Khan, *Glimpses of Medieval Indian Culture* (1959), p. 66; Schimmel, *Gabriel's Wing*, p. 100. Dard's father, too, blames the Sufis who invent so many useless and meaningless names for God, like Absolute Existence, Essential Unicity, Pure Being, etc (*NA* I: 251).

49 This description is given under the heading 'Technical terms of the Muhammadans' and refers to Ghazili's *miškāt al-anwār*; cf. Gairdner's translation of

The concept of God as Light—not of light as the first divine manifestation—allows Dard an elaboration of his theories of contemplation and vision, although he does not develop a range of colour experiences.[50] Once the self is negated the mystical path will lead man to that light which is the path of salvation;[51] eventually, light will fill the world from the Throne to the earth, and 'Whithersoever ye turn there is the Face of God' (*sūra* 2: 109, Dard's favourite Ḳur'ānic quotation),[52] and everything besides God will disappear, just as the stars become invisible in the overwhelming daylight (*K.* 309*f.*). Man, too, can become so

filled with this spiritual Light that the candle of his spirit is no longer veiled by the body's lampshade. [*N* 284]

Dard often craves, in his prayers, for more light,

a light that should enable me to see God's face everywhere, so that He may put me squatting [*murabbaʿ*, 'fourfold'] on the four cushions of the state 'I did not see anything without seeing God before it, with it, in it and behind it'. [*S* 29][53]

Since God is addressed as

the spring of the rose garden of *tanzīh* (exclusion of likeness with created things

---

the *miškāt* (1924) p. 53. The article 'Nur' in the *Shorter Encyclopedia of Islam* mainly discusses the aspects of light-mysticism, as developed by the Išrāḳī school.

50 About colour experiences on the mystical path cf. Fleischer, 'Über die farbigen Lichterscheinungen der Sufis', *Zeitschrift der Deutschen Morgenländischen Gesellschaft* XVI 16 (1863); and particularly Meier, *Die fawā'iḥ al-ǧamāl wa fawātiḥ al-ǧalāl des Naǧm ud-dīn al-Kūbrā* (1958), pp. 115*ff.*

51 Cf. the commentary of *sūra* 24: 35 in *K* 102*ff.* The danger is, as Dard points out, that the atom exclaims *ʿana'š-šams*, 'I am the sun' (like Ḥallāǧ's *anā'l-ḥaḳḳ*), 'but do not turn your head from the enclosure of atomhood and know that this sun is always present, looking towards you and manifesting itself upon you' (*ibid.*, 103).

52 This Ḳur'ānic verse, so pertinent to mystical feeling, occurs in Sufi poetry at least as early as in ʿAṭṭār's work (*Dīwān*, ed. Nafīsī [1339 s], *kaṣīda* 16, p. 50).

53 In a shorter form, attributed to the early Ṣūfī Muḥammad ibn Wāsiʿ, in Huǧwīrī, *kašf al-mahǧūb, ed. cit.*, pp. 91*f.*; a meditation upon it in Sanā'ī 'ṭarīḳ at-taḥḳīḳ', verses 561–91 (*Matnawīhā-yi Sanā'ī*, ed. Rażawī, [1348 š], pp. 121*f.*). Ḥamza Fanṣūrī makes each of the four Righteous Caliphs pronounce one part of the formula. Abū Bakr said, 'I did not see anything without seeing God before it'; ʿAlī said '. . . in it' etc. (Al-Attas, *op. cit.*, p. 265.)

who strangely plays in his manifestations in the rose parterre of *tašbīh* (likeness, anthropomorphism),

man should

from every form in this worldly rose bed pluck nothing except the rose of vision of God. [*A* 192]
Existence and non-existence are completely drunk from His wine-house,
Contingency and necessity are intoxicated by His goblet.
If your heart's eye is such that it sees Reality—
Then each atom of creation is a window of His house. [*P* 83]

Dard does not shun the imagery of traditional Persian poetry, e.g. the juxtaposition of faith and infidelity, Ka'ba and idol temple, when he prays (*A* 96):

We, beguiled by Thy perfect beauty, do not see in all the horizons anything but Thy open signs . . . [*sūra* 2: 109] The light of faith is a sign of coquetry from the manifestation of Thy face, and the darkness of infidelity is dressed in black from the shade of Thy tresses . . .

The one light behind the changing colours (cf. the great prayer, *K* 599) manifests itself in *madrasa* and convent, in the Kaʿba and the monastery, but

we, the guests, have seen Thee as the Master of the House [*U* 2]

from whom everything comes (*hama az ōst*, as contrasted to the monists' creed *hama ōst*, 'Everything is He').

It is typical that Dard's last words as noted down in the *šamʿ-i maḥfil* (*S.* 341), a few days before his death, are an Arabic prayer for light, as ascribed to the Prophet and often repeated in devotional literature.[54]

The equation God = Light is also helpful in elaborating the idea of the Light of Muḥammad, which had been invented in the early days of Islamic mysticism and can be observed in the works of Sahl at-Tustarī (d. 896) and Ḥallāğ (d. 922).[55] The *ḥaḳīḳa Muḥammadīya* as the first individuation is conceived as the dawn by which the

54 Cf. Farīd, *Prayers of Muhammad* (1959), p. 140; in Abū Talib al-Makki's *ḳūt al-ḳulūb* 1: 6 (cf. Smith, *Readings from the Mystics of Islam* [1950], No. 47).

55 Cf. Andrae, *Die Person Muhammads*, pp. 319*ff.*; a *ḥadīṯ* attributed to Muḥammad is 'The first thing that God created was my light . . .' (*Aḥādīṯ-i māṯnawī*, p. 113, No. 342.) There is a beautiful example in Ḥallāğ's *kitāb aṭ-ṭawāsīn*, ed. Massignon (1914), *ṭāsīn as-sirāğ*.

eternal divine Light becomes first visible in creation (*K* 111; *D* 203),[56] and

one must see the divine Beauty in the Muṣṭafian [= Muḥammad's] mirror

Hence the rays of the divine names enter the world, and are made manifest in man, who is the stage for the manifestation of the names and attributes (*K* 464), the microcosm reflecting the divine attributes (*K* 139), so that Dard can proudly address God:

Whatever we have heard of Thee, we have seen in man. [*U* 28][57]

For it is the heart of man in which God dwells rather than in heaven or earth (*A* 302), as Dard says, quoting a well known *ḥadīt ḳudsī*;[58] it is man who is

the seal of the degree of creation, for after him no species has come into existence and he is the sealing of the hand of Omnipotence, for God Most Exalted has said 'I created him with both my hands.'[59] He is, so to speak, the divine seal which has been put on the page of contingency, and the Greatest Name of God has become radiant from the bezel of his forehead. The *alif* of his stature points to God's unity, and the *ṭuġrā* of his composition, e.g. the absolute comprehensive picture of his eyes, is a *hā'* with two eyes which indicates divine ipseity (*hūwīya*). His mouth is the door of the treasure of divine mysteries which is open at the time of speaking, and he has a face which everywhere holds up the mirror of the face of God (*sūra* 2: 109), and he has an eyebrow for which the word 'We honoured the children of Adam' (*sūra* 17: 72) is valid . . . [*K* 422]

In fact,

Although Adam had not wings,
He has reached a place that was not destined even for angels [*U* 9]

It is this high rank of man which enables him to ascend through the stages of the prophets towards the proximity of Muḥammad,[60] and thus towards the *ḥaḳiḳa Muḥammadīya*, the first principle of individuation. Dard has experienced this way—as have a number of mystics

56 Rumi speaks of the 'quality of messenger [*rasūlī*] inherent in the dawn', *Dīwān-i kabīr*, No. 1480.

57 *K* 279 (Arabic): 'He created man according to His love and formed him in His image, and He looks at Him always with longing eyes just as the beautiful person looks with the view of yearning into the mirror in his hand.'

58 *Aḥādīt-i maṯnawī*, p. 26, No. 4.

59 Slightly changed from Ḳur'ān, *sūra* 38: 75.

60 The best introduction to the peculiarities of the prophets is Ibn 'Arabī's *fuṣūṣ al-ḥikam* (German translation, '*Die Ringsteine der Weisheit*' by Kofler, (1970]); cf. also *Commentary on Rūmī's Maṯnawī* VII, 361.

before him—and it may be interesting to give his spiritual autobiography in full (*K* 504*ff*.). He speaks—in the Arabic text—in the third person. After having discussed extensively the problem of the vicegerency of the Prophet, he continues:

And He made him his closest Friend [*ṣafī*] and his vicegerent on earth by virtue of the Adamic sanctity [*sūra* 2: 31 etc],

And God saved him from the ruses of the lower self and from Satan and made him His friend [*naǧī*] by virtue of the Noachic sanctity,

And God softened the heart of the unfeeling before him and sent to him people of melodies by virtue of the sanctity of David,[61]

He made him ruler of the kingdom of his body and his nature, by a manifest power, by virtue of the sanctity of Solomon,[62]

And God made him a friend [*ḫalīl*] and extinguished the fire of wrath in his nature so that it became 'cool and peaceful' (*sūra* 21: 70) by virtue of the Abrahamic sanctity;[63]

And God caused the natural passions to die and slaughtered his lower soul and made him pure from worldly concerns, so that he became completely cut off from this world and what is in it, and God honoured him with a mighty slaughtering [*sūra* 37: 107] in front of his mild father, and his father put the knife to his throat in one of the states of being drawn near to God in the beginning of his way, with the intention of slaughtering him for God, and God accepted him well, and thus he is really one who has been slaughtered by God and remained safe in the outward form, as his father gave him the glad tidings: 'Who ever has not seen a dead person wandering around on earth may look at this son of mine who lives through me and who moves through me'! In this state he gained the sanctity of Ishmael.

God beautified his nature and character and made him loved by Himself and accepted by His beloved [Muḥammad]; He attracted the hearts to him and cast love for him into his father's heart—a most intense love—, and he taught him the interpretation of prophetic traditions by virtue of the sanctity of Joseph [*sūra* 12: 45f.];

God talked to him in inspirational words when he called: 'Verily, I am God, put off the shoes [*sūra* 20: 12] of the relations with both worlds from the foot

61 David softened the iron (*sūra* 21: 80; 34: 10), he was the master of music (*sūra* 21: 79; 34: 10; 38: 17). Since Dard was very fond of music and *samāʿ* and had composed a book, *ḥurmat-i ġināʾ*, he had often to defend himself against the other Naḳšbandī leaders, since the *ṭarīḳa* does not approve of music. Cf. *N* 35; about his singing Indian ragas, cf. *Maiḫāne*, 147*f*.

62 Sulaimān is the ruler of men and *ǧinn*, cf. *sūra* 21: 84, 38: 37.

63 Nimrūd's fire into which Abraham was thrown is here spiritualised: God's grace has quenched the fire of Dard's wrath. One may think of the *ḥadīṯ*: 'Wrath is from Satan, and Satan is created from fire . . .' (*Aḥādīṯ-i maṯnawī*, p. 88, No. 243.)

of your ascent and throw away from the hand of your knowledge the stick with which you lean on things besides Me, for you are in the Holy Valley' [by virtue of] the sanctity of Moses.

God made him one of His complete words and breathed into him from His spirit [*sūra* 15: 29; 38: 72], and he became a spirit from Him [*sūra* 4: 69] by virtue of the sanctity of Jesus. And God honoured him with that perfect comprehensiveness which is the end of the perfecting by virtue of the sanctity of Muḥammad, and he became according to 'Follow me, then God will make you loved by His beloved' and he was veiled in the veil of pure Muhammadanism and annihilated in the Prophet, and no name and trace remained with him,

And God manifested upon him His name The Comprising [*al-ǧāmiʿ*] and helped him with angelic support.

And he knows through Gabriel's help without mediation of sciences written in books, and he eats with Michael's help without outward secondary causes,[64] and he breathes through Isrāfīl's breath and loosens the part of his body and collects them every moment, and he sleeps and awakes every day and is drawn toward death every moment by ʿAzrāʾīl's attraction.

God created him as a complete person in respect to reason, lower soul, spirit and body, and as a place of manifestation of all His names and the manifestation of His attributes, and as He made him His vicegerent on earth in general for humanity generally, so he also made him the vicegerent of His vicegerent on the carpet of specialisation, especially to complete His bounty upon him in general and in special, and to perfect his religion in summary and in detail, and He approved for him of Islam outwardly and inwardly [cf. *sūra* 5: 5] and made him sit on the throne of vicegerency of his father, as heritage and in realisation, and on the seat of the followers of His prophet by attestation and Divine success . . .[65]

This description, with its numerous allusions to the Ḳurʾānic prophets, is highly revealing although we do not know to which event in his youth Dard alludes with the state of 'Ishmaelian sanctity'. Does it refer to the sufferings the young Dard experienced when his father had his great vision at the beginning of the Muhammadan path (*K* 85)?

64 Michael is the angel in whose hands is, *inter alia*, the nourishment of living beings, cf. Sanāʾī, *Ḥadīḳat al-ḥaḳīḳa* VIII, p. 609; ʿAṭṭār, *Muṣībatnāme*, chapter 3. Rūmī has several times alluded to this peculiarity of the archangel, and the idea is alive among Persian writing poets up to Ghalib in the nineteenth century (cf. his *Ḳaṣīda*, No. 17). Cf. Horten, *Die religiöse Gedankenwelt des Volkes im Islam* (1917), p. 62.

65 Dard mentions in the following paragraph that he had been given a special throne and the 'Muhammadan banner', which was, according to his father's account (*NA* I: 322, 834; II: 868) and to *Maiḫāne* 92, a kind of lance which guaranteed victory and safety in every situation.

Or was his father indeed willing to sacrifice even his most beloved son? It seems typical that a later biography of Dard by a descendant of his skips the details of the 'Ishmaelian sanctity'. The chain of prophets is by no means complete; it differs from the Ḳur'ānic list as well as from that elaborated by Ibn ʿArabī in the *fuṣūṣ al -ḥikam*, and from his father's prophetology (*NA*[I]: 243, 259; *NA*[II]: 652).

The relations with the archangels are strange; the passage where his limbs were loosened and put together every day by virtue of Isrāfīl points to a spiritualisation of the body which could, in some cases, be witnessed in outward form.[66]

Dard mentions still more signs of divine blessings, and has asserted that things were unveiled to him which were even beyond the state of the venerable *šaiḫ* Ibn ʿArabī (*K* 402). Members of the Naḳšbandīya school often claim that they have surpassed the delusive state of *waḥdat al-wuǧūd* as experienced by the followers of Ibn ʿArabī, but Dard's vision is of a still different kind. He has recorded an audition (in Arabic, of course, for that is the language of the Ḳur'ān), which ends in the divine words:

> And He said, 'Say: if Reality were more than that which was unveiled to me, then God would verily have unveiled it to me, for He Most High has completed for me my religion and perfected for me His favour and approved Islam for me as religion, and if the veil were to be opened I would not gain more certitude—verily my Lord possesses mighty bounty.' [*K* 61][67]

After this report of an experience in which he was invested as the true successor of the Prophet, Mīr Dard goes on to speak of the names which God has bestowed upon him. There had been mystics who had knowledge of their heavenly names, like Naǧmuddīn Kubrā,[68] but

66 The loosening of the limbs is a typical initiation experience in Shamanism; cf. *Schamanengeschichte aus Sibirien*, trans. from the Russian by Friedrich and Buddrus (1955), p. 28, with many examples; it is also sometimes told about Muslim saints, especially in India, when the mountain of the bodily nature has been demolished and they are free for the influx of the divine spirit. There is a fine example in Muḥammad Aʿẓam Tattawī, *Tuḥfat aṭ-ṭāhirīn*, ed. Durrānī (1956), p. 159, about the sixteenth century Sindhi saint Pīr Chhata: 'Somebody saw [during the *ḏikr*] that the limbs of this love-slain man fell apart, and each of them with a separate tongue proclaimed the name of God'. Further: Dārā Šikōh, *Sakīnat al-auliyā'*, ed. Tara Chand and ǧalālī Nā'inī (n.d.), p. 207.

67 Cf. the detailed translation in 'German scholars on India'.

68 Meier has dealt with the problem of Naǧmuddīn Kubrā's heavenly names, *op. cit.*, p. 135; one may also remember that Ḥallāǧ assumed a large number of different names. Cf. *Commentary to Rūmī's Maṯnawī* VII, 82, 85.

Dard first gives a list of his 'attributive and relative names', and then explains that God

> taught Adam all the names (*sūra* 2: 29); that means He made man the place of manifestation for all His names and cast the light of His perfections into this mirror, But according to the custom of the Lord I shall show before you ninety-nine names which point to my all-comprehensive human reality, and at some times I have been elected with them . . .

Among these divinely inspired names are found even those which are exclusively used for God—such as *nūr*, 'Light', and 'Beyond the Beyond'—together with many others from the list of the Most Beautiful Names, and this aspect of Dard's mysticism deserves a special study; it is closely connected with the mystic's search for identity, on the one hand, and with a psychological trend peculiar to many oriental peoples, on the other.[69]

One would expect that a 'sincere Muhammadan' like Dard would be perfectly invariable and steadfast in his words and addresses, in his prayers and advice; but it is touching to see how, notwithstanding his deep mystical experiences, he never ceases asking 'Who am I?'[70] The mystery of his self escaped him—even as much as the ineffable mystery of God, so often described by him in technical terms as if it were perfectly clear and sometimes experienced in wonderful lucidity, remained beyond description. God's manifestations could be perceived, but how is one to reach the pure Light? The large number of strange poetical and philosophical addresses to God in Dard's prayers show his attempt to come closer to this Absolute Light from different angles, through different prisms and mirrors.[71] But he, 'the Sacred Valley of Absolute Existence', remains hidden behind the sand dunes of individuations which change their forms every moment, and the weary wayfarer becomes aware that the Desert of Absoluteness is caught each moment in new limitations (*taḳayyud*) (*A* 123).

69 'Andalīb, too, was very fond of surrounding his heroes with numerous names (see 'German scholars on India'). The long chains of names and titles are typical of the Mughal feudal culture, as they are of the Indian mind; even Kipling points to this indulging in name mysticism in the eleventh chapter of *Kim*.

70 The aged Dard still remembers his question, at the age of about three years, 'Who am I?' (š 122).

71 The addresses in Dard's prayers, from the simple *ilāhī*, 'My God', to 'Absolute Beloved' or 'Sun of the Sphere of Lordliness', deserve special interpretation just as his prayers, scattered through his books, are worth studying both for their contents and for their poetical beauty.

How can one find God but by losing one's self? The mystic may discover that the *dulcis hospes animae* has secretly entered his heart so that this desolate house is radiant with his light. How can he mysteriously inhabit it without expelling its owner (*N* 228)? In this state of selflessness,

the hand of the gnostics' prayer turns over the leaves of the booklet of involuntariness, similar to the leaves of the plane tree, whose object is not to grasp the skirt of the rose of wish.[72] They must follow the blowing of destiny's wind; in whatever manner it moves them they are moved . . . [*Š* 118]

Although to Mīr Dard it had been granted to reach 'proximity to the Prophet' and to be invested as 'true vicegerent' and as 'first of the Muhammadans', blessed with visions and strange experiences, he never ceased relying upon the acts of worship as absolutely necessary for salvation, and constantly asked forgiveness, completely trusting his Prophet, the intercessor at Doomsday, trusting also his father, whose help he implored over and over again—not only for himself, but for his family and all those who follow the Muhammadan path as well.[73]

He would have agreed in full with his father's verse:

> Strive that you may find the eternal Kingdom,
> and this you will find from the Muhammadan law.
> [*NA* II: 791]

But he knows also that

a complete submersion in contemplation cannot be acquired [by personal effort] but solely by divine grace. [*K* 311]

And thus his whole religious system of the reflection of the divine names, all his theories of recollection and contemplation, and likewise his overwhelming experiences on the Path, of which he was so proud, are summed up in the humble prayer for salvation through grace:

My request is only that the king-bird [*humā*] of happiness, namely of being accepted by Thee, may open his wings upon me . . . [*A* 160][74]

---

72 The comparison of the leaves of the plane tree to human hands goes back to Persian poetry in Ghaznawid times, cf. de Fouchécour, *La Description de la nature dans la poésie lyrique persane du XIe siècle* (1969).

73 Cf. *P* 112: 'I, as a Muhammadan, have an intercessor at Doomsday—I bring a hundred heaps of sins and say "Forgive"!' 'Do not despair' (*sūra* 39: 54) is the axis of Dard's faith; cf. *D* 10; *N* 131, 303; *A* 233.

74 The king-bird, *humā*, transforms the person upon whom his shade falls into a king, as Persian mythology often repeats.

17

Eric J. Sharpe

Salvation, Germanic and Christian

The subject of the encounter of religious traditions in northern Europe, well documented and signposted though it is, cannot be said to have received the attention it deserves from historians of religion, at least from those writing in English. It is difficult to account in full for this neglect. Doubtless it is partly due to the general position of Germanic and Scandinavian studies in the English-speaking world, where they remain largely the province of the linguist. In part it would seem to be due in a negative sense to the influence of the great triad of Classics, Semitics and Indology in shaping comparative religion in their own image. Certainly there have been a few British historians of religion who have been prepared to consider the ground beneath their own feet; but they have been remarkably few. Even a scholar of such far-ranging sympathies and such vast erudition as the late Professor Brandon was always cautious in dealing with the religious history of the north—and this despite his profound interest in, for instance, the iconography of the medieval Christian Church. And significantly, Brandon's studies of man in time, *Time and Mankind*, *Man and his Destiny in the Great Religions*, and *History, Time and Deity*, make no mention of man in the specifically Germanic and Scandinavian setting.

Nevertheless, towards the end of the chapter on Christianity in *Man and his Destiny* Brandon did observe that as a result of the earliest Christian centuries the stage was set for 'the great synthesis of human thought, needs and aspirations, which the faith and practice of medieval Christendom achieved'.[1] And he went on to observe that

Accordingly, the Christian was taught to regard his life as a pilgrimage through the sorrows and temptations of a fallen world, since the original sin of Adam and Eve had brought the whole human race into the power of Satan and

1 Brandon, *Man and his Destiny in the Great Religions* (1961), p. 233.

rendered its members objects deserving of the wrath of God; but he made this pilgrimage in hope, because the Son of God had redeemed him from Satan's power and made atonement to God on his behalf.[2]

No one, I feel, would want to quarrel with this general statement of the ethos of medieval Christianity. The theologians and doctors of the Church indeed represented man's position in the world in precisely these terms, and impressed upon the faithful—and the less faithful—that their salvation was to be gained on no other ground than through the sacrificial death of Christ. To quote Professor Brandon once more,

> . . . the Christian was taught to see the purpose of his life as the attainment of his soul's salvation—born in the inherited sin of his race, he was placed by the sacrament of baptism on the way to salvation, and, fortified by constant communion with God in the holy Mass, he looked forward beyond death to the achievement of his eternal salvation.[3]

Again I should emphasise that this is not really disputed territory, as long as one views medieval Christendom, as it were, from within. The didactic and homiletical tradition, reinforced at many points by iconography, placed man and his salvation firmly within that cosmic drama played out at Jerusalem, and repeated year by year in the liturgical cycle. This was certainly how the Christian was taught to hope for salvation.

But during the long period from the fifth to the twelfth centuries, northern Europe was only *becoming* Christian. Scandinavia, in particular, remained pre-Christian across the millennium, and the adoption of Christianity by the Icelandic *Althing* in the year 1000 was a type of decision possible only in a compact territory, ruled centrally—conditions that did not really apply in 'mainland' Scandinavia. Certainly the 'Christianisation' of Britain had taken place some centuries earlier; the 'conversion' of Sweden, on the other hand, came considerably later. Thus the entire period was a missionary period, in which the Christian message had to be addressed not to Christians only, but to people whose cultural and spiritual roots were to be found in the pre-Christian Germanic religious traditions. Not only the Christian but the non-Christian too had, in the Church's eyes, to be taught to consider the salvation of his soul.

The question before us, then, is whether the Germanic mind of the early Middle Ages was soteriologically a *tabula rasa*, upon which the

2 Brandon, *Man and his Destiny in the Great Religions* (1961), pp. 233*f*.

3 *Ibid.*, p. 234.

Christian scheme of salvation could easily be written; or whether certain presuppositions were present which caused the Christian message to be received and understood in a distinctive way, and which brought about the emergence of an equally distinctive Germanic Christian view of salvation. But before we proceed to a consideration of some at least of the evidence there are a number of preliminary remarks which would seem to be in order.

The first must be the truism that the interpretation of the conversion period in northern Europe is a highly complex undertaking.[4] Geographically and historically, the problem spans a very wide area, and precise lines of demarcation are equally difficult to draw in either respect. In what follows our material will be drawn largely from the period between the ninth and eleventh centuries, and from Scandinavia (including, of course, Iceland) and Anglo-Saxon Britain. These are fairly arbitrary boundaries, but otherwise the treatment would be diffuse in the extreme—though I am not personally convinced that a broader selection of evidence would necessarily alter the picture materially. Further complications arise from the nature of the pre-Christian source material, much of which was either preserved in a Christian setting or deliberately subjected to an *interpretatio christiana* or an *interpretatio ecclesiastica*.[5] It is, however, no part of my present purpose to enter into an overall discussion of the extent of Christian influence on the transmission of pre-Christian material. We may observe merely that the Old Norse and Anglo-Saxon (Old English) sources are for the most part Christian sources, and that where they discuss or refer to matters of pre-Christian belief they do so in their own perspective.

The second preliminary observation is mainly a methodological one: that certain stereotypes have long been prevalent concerning the way in which the north of Europe became Christian. Again, I do not wish to discuss these in great detail, but it will be necessary at least to identify them. According to one such stereotype, the Germanic peoples (and

4 The subject has been dealt with by many writers, among whom may be mentioned: Paasche, *Kristendom og Kvad* (1914), *Hedenskap og Kristendom* (1948); Schmidt, *Die Bekehrung der Germanen zum Christentum* (1935*ff.*); Ljungberg, *Den nordiska religionen och kristendomen* (1938); Sverdrup, *Da Norge ble kristnet* (1941); Ellis Davidson, *Gods and Myths of Northern Europe* (1964), pp. 211*ff.*; de Vries, *Altgermanische Religionsgeschichte* II (1970), pp. 406*ff.*

5 De Vries, *op. cit.*, I, pp. 166*f.*, with reference to Achterberg, *Interpretatio Christiana* (1930).

others) were converted abruptly and *en masse*, usually because the missionaries were successful in persuading a king—or, not infrequently, a queen—to accept baptism.[6] Although the old religion was able to put up a token resistance, and although reversions to paganism occurred from time to time (as on the death of Edwin of Northumbria), the final 'victory of Christianity' was only a matter of time, and once it had been achieved nothing was quite the same again. Speaking of the 'striking innovations' which the coming of Christianity brought with it to Scandinavia, K. S. Latourette writes that 'The bright aspect of early Scandinavian Christianity was the opposite of the grim inescapable fate which characterized pre-Christian Northern religion'.[7] The stereotype here is, I fear, an evangelical one. Other historians may recognise that the 'struggle' between the adherents of the old faith and the new was very lengthy. This is true enough in a way. But when C. J. A. Oppermann, writing in this vein about Sweden, goes on to observe that

> Well over three hundred years had elapsed since the time when the Gospel was first proclaimed by the shores of Lake Mälar before its victory was completely secured; and even then heathenism lingered for some time in the more remote districts . . .[8]

one cannot but suspect that a further stereotype has emerged: that which interprets the encounter of religions as the encounter of religious *systems*, and the abrupt replacement of the one by the other just as soon as some kind of official decision had been made to embrace Christianity. Of course, a corollary of this view is that 'in the more remote districts' people remained heathen, and elsewhere the peasantry and even the lesser clergy remained incurably superstitious (though in fact the ecclesiastical historians are not fond of dwelling on this side of things). Nor do I wish to dwell on it, but merely to suggest that once 'systems'—Christian or otherwise—have been eliminated from the picture, the actual encounter becomes far more easily comprehensible. It was, of course, not a monolithic take-over that took place but

6 For a balanced estimate see Sundkler, *The World of Mission*, English translation (1965), pp. 81*ff*. On p. 89 he writes: 'The conversion was neither sudden nor complete. Only gradually did pagan beliefs, customs and ceremonies fall into abeyance, particularly since the protagonists were an ancient popular religion and a Church prepared to exercise a measure of cultic tolerance.'

7 Latourette, *A History of the Expansion of Christianity*, II (1938), p. 349.

8 Oppermann, *The English Missionaries in Sweden and Finland* (1937), p. 34.

a gradual modification of cumulative traditions in a Christian direction;[9] I shall attempt to show how this happened with respect to one particular concept, that of salvation. And this leads me on to my third and last preliminary observation.

It is this: that it is often assumed to be proper to speak of 'salvation' only in the context of certain types of deity, preferably 'dying and rising' gods (or goddesses) with whom the individual worshipper might be ritually united, in order to secure his or her protection and guidance in the world beyond the grave. Certainly this is a type of soteriology dominant in the Mediterranean world; that is not the point at issue. The point is that should this pattern be accepted as the only *genuine* pattern of salvation, then the Germanic religious traditions would inevitably stand out in the sharpest possible contrast to Christianity as, in effect, non-soteriological.[10] This is not to say that the north knew of no vegetation and fertility deities, celebrated in a seasonal cult. Freyr was, of course, such a deity, and so too, in a measure, was Baldr. But extensive consequences for the religious life of the individual do not appear to have been drawn in either case. The conversion of the north might then seem to have been a matter of the introduction of a new and exciting prospect of eternal life to people otherwise believing that their only hope of immortality lay in their continuing 'good name'. After all, did not one of Edwin's chief men compare the life of man to the flight of a sparrow out of, and into, the darkness and point out that '. . . man appears on earth for a little while, but we know nothing of what went before this life, and what follows. Therefore if this new teaching can reveal any more certain knowledge, it seems only right that we should follow it.'[11]

No one would wish to under-estimate the eschatological aspect of Christian soteriology; but I find it hard to accept either that Germanic religion was innocent of elements of soteriology, or that there was such a total acceptance of Christian eschatology *as a dominant element* in the

9 I am using the term 'cumulative traditions' in the sense advocated by Cantwell Smith, *The Meaning and End of Religion* (Mentor Books edition, 1964), pp. 139*ff*.

10 It is always dangerous to use an *argumentum e silentio*, but it is perhaps not without some significance that the recent symposium *Religions de salut* (1962) should make no mention of the Germanic material. Some of the observations made in this volume about shamanism (e.g. p. 18, pp. 113*ff*.) would seem, however, to be relevant in the Germanic setting.

11 Bede, *A History of the English Church and People*, trans. Sherley-Price (1955), p. 125.

new view of salvation that other perspectives—Germanic perspectives—were thereby ruled out. Indeed, it seems more than likely that, of Edwin's advisers, it is Coifi the high priest who sounds the more authentically Germanic note in response to the message of Bishop Paulinus than does the anonymous *thegn*. Coifi's argument—which Bede very appropriately describes as 'prudent'—was apparently thoroughly utilitarian:

Your Majesty, let us give careful consideration to this new teaching, for I frankly admit that, in my experience, the religion that we have hitherto professed seems valueless and powerless. None of your subjects has been more devoted to the service of the gods than myself, yet there are many to whom you show greater favour, who receive greater honours, and who are more successful in all their undertakings. Now, if the gods had any power, they would surely have favoured myself, who have been more zealous in their service. Therefore, if on examination these new teachings are found to be better and more effectual, let us not hesitate to accept them.[12]

And a little later Bede represents Coifi as saying that the Christian teaching 'clearly reveals truths which will afford us the blessings of life, salvation, and eternal happiness'.[13] Whatever we may think of the former argument about the value of the pre-Christian religion (surely Bede's rather than Coifi's), the latter places Christian salvation squarely *between* this world and the next, so to speak. It may well be true, then, that Germanic religion was not consistently hopeful about eschatology,[14] but if salvation is understood as deliverance from present ills and the granting of temporal benefits from divine sources, then the Germanic peoples did at least have certain expectations which it was not necessary to die to enjoy. Eternal life might be an added incentive; but there was always a Judge to be faced—and it is at least questionable how attractive this aspect of the Christian message in fact proved.

Gerardus van der Leeuw argued that salvation is that 'at which all religion without exception aims',[15] and that 'religion is always directed towards salvation, never towards life itself as it is given; and in this respect all religion, with no exception, is the religion of deliverance'.[16]

12 Bede, *A History of the English Church and People* (1955), p. 124.

13 *Ibid.*, p. 125.

14 On the difficult subject of Germanic personal eschatology, see Ellis [Davidson], *The Road to Hel* (1943); cf. Turville-Petre, *Myth and Religion of the North* (1964), pp. 269*ff*.

15 Van der Leeuw, *Religion in Essence and Manifestation*, English translation (1938), p. 536.

16 *Ibid.*, pp. 681*f*.

There is, it seems to me, nothing in the Germanic traditions which would contradict this admittedly broad view of the nature of salvation. For 'deliverance' from oppressive powers and conditions may well be —indeed, I believe it usually is—a matter to be experienced by *homo religiosus* here and now, in this life. We may, then, speak of an element of salvation in Germanic religion in the sense of a belief in the protection afforded by a god or gods from other destructive powers—protection sufficient to gain the individual honour, victory and ultimately, perhaps, peace in the grave and beyond it. It was in this sense that S. G. Youngert wrote of the Germanic ideal of salvation as '. . . the getting rid of those things which . . . were absolutely evil' and as 'a state of happiness' to be achieved 'only by fight and honest victory'.[17]

Significantly, key terms in the Germanic (Scandinavian) tradition frequently reflect the exercise of power—not an impersonal power, such as an older generation of scholarship believed to be reflected in terms like the Melanesian *mana*, but a power exercised particularly by the great gods Thor and Odin, and capable of being appropriated by man.[18] Two words in particular are *megin* and *máttr*, the former of which had divine provenance as *ásmegin*, 'the power of the gods'. It is true that by the mission period there were those who were practically atheists, who were said to believe in their own power and strength (*trúa á mátt sinn ok megin*) and to care nothing for divine assistance; but this was sufficiently rare to warrant special mention. Far more typical is the assumption that the gods were willing and able to make their *megin*, or in the case of kings *magna*, available in return for sacrifice (*blót*). In the Icelandic literature this latter aspect is stressed very frequently; we must remember that the milieu of this literature is that of the royal assembly, and that battle and victory (less often defeat) are constantly celebrated. As an example we may perhaps quote a verse from Einarr Helgason skálaglamm's *Vellekla*, which dates from the 980s:

Valfǫllum hlóð vǫllu,
varð ragna konr gagni,
hríðar ǫ́ss, at hrósa
(hlaut Oðinn val) Fróða;

17 *Encyclopaedia of Religion and Ethics*, ed. Hastings, XI (1920), p. 149b.

18 De Vries (*op. cit.* I, p. 276) appears to hold to the older view. Against this, see, for example, Baetke, *Das Heilige im Germanischen* (1942), Widengren, *Religionsphänomenologie* (1969), pp. 10*ff.*, 30*ff.*

hver se if, nema jǫfra
ættrýri goð stýra?;
rammaukin kveðk riki
rǫ́gn Hǫ́konar magna.[19]

An approximate translation would be: 'He, the descendant of the gods, piled up the corpses of the fallen on the battlefield. The god of Frode's storm [battle] could praise his victory, but Odin had the fallen. Doubtless the gods guide this bane of the line of kings. I say that the gods, strengthened by sacrifice, establish Hákon's power.'[20]

Sacrifice was clearly the means by which protection of this order could be gained and maintained. But there were other, less spectacular (and less bloody) purposes for which the power of the gods might be sought. After all, the Germanic peoples were not all kings and warriors. Most were farmers; and either in the great sanctuaries, such as that described by Adam of Bremen at what is now Gamla Upsala in Sweden, or more frequently in the main building of a large farm, rituals were observed in which various aspects of life were brought within the divine protection.

The main semi-private ritual form was that called *veizla*, or sacrificial feast, which was held in front of an image of one or other of the great gods. It began with an act of consecration, continued with a ceremonial and in some sense sacramental meal, and reached its climax in the drinking of solemn toasts (*full*, *minni*; the English word is weak), regulated by strict formulas. Horns were emptied to the gods and to the dead, thus ensuring their help. Gods particularly named included Thor, Odin and Frey; Odin's *full* was drunk 'til sigrs ok ríkis konungi sinum', Frey's 'til árs ok friðar'—to a good year and to peace.[21] The horn might also be consecrated by making the sign of, for instance, Thor's hammer over it.[22] The *veizla* might also have the form of a seasonal (autumn–winter) sacrifice to lesser supernatural beings, and thus be called *dísablót*, as in *Víga-Glúms Saga* 6 ('þar var veizla búin at vetrnóttum ok gert dísablót, ok allir skulu þessa minning gera').

19 Jónsson, *Den Norsk-Islandske Skjaldedigtning* (1908), II: B, p. 123.

20 Cf. Ohlmarks, *Tors skalder och Vite-Krists* (1958), p. 387: 'Every line in this verse breathes sacrifice and heathen magic, ancient sorcery and belief in the power of the old gods.'

21 The latter formula continued to be used by Christians. The *Gulatingslagen* laid down that drink should be consecrated to Christ and the Virgin Mary 'til árs ok til friðar'; cf. Ström, *Diser, nornor, valkyrjor* (1954), pp. 19*f*.

22 Sverdrup, *Da Norge ble kristnet*, pp. 47*ff*.

Similar references are found in *Flateyjarbók* 1 and *Egils Saga* 44 ('ok skyldi þar vera dísablót, ok var þar veizla in bezta ok drykkja mikil inni í stofunni').[23] From these examples it is clear that the practice was aristocratic, confined to a close circle of relatives and friends associated with a particular *garðr*, and liable to be rendered null and void by the presence of strangers, as Sigvat skald found on his visit to Västergötland in Sweden.[24] The main object of this particular form of sacrifice was to secure the benevolence of the lesser, rather than the greater powers, the *dísir* and *alfar* rather than Thor and Odin. Of the two classes, it would seem that the *alfablót* was the more private and personal, and hence in the long run much harder for the Christian Church to come to terms with.[25]

The power of the *dísir* and *alfar* was of course limited—though not for that reason unimportant to the agriculturalist. The great gods, on the other hand, wielded power on a genuinely cosmic scale, and those to whom the personal exercise of power was itself a matter of everyday concern were on the one hand particularly wary of offending them in any way, and on the other able to strike up a distinctively personal relationship, perhaps especially with Thor.[26]

At this point it is necessary to remember that the Scandinavian myths contain a great deal of well known material concerning the means by which these deities obtained and maintained their power. In Thor's case it was mainly a matter of the exercise of sheer force over against all threatening powers. In the prologue of Snorri's *Gylfaginning* we read at once that

> At twelve years old he had come to his full strength and then he lifted twelve bear pelts from the ground at once and killed his foster-father Loricus, with his wife Lóri or Glóri, and took possession of the realm of Thrace—we call that Thrúðheim. After that he travelled far and wide, exploring all the regions of the world, and by himself overcoming all the berserks and giants and an enormous dragon and many wild beasts.[27]

The explanation is late and euhemeristic, and yet contains genuine insight into Thor's character. The parallel to the Vedic Indra is very apparent: he is constantly fighting, particularly with giants; with his

23 Ström, *op. cit.*, pp. 12*ff.*

24 Sverdrup, *op. cit.*, pp. 54*f.*

25 *Ibid.*, pp. 16*f.* Ström regards the *alfablót* as the genuine precursor of the Christian midwinter celebration in Scandinavia. On this whole subject see Celander, *Förkristen jul enligt norröna källor* (1955), especially pp. 37*ff.*

26 The most comprehensive study is Ljungberg, *Tor* (1947).

27 *Snorri Sturluson: the Prose Edda*, trans. Young (1966), pp. 25*f.*

weapon, the hammer (cf. Indra's *vajra*), he strikes down all opposition; and as such he is the protector of men and gods, the defender of the world against all the forces of chaos.[28]

But at the same time that Thor was genuinely the object of men's devotion is clear, not least from the work of the skalds of the ninth to the eleventh centuries, some of whom have been characterised by Åke Ohlmarks as making verses to 'Thor the strong, the anti-Christian saviour god and symbol of unity of late paganism'.[29] It is, I think, significant that Ohlmarks should have chosen to call Thor at this period a 'saviour god' (*frälsargud*) in opposition to the White Christ—significant and entirely correct, for the qualities for which Thor was revered were precisely those of the saviour: power, benevolence, dependability and availability. This is not to say, however, that Thor was ever treated in a cavalier fashion. But he might well be called a 'good friend' (*ástvinr*), in whom the individual and the family might well place their trust (*fulltrúi*), and who could be relied on to guide them in their day-to-day activities. Perhaps the best known example of this would be the settler Thorolf Mostrarskegg, who asked Thor's advice before setting off from Norway for Iceland, and who left it to Thor to choose where he would actually live, once he had arrived.[30] Also there is evidence that Thor was able to ensure at least peace in the grave, since the hammer symbol has been found on gravestones and among grave-goods in certain parts of Scandinavia, and inscriptions accompanying the symbol ask Thor to take to himself the body of the deceased.[31]

In the case of Odin the evidence is not so clear. If Thor won his power by sheer force, Odin's power was gained by much subtler means, probably not far removed from the practices of shamanism. Accordingly, it is harder to think of Odin as in any sense a saviour god; harder, but not impossible, provided that one recognises his proper sphere of activity, first as god of death and the dead, and second as the god who had won for himself resources of a subtlety unmatched in any other Germanic deity. Clearly, we cannot here enter into a dis-

28 Turville-Petre, *op. cit.*, p. 85. Cf. Ellis Davidson, 'Thor's hammer', *Folklore* LXXVI (1965), pp. 1*ff.*

29 Ohlmarks, *op. cit.*, p. 14.

30 *Eyrbyggja Saga* IV.

31 Ellis Davidson, 'Thor's hammer', pp. 13*f.* (offprint pagination). She concludes that 'The hammer-sign . . . stood for the continuing protection of the god, and may indeed have signified the idea of continuing life after death' (p. 14).

cussion of this extremely complex subject; but one point in particular is deserving of mention, *viz.* his mastery of writing, and particularly of the runes.[32]

The ultimate source of Odin's *gnosis* is said in one celebrated source (*Hávamál* v) to have been his act of self-sacrifice:

I know that I hung in a windy tree
For nine nights,
Stung by the spear-point, given to Odin,
Myself to myself.

I drank not from the horn, nor did I eat bread—
I gazed downward,
I took up the runes, called and took,
Then I fell from the tree.

And a later strophe reads:

Do you know how to carve? How the runes are interpreted?
Do you know how the runes are painted, what they say?
Do you know how to pray, how to make sacrifice?
Do you know how to offer gifts, how to sacrifice?

This is the language of the powerful signs, controlled by the shaman and to some extent also by the skald, the master of words. And again and again the assumption is made that the source of this particular power is Odin—'aldingagautr ok ásgarðs jǫfurr, ok valhallar vísi' ('aged Gautr and prince of Asgard and lord of Valhalla').[33] On the one hand, this might express itself in the activities of the 'religious underworld', among charms and spells;[34] but on the other, there is evidence of genuine devotion to Odin on the part of the professional word-smith. For instance, we have the words of the newly converted Hallefreðr Vandræðaskáld (*c.* 996):

Ǫll hefr aett til hylli
Oðins skipat ljóðum,
algilda mank, aldar
iðju várra niðja,

32 See, for example, de Vries, *op. cit.*, II, pp. 73*ff.*

33 *The Icelandic Runic Poem* 4, in Dickens, *Runic and Heroic Poems of the Old Teutonic Peoples* (1915), pp. 28*f.*; cf. p. 13.

34 The celebrated passage in Snorri's *Ynglinga Saga* 7 ('Odin moved on. Although his body lay as it were asleep or dead, he was at that time a bird or animal, fish or serpent, and went voyaging to far-off lands on his own or others' business.'), although late, emphasises the relevant shamanistic element with full clarity.

en trauðr, þvit vel Viðris
vald hugnaðisk skaldi,
legg ek á frumver Friggjar
fjón, þvit Kristi þjónum.[35]

—'Every race of men has made songs to honour Odin; I remember the excellent poetry of our fathers' day. I do not willingly hate Frigg's mighty husband just because I serve Christ—for the power of Vidrir [Odin] served the poet well.' It has been suggested that devotion to Odin in the last years of pre-Christian Iceland was itself a sign that some of the old social ties were breaking down, and that in the earlier period there was little or nothing of personal salvation in the worshipper's attitude to the Germanic god or gods.[36] From this it would follow that elements of soteriology in Germanic religion emerged only in answer to the pressure of Christian soteriology and at a very late date. I am not convinced that this was so, although clearly there is a certain reaction-formation to be observed in the Germanic religion of this period. On the whole, it seems safer to assume that soteriological elements were latent in Germanic religion from a very much earlier period—the element of conflict and victory (embodied particularly in the cosmic struggle of Thor), and the element of appropriation of supernatural power by occult means (of which Odin was the outstanding embodiment), and that these were the forces with which Christianity had to contend in the Middle Ages. But was Christianity itself a stranger to these ideas?

Certainly the normative Christianity of a later period, as expounded in the schools, Catholic and Protestant, tended to have its sights fixed at a different, more forensic, level. This point needs no elaboration, save perhaps to stress once more that this may serve in part to explain some of the stereotypes with which the study of the conversion of northern Europe has been unnecessarily complicated.

Implicit in all that we have said thus far has been the view that Germanic religion was in a sense dualistic, in that it recognised the influence in the world of powers of chaos and destruction—Thor and the giants, for example, or the contrasted regions of Midgard and Jotunheim; and that as far as this present order goes, the powers of creation are dominant, though threatened, and establish their power in an on-going drama of conflict. The existence of a parallel series of dramatic-dualistic beliefs in early Christianity has never been seriously

35 Jónsson, *op. cit.*, I: B, p. 158.

36 Sverdrup, *op. cit.*, pp. 81*f.*, 89.

questioned, although it has frequently been overlooked, or at least relegated to a subordinate position. Professor Brandon, for instance, noted that Paul was preoccupied with a *mythos* of redemption or salvation which differed fundamentally from the original form of the faith:

> By virtue of it Paul was enabled to lift the crucifixion of Jesus out of its location in time and space and to proclaim it as a divinely pre-ordained event of universal relevancy. Mankind, as a whole, lay enthralled to the daemonic powers of the cosmos, and from that state, and all that it implied in spiritual evil, the race of man had been delivered by this *deuteros theos*, who, by becoming incarnate as a man and dying on the cross, had in some way tricked these daemonic masters of men and caused them to forfeit their hold over them.[37]

Bearing in mind certain passages in Galatians, Colossians and 1 Corinthians, there is no doubt that this element of redemption from daemonic powers by the victory of Christ is very much present; and I do not wish to enter into the problem of what is, and what is not, 'original' in this view. But as Gustaf Aulén has pointed out in various contexts, notably in his celebrated *Christus Victor* (first published in 1930 as *Den kristna försoningstanken*), the dramatic–dualistic view here represented dominated the early Church and the world of the Fathers. In it

> God is pictured as in Christ carrying through a victorious conflict against powers of evil which are hostile to His will. This constitutes Atonement, because the drama is a cosmic drama, and the victory over the hostile powers brings to pass a new relation, a relation of reconciliation, between God and the world.[38]

Aulén also quotes Irenaeus (*Adv. Haer.* II: 20, 3):

> The passion of Christ brought us courage and power. The Lord through His passion ascended up on high, led captivity captive, and gave gifts to men, and gave power to them that believe in Him to tread upon serpents and scorpions and upon all the powers of the enemy—that is, the prince of the apostasy . . .[39]

Many other examples might have been given, but Aulén's summing up is surely correct, that although this kind of view gradually gave way to more forensic ideas, for the first thousand years of Christian history this was 'the ruling idea of the Atonement'.[40] Christ had, in other words, conquered the forces of evil by the exercise of superior divine power, and made that divine power of salvation available to

37 Brandon, *Man and his Destiny*, p. 216.
38 Aulén, *Christus Victor*, English translation (1931), p. 21.
39 *Ibid.*, p. 48. 40 *Ibid.*, p. 23.

men through baptism and the holy Eucharist. The problem was perhaps, as the Church moved north, to 'identify the enemy'.

In one sense, the powers of evil from which man in northern Europe prayed to be delivered remained precisely the same under Christ as they had been under Thor and Odin—the evils of imbalance in nature, famine, disease and death. The peasant knew precisely what measures were appropriate in these cases; and he continued to take them. As Sverdrup has so well said, the Scandinavian peasant (and this applies elsewhere in equal measure) gave up his gods, but he did not give up his religion.[41] The White Christ might have ultimate power over life and death, and might be the highest ruler of the heavens, but was it so sure that he knew about the everyday concerns of the farmer in field and forest and stable? There were adjustments, of course; the *dísir* and *alfar* might themselves now acknowledge a new overlord, and have to be called by different names. But the not inconsiderable body of Germanic charms which survived well into modern times witness to the continuity of popular belief on this level. The Anglo-Saxon *Land-Remedy* on making the first furrow:

> Hail to thee, Earth, mother of men!
> Be fruitful in God's embrace,
> Filled with food for the use of men.

is clearly of vast antiquity, but must certainly have been used by Christians.[42]

But in the *interpretatio ecclesiastica* the forces of imbalance and evil now had powerful allies in the old gods themselves, the ancient saviours as well as their lesser minions. All were lumped together under Hebraic condemnations of 'idolatry'—with the results we know so well. From the eighth century we have Charlemagne's sinister list of *malefici, venefici, sortiarii, cauculatores, incantatores, tempestarii vel obligatores* as examples of the forces from which the Christian was urged to dissociate himself.[43] And unless he did so openly and publicly

41 Sverdrup, *op. cit.*, p. 171.

42 An English version of the *Land-Remedy* is found in *Anglo-Saxon Poetry*, ed. Gordon (1964), pp. 88–90. The subject of the continued use of charms is extremely interesting, and would certainly repay further study. See Grendon, 'The Anglo-Saxon charms', *Journal of American Folk-lore* XXII (1909), pp. 105*ff.*, and Grattan and Singer, *Anglo-Saxon Magic and Medicine* (1952). A survey of similar Swedish material is found in af Klintberg, *Svenska troll-formler* (1965).

43 Boudriot, *Die altgermanische Religion in der amtlichen kirchlichen Literatur . . .* (reprinted 1964), p. 63.

he could not be admitted into the fellowship of Christ's flock. The renunciation of the old high gods was sometimes very explicit indeed, as in the Saxon baptismal formula: '. . . . ec forsacho allum diaboles wercum ende wordum, Thunaer ende Woden ende Saxnote ende allum them unholdum, the hira genotas sint.' Thunaer is of course Thor, Woden is Odin, Saxnot appears to be *Tiwaz < Týr.[44]

This was, however, very far from being the whole story: cumulative traditions are not broken so easily, and what went on in the mind and heart of the newly christened northerner cannot be evaluated in terms of such abrupt change. Eleventh century Sweden was spoken of in one source as a country 'cuius terrae populi partim se Christianos esse dicunt, sine fide quidem et sine confessione et sine babtismate, partim vero cum similiter sint Christiani, Jovem et Martem colunt'.[45] And on the individual level there were certainly many who, like the Icelander Helgi inn Magri in the *Landnamabók* (III: 14, 3), who were 'of mixed faith' ('blandinn i trú'): 'he believed in Christ, and named his homestead after him, but turned to Thor when at sea or in danger'; or like Redwald, king of the East Angles in the early seventh century, who 'had in the same temple an altar (*altare*) for the holy Sacrifice of Christ side by side with an altar (*arula*) on which victims were offered to devils'.[46] There were certainly others who were more like the skald Hallfreðr Óttarson, whose conversion was very much a matter of personal attachment to King Olav Tryggvason, and who left the old gods with real regret.[47] And others again to whom Thor in particular appeared in visions, alternately threatening and cajoling, and showing every sign of distress at being abandoned for a foreign god.

There is a great deal of evidence to show that amid these experiences of conversion, some traumatic, some less so, one image in particular retained all its old power: the image of salvation as resulting from a cosmic conflict between forces of good (law) and evil (chaos). Previously Thor had been the victor; now he in his turn had been overcome by the White Christ, and all Christ's symbols became symbols of victory. This, it seems, the Germanic mind could accept without question as an integral part of a long cumulative tradition. Thor's victories

44 *Ibid.*, pp. 57*f.*

45 Quoted by de Vries, *op. cit.*, II, p. 429, note 2.

46 Bede, II: 15; cf. de Vries, *op. cit.*, II, pp. 429*f.*

47 On Hallfreðr's conversion, see Paasche (*Kristendom og Kvad*, pp. 9*ff.*), who was in no doubt as to the genuineness of his new faith; Jónsson, *Den Islandske Litteraturs Historie* (1907), pp. 122*ff.*, was equally convinced that it had no depth. See also Ohlmarks, *Tors skalder*, pp. 111–40.

over the giants gave place to Christ's victory over the powers of darkness and death; but the terms of the conflict remained virtually unaltered. The extensive body of Christian Anglo-Saxon writing is especially rich in material of this kind.

The official terms of the conflict were laid down in the poem *Christ* (II: 1), where the Saviour says:

Go now throughout all the wide earth, throughout distant regions; make known to multitudes, preach and proclaim the fair faith; and baptise people beneath the sky, turn them to heaven; cut down the idols, fell and destroy them; abolish hatred, sow peace in men's hearts *by your fullness of power.*

This fullness of power was derived directly from Christ's victory on the cross, and made available to '. . . . the people whom He took from the fiends by His own triumph' (*Christ* II: 2). But the conflict extended beyond the land of the living; among the many references to the 'harrowing of hell', we find this battle scene, from *Christ and Satan*:

Then God by His might entered hell to the sons of men; He was minded to bring forth many thousands of men up to His home. Then came a sound of angels, a noise at dawn. The Lord Himself had laid low the fiend; the struggle was yet to be seen at daybreak; then the dread strength was made manifest.[48]

Perhaps it would not be too much to claim that the triumph of the cross was a triumph to the Germanic mind mainly because it concealed the harrowing of hell, as though the killing of 'the Lord of victories' gave him precisely the opportunity he needed to free those held enchained by the 'evil spirits, malicious fiends'. Christ's victory thus gave man above all present protection, salvation here and now, since the power of the Adversary had been decisively broken. Again we hear the authentic Germanic voice in *Christ* (II: 5):

No one on earth of the race of men need dread the darts of the devils, the spear-flight of foes, if God, the Lord of hosts, is his shield.

It should perhaps be added that close distinctions between Christ and God were not always drawn.

There remains to mention briefly two particular symbols of Christian salvation in northern Europe, the cross and the Pater Noster. There is, of course, no suggestion that either was geographically confined to the north; it is suggested merely that both were appropriate to the north, for the reasons already stated.

48 *Anglo-Saxon Poetry*, p. 131. The quotations from *Christ* are also taken from this collection.

Snorri's *Heimskringla* (*Hákonar Saga Goða* 17) tells the story of the Christian king Hákon and the *veizla* at Lade in Norway. Hákon sat in the place of honour, and the first horn, after having been consecrated to Odin, was passed to him. He received it, and made the sign of the cross over it. A man called Kár said: 'Why did the king do that? Will he still not sacrifice?' Diplomatically Sigurd Jarl (who was giving the banquet) answered, 'The king is doing as all those do who trust in their own power and strength; he consecrated the horn to Thor, and that was the sign of the hammer he made, before he drank.'

I mention this merely to show how interchangeable signs of power could be in this setting, and how easily the sign of Thor could give way to the sign of Christ. Not that hammers were set up in our villages before the crosses; but a king in particular could adopt a new symbol and use it in functionally similar ways, and in precisely similar situations. To be sure, the old religion had no literature to compare with Cynewulf's *Elene* or with the *Dream of the Rood* in its concentration on a particular symbol. But within this literary *genre* there are instructive glimpses of the pure symbolism of power existing quite apart from whatever conceptual content might be given to the symbol in question. This is perhaps only marginally a matter of soteriology; but it is certainly part of the overall symbolism of salvation.[49]

Thus in the account in Cynewulf's *Elene* of the conversion of Constantine, the emperor sees the vision of the cross while asleep 'covered with his boar-helmet' ('eofurcumble beþeah')—probably a symbol of heathen power. He takes heart, has the sign of the cross made, and carries it into battle. 'Then the banner was raised, the sign in front of the troops; the song of victory was chanted' (*sigeleod galen*—which may have overtones of incantation). And victory is won; but only *after* the victory does it occur to Constantine to ask his advisers whose sign it was which had brought him victory. The sign was a repository of power, whether anyone knew the name and the story of Christ or not. We may if we wish label this 'superstition', but it sounds authentic—not authentically Constantinian, for with the best will in the world one cannot accept that he was totally ignorant of Christ before his vision, but authentically Germanic. It is from this same source, and

49 Limitations of space have prevented a fuller consideration of the symbolism of the cross. But mention should be made of the recent edition by Swanton of *The Dream of the Rood* (1970), for its bringing together of archaeological and literary material; the religio-historical interpretation is not, however, exhaustive.

from this same part of the world, that we have the two magnificent hymns of Venantius Fortunatus, *Vexilla regis prodeunt* and *Pange, lingua, gloriosi proelium certaminis*, written in A.D. 569.[50]

My other example of a repository of power concerns the Pater Noster, as apostrophised in the remarkably little known and little studied *Dialogue of Solomon and Saturn*.[51] In this Anglo-Saxon poem Solomon represents Christian wisdom, Saturn (on the whole) pagan wisdom, and Solomon describes to Saturn all the virtues inherent in the 'palm-twigged' Pater Noster. But these have remarkably little to do with the relationship between God and man of which the prayer properly speaks. Instead, the two words 'Pater Noster' are broken down into letters, each of which is then reproduced by means of its proper runic symbol. Each one separately exercises its own influence, or rather serves as a mediator of some distinct aspect of the divine power of God. To the 'word of God' (*Godes cwide*) the anonymous author ascribes cosmic powers. By its power the fetters of the evil one (*se feónd*) are broken, and his cunning (*cræft*) is torn apart; it is the refuge of beasts and fishes, as well as of men, but most important is its power in putting to flight 'the fighting fiend' (*fechtende feónd*):

> Mæg simle se Godes cwide   gumena gehwylcum
> ealra fēonda gehwane   flēonde gebrengan.[52]

And as with the whole, so with each of its parts: each single rune afflicts the fiend with a separate torment.

We cannot here enter into a detailed discussion of the early Christian interpretation of the runes; it is sufficient for our purposes to point out

50 Cf. Every, *Christian Mythology* (1970), pp. 62*f.*

51 There have been two editions. The first, by Kemble, was published, with a valuable introduction and translation, in 1848; the second, by Menner, without translation, in 1941.

52 I: 146*f.* (Menner): 'Ever may the Word of God for every man put to flight every fiend.' The prose section of *Solomon and Saturn* describes in detail a conflict between the devil and the Pater Noster, in which the devil changes shape constantly, only to be met by a corresponding (and superior) stratagem on the part of a thoroughly hypostasised Pater Noster. A random quotation will illustrate the degree of hypostasisation: 'The Pater Noster has a golden head and silver hair; and although all the waters of the earth should be mingled with the waters of heaven above into one channel, and it should begin to rain them together upon the earth and all its creatures, yet might it stand dry under a single lock of the Pater Noster's hair.' (Kemble's translation, *Solomon and Saturn*, p. 149.)

that here we see a line of continuity stretching far back into the Germanic religious past, and a further means by which Christian soteriology was given a typically Germanic framework of symbolism.

It is difficult to sum up in a few words the extremely disparate material which I have tried to pass in review in this paper. Clearly there are vast problems involved in the interpretation of the conversion process in northern Europe, problems which I have been able only to hint at in this context. Religiously, however, the Germanic mind was very far indeed from being a *tabula rasa* on which the first words of salvation were to be written by the Christian Church. The presentation of Christ as the cosmic victor and the symbolism in which that act of salvation was depicted fell into prepared soil. From the standpoint of the history of religions it is simply impossible to dismiss the Christian application of Germanic symbols of power, or the apparent Germanic unconcern with the finer points of Christian doctrine, as evidence of incurable superstition. We must remember, as Christopher Dawson put it, that

> . . . the German warrior and the Celtic peasant looked on the world with other eyes than did the civilized Roman magistrate or the Greek scholar or the oriental ascetic, and there was nothing in their culture and their social traditions that could help them to understand the religious thought and the moral ideals of the civilized Christian world of the patristic age.[53]

True enough, perhaps; but one thing they could, and did, understand. They understood the drama, the *mythos*, of salvation; and they understood the power of the risen and ascended Christ, the judge of all men. To this end they took and reshaped their ancient symbols and their ancient concepts, conscious that they were now part of a greater Empire, but conscious equally of their own distinctive heritage.

Perhaps we may give the last word to Olav Tryggvason's 'difficult poet', Hallfreðr Vandræðaskáld. Facing death at sea in the year 1007 he made his last verse:

> Death I dare to face, though
> once I was sharp in speech,
> if only I see my soul
> saved on the farther shore.
> Death is our due, the Lord's doom
> certain whatever our way:

53 Dawson, *Mediaeval Religion* (1934), p. 7.

here I was hindered by naught—
but the fires of hell I fear.[54]

54 Ek munda nú andask,
ungr vask harðr í tungu,
senn, ef sglu minni,
sorglaust, vissak borgit;
veitk, at vetki of sýtik,
valdi goð hvar aldri,
(dauðr verðr hverr) nema hræðumk
helvíti, skal slíta.
(Jónsson, *op. ict.*, I: B, p. 163)

18

Marcel Simon

On some aspects of early Christian soteriology

Christianity has often, and with good reason, been described as a salvation religion, and even as the salvation religion *par excellence*.[1] It is also commonly admitted that this feature is most apparent in the Pauline interpretation of the Gospel, with its particular emphasis on Christ's atoning death and glorious resurrection as the means whereby salvation is achieved or at least initiated. Most scholars would agree that this particular aspect of the Christian message can hardly be accounted for by the Jewish background of the early Church, but proceeds mainly from non-Jewish roots: the Christian Saviour appears as a very close counterpart of the pagan saviour gods worshipped in the Graeco-Roman world.

It is, however, important, in this respect, to distinguish between salvation and redemption. The gods of the pagan mystery religions are saviour gods, since they lead the faithful to immortality. None of them is a redeemer in the etymological meaning of this term (*redimo*, 'to purchase back'). They do not suffer death in order to atone for the sins of Man. Their passion is not, to use the words of the Book of Common Prayer, 'a full, perfect and sufficient sacrifice, oblation and satisfaction for the sins of the whole world'; it has no vicarious efficacy. The Pauline idea of redemption cannot therefore be traced back exclusively, despite evident affinities, to any pagan model. It must either be ascribed to Paul's own creative genius, or explained, at least in part, by some Jewish antecedent. It seems, in fact, impossible to understand Pauline soteriology and its most original features if one leaves Judaism completely aside. On the other hand, it is by no means certain that the Pauline soteriological teaching is really representative of the early Christian position at large. The purpose of this paper is to develop a few remarks on these two points.

1 Brandon, *Man and his Destiny in the Great Religions* (1962), p. 223.

There can be little doubt that the idea of salvation, though not so central and prominent by far as it is in Christianity, is present in Judaism. God's repeated intervening in history from the very beginnings of mankind constitutes one continuous process of salvation, which will find its completion in the messianic kingdom and at the end of time. The verb σῴζω is commonly used by the Septuagint to describe divine action at work in what modern theologians call *Heilsgeschichte*. The Old Testament provides numerous examples of 'salvation'. It is important to note the distinctive characteristics of this Israelite Jewish concept, as contrasted with the Christian one. First, salvation means always primarily rescue from some physical or material evil: from danger, from the hands of one's enemies, from the death of the body.[2] Noah is saved from the flood,[3] Lot from destruction,[4] the Hebrew people from bondage in Egypt.[5] The fruit of salvation is 'life'. What is meant by this term is made clear by a number of biblical passages. It is in most cases the present life: 'All the commandments which I command thee this day shall ye observe to do, that ye may live, and multiply, and go in and possess the land which the Lord sware unto your fathers.'[6] It was only gradually, as the Israelite beliefs about after-life became more precise, that salvation was extended beyond the limits of the present world and became eternal salvation.[7]

Second, there is neither need nor room in such a conception for a saviour in the Christian sense of the word. The traditional figure of the Messiah is, of course, invested with some features which might be considered as soteriological. His main task is to rescue the righteous from the tyranny of the wicked, which means primarily, in the nationalist context which was still predominant in Israel at the beginning of the Christian era, that he will bring to an end foreign domination over the Holy Land and the chosen people.[8] But then, the Messiah is only an instrument in the hands of God. The initiative

2 E.g. Ps. 106: 10; Luke 1: 71. On the various meanings of the concept of salvation in Jewish thought, see Kittel, *Theologisches Wörterbuch zum Neuen Testament*, art. σῴζω, σωτήρ, σωτηρία.

3 Gen. 6: 8*ff.*; Heb. 11: 7; 1 Pet. 3: 20.

4 Gen. 19: 17.

5 Exod. 15: 2.

6 Deut. 8: 1.

7 Bousset, *Die Religion des Judentums im späthellenistischen Zeitalter*, third edition, ed. Gressmann (1926), pp. 242–301; Oesterley, *The Jews and Judaism during the Greek Period* (1941), pp. 186*ff.*

8 Mowinckel, *He that cometh* (1956), pp. 280*ff.*

of his saving action lies entirely with God, who is thus the one and only real Saviour.[9]

Third, God is Saviour essentially in his capacity as a legislator. Noah was saved because 'he was a righteous man',[10] and obeyed God's commandments. It is faithful observance of the divine ordinances which ensures what the Old Testament calls 'life'.[11] More precisely, the Mosaic law has been instrumental, ever since its promulgation, in the achievement of salvation and can therefore be rightly described as *προστάγματα ζωῆς*.[12] Salvation is, to begin with, a privilege imparted to a small part of mankind, namely the holy men of the remote past who lived in accordance with the still unwritten divine will, and, subsequently, God's own people. Salvation is implied in Israel's election and could therefore almost be considered as an event of the past. It took place, by a free decision of divine grace, on Mount Sinai, which, seen from this angle, appears as the Jewish counterpart of Calvary. A Jew is virtually saved by the very fact that he was born into the chosen people. It is for him to actualise this salvation by his pious behaviour.[13]

There is little concern, in the primitive Israelite perspective, for the gentiles, who are mostly thought of, being Israel's enemies, as an obstacle to 'salvation' and who cannot, at any rate, partake of it: their lot is death, not life. In the course of time the Jewish view of salvation was spiritualised and at the same time became more universalistic. The idea of eternal salvation became more and more accepted, along with the idea that it was not necessarily restricted to the Jews only, and that gentiles could, under certain conditions, share in it.[14] But even at this comparatively late stage in the evolution of Judaism it is the Law which provides the means of salvation. If a gentile wants to be saved he must either become a proselyte and keep the whole Law, or at least observe a minimum of precepts, the essentials of the Law as summarised in the so-called Noachian commandments.[15]

This view of salvation, briefly sketched, has at first sight little in common with the Pauline conception, which emphasises the redeeming action of a heavenly Saviour, distinct from God, and makes grace

9 Bonsirven, *Le Judaïsme palestinien au temps de Jesus-Christ* I (1935), p. 356.

10 Gen. 6: 9.

11 E.g. Deut. 4: 1; 8: 1; 30: 15–16, 19–20; 32: 46–7.

12 Ezek. 33: 15; cf. Baruch 3: 9; also Acts 7: 38: *λόγια ζῶντα*.

13 Moore, *Judaism in the First Centuries of the Christian Era* II (1930), pp. 94–5.

14 Moore, *op. cit.* II, pp. 385*ff*.

15 Moore, *op. cit.* I, p. 274; Bonsirven, *op. cit.* I, p. 251.

freely offered to all those, irrespective of their birth, whom God has chosen, the source of salvation. There are, however, a few trends in Jewish soteriology which foreshadow Paul's teaching. It is to be remembered that divine Wisdom is, in some late Jewish writings, hypostatised and presented as a personal being whose function it is, amongst others, to lead man to immortality.[16] It is in Ecclesiasticus explicitly identified with the revealed Law of God.[17] This is of some importance for the understanding of Paul's soteriology: Christ is the incarnate Wisdom;[18] he is Saviour not only by virtue of his death on the cross, but also *qua* Wisdom, as bearer of the new revelation.[19]

Another aspect of Jewish soteriology is probably more momentous with regard to Pauline thought, namely the idea that the merit of the righteous is able to atone for the sins of other people. It is deeply rooted in Jewish tradition. It is very strikingly expressed in the biblical episode of the destruction of Sodom: God is prepared to spare the sinful city if only ten righteous men are found among its inhabitants.[20] The belief in the merit of the Fathers (*zekut abot*) is an important tenet of rabbinic doctrine.[21] This is redemption in the very precise meaning of the word, and possibly the main source of Paul's conception of a Redeemer and of Christ's vicarious sacrifice. Some scholars would find an even closer and more precise parallel in the sacrifice of Isaac (*aqedat Jizhaq*), which was interpreted by the typological exegesis of the ancient Church as a figure of Christ,[22] and which plays an important part both in rabbinic thought and in the liturgy of the synagogue. It has indeed been interpreted by the rabbis as a redeeming act for the sins of Israel and should therefore, so we are told, be considered as the very pattern after which early Christian and, more precisely, Pauline thought explained Christ's death.[23] The idea is certainly very attractive. But on closer investigation it appears that it rests almost exclusively on rabbinic texts which are all, in so far as they can be dated, post-Christian. The episode of the sacrifice of Isaac is already commented

16 Wisd. 8: 13–17; 9: 18.

17 Eccles. 24.

18 1 Cor. 1: 24.

19 Davies, *Paul and Rabbinic Judaism* (1948), pp. 147*ff.*

20 Gen. 18: 32.

21 Moore, *op. cit.* I, pp. 538*ff.*; Marmorstein, *The Doctrine of Merit in Old Rabbinical Literature* (1920).

22 Gen. 22: 1*ff.*; cf. Daniélou, 'La typologie d'Isaac dans le christianisme primitif', *Biblica* XXVIII (1947), pp. 363–93; Lerch, *Isaaks Opferung, christlich gedeutet* (1950).

23 Schoeps, *Paulus* (1959), pp. 144*ff.*

on in pre-Christian writings, but it is then presented as illustrating perfect obedience and faith, and not yet as a redeeming act. A precisely soteriological interpretation of it is not to be excluded altogether before the appearance of Christianity.[24] But it cannot be affirmed either. It is quite possible, and in my opinion likely, that it is due to Christian influences and constitutes a Jewish reply to the Pauline conception of Christ's atoning death. It is best understood against the background of Jewish–Christian controversy during the first centuries.

Rabbinic tradition insisted not only on the virtues and exemplary life of the righteous but also, and even more, on their suffering. In the case of Isaac, 'his willingness to lay down life at God's bidding is reckoned by God as though the sacrifice had been accomplished, and was pleaded by his descendants as a ground for the remission of their sins'.[25] Still higher value was, quite naturally, set on the efficacy of suffering and death really endured. The question of a suffering and/or dying Messiah in Judaism has been much discussed. Though the Dead Sea scrolls have provided some new material, it still remains open.[26] It seems at least likely that the idea of a triumphant warrior Messiah was not, at the beginning of the Christian era, the only one accepted in Judaism. Some quarters seem to have favoured a messianic interpretation of Isa. 53 and more or less explicitly identified the Messiah with the suffering Servant.[27] But here again it is difficult to distinguish what is really pre-Christian and what is an appropriation of Christian doctrine.

One thing at least is certain: whether or not the figure of the Messiah himself was involved, atoning and redeeming efficacy was attributed to the suffering of the righteous. This is most clearly expressed in 4 Maccabees. Eleazar, who is enduring the torments of

24 Simon, *Recherches d'histoire judéo-chrétienne* (1962), pp. 195*ff*.

25 Moore, *op. cit.* I, p. 549.

26 Brierre-Narbonne, *Le Messie souffrant dans la littérature rabbinique* (1940); Mowinckel, *op. cit.*, pp. 325*ff*.; Schoeps, *op. cit.*, pp. 136*ff*. The main problem, as regards the Dead Sea scrolls, is whether the Teacher of Righteousness was martyred and was considered the Messiah designate, whose coming was expected by his disciples: Dupont-Sommer, *Aperçus préliminaires sur les Manuscrits de la Mer Morte* (1950), p. 116; *Les Ecrits esséniens découverts près de la Mer Morte* (1959), pp. 375*ff*.; cf. Philonerko, *Les Interpolations chrétiennes des Testaments des Douze Patriarches et les manuscrits de Qoumran* (1960).

27 Rowley, 'Suffering Servant and Davidic Messiah', in *The Servant of the Lord* (1952), pp. 61–8; Bonsirven, *op. cit.*, I, pp. 380*ff*.; Manson, *Jesus the Messiah* (1943), pp. 173*ff*.; Davies, *op. cit.*, pp. 279*ff*.

martyrdom, prays to God in the following words: 'Be gracious to thy people, being satisfied with our punishment in their behalf. Make my blood a sacrifice for their purification [καθάρσιον] and take my life as a substitute [ἀντίψυχον] for theirs.'[28] And the author expresses the same idea even more strikingly when he writes, 'They have become, as it were, a substitute, dying for the sins of the nation; and through the blood of those godly men and their propitiatory death divine Providence saved Israel, which was before in an ill plight.'[29]

Important though it may be, the role attributed in Jewish thought to the vicarious merit and suffering of the righteous is none the less subordinate to the efforts of the individual. Salvation is primarily a matter of personal obedience to the Law of God. It is important at this point to see what the Jewish Christian position was with regard to soteriology. The question is a difficult one to answer for lack of reliable and precise sources. The main problem, obviously, was to bring into accord the traditional Jewish view of the Law as the instrument of salvation and the conception of Christ as the Saviour. While to Paul the Law and Christ were mutually exclusive, and salvation could be achieved only by Christ and through faith in him, and included salvation from the Law,[30] it can be safely assumed *a priori* that to the Jewish Christians the Law had a part to play, along with Christ, in the process of salvation. Thus only is their stubborn clinging to legal observance to be satisfactorily explained. It appears that the most extreme and uncompromising among them attempted to enforce these views even upon the gentile converts: 'Except ye be circumcised after the manner of Moses, ye cannot be saved'.[31] The crux of the matter was to define the precise relation between Christ and the Law.

The inherited Jewish conception of salvation is clearly expressed in the Gospel episode of the young man who asks Jesus what he must do to inherit eternal life.[32] Jesus' answer could just as well have been given by any of the Pharisees: 'Thou knowest the commandments: Do not commit adultery, do not steal . . .' The decalogue, as summarising divine Law, is the true way to heaven: this is salvation without a saviour. When the young man has replied that he has kept all these

28 4 Macc. 6: 27–9.

29 4 Macc. 17: 20–2. Salvation here is still nothing other than rescue from earthly danger. But the author also knows eternal salvation as distinct from, and opposed to, earthly salvation (15: 3).

30 Gal. 3: 13; Rom. 5: 20–1; 7: 4–6; 1 Cor. 15: 56.

31 Acts 15: 1.

32 Mark 10: 17*ff*.; Matth. 19: 16*ff*.; Luke 10: 25*ff*.

ordinances since he was a boy, Jesus asks him to sell all he has and give to the poor, adding that he will thus have treasures in heaven,[33] which corresponds exactly to the traditional Jewish conception of merit. There is still nothing specifically Christian about this supererogatory element proposed by Jesus to his interlocutor, since the ideal of absolute renouncement and poverty was already that of the Essenes.[34] The Christian element appears only in Jesus' concluding injunction: 'Come and follow me.'[35] Jesus is still nothing more, in this perspective, than a model. He does indeed show the way to moral perfection, which is the surest means of being saved. But he is not really instrumental in the process of salvation. This consists of an *imitatio Christi*, which develops along the line drawn by the moral code of the decalogue, but goes beyond what is requested of the rank and file in Israel.

Jesus thus appears as the messenger sent by God to fulfil the Law, that is, to bring it to its perfection and also, it seems, to keep it himself more perfectly than anybody else. A curious passage of Hippolytus may be quoted in this connection. The Ebionites, he says,

> live according to Jewish customs, thinking that they will be justified by the Law and saying that Jesus was justified in practising the Law; wherefore he was named by God Christ and Jesus, since none of them has fulfilled the Law. For if any other had practised the commandments which are in the Law, he would be the Christ. And they say it is possible for them if they do likewise to become Christs; and that He was a man like unto all men.[36]

This sounds very strange. That Jesus should be thought of as a model of legalism and as having been elected, because of his own merits, to the messianic dignity is consonant with the Jewish Christian emphasis on works. But the ideas expressed in the following sentences—the impossibility of observing the Law perfectly, identification of the faithful with Christ—smack of Paulinism. To Paul, however, the utter impossibility of observing the Law is a reason for rejecting it.[37] And it is through a mystical process, by which he is made participant in divine grace and absorbed in the *pneuma* of the Lord, that the Christian can be

33 Mark 10: 21.
34 Josephus, *Bell. Jud.* 2: 8, 3; *Ant. Jud.* 18: 1, 5; Rule of Qumran (1 QS), 6: 19–20.
35 Mark 10: 21. Some manuscripts, followed, among others, by the Authorised Version and by Luther, add after 'come', 'take up the cross': cf. Matt. 16: 24–5.
36 *Philosoph.* 7: 34.
37 Gal. 3: 10; 5: 3; Schoeps, *op. cit.*, pp. 183*ff*.

identified with Christ.[38] On the contrary, in the Ebionite perspective, it is by keeping the Law as accurately and faithfully as Christ himself that this identification is achieved. We are thus faced with something like inverted Paulinism. And it still remains to be explained how, whereas the Jews were so far unable to keep the Law, this becomes possible to the Jewish Christians. The answer is obviously: through divine grace, of which Christ is the dispenser. Something more is needed here than just to follow his example, namely living 'in Christ'. We are thus back again on Pauline ground. The picture drawn by Hippolytus may not be perfectly adequate. But it is not to be excluded altogether that he has summarised a more or less successful attempt, on the part of some Jewish Christian sect, to come to terms with the fundamental tenets of the Pauline Gospel and to bring them into agreement with its own legalistic soteriology.

Even if the doctrine analysed by Hippolytus is not the product of an arbitrary or mistaken reinterpretation by the author himself, it must have been rather exceptional among the various shades of Jewish Christianity. What seems to be a common Jewish Christian feature is the impossibility of thinking, or the refusal to think, of salvation in other than legalistic terms. What is of fundamental importance in Christ's redeeming work is not his sacrifice on Calvary but his attitude to the Law, and this attitude cannot but be positive. Though Paul himself may refer to the *νόμος τοῦ Χριστοῦ*,[39] it is obvious that to him Christ's person rather than his teaching is the new Law, which is not to be reconciled with the old one, and abolishes it.[40] He performs by his death the saving task which the Jews wrongly attributed to the Law. On the contrary, in the sermon on the mount Jesus appears as the legislator of the new covenant which brings the old one to its perfection: he is the new Moses.[41]

This character appears very clearly in the Pseudo-Clementines, where Jesus is presented as one more avatar of the only true Prophet. His

38 Rom. 6: 3; 2 Cor. 5: 17; Gal. 2: 20; 3: 27; Col. 2: 12.

39 Gal. 6: 2.

40 Davies, *op. cit.*, p. 148: 'In a real sense conformity to Christ, His teaching and His life, has taken the place for Paul of conformity to the Jewish Torah. Jesus himself—in word and deed or fact—is a New Torah . . . Not only did the words of Jesus form a Torah for Paul, but so also did the person of Jesus.' I personally should insist more on the 'person' and less on the 'words'. In Rom. 3: 27 'law of faith' as opposed to 'law of works' is just another way of saying 'faith'.

41 Davies, *op. cit.* p. 149; Windisch, *Der Sinn der Bergpredigt* (1929), pp. 97*ff*.

main task is to proclaim the new form of divine revelation, which expresses itself in terms of commandments, and to restore in its original purity the eternal Law revealed first to Adam, then to Moses, and which had in the meantime been adulterated.[42] While the Pseudo-Clementine homilies never mention his Passion, they insist on the necessity for salvation of knowing the message he proclaims.

Knowledge is thus fundamental in the redeeming process, for ignorance—*ἄγνοια*—is the main obstacle to salvation: it leads inevitably to evil doing and is thus in itself a cause of perdition.[43] The object of knowledge is the Law, and knowledge can be described as *νόμιμος γνῶσις*.[44] This element of knowledge is, of course, present also in the Pauline interpretation of Christianity, but it is focused on the soteriological significance of Christ's death and resurrection, and is much less central than faith, *pistis*, which in its turn is not absent from other forms of early Christianity. The two elements are closely linked with each other. This is clearly expressed in Peter's words in the fourth Gospel: 'Lord, to whom shall we go? Thou hast the words of eternal life. And we believe [*πεπιστεύκαμεν*] and know [*ἐγνώκαμεν*] that thou art the Holy One of God.'[45] But even in this passage the object of knowledge, which brings forth faith, is not the redeeming act on Calvary but the teaching which Jesus imparts to his disciples, for which there is little room in Paul's interpretation of Christianity, and which is here described as *ῥήματα ζωῆς αἰωνίου*. The words which sum up the teaching of the fourth Gospel are to be interpreted along the same lines: 'These things are written that ye might believe that Jesus is the Christ, the Son of God, and that believing ye might have life through his name':[46] belief is grounded on knowledge, which is thus the very source of salvation.

The verb *γιγνώσκω* and the substantive *γνῶσις* can in some cases, but do not necessarily, carry a 'gnostic' connotation, in the precise and, so to speak, technical meaning of the term 'gnostic'. They can also just signify the fundamental importance of right teaching, a teaching which is not only, nor even primarily, *about* Christ but which has been first revealed *by* Christ. The passage from knowledge in the broadest

42 *Hom.* 2: 38–9, 43–44, 52; 3: 9, 43, 47; Schoeps, *Theologie und Geschichte des Judenchristentums* (1949), pp. 148*ff.*; Strecker, *Das Judenchristentum in den Pseudoklementinen* (1958), pp. 166*ff.*

43 *Epist. Clem.* 6: 1; *Hom.* 11: 11, 20; G. Strecker, *op. cit.*, p. 203, note 2.

44 *Hom.* 11: 19; Strecker, *op. cit.*, p. 152.

45 John 6: 68–9.

46 John 20: 31.

meaning of the term to specific *gnosis* is illustrated by a quotation from Clement of Alexandria by Eusebius: 'To James the Just and John and Peter, the Lord after the resurrection committed the *gnosis*; they committed it to the other Apostles and the other Apostles to the Seventy, of whom Barnabas also was one.'[47] The esoteric and properly 'gnostic' character of this teaching is made clear by the fact that it is not imparted during Christ's earthly life but after the resurrection, and that its transmission is limited to the inner circle of his closest disciples and thus constitutes the core of genuine apostolic tradition.[48]

Whatever our opinion may be on the vexed question of the relationship between Judaism, or Jewish Christianity, and Gnosticism, there can be little doubt about the importance of knowledge, as the very condition of right behaviour, in Jewish Christian soteriology. Jesus is the Saviour because he is the herald of the new dispensation, which does not, however, necessarily supersede the former one. In fact, according to the Pseudo-Clementines, salvation can be achieved by following either the Christian or the Jewish way of life. 'Jesus is hidden from the eyes of the Hebrews, who received Moses as their teacher, and Moses is hidden from the eyes of those who believe in Jesus. As the teaching transmitted by the one and by the other is the same, God receives anyone who believes in either of them.'[49] But the most privileged among men is the one who knows both Moses and Jesus: 'He is to be reckoned rich before God, for he understands that the things of old are new in time and that the things new are old.'[50]

The emphasis, once more, is on works. But here again, despite the violent hostility displayed by the Pseudo-Clementines against Paul, there appears something of a Pauline influence. Salvation is indeed procured by works, but conditioned by divine grace: 'It is God who bestowed on the Hebrews, and on those among the gentiles who have been called, their faith in the teacher of truth. What was left to each one's own decision is to perform good works.'[51] But this recourse to grace, which engenders faith, finally turns against the Pauline idea of salvation *sola fide*. The fundamental, and typically Jewish, idea is that of personal merit. There is no merit in being called by God: 'This

47 *Eccl. Hist.* 2: 1, 4.

48 In the Pseudo-Clementines (*Epistle of Peter to James*) the same precautions are taken concerning Peter's authentic teaching. Its transmission must be effected after the method used by Moses when he transmitted his teaching to the seventy elders.

49 *Hom.* 8: 6.

50 *Hom.* 8: 7.

51 *Hom.* 8: 5.

call is not men's own work, but that of God, who called them. It is not sufficient to obtain them a retribution, for the initiative is not theirs, but that of Him who inspired them. If, having been called, they achieve good works, which precisely is their own task, then they will deserve a retribution for it.'[52] In fact, baptism and good works are the two main conditions of salvation.

The mutual relation of these two elements in the Pseudo-Clementine conception is not perfectly clear. The necessity of baptism is frequently and insistently proclaimed. The efficacy of good works is dependent on baptism: 'Even if your piety transcends that of all pious men who have ever existed, you are unable without baptism to attain the object of hope. You will have to suffer a punishment all the greater for not performing good works rightly. For a good work is agreeable only when it is done as God has commanded it.'[53] What this means is made clear by the context: works can be considered good only if they are done in connection with, or more precisely after, baptism: for it is impossible without baptism to attain salvation.[54]

The necessity of baptism is obvious as regards the unrighteous—that is, the heathen, who have not, so far, known the Law: 'If you are unrighteous you need baptism to obtain remission of the sins you have committed through ignorance.'[55] But since the *Kerygmata Petrou* proclaim that Christians and—unbaptised—Jews alike, provided they keep the Law, can be saved, it is difficult to see what additional benefit baptism could bring to those who have already achieved righteousness by observing the divine commandments. And still, to them also it is indispensable to take recourse to the 'living water' in order to obtain salvation: 'Go ye therefore to it, whether you are righteous or unrighteous. If you are righteous you only lack baptism to be saved.'[56]

There is an evident contradiction in admitting that righteousness can, and in fact often does, precede baptism and that baptism is still the necessary prerequisite to true righteousness and thus to salvation. G. Strecker is certainly right in noting that baptism does not fit in very well with the rationally constructed moralism of the *Kerygmata Petrou*: 'It is just an inherited necessity, which he feels bound to maintain, an initiation rite whose real significance is no longer self-evident to him.'[57]

The reason for this rather unsuccessful attempt to reconcile a purely ethical and a sacramental conception of salvation seems to lie, at least

52 *Hom.* 8: 4.
53 *Hom.* 11: 25.
54 *Hom.* 11: 26.
55 *Hom.* 11: 27.
56 *Ibid.*
57 *Op. cit.*, p. 204.

in part, in the peculiar cosmology professed by the *Kerygmata Petrou*. Water is the primeval element, the first of all creatures,[58] on which God's *pneuma* breathed and out of which it shaped the whole creation.[59] It is opposed to fire, and this cosmic opposition is reflected at the ritual level. Even as ordinary water extinguishes fire, so did Jesus, 'by the grace of baptism, extinguish the fire of sacrifices kindled by Aaron because of the sins of the people', and which, in some way, prefigures the fire of eternal damnation.[60] Water is the purifying and life-giving element. This aspect is stressed even in connection with the Flood, where the function of water seems at first sight merely destructive. It does indeed destroy sinful mankind. But the main purpose of the Flood is that 'the purified world might be handed over stainless to the righteous one who was saved in the ark for a new beginning of life'.[61] Baptism, like the Flood, operates a new beginning. Through it man is regenerated; 'his natural birth is changed';[62] he thus 'extinguishes the fire of his former birth, for this was brought forth by the fire of concupiscence': 'Prima enim nostra nativitas per ignem concupiscentiæ descendit et ideo dispensatione divina secunda haec per aquam introducitur, quae restinguat ignis naturam.'[63] The effects of sin are thus abolished. Through the rebirth which it operates, baptism re-inserts man into the original order of the universe, which was born of water, and at the same time it saves him from the eternal flames: 'Seek ye therefore refuge in water, which alone can extinguish the ardour of flames.'[64]

The *Kerygmata Petrou* seems here to be once more influenced by Pauline thought. One of the fundamental differences between Paul's soteriology and salvation as conceived by Judaism lies in the fact that to Paul a new birth is requested, as a consequence of the Fall, for a man to be saved. This necessity is unknown to the traditional Jewish conception: nothing else is needed for salvation than observing the Law. Sins can be washed away by the sinner's own efforts; repentance and moral conversion provide the normal way to salvation. In the Pauline view, on the contrary, there is no such thing as moral conversion achieved by mere human will. Rebirth is a mystical process, where divine grace is the agent, and through which the spiritual element supersedes the earthly or psychical one. It is achieved by baptism 'into Christ'[65] through which the Christian, made participant of Christ's

58 *Hom.* 11: 24.
59 *Hom.* 11: 22–4.
60 *Recog.* 1: 39.
61 *Hom.* 8: 17.
62 *Hom.* 19: 23.
63 *Recog.* 9: 7.
64 *Hom.* 11: 26.
65 Rom. 6: 3; Gal. 3: 27.

death and resurrection, has become 'a new creature' and has been raised 'to walk in newness of life'.[66] This conception, more or less happily interpreted and transposed, seems to be underlying the Pseudo-Clementine view of salvation and baptism.

But here again Jewish thought and practice cannot be left completely aside. Recent research has made it clear that Jewish proselyte baptism was more than a mere levitical purificatory rite. It was accorded by rabbinic opinion, probably as early as the beginning of the Christian era, a truly sacramental significance.[67] Not only is the proselyte likened to a new-born child,[68] but Hillel and his school state, even more strikingly, that 'he who separates himself from the uncircumcision is like him who separates himself from the grave', which amounts to saying that 'conversion meant a passage from death to life'.[69] D. Daube has argued, in my opinion convincingly, that this relates precisely to the baptismal rite and that 'the decisive moment in proselyte baptism was the "going up" or "coming up"—no doubt because of its symbolical value'.[70] 'When the proselyte has undergone baptism and come up, *tabhal we'ala*, he is like an Israelite in all respects.'[71]

This seems very close to the Pauline conception of baptism. Two differences must, however, be noted. First, whereas the proselyte, before his baptism, is dead by the very fact that, being a heathen, he is outside the sphere of salvation, the Christian 'is baptised into death';[72] he is both 'buried with Christ in baptism and risen with him'.[73] Baptismal symbolism is here more elaborate than in the case of proselyte baptism. It includes the 'going down' as well as the 'coming up', because the rite reproduces both the death and the resurrection of Christ. Its meaning is nonetheless fundamentally the same on the Jewish and on the Christian side, for it signifies the passage from death to life and operates a new birth.

The second difference is more important. Proselyte baptism is for converts only It is useless for the Jews, who, having been trusted with the divine revelation, have thus already been called to life and are in no need of a new birth. In Paul's view, on the contrary, since the Law

66 2 Cor. 5: 17; Rom. 6: 4.
67 Daube, *The New Testament and Rabbinic Judaism* (1956), pp. 106*ff.*
68 *Yebam.* 48b; Davies, *op. cit.*, p. 119.
69 Daube, *op. cit.*, pp. 109–10.
70 *Op. cit.*, p. 111.
71 *Yebam.* 47b.
72 Rom. 6: 3.
73 Col. 2: 12.

is unable to procure salvation, the Jews are in no better position than the heathen. To be under the Law, under the curse of the Law[74] is tantamount to being 'in bondage under the elements of the world'.[75] Heathen and Jews alike must become a new creation: baptism is for all of them.

This universal necessity of the sacrament of regeneration springs quite logically from Paul's rejection of the Law. The position of the *Kerygmata Petrou*, on the other hand, lacks coherence. While it unreservedly accepts and even emphasises the idea of baptismal regeneration and even seems to make baptism instead of circumcision the only initiation rite,[76] it still insists on the saving efficacy of works and of the Law. Since the validity of the Law as a means of salvation is not called in question, it seems that baptism should be prescribed for pagan converts only. The Pseudo-Clementine conception appears thus as a rather awkward compromise between the traditional Jewish view of proselyte baptism and Pauline soteriology. It testifies in its own way to the pervasive influence of Paul's thought even in those quarters which were least prepared to accept it and were strongly hostile to the apostle.

Christian thought in post-apostolic times appears rather hesitant as regards the precise relation between Christ and the Law—some sort of Law—in the scheme of salvation. Paul's position is hardly represented in its original radicalness. This is to be accounted for both by the intrinsic difficulty of Pauline doctrine and by the tenacious persistency in almost all sections of the Church of the Jewish, or Jewish Christian, ways of thinking. Early Christianity is far from identifying itself with Paulinism.

The Pauline conception of Christ's person as the new Law is expressed now and then. In the *Kerygma Petrou*, quoted by Clement of Alexandria, 'the Lord is called Law and Word'.[77] According to Justin Martyr, 'Christ has been given to us the eternal and final Law, a secure covenant after which there is neither Law, nor precepts, nor commandments'.[78] This is in line with Pauline thinking, and has a definitely antinomistic and anti-Jewish sting. In the *Shepherd of Hermas*

74 Gal. 3: 13.

75 Gal. 4: 3.

76 Molland, 'La circoncision, le baptême et l'autorité du décret apostolique dans les milieux judéo-chrétiens des Pseudo-Clémentines', *Studia Theologica* IX (1955), pp. 1–39; reprinted in *Opuscula Patristica* (1970), pp. 25–59.

77 *Strom.* I: 29.

78 *Dialogue*, 11: 2; 43: 1.

'the Law given to the whole world is the Son of God, who is preached unto the limits of the earth'.[79] Here, however, the inspiration is fundamentally Jewish Christian,[80] and the identification of Christ with the new Law seems to be hardly more than an inherited way of speaking, whose bearing has been lost sight of. It is not certain, moreover, that the sentence belongs to the original text. It might be interpolated.[81] For immediately after that the archangel Michael—who here is probably Christ[82]—is presented as the one who gives the Law. And the image of Christ as a legislator is certainly more consonant with the general inspiration of this curious work than the idea of Christ the new Law.

In fact the *Shepherd* voices a strictly legalistic form of Christianity. Faithful observance of the Law is the condition of salvation. The crown of immortality is granted to those who have fought against the devil and defeated him. Repentance is the way to life, and life is for all those who keep the commandments of the Lord.[83] The role assumed by Christ is described in significant terms: 'Having washed away the sins of the people, he showed to them the paths of life by giving them the Law which he had himself received from his father'.[84] The Passion is thus presented as a mere preamble. The decisive moment, in the process of redemption, is the promulgation—apparently after the resurrection—of a Law which must be closely akin to that of Sinai: this may be inferred from the fact that the Son receives it from the Father, which underlines the continuity in the unfolding of the divine plan. It seems that the ancient legislation is not abolished, except perhaps as regards its merely ritual parts. Christ's sacrifice is described in curiously obscure words: 'He purified the people of its sins, at the cost of immense pain and great toil'.[85] But it is not even certain that this does really refer to Christ and his Passion.[86] However this may be, we are very far here from Pauline christology and soteriology.[87]

79 *Simil.* 8: 3, 2.
80 Daniélou, *Théologie du Judéo-Christianisme* (1958), pp. 46*ff.*; Giet, 'Un courant judéo-chrétien à Rome au milieu du IIe siècle?' in *Aspects du Judéo-Christianisme* (1965), pp. 95–112.
81 Giet, *Hermas et les Pasteurs* (1963), p. 239
82 Daniélou, *Théologie du Judéo-Christianisme*, pp. 173*ff.*
83 *Simil.* 8: 6, 6; 8: 7, 6.
84 *Simil.* 5: 6, 3.
85 *Simil.* 5: 6, 2.
86 Giet, *Hermas et les Pasteurs*, pp. 218 *ff.*
87 *Simil.* 9, which develops a doctrine of baptism as the condition of salvation (9: 16) very similar to that of Paul, is not by the same author as the other *Similitudes*: Giet, *Hermas et les Pasteurs*, pp. 139*ff.*, 289*ff.*

The importance of the *Shepherd* must not be undervalued, since it enjoyed considerable popularity in the ancient Church and was regarded as quasi-canonical 'by Irenaeus, Clement of Alexandria, Tertullian and apparently Athanasius in his earlier years, and was also included in the Codex Sinaiticus in the New Testament'.[88]

This conception of Christianity and of salvation in terms of law is by no means exceptional. It appears, diversely expressed, in a number of early Christian writings.[89] Two main reasons, it seems, explain such a view. It represents a sort of a compromise between the Pauline position and a more traditional and Judaising interpretation of the Gospel. And it also corresponds to the necessity of formulating in a satisfactory way the relation between the Old and the New Testaments, considered as two successive stages of one and the same undivided divine revelation. Christ can consequently be described as the new legislator, *ὁ καινὸς νομοθέτης*.[90] The distinction between Christ who is the new Law and Christ who promulgates it tends to vanish, and so also does the sharp distinction drawn by Paul between Law and faith, between the old and the new Covenants. According to Clement of Alexandria, both the new and the old Law have been given by the Logos, *ὑπὸ τοῦ Λόγου*, the new one directly, the old one through Moses, *διὰ Μωσέως*.[91] The Gospel is the new Law. Conversely, the Mosaic law is the grace of old, *χάρις παλαιά*.[92] There can thus be no conflict between faith and law, which are ultimately one and the same thing. The Law, by which is meant the moral law, is the necessary schoolmaster, not only in the past, 'unto Christ, that we might be justified by faith',[93] but even after Christ's coming, unto salvation: 'Let us take the Logos as our law; let us recognise that his precepts and advices open short and rapid ways unto eternity.'[94] Salvation, therefore, is achieved by making one's conduct conform to Christ's ethical teaching.

One could perhaps be tempted to trace such a conception back to Paul himself, who states that 'in Christ Jesus the life-giving law of the Spirit has set us free from the law of sin and death'.[95] But it is obvious

88 Cross, *Early Christian Fathers* (1960), p. 24.
89 E.g. Jas. 1: 25; 2: 8; 2: 12 ('law of freedom'); Barnabas 2: 6 ('the new law of our Lord Jesus Christ, free from the yoke of compulsion').
90 Justin, *Dialogue* 18.
91 *Paed.* 1: 60, 1.
92 *Ibid.*
93 Gal. 3: 24.
94 *Paed.* 1: 9, 4.
95 Rom. 8: 2.

that the Pauline oppositions are no longer understood by Clement.[96] Paul's views have been distorted, probably under the combined influence of Jewish concepts and of the philosophical, mainly Stoic, ideal of moral perfection, achieved through individual effort, in conformity with, and submission to, the universal law of nature.

96 Prunet, *La Morale de Clément d'Alexandrie et le Nouveau Testament* (1966), p. 230.

19

Ninian Smart

Living liberation

Jīvanmukti and nirvāṇa

Too often the understanding of the early Buddhist idea of *nirvāṇa* has been hampered by the failure to note the two aspects of liberation. Or to put matters another way, nirvana has not been looked at sufficiently as a case of *jīvanmukti* or 'living liberation'. Such a conception has, of course, proved highly influential in the Indian tradition; and perhaps its most natural milieu has been that of a yogic tradition. That is to say, it implies the overcoming of those forces impelling the individual to further involvement in the round of *saṁsāra.* in such a way that the individual has only to finish off the remains of his current life; then there will be no more rebirth. Typically, the means of achieving this state of *jīvanmukti* are yogic meditation and austerity. Different schools and movements have differing emphases.

Let us consider, by way of illustration, the situation in Sāṃkhya-Yoga, as this dual school came to formulate itself. Here innumerable *puruṣas* are implicated in rebirth; but more generally they are implicated in *prakṛti.* i.e. nature. The material, natural world is one great system, breathing in and out, so to speak, as the cosmos forms out of chaos through the interplay of the *guṇas*, and then relapses at the end of an enormous cycle into grey equipoise once more, waiting secretly for the next evolutionary process to begin. In this great system are dotted an infinity of transmigrating souls, experiencing *duḥkha* or illfare, moving perhaps towards release. Release means, of course, the freeing of the *puruṣa* from the psycho-physical organism to which it has been wedded hitherto forever. Imagine, therefore, what strain and self-control, what knowledge and meditative skill, are required to achieve assurance of release—to achieve assurance through actuality, and to be released here and now.

However, we would be a little anachronistic in comparing directly this Sāṃkhya-Yoga system with that of early Buddhism. Yet undoubtedly the *general* form of such a belief in rebirth, yoga, souls and *mukti* was present in the Buddha's environment. And we also have to look towards the pattern of Jaina belief and practice, not at all dissimilar; stressing, however, *tapas* and *ahiṃsā*.

Yet it was more than in practice that early Buddhism trod a middle path. In theory also it steered between souls and materialism, rejecting the former but asserting rebirth. This mediation meant an entirely original perspective upon rebirth and salvation. For whereas other movements—Ājīvakas and Jainas, for example—postulated souls and so something which could, *post mortem*, achieve 'final liberation', Buddhism could not treat its *jīvanmukti* in this mode at all. And that, as is well known indeed, was bound to lead to the question as to what becomes of the Buddha or saint (*arhant*) after death. That *nirvāṇa* can, however, be looked on profitably as a form of *jīvanmukti* should not on that account be doubted, and Louis Finot was right to insist upon the point.[1] Yet what is at first sight puzzling is that in the case of Buddhism there is nothing to be liberated, or rather (to put it more particularly) there is no soul (*puruṣa*, *jīva* or *ātman*) to be liberated.

Nevertheless it is unwise to be *too* puzzled by this. For consider the situation in our previous 'model', namely Sāṃkhya–Yoga. The *puruṣa* there is only in one sense individual. It is individual in the sense, first, that it is not numerically identical with any other *puruṣa*, and, second, it is uniquely co-ordinated to a given psycho-physical organism (and its predecessors in the transmigratory sequence). For the sake of clarity I shall refer to the individual in a given (e.g. the current) life as 'individual' and to the sequence as the 'macro-individual'—so that John Jones is an individual but the sequence up to and including him (and stretching into the future, unless he is a *jīvanmukta*) is the macro-individual.[2] To recapitulate, the *puruṣa*, in the Sāṃkhya–Yoga system, is uniquely correlated to a particular macro-individual. Similarly, the *jīva* in the Jaina system is so correlated. However, though the *puruṣa* is uniquely correlated to a macro-individual, the characteristics and elements which make up the latter do not belong to the soul. To put it more concretely, what makes up the individual Surasena and his predecessors in the sequence is not carried over into the *post mortem* liberated state. Thus it is characteristic of systems of salvation of the

1 In his review of Rhys Davids, *Buddhism: its history and literature*, *Revue de l'histoire des religions* XXXVII, pp. 247–448 [see Welbon, *The Buddhist Nirvana and its Western Interpreters* (1968), p. 239 note 53].

2 This is a convenient distinction which I first made in my *Doctrine and Argument in Indian Philosophy* (1964).

relevant sort—mainly Śramanic—not to consider final *mukti* as belonging strictly to the psycho-physical individual. All this can be put another way: the soul is *beyond* the mental constituents of the individual. The soul–organism distinction is not at all to be equated with the mind–body distinction. So the Western question 'Can there be disembodied existence after death?' is not strictly relevant to the Indian case.

This is brought out at the cosmological level also. As is well known —and it is a striking aspect of Buddhist cosmology in particular—many Indian systems of belief do not equate *post mortem* liberation with heavenly existence. *Nirvāṇa* lies beyond heaven. One can have a glorious disembodied existence in one of the heavens, say as one of the Brahmās. But this is still impermanent and in principle shot through with *dukkha*. Thus imaginatively the line between unsatisfactory existence and liberation is drawn in a different place and in a different way from its analogues in the traditions of the West and the Middle East.

This match between the cosmic and the individual levels may in part help us to understand why the question of the infinity (endlessness) of the *loka* as to space and time was also undetermined, as well as the question of the survival of the 'thus gone' person after death. A. K. Warder writes,

> These extracts would seem to confirm that the notions of 'soul' and 'universe' are very closely associated, belong to the same realm of ideas, from the standpoint of the Buddha. If we are right in concluding that for the Buddha there was no such thing as the 'universe', then we must conclude that for him the question of its being infinite or infinite in space and time is meaningless instead of being beyond our knowledge.[3]

However, something more than this needs to be said.

First, the question of the survival of the *Tathāgata* after death seems to be meaningless in a deep sense, as K. N. Jayatilleke pointed out; the parallel with Wittgenstein's doctrine of certain utterances as being meaningless is plausible.[4] Perhaps one can put the point by the following example. It is not the case that the present king of France is bald; nor is he not bald—and the reason is that there is no king of France. And the survival of the *Tathāgata* cannot be affirmed or denied, in that there is no soul to 'carry over'. But whereas it merely *happens* to be the

3 Warder, *Indian Buddhism* (1970), p. 149.

4 Jayatilleke, *Early Buddhist Theory of Knowledge* (1959), pp. 384*ff*.

case that there are no kings of France these days, the non-existence of the *ātman* is not thus contingent. It is part of 'the nature of things' as revealed by Buddhist analysis and experience.

It might be replied that this interpretation of meaninglessness depends heavily on the passage about the fire going out (whither does it go when it goes out?—a wrongly posed question);[5] whereas there is also a pragmatic interpretation, implied by the simile of the arrow: work out your salvation without bothering yourself with the distractions of metaphysical speculation. But of course the two accounts are up to a point compatible. Theory and practice go solidly together in the teaching of the Buddha. There might be incompatibility in so far as the pragmatic interpretation can easily be taken to mean that one *can* answer the question about the *Tathāgata*, that there are possible theories here. And this is in conflict with the notion that the question is wrongly put and so unanswerable. Incidentally, it is of the utmost importance to notice that in early Buddhism, and in the later Theravāda, it is only a certain set of questions that is held to be unanswerable. There is no necessity for the inference that *all* metaphysical views were excluded; for instance, the analysis of the *skandas*, the doctrine of dependent origination, more generally the account of causation—these and many other aspects of Buddhist teaching are in an important sense metaphysical. (The Mādhyamika, of course, was bold enough to generalise the fourfold negation; but this is only one interpretation of the Buddha's meaning, not shared by most other schools.) In brief, then, one needs first to note that a partial pragmatic account is not inconsistent with the 'Wittgensteinian' interpretation; and second to bear in mind that particular questions are undetermined —and this means that we need to see in particular why this is so. In the case of the survival of the *Tathāgata*, part of the reason is the non-existence of the *ātman*, the *necessary* non-existence of it, on Buddhist analysis. It is only part of the explanation, in that we have to consider positively why there is a *nirvāṇa* without substrate (*anupadhiśeṣa*). But in the meantime let us apply the present account to the question of the everlastingness of the universe, etc. As we have seen, Warder considers that the Buddha essentially rejected the very idea of the *loka*, just as he rejected the *ātman*. But is this correct? Certainly there are plenty of uses of the term in the Pāli canon, yet this is a very indecisive argument, for the term *atta* is also used in a conventional (*vyāvahārika*) way.

5 *Majjhimanikāya* 72

First, note a parallel between the question about the *Tathāgata* and the question about the *loka*. In the former the question is about continued existence, but there is no question about the existence of the *Tathāgata* here and now (so to speak)—this is assumed. So is it not more proper to look on the question of the *loka* as about its continued existence, but without any implication that there is no such thing as the *loka*? In the discussion preceding the conclusion which I have quoted above, Warder rightly draws attention to the connection between ideas of continued existence (of the *loka*) and survival (i.e. of the macro-individual). But it would be more apposite to conclude that the reason for the *loka*'s neither being nor not being endless in space and time has to do precisely with the question of 'how you come to the end of the *loka*', that is, with the question of *nirvāṇa*.

Let us look at this from the temporal aspect. Virtually Buddhism treats rebirth as endless—so that the macro-individual always was and always will be unless he attains *nirvāṇa*, in which case rebirth ceases and there is a state of ultimate liberation, but of whom we cannot properly inquire. All this implies that in some important sense the *loka* or cosmos always was and in principle always will be. True, it cannot be treated as a timeless entity, it is made up of events—of impermanencies. Still looking at the *loka* existentially—that is, from the point of view of experience, or from the point of view of the indissoluble wedding between theory and practice which so characterises the Buddhist approach—it has a sort of end. The question, however, is wrongly put if it is asked simply about what is 'out there', for the spiritual relevance of the question necessarily connects with the possibility of our 'making an end'. There is a sort of end of the cosmos as we disappear 'into' *nirvāṇa* and there is no rebirth any more for the particular macro-individual. On the other hand, the disappearance of one macro-individual from *saṃsāra* does not entail the disappearance of others. *Saṃsāra* still goes on. If the question 'Is there an end to the *loka*?' is asked simply from an autobiographical point of view, then the answer is that there is a possible end to the macro-individual, but it is not a spatial limit, so to speak. From the autobiographical point of view, where the existential question has to do with liberation, the question about the endlessness of the world in space is wrongly put, i.e. irrelevant.

However, if there is an end of the macro-individual through the onset of *nibbāna*, surely there is a temporal end to the cosmos, for *me*? But here the question becomes virtually identical with the question about whether the saint exists after death. Further, there is a question about whether the *nibbāna* element is to be counted as part of the *loka* or not. We must remember the very fine gradations of existence which are to be found in the Buddhist cosmology. The matching of differing types of existence to the range of *jhānas*, right up to the sphere of neither-perception-nor-non-perception,[6] indicates a partly psychological approach to cosmology, one which could perhaps be characterised as 'existential' in the modern sense. However, the fineness of the gradations means that at the most elevated level of consciousness and existence one is getting to what in other systems of belief could be regarded as liberation. *Nirvāṇa* lies beyond, of course; but the Buddhist mood is not one of a sharp line to be drawn between the *loka* with all its invisible and divine realms and the state of ultimate liberation. The Buddha, as a liberated one, could come to be regarded as transcendental or *lokottara*; and there is an important sense in which *nirvāṇa* is transcendent. But the distinction between the highest spheres of the *loka* and *nirvāṇa* is a delicate one. It turns, of course, essentially on the idea of permanence, to which I shall return in a moment.

As to the distinction between transcendental *nirvāṇa* and the *loka*, another point is worth seeing—namely that it is (roughly speaking) the same distinction as that between *anupādisesa* and *saupādisesa nibbāna*.[7] *Nirvāṇa* with substrate is a dispositional state of an identifiable individual, one which accrues upon a form of *gnosis*, or existential knowledge of the truth of things accompanied by complete serenity. It is a dispositional state in the sense that the person who is *nibbuta* is no longer in the grip of craving and ignorance, and this shows through in his actions, words, gestures and so on. On the orthodox line, it is an unbreakable disposition—the *arhat* cannot fall away. (If he appears to do so, it only goes to show that he was not *nibbuta* in the first place.) Since, however, *nirvāṇa* without substrate involves, as we have seen, the disappearance of the macro-individual, we cannot speak of anything or anybody as now identifiable, so that the dispositional analysis of *nirvāṇa* cannot any more apply. And in so far as the saint in this life can be said to have 'seen' or 'tasted' *nirvāṇa* and to have, as it were, crossed to the other shore, we can also quite legitimately think of *anupādisesa nibbāna* as being, as it were, a transcendent state already present to the saint. Or, to put this another way, the

6 Eliade, *Yoga: Immortality and Freedom* (1954), pp. 167–73.

7 Or Sanskrit *Anupadhiśeṣa* and *Saupadhiśeṣa*; for an interesting discussion see Welbon, *op. cit.*, pp. 208*ff*.

nirvāṇa with and without substrate coexist as well as succeed one another in time, in relation to a given macro-individual. Empirical *nirvāṇa* (*nirvāṇa* with substrate) involves 'seeing' transcendent *nirvāṇa*. The saint sees and is in contact with the changeless.

Here we need to turn to the question of permanence. The whole way of analysing the world from a Buddhist point of view turns on the distinction between that which is impermanent and that which is permanent. It may not be the whole of the doctrine of *dukkha* that what is impermanent is therefore unsatisfactory and painful. But yet there is some plausibility in seeing the other two marks of existence (*anattā* and *dukkha*) as flowing from the impermanence of things (*anicca*). The impermanence of individuals entails that they do not consist partly in changeless souls. Likewise the *loka* has no eternal changeless heart (so to speak), even if it may in effect be everlasting, continually in flux. It is no great exaggeration to say that the whole Buddhist metaphysical and existential analysis depends on where the line is drawn between the changing and the changeless. (More generally, it is this distinction which is vital in most Indian systems of salvation; thus, for example, Śaṃkara's doctrine of *māyā* boils down essentially to the notion that the world is changeable and impermanent and so does not bring the higher satisfaction, the realisation of one's identity into the eternal Brahma.)

But whereas Śaṃkara, for example, could be said to draw a dualism between substance and substance—between Brahma and the visible universe, etc—which has some analogues at least between the God's world distinction in the Western tradition, the Theravādin distinction between the temporal and the changeless is more a state–state dualism (or an element–element dualism). That is, in the one case the distinction is between a permanent entity and a congeries of impermanen entities; in the other the division is between the eternal state of *nirvāṇa* and the impermanent state or events of the empirical world (including the various heavens and purgatories).

Since Śaṃkara was a bit influenced by the Mahāyāna and in particular by the Mādhyamika school, it is interesting to bring into the comparison the idea of *Śūnya*, the Void, also called *tathatā*. These words are used fleetingly to refer to 'ultimate reality'. And yet *Śūnyatā* suggests a phantasmogorical ultimate *unreality*. The 'higher truth' of the Void confronts the 'empirical truth' of ordinary experience. It goes without saying, in the Buddhist context, that the Void has a reference in meditational experience. However, the atmosphere (if I can put the matter so vaguely) of the Mādhyamika is more that of substance-substance dualism than of state–state dualism.[8] This connects, perhaps paradoxically, with the *nirvāṇa–saṃsāra* identification, which looks like a kind of monism. The identification can without too much strain, but alas with a certain crudity, be explicated in the following way. Liberation means the attainment of Buddhahood. The essence of the latter is the *dharma* (or the *dharmakāya*), which is what the teaching refers to. This is the Void, which has two aspects, one experiential and the other metaphysical. (These two aspects, indeed, correspond loosely to the two aspects of the Buddhist doctrine of the *loka*—both metaphysical or analytic and at the same time practical and experiential.) The experiential aspect is that the perception of the higher truth (in brief, enlightenment) is non-dual and uncharacterised, therefore, by the distinctions of everyday existence. From the latter point of view it is empty, and it is in fact devoid (or one should, no doubt, say *void*) of the distinctions and distractions of discursive thought and ordinary emotions, etc. On the metaphysical front, the world of everyday entities is empty, for nothing has real substance, and every theory of reality contains contradictions. The tangible and the real—these turn out to have no real permanence and no 'inner stuff'. Their real nature is the void. It follows that *saṃsāra* has the Void as its inner reality. But the Void is the true nature of the Buddha. So the essence of Buddhahood, which is also *nirvāṇa*, is the essence of the phenomenal world. Therefore *nirvāṇa* and *saṃsāra* are the same! A meaningful and intelligible paradox.

The identity signifies a kind of monism; but there remains the dualism, for there are two levels of reality or truth to notice. The main difference between this idea and the main distinction of the Theravāda is that the void is 'the true nature of things' while also being the essence of liberation, while in the Theravāda liberation is not the 'true nature of things' (the latter is dealt with rather separately through the idea of the three marks of conditioned existence) but a distinct state. It is possible to evolve a theory of why the Mahāyāna went for what I have referred to as a 'monistic' account, and I have tried to give some sort of an explanation elsewhere.[9]

It might further be remarked that the Mahāyāna dualism is marked, more positively than in the Pāli tradition, by a doctrine of two levels

8 This point is elaborated somewhat in my *Doctrine and Argument in Indian Philosophy*.

9 In *Reasons and Faiths* (1958), chapter v.

of truth. Though the distinction exists in the Theravāda, it is there treated (if I may put it so) 'less ontologically'. And being less systematically applied, it turns out to mean that the analysis of reality is hampered by the conventional acceptance of words: once analysis unmasks reality, however, it is entirely legitimate to carry on talking 'conventionally' (even if the illusions of language have now been dissipated, so that ordinary language suffers a sort of a sea change).

Perhaps we can now return, after these excursions, to the idea of *nibbāna* or liberation as it is to be found in the Pāli canon. Although the analysis of the world in terms of the three characteristics of existence is itself a means of liberation and so to be interpreted up to a point as 'existential', the analysis leans towards the realistic (just as by contrast the Mahāyāna analysis leans towards the subjective and the ideal). The fact that the Theravādin analysis is of this kind is no coincidence. The equation between *nirvāṇa* and *saṃsāra* implied that knowledge was the key—for the adept had only to realise that there was no difference in order to be liberated: the realisation of the non-difference makes the difference. This doctrine (whatever its other merits and defects) was one which was favourable to laymen. They were, so to speak, already there, if only they could realise this truth; and the lack of distinction between the 'beyond' and 'here' was also reflected in increasingly strong feelings that the laymen would here and now attain conversion and release. By contrast the state-state dualism of the Theravāda did not encourage lay optimism, and there was and is a very powerful insistence on methods of meditation as the key to the way upward and ultimately to *nirvāṇa.* This emphasis is, of course, not absent from the Mahāyāna. But the Theravāda retains an emphasis on the effort of the individual as the key to liberation.

It is a strong, strong effort, because of the way in which lives previously led and previously conceived to have generated a lot of *karma* may strongly jeopardise the vocation of the monk. The whole pattern of belief in rebirth and *jīvanmukti* implies strenuous self-training, as also in the Jaina tradition. Further, the pursuit of liberation as it is represented in the Pāli canon does not imply anything about reliance upon divinity.[10] On the other hand, the celestial Buddhas and Bōdhisattvas of the Mahāyāna provide a means towards liberation where individual effort is stressed much less.

At all events, the realism of Theravāda metaphysics and the dualism

10 See my 'The work of the Buddha and the work of Christ', in *The Saviour God*, ed. Brandon (1963).

of impermanent states and permanent state fits in with the ethics of energetic striving after liberation. At the same time I have in this analysis been concerned also to stress the 'existential' aspects of Theravādin cosmology, and it is partly because of these that the questions about survival after death and the everlastingness of the cosmos are undetermined. I have attempted to indicate how it is that both the Wittgensteinian and the pragmatic accounts are relevant to the understanding of the Buddha's teaching on these matters. It is difficult to solve the historical question of what early Buddhism said without trying to penetrate to what it meant.

20

D. Howard Smith

Conflicting ideas of salvation in A.D. fifth century China

The religious situation in China during the fifth century of our era is of particular interest to the student of comparative religion. Throughout the previous century Buddhism had had a phenomenal success, particularly as regards its Mahāyāna forms. In the north nearly the whole of the population had been converted, through the efforts of such missionaries as Fo T'u-têng (d. A.D. 349), whilst in the south Buddhism had penetrated court circles and attracted many of the educated gentry. The time was come when leading Confucians and Taoists, envious of the success of the Buddhist religion, were prepared to engage in controversy and even acrimonious discussion with the Buddhists, and one question of great concern was the different interpretations of the nature of man and his ultimate destiny. Much of the debate centred on the question as to whether or not there exists a permanent spiritual principle in man, and if so what happens to it on the dissolution of the body at death.

On the whole, it was Confucians who, in this period, tended to deny that there is a spiritual element in man which survives death, and this in spite of the universal appeal of the cult of ancestors, with its detailed prescriptions as to mourning and sacrificial rites. These seemed to imply the recognition of at least some form of survival. But the influence of Hsün-tzŭ's (*c.* 298–238 B.C.) naturalism had been strongly reinforced by the scepticism and rationalism of Wang Ch'ung (A.D. 27–97?), who completely rejected the idea of a soul living on after death. 'After a man dies he does not become a spiritual being, has no consciousness, and cannot speak'.[1] During the Han dynasty Confucianism had found a reasonable and logical basis for the view that human existence, beginning with conception and birth, terminates at death, by taking up into itself the *yin–yang* philosophy, which argued that everything in the universe, including man, results from the interaction

1 Chan, Wing-Tsit, *A Source Book in Chinese Philosophy* (1963), p. 302.

of two complementary material elements, the *yin* and the *yang*, which are constantly engaged in producing all things. Everything is evolving in an ever-changing flux. Human life, being part of Nature, and also a product of this interplay of *yin* and *yang*, persists so long as these forces are held together in mutual harmony, but death results when they disperse. What is called 'mind', 'soul' or 'spirit' is but the functioning of the material body. It is inseparable from the body, so that when the body perishes the soul perishes likewise. The soul (*shên*) is recognised to be something mysterious, but it too is a product of the interplay of *yin* and *yang*, which by their coalescence bring about the beginning of a life, and by their dispersal bring about the end.

For the Confucian, therefore, there was no persisting spiritual element which lived on after death. Consequently, the salvation about which he was concerned was not so much a personal salvation as a political and social change within the present world order which would result in the establishment of the just and benevolent rule of a sage king, and an era of universal peace, justice and prosperity. To his way of thinking those who spoke of a blessed realm beyond death to which the saved and purified soul might hope to go were but deluding the people.

The position taken up by leading Taoists differed from that of the Confucians. One form of Taoism known as the Huang-Lao philosophy was influenced by the mysticism of Chuang-tzŭ (fourth century B.C.). Whilst they also accepted the *yin-yang* theory, they believed that by means of prescribed disciplines and techniques the two complementary elements whose interaction had resulted in a human life could be held together for an incredibly long time. Throughout life all kinds of influences tended to break up that harmony between the *yin* and the *yang* elements, causing sickness and death. These must be thoroughly studied with a view to their elimination, whilst everything that helped to harmonise the *yin* and the *yang* must be encouraged. If one carefully followed all the prescriptions and mastered the disciplines the result would be, for all practical purposes, an immortal life. It would be a life in which the grosser and coarser elements of one's nature had been gradually purged away. Hence salvation for these Taoists was the attainment of an immortal life in a body that had become so tenuous as to be invisible and lighter than air, free to wander, if it so desired, to the confines of the universe.

A strong religious Taoist movement which emerged in the closing decades of the Han dynasty had attracted hundreds of thousands of peasants. This form of Taoism developed a cultic organisation, with its priests and libationers, its rituals of purification, penance and atonement. It promised the believer salvation from sin, the cure of sickness, disease and devil-possession, a happier life in this world and the hope of immortality beyond the grave. It was this form of Taoism which proved a fertile field for the propagation of popular Buddhism among the peasantry throughout the fourth century.

In the early centuries of the Christian era Confucians and Taoists alike accepted the belief that man is essentially a part of Nature, and therefore, like everything else in nature, man is in a state of evolution and change. He has his beginning and end, his birth and death. As Chuang-tzŭ had so pertinently said, 'Life follows upon death. Death is the beginning of life. Who knows when the end is reached? The life of man results from convergence of the vital fluid. Its convergence is life; its dispersion, death. If therefore life and death are but consecutive states, what need have I to complain?'[2] Whereas the Confucian believed that over his *fate* or *destiny* the individual man had little or no control, the religious Taoist believed that techniques had been evolved by which the future might be greatly modified. But the philosophically minded, whether Confucian or Taoist, believed that human life was tragically fleeting and inevitably bounded by the complete annihilation of the person as such in death. This is well expressed in the *Book of Lieh-tzŭ*, which most Chinese scholars attribute, at least in its present form, to the third century A.D.[3]

Some in ten years, some in a hundred, we all die. In life they were Yao and Shun [two sage kings], in death they are rotten bones; in life they were Chieh and Chou [two evil tyrants], in death they are rotten bones ... Once I am dead, what concern is it of mine? It is the same to me whether you burn me or sink me in a river, bury me or leave me in the open, throw me in a ditch wrapped in grass or put me in a stone coffin dressed in a dragon-emblazoned jacket and embroidered skirt... While you are alive, resign yourself and let life run its course; satisfy all your desires and wait for death. When it is time to die, resign yourself and let death run its course; go right to your destination, which is extinction.[4]

It was into this climate of thought that Buddhism came with its call to a high morality linked to a dynamic message of hope and

2 See Giles, *Chuang Tzŭ* (1926), p. 210.

3 See Fung Yu-lan, *History of Chinese Philosophy* II (1953), p. 191; Graham, *The Book of Lieh-tzŭ* (1960), p. 1.

4 Graham, *op. cit.*, pp. 140, 143, 148.

comfort. It was a message, however, which in certain fundamentals was completely misunderstood by the Chinese, at least during the early centuries. The religion which in India had opposed the Hindu beliefs in *ātman* and Brahman by its doctrines of *anattā* and *nirvāṇa*, and was dominated by concepts of *karma*, rebirth, universal suffering and impermanence, made its strongest appeal to the Chinese by teaching that it is the 'self' or 'soul' which alone is 'real', and therefore imperishable. The message proclaimed by early Buddhist preachers in China spoke of the self persisting through successive rebirths, but it held out the hope that the faithful would attain to what for all practical purposes was a life of endless bliss in the Tushita heaven of Amitābha Buddha. E. Zürcher puts the position succinctly when he writes,

> The doctrine of the non-existence of the permanent ego was completely misunderstood by the Chinese, monks and laymen alike, before the fifth century A.D. The Chinese, not unreasonably, were unable to see in the doctrine of rebirth anything else than an affirmation of the survival of the soul (*shên*) after death. Thus we find the queer situation that in the fourth and fifth centuries the Chinese Buddhists defended the immortality of the soul.[5]

It was partly in consequence of this insistence on the immortality of the soul during the period known as the 'period of disunity' (A.D. 221–589) that Confucianism and Taoism lost ground to Buddhism, which emerged in China as a major religious force and won over and absorbed the energies of the most philosophically minded of the Chinese. As the name given to the period suggests, it was a time of great political disturbance, resulting in suffering and misery, vast movement of population, and the division of the country politically into north and south. Several Chinese dynasties in turn controlled south China, whilst non-Chinese dynasties ruled in the north. It was a period of intense intellectual activity, not only of controversy between Confucians and Taoists on the one hand and Buddhists on the other, but the gradual emergence of several different schools of Chinese Buddhism with very different interpretations of man's nature and destiny. Buddhism in China began to crystallise into different schools after the great missionary translators had made available in literary Chinese most of the great Mahāyāna sutras which had been written in Sanskrit. When Kumārajīva died in A.D. 413 most of the important treatises of the Mahāyāna, together with the Vinaya of the Sarvāstivādins, had been rendered into excellent literary Chinese.

5 Zürcher, *The Buddhist Conquest of China* (1959), p. 11.

From A.D. 402 until his death Kumārajīva and his band of translators and copyists, working in the northern capital of Ch'ang-an, had poured out a steady stream of translations. One of his disciples, Sêng-chao (A.D. 374–414), became an outstanding interpreter of the Mādhyamika system of *Nāgārjuna*. About the same time, at Liang-chou, the capital of the northern Liang dynasty, Dharmakshema was translating the Mahāparinirvāna sutra, whilst at Tun-huang, at the eastern confluence of the two great caravan routes across central Asia, Dharmaraksha was providing through his translations a powerful aid to the propagation of Buddhism in the far north-west. In the year A.D. 399 Fa-hsien left for India on his famous pilgrimage,[6] returning after thirteen years with many precious manuscripts. Thus was inaugurated a series of pilgrimages to the Holy Land of Buddhism by intrepid Chinese monks, eager to study under Indian masters, to learn Sanskrit, to collect sacred texts and relics, and to persuade Indian monks to return with them as missionaries of the faith. By the year A.D. 420 the Chinese possessed a vast volume of Buddhist literature in translation, the important Mahāyāna sutras and the Vinaya rules for the governing of monastic life. At the same time Buddhists in China could look back on a long line of illustrious monks, both Chinese and missionary, who had spent their lives in spreading the influence of Buddhism among all classes of Chinese society.

We will first take note of the controversy during the fifth century A.D. between the Buddhists and their Confucian and Taoist opponents as to the soul and its salvation, and then examine the development within Buddhism itself of the positive idea of the Buddha nature in all sentient beings which, just because it was *real and eternal self*, guaranteed an ultimate universal salvation.

The controversy between the Buddhists on the one hand and the Confucians and Taoists on the other hand as regards the existence of the soul and its ultimate destiny came to a head with Hui Yüan (A.D. 344–416) and his famous treatise on the indestructibility of the soul, *Shên-pu-mieh lun*.[7] If, as many scholars believe, the work known as *Mou-tzŭ Li-huo lun* can be attributed to the third century A.D.,[8] the question was already being debated among Chinese scholars as to how the Buddhists could say that when a person dies he is reborn in another life. Mou-tzŭ answers the question by saying that at death only the

6 Giles, *The Travels of Fa-Hsien* (1923).

7 Zürcher, *op cit.*, p. 239; Ch'ên, *Buddhism in China* (1964), pp. 111–12.

8 Zürcher, *op. cit.*, pp. 12*ff.*; Ch'ên, *op. cit.*, pp. 36*ff.*

material body perishes. The soul or spirit lives on. He likens the body to the leaves and roots of plants, while the soul is likened to seeds, which continue to produce new plants again and again. The Confucian *Classics* are cited to show that the practice of the calling back of the soul of a deceased person implies its existence after death.[9] Already by the fourth century the doctrine of karmic retribution had become widely accepted among the Chinese, together with the concept of rebirth, which, as interpreted by the Chinese, meant the immortality of the soul. For instance, Yü Fa-k'ai (*c.* A.D. 310–70) taught the existence of a permanent soul (*shên*) in man, a soul which had become polluted and darkened by the influences of the world. Purified and freed from the fetters of the body, this soul would enter on a higher plane of existence. Other Buddhists maintained that the *dharmakāya* (*fa shên*) means the pure existence of the spirit without any material support.[10] The prominent Buddhist master, Chu Tao-i (*c.* 330–440), maintained that whilst all phenomena are illusory and form the worldly truth, the spirit (*shên*), as the base of wisdom and enlightenment, is not *empty*, but on the contrary is the principle of the highest truth.[11]

Probably the greatest exponent of Buddhism during the fourth century was Tao-an (A.D. 312–85). who, recognising the fundamental difference between Buddhism and the Chinese cultural heritage with which he had become increasingly dissatisfied, set out on a lifelong quest for a true understanding of Buddhism. It was while he was living at the Buddhist centre of Hsiang-yang that he was responsible for organising the cult of Maitreya, who was regarded as the future Buddha, destined to descend on earth from the Tushita heaven as the saviour of men. Together with eight disciples, he appeared before an image of Maitreya, where they made a corporate vow to be reborn in the Tushita heaven, where Maitreya was abiding until such time as the world was prepared for his advent. It was Tao-an's still more famous disciple, Hui-yüan, who in A.D. 402 assembled the monks and laymen of his community before an image of Amitābha, and there made a corporate vow to be reborn in his western paradise. This event in later times was taken to mark the beginnings of the Pure Land school of Buddhism, which was to capture the hearts of millions of devotees in China, Korea and Japan through preaching faith in the saving merit

9 See Legge, *Sacred Books of the East*, ed. Müller (1885; reprinted 1966), XXVII, pp. 108, 112, 129, 157, 167, 340, 368–9; XXVIII, pp. 132, 136, 143, 174–5.

10 Zürcher, *op. cit.*, p. 143.

11 *Ibid.*, p. 144.

of Amitābha and his two assistant *bodhisattvas*, Ta-shih-chih (Mahāsthāmaprāpta) and Kuan-yin (Avalokiteśvara). This collective vow bound the participants not only to strive their utmost to attain salvation, but to help each other, so that if one of them should reach the western paradise first he would not enjoy his bliss in solitude, forgetting to share his salvation with the others.[12] The only effective reply that religious Taoism could make to this Buddhist belief in mighty and compassionate saviour gods was to make the Taoist immortals into divine instructors who taught the Taoist adept how to follow in their footsteps and thus achieve immortality. Taoism was forced to invent a pantheon of immortal gods and spirits to match the Buddhas and *bodhisattvas* of Buddhism.[13]

Early in A.D. 404 Hui Yüan wrote his most important treatise, the fifth and last section of which is on the indestructibility of the soul. In it he describes the process by which the soul (*shên*) is purified and emancipated from the fetters of lust until it finally attains to *nirvāṇa*. Hui Yüan defines the soul as an extremely subtle, immaterial and everlasting principle in man. As long as the emotions keep it bound to existence it transmigrates from one body to another, like a flame which leaps from one faggot to another.

As for the soul [he wrote], it responds perfectly and has no master; it is extremely mysterious and nameless. It moves in response to things and it functions in individual destinies. Though it responds to things, it is not a thing; therefore the thing may change but it does not perish. It is attached to individual destinies but it is not bound to them, so that it is not exhausted when the destiny is terminated. Because it has feelings it can be encumbered by things; because it has intelligence it may seek an individual destiny. Since there are fine and coarse destinies, their natures are different, and since there are bright and dull intelligences, their lights are not the same . . . The transmission of fire to firewood is like that of the soul to the body. The transmission of fire to another firewood is like that of the soul to a new body . . . The former body is not the latter body . . . A deluded person, seeing the body destroyed in one life, assumes that the soul and feelings also perished with it, as if fire would be exhausted for all time when a piece of wood is burned.[14]

At the time of Hui Yüan controversy between Confucians, Taoists and Buddhists centred on this Buddhist contention that there is a self or soul which is indestructible. The Confucians were agnostic as regards

12 *Ibid.*, pp. 219–20; Ch'ên, *op. cit.*, pp. 106*ff.*

13 Welch, *The Parting of the Way* (1957), pp. 137*f.*

14 Ch'ên, *op. cit.*, pp. 111*f.*

what comes after death, though some of them scorned the idea that any element of personality lives on. One strong argument which they used against the Buddhists was that, whereas Buddhism is supposed to teach the suppression of craving, it actually increased craving in the minds of the multitudes by its gruesome pictures of the torments of the various hells to frighten people, and by its rosy pictures of the paradises of the blessed.

Probably the most able of the opponents of Buddhism in the latter part of the fifth century and the early years of the sixth was Fan Chên (*c.* A.D. 450–515), who was a Confucian scholar, an official, and the author of a famous essay on *The Destruction of the Soul* (*Shên-mieh lun*). In this work he takes up the typically Confucian attitude.

The body is the substance of the soul, the soul is the functioning of the body . . . The relationship of the soul to its substance is like that of sharpness to a knife, while the relationship of the body to its functioning is like that of the knife to its sharpness. The sharpness is not the same as the knife, and the knife is not the same as the sharpness. But there can be no knife if the sharpness is discarded, and no sharpness if the knife is discarded. I have never heard of the sharpness surviving if the knife is destroyed, so how can it be admitted that the soul can remain if the body is annihilated?[15]

He attacked the Buddhist doctrine of *karma* and the indestructibility of the soul by claiming that birth and death follow a natural sequence. There is no need to postulate the operation of *karma*. As the soul is the functioning of the body, the two cannot be differentiated. In reply the Buddhists were able to cite the Confucian *Classics*, and especially the *Classic of Filial Piety* (*Hsiao Ching*), which emphasised and esteemed filial piety and the worship of ancestors. If this worship was not mere mockery and if it had any real meaning at all, then the Confucians must accept that the soul persists and lives on in a conscious state after death. One does not sacrifice to a non-entity.

We now turn from this controversy between these rival systems of thought in order to consider the great change of emphasis within Chinese Buddhism and which seems to have affected most of the Buddhist community.

When Buddhism first came to China during the Han dynasty, two trends were developing side by side. Hīnayānist influence was very

15 Quoted from Fung Yu-lan, II, p. 299, and taken from the *Hung Ming Chi*, Chapter 9: 55, a collection of essays of an apologetic and controversial nature by Sêng Yu, probably written *c.* A.D. 515–18.

strong in the emphasis made on *dhyāna* techniques for the control and concentration of the mind and the suppression of passions. At the same time great interest was shown in the Prajñā school, Mahāyānist in spirit and concerned with the problems of ultimate reality, the transience of the phenomenal, and the relationship of these transient dharmas to the eternal Buddha nature. It was the Prajñā school which brought Buddhism into close relationship with Lao-Chuang philosophy. The voluminous *Perfection of Wisdom* literature was early translated, and was condensed during the fourth century into the Heart sutra and the Diamond-cutter sutra, which taught that all existences possess no self-nature of their own. The attainment of wisdom is the recognition that all phenomena (*dharmas*) are void and non-existent. That being so, there is no duality between subject and object, between affirmation and negation, between *saṃsāra* and *nirvāṇa*. Until about the end of the fourth century the influence of Prajñā philosophy was paramount. Both Buddhism and neo-Taoism came together in a recognition that the fundamental essence of things lies beyond the phenomenal world and can best be described, if described at all, as non-being. Under the influence of the great Prajñā sutras of the Mahāyāna, Chinese Buddhists of the fourth century A.D. had emphasised the antithesis between the Absolute and the temporal, between permanence and change, between *nirvāṇa* and *saṃsāra*. Both Taoists and Buddhists saw little difference between these concepts and the Taoist concepts of non-being and being, quiescence and movement, non-activity and activity. The Prajñā sutras taught that the state of *nirvāṇa* consisted of an intuitive grasp of *śūnyatā*, or the unreality of all elements of existence. It was non-being or the *void* (*pên wu*) which was considered to be the ground of all being, and it was the negative aspects of *nirvaṇa* that were stressed. But with the popularisation of the Mahāparinirvāna sutra, as translated by Dharmakshema, the positive, joyous and eternal nature of *nirvāṇa* was seized upon and with it the doctrine that the real self in every creature is the Buddha nature, which is imperishable. The early Buddhists had taught that there is no permanent self in *saṃsāra*, but only a conglomeration of the five constantly changing aggregates (*skandas*). This was still recognised, but the Mahāparinirvāna sutra taught that there is a permanent self in *nirvāṇa*, and this self is in reality the Buddha nature in each individual. The final state of *nirvāṇa*, to which all sentient beings aspire, is one of bliss and purity enjoyed by this eternal self. Salvation to this state is universal, since all living creatures possess the Buddha nature. This teaching at first appeared to be heretical to those who had been nurtured on the Prajñā sutras with their doctrine of *śūnyatā*, but it proved to be a teaching peculiarly suited to the needs of the Chinese people.[16] It was enthusiastically taken up by Tao Shêng (*c.*360–434), whose influence on Buddhism was great in both north and south. To him the *śūnyatā* of the Prajñā sutras and the Buddha nature of the Nirvāṇa sutra were the same, ultimate truth without characteristics and transcending symbols and forms. Yet he taught that within every creature there is this Buddha nature which everyone could realise and that instantaneously and completely. This attainment of Buddhahood by a sudden and complete enlightenment was to be taken up later and expanded by certain forms of Ch'an (Zen).

Though Tao-shêng preached salvation through the realisation of one's Buddha nature, he set his face against the idea that meritorious deeds would be rewarded, and he denied the existence of the Pure Land of Amitābha. In his day the idea of salvation and rebirth in the Pure Land of Amitābha had taken hold of the imagination of the common people. It was being fostered by preachers and by the vivid pictures painted on the walls of temples and *stupas*. People were being encouraged by avaricious and unworthy monks to believe that meritorious deeds such as gifts to temples and monasteries would ensure escape from the miseries of hell and entrance into paradise.

Whilst in south China throughout the fifth century the greatest success of Buddhism lay in its penetration into the higher strata of society and the development of what has been called 'gentry' Buddhism, in north China, through the missionary activities of many devout monks such as Fo T'u-teng and Tao-an amongst the general populace, the majority of the population was converted to Buddhism. Throughout the fifth century the most powerful State was the nothern Wei dynasty (A.D. 386–534) founded by a non-Chinese people known as T'o-pa and probably of Turkic origin. By A.D. 440 they had conquered practically the whole of north China and adopted Chinese civilisation and culture. The emperors of this dynasty encouraged Buddhism, except for a short period of intense persecution about the middle of the century, a persecution which had been engineered by a Confucian scholar called Ts'ui-hao and the Taoist K'ou-ch'ien-chih. The latter's main concern seems to have been the establishment of a holy empire on earth under Taoist auspices with himself as a sort of Taoist pope. In

16 See Ch'ên, *op. cit.*, pp. 114*f.*

contrast, the aspirations of the Buddhists reached out beyond this life of suffering to the eternal life of purity and joy pictured in the Nirvāṇa sutra. Much of the appeal of Buddhism had been made to the illiterate peasantry, inculcated by vivid stories about the Buddhas and *bodhisattvas*, by the elaborate decorations of temples and *stupas* and by the carving of images. After the persecution the revival of Buddhism was accompanied by great building activity. The great images and inscriptions carved in the Yün-kang caves, about ten miles west of the capital city of Ta-t'ung, belong to this period. Some of the inscriptions testify to the intense longing and prayer of devout Buddhists that their ancestors, their teachers and all their relations might be reborn in the Pure Land and live there without blemish, being nurtured on the lotus.[17] In the early decades of the sixth century the northern Wei moved their capital to Lo-yang, and once more there began an intensive period of rock-carving at Lung-mên, eight to nine miles south of the city. The leading deities portrayed there were Śākyamuni and Maitreya. It seems that millennialist ideas were very much in the air. It was about a thousand years since Śākyamuni had lived on earth, and there was a widespread belief that the time was ripe for the appearance on earth of the future Buddha, the saviour Maitreya, to establish a reign of peace and righteousness. For a short time hopes of salvation centred in these millennialist ideas and on the worship of Maitreya, but as millennialist expectations died down the Pure Land doctrines grew in popularity and more and more people turned for salvation to Amitābha, the Buddha of eternal life and light, and to the compassionate *bodhisattva* Kuan-yin, who could be relied on to answer the cry of faith and fly to the succour of the needy.

Throughout almost the whole course of the fifth century, the Lotus sutra was being increasingly disseminated in China in the translations of Dharmarāksha (A.D. 286) and Kumārajīva (A.D. 406), and proclaimed as the final truth given out by Śākyamuni before his decease. In this work, according to Soothill,[18]

> he at last makes known the All-Truth, which confers Perfect Enlightenment and Final Nirvāna, or Liberation. This supreme liberation cannot be attained by self-discipline and works; it can only be attained by faith and invocation. Salvation by faith is then the fundamental doctrine of the Mahāyāna School. According to the Lotus teaching no sacrifice is required, no expiation, no atonement, no remorse, no repentance in the sense of contrition, nothing but

17 *Ibid.*, p. 168.
18 Soothill, *The Lotus of the Wonderful Law* (1930), pp. 34*f*.

faith in the infinite mercy and infinite power of the Infinite Buddha, who lives and reigns for ever.

This call to faith in the infinite mercy of the Buddha is set in the context of a stupendous apocalyptic vision in which the promise of salvation is given to all, even to the devils in hell. Here is the firm assurance that all the sentient creation is destined ultimately to become enlightened.

The Buddhism of the Lotus sutra, however it may have been interpreted by the learned and enlightened scholar, undoubtedly came to the unlettered multitudes of fifth century China as a gospel of hope. It became

> the most popular sutra in China because it was studied and recited by practically all the Buddhist schools there, because it contained the most comprehensive statement of the revolutionary Mahāyānist doctrines of the eternal Buddha and universal salvation, and because it had been the inspiration for Buddhist art and practices during the past millennium and a half in China.[19]

There was, however, another important work, and this much shorter, and quite possibly of Chinese origin,[20] which witnesses to the keen interest in universal salvation among Buddhists of fifth century China. It was about the middle of the sixth century that a text known as *The Awakening of Faith in the Mahāyāna* (*Ch'i Hsin Lun*)[21] appeared. Although attributed to Ashvaghosha of the first century A.D., and its translation into Chinese to Paramartha (*c.* 498–569), the authorship and provenance of this important work are still in dispute. It exists today in two Chinese versions. The work is a short but extremely competent summary of Mahāyāna Buddhism, and a brilliant synthesis of the teachings of those schools of Buddhism which are known to have flourished in China in the course of the fifth century. The treatise refers to the confusion brought about by the very existence of a huge corpus of Buddhist scriptures, sutras with seemingly divergent teachings difficult for monks and laity alike to understand. Already in north China during the Wei dynasty serious attempts had been made to organise and classify the Buddhist scriptures, and we know that diverse

19 Ch'ên, *op. cit.*, pp. 381–2.

20 A thorough discussion of this question is to be found in an essay by Liang Ch'i-ch'ao entitled *Ta Shêng Ch'-i-hsin-lun k'ao chêng* in *Ta Shêng Ch'i-hsin-lun chên-wei pien* (1956).

21 There are four translations of the *Awakening of Faith* into English. The most recent and the best is by Hakeda (1967).

teachings were creating a serious problem. Whilst the *Awakening of Faith* applied itself to the philosophical problems, it also emphasised the deep concern for salvation felt by devout Buddhists of the fifth century in China, and indeed by Chinese Buddhists ever since. After an invocation in which refuge in the Buddha is sought, 'the greatly compassionate one, the saviour of the world, omnipotent, omniscient, omnipresent', the author gives his first and greatest reason for writing the treatise as 'to cause all men to free themselves from suffering and gain final bliss'. Towards the end of the treatise the author writes of the man who seeks after true faith but lacks courage and strength. He is immersed in a world of suffering, fears that his capacity is unequal to the task of maintaining contact with the Buddhas and worshipping them aright. He knows that faith is difficult to bring to perfection, and he is inclined to give up.

He should know that the *Tathāgatas* have an excellent expedient means by which they can protect his faith: that is, through the strength of wholehearted meditation on the Buddha, he will in fulfilment of his wishes be able to be reborn in the Buddha-land beyond, to see the Buddha always, and to be for ever separated from the evil states of existence. If a man meditates wholly on Amitābha Buddha in the world of the Western Paradise, and wishes to be born in that world, directing all the goodness he has cultivated towards that goal, then he will be born there.[22]

It was this hope of salvation, positive, personal and joyous, preached so persuasively in the Nirvāṇa sutra, and so attractively set forth in the 'imagery, pageantry, vision, similes and parables'[23] of the Lotus sutra, which won over the majority of the Chinese of the fifth century to the Buddhist faith and gave Buddhism an appeal that could be matched neither by Confucianism nor by Taoism.

22 Trans. Hakeda, p. 102.
23 *Ibid.*

21

R. J. Zwi Werblowsky

Mysticism and messianism

The case of Hasidism

Mysticism and messianism are discussed—in the jargon of comparative religionists—as distinct forms of salvation. In fact they are considered as polar opposites, *viz.* as two 'ideal types' at the extremes of the spectrum constituting the so-called religions of salvation. The distinction has been a commonplace among historians and phenomenologists of religion for some time, and it has found its classical and definitive expression in the masterly account of 'prophetic' versus 'mystical' religion given by F. Heiler in *Das Gebet.* Chapter 6 of Heiler's well known classic is devoted to a comparative analysis of the general characteristics of mysticism and prophetic religion. His paragraphs on the concepts of salvation, on the relation to society, and especially on the 'evaluation of history' and the time process in the two types of religion are of particular relevance to the subject of 'messianism'.

Whilst the distinction between mysticism with its ahistorical (*viz.* trans-historical) emphasis on the one hand, and the historical and social character of prophetic messianism[1] on the other, is generally accepted, there is even more emphatic agreement to the proposition that typological distinctions are of doubtful value unless covered by historical facts.

> For phenomenology to fulfil its task, it stands in need of constant correction by the most meticulous philological and archaeological scholarship. It must ever be ready for a confrontation with the facts . . . [Phenomenological 'understanding' threatens to become] a pure art or an exercise of sheer fantasy if it avoids control by philologico-archaeological interpretation.[2]

This is not the occasion to inquire whether van der Leeuw's own phenomenological work always lived up to these admirable words of

1 Cf. also the use of terms such as 'prophetic movements' for messianic, millenarian or eschatological movements.

2 Van der Leeuw, *Phänomenologie der Religion*, third edition (1956), pp. 776–7.

warning. It is taken for granted by all students of religion that *Idealtypen* are rarely, if ever, encountered in actual reality, and that concepts which are useful for constructing a 'grid' or system of co-ordinates designed for helping us to place a phenomenon in a comparative context are not to be misused for simple labelling. The history of religion knows many examples of two-way traffic from apocalyptic and messianic eschatology to mystical spirituality and vice versa. Many are the messianic movements that ended by spiritualising themselves into pure interiority, whilst often enough mystical movements have generated explosive chiliasms. There are many intermediate points along this spectrum; the transition of early Quaker enthusiasm (with James Nayler riding into Brighton amidst shouts of 'Hosanna!' in 1656) to Quaker silence is but one example.

The history of Jewish mysticism is of special interest to the student of religion, as it represents a mystical phenomenon that grew in a tradition that had acquired a thoroughly messianic orientation. The history of the development of messianic ideas, beliefs and movements in Judaism is not our concern here.[3] Suffice it to say that between the Second Temple period and the final crystallisation of rabbinic (normative) Judaism, messianism had established itself as one of the central elements of Jewish faith and hope. There were differences in emphasis as well as in the degree of acuteness of this belief and of the intensity of expectation. There were periods of 'quiescent' messianism (i.e. messianic belief as a theological dogma and as an earnest religious hope) and periods of 'hot', i.e. acute and imminent eschatological expectation exploding into messianic movements—but the messianic factor had become a constant element of Judaism.

Nevertheless, Jewish mystics until the sixteenth century had no markedly messianic concerns. Neither the semi-gnostic, ecstatic visionaries of early Markabah mysticism[4] nor the contemplative mystics of the classical Kabbalah were much concerned with eschatology. No doubt, as pious and orthodox Jews, they earnestly believed in and prayed for the coming of the Messiah and the redemption of Israel, but the centre of gravity of both their mystical life and their systematic mystical doctrine was elsewhere. It was only in the 'new Kabbalah' produced by the great sixteenth century mystical revi-

3 Cf. R. J. Z. Werblowsky, 'Messianism in Jewish history', *Journal of World History* XI (1968), pp. 30–45.

4 Cf. G. Scholem, *Major Trends in Jewish Mysticism*, second edition (1946), chapter 2.

val (whose centre was in Galilee) that messianism became a central and determinative element in the Kabbalah. The subject has been fully described and analysed by G. Scholem[5] and there is no need to go once more over well known ground. But even the new Kabbalah of Safed exhibits complex variety as far as our subject is concerned. There were kabbalists (like Moses Cordovero and his school) whose mystical theology, *viz.* kabbalistic doctrine, is pure mystico-speculative theosophy without any marks of messianic tension or imminent eschatological adventism. Yet what we know of their devotional life and practice leaves no doubt that their spirituality was permeated by acute and active messianic aspirations. Lurianic Kabbalah, on the other hand, was thoroughly messianic not only in terms of devotional life but in its doctrinal structure. Messianism was an essential ingredient of the theoretical system and provided much of its dynamics. The Lurianic Kabbalah generated a messianic high-tension which found its explosive and catastrophic discharge in the great awakening of 1665–7 connected with the name of Sabbatai Sevi.[6] The disgraceful *débâcle* left an aftermath of antinomian heresy, of outright mystical nihilism (in the circles of the more radical Sabbatian sectarians) and of spiritual disarray (among the spiritually more sensitive in the orthodox camp).

The great religious and mystical revival of the eighteenth century initiated by R. Israel Ba'al Shem Tob (*c.* 1700–60) and known as Hasidism did not take place in a vacuum. It was a response to a specific historical and social situation and its spiritual needs, the background of which bore the imprint of the preceding Sabbatian and post-Sabbatian (Frankist) crisis.[7] Eighteenth century Judaism was a burnt child that had good reason to dread the fire of mystical enthusiasm and of the messianic dynamite contained in the traditional and practically canonical Lurianic Kabbalah. What options were there left for Jewish mystics and *spirituales*? According to Scholem,[8] three possibilities were open: (1) an orthodox continuation of traditional Lurianism, shut up in its own kabbalistic word and behaving (with or without *mauvaise foi*), as if nothing had happened; (2) a retreat of kabbalism from the market-

5 Scholem, *Major Trends in Jewish Mysticism*, chapter 7; *id.*, *Sabbatai Sevi: the Mystical Messiah* (1973), chapter 1; *id.*, *The Messianic Idea in Judaism and Other Essays* (1971).

6 Scholem, *Sabbatai Sevi*, and *id.*, *Major Trends in Jewish Mysticism*, chapter 8.

7 Scholem, *Major Trends in Jewish Mysticism*, chapter 9.

8 *Ibid.*, pp. 328–9.

place to the conventicles of a small elite of initiates—Lurianism would give up its role as the dominant influence on popular piety and devotion, and as basis of the generally accepted theology, and would become the preserve of a minority, exactly as classical Spanish Kabbalah had been in the thirteenth and fourteenth centuries; (3) a popular mystico-pietist revival with spiritual appeal to the masses, but purged of all dangerous, i.e. messianic, elements. According to Scholem, this is precisely what early Hasidism succeeded in doing. By appearing to assume the inheritance of Lurianic kabbalism yet with the messianic sting of the latter removed, Hasidism could become a mass movement and infuse a new spirit into the Jewries of eastern Europe. Scholem did not suggest that Hasidism tried to abolish messianism. The early Hasidic masters were pious and orthodox Jews, and they prayed and hoped for the advent of the Son of David like all other good Jews. But in their spirituality, as it was intensely lived and preached, the centre of gravity was in contemplative-mystical values such as communion with God, rather than in eschatological adventism. A similar phenomenology of spirituality can be found in earlier and non-kabbalistic forms of Judaism, the best example being the great twelfth century philosopher and theologian Moses Maimonides. To describe this particular achievement of the Hasidic masters Scholem coined the term 'neutralisation' of the messianic elements.

Whether or not Hasidism was a 'messianic' movement or, at least, a revival movement with significant messianic qualities or overtones has been a hotly disputed issue among students of Jewish history and religion. The protagonists in the debate include such illustrious names as S. Dubnow, B. Dinur and Martin Buber, but much of the relevant discussion was conducted in Hebrew and hence remained unknown to general historians of religion. Recently, however, the debate has spilled over into non-Hebrew publications and it may be useful, therefore, to take another look at the problem, and especially at the kind of Hasidic texts invoked as evidence.[9]

9 Scholem's thesis has been attacked in a long and well documented article (in Hebrew) by I. Tishby, 'The messianic idea and messianic trends in the growth of Hasidism', *Zion* XXXII (1967), pp. 1–45 (with an English summary at the end of the same volume). Scholem has replied to Tishby's criticism in an article (in English), 'The neutralization of the messianic element in early Hasidism', *Journal of Jewish Studies* XX (1969), pp. 25–55, reprinted in Scholem, *The Messianic Idea*, pp. 176–202. The articles by Tishby and Scholem have references to the relevant literature on the subject. Mrs Schatz-Uffenheimer has argued Scholem's thesis in a more extreme

As has been remarked before, the question is not whether the early Hasidic masters shared or repudiated the traditional beliefs and longings regarding the messianic advent. Of course they believed in the Messiah and waited for his coming. Many of their writings are full of references to this desired consummation. But the problem is not one to be solved by statistics:[9a] how often the messianic hope is mentioned in this or that Hasidic text. The question is a 'qualitative' one: what is the specific weight of such references and utterances, and what is their place in the total *Gestalt* of early Hasidic spirituality? There is a methodological problem involved here, and there is—alas—no rule-of-thumb procedure for dealing with it. An orthodox Christian author may have a long chapter on the Second Coming, and yet there will be a world of difference between him and a medieval or modern chiliast.

In an article entitled 'Contemplative mysticism and "faith" in Hasidic piety'[9b] the late Joseph Weiss tried to show how a radically mystical form of Hasidism (HaBaD) practically liquidated the messianic dimension, whereas in the Bratzlav school of 'dialectical' faith it had a more central place. Weiss's desire to illustrate two *Idealtypen* inevitably made him over-state his case by 'over-interpreting' the evidence. But his essay provides an instructive illustration of both the complexity of the Hasidic movement and the seductive dangers of correlating historical phenomena with phenomenological types. Tishby[10] was undoubtedly right in insisting that

> there is no basis for theoretical statements concerning a certain course which the new movement had to follow by virtue of historical circumstances obtaining at the time of its formation. A decisive answer . . . depends only on information concerning the actual position of the messianic ideas in the Hasidic movement . . . [and] after a study of extant sources with no prior assumptions.

Nobody would want to quarrel with this methodological precept. Let us, therefore, turn to the 'information concerning the actual position of the messianic ideas in the Hasidic movement' and—what is even more important, although not sufficiently emphasised by Tishby—to the problem of how to assess the information available.

A large part of Tishby's article[11] is devoted to an examination of the writings and views of kabbalistic teachers and moralist preachers

---

form; cf. her (English) essay 'Self-redemption in Hasidic thought', in *Types of Redemption*, ed. Werblowsky and Bleeker (1970), pp. 207–12.

9a See p. 314 9b *Journal of Jewish Studies* IV (1953), pp. 19–29.

10 *Loc. cit.* 11 *Loc. cit.*, pp. 3–24.

belonging to the kind of religious and social *ambiance* from which also the early Hasidic masters were recruited, and to showing that their messianic orientation and ideas were more or less in the line of traditional Lurianic kabbalism. Scholem[12] dismisses these works by 'non-hasidic authors of that period, written in the traditional vein of Lurianic kabbalism' as 'altogether irrelevant' for the issue under consideration. This cavalier dismissal seems unjustified. The texts analysed by Tishby are eminently relevant, though they actually prove the exact opposite of what Tishby meant them to prove. They show that there were indeed kabbalists speaking of things messianic in 'the traditional vein of Lurianic kabbalism'. But it is precisely these kabbalists who did *not* create a mystical revival, precipitate a religious mass movement and produce a spiritual renewal that embraced creative charismatic mystics as well as the popular levels of piety and devotion. The question is not whether or not the old-type messianism was still possible but whether —given the situation of eighteenth century Jewry in eastern Europe— it could produce a spiritual mass revival.

Limitations of space make it impossible to review, even in cursory fashion, the literature produced by the early (i.e. eighteenth century) masters. For our purpose the more interesting works are not those which neglect the messianic theme because of their preoccupation with spiritual states of *devekuth* (communion with God), but precisely those writings which time and again express messianic longing. These expressions are undoubtedly far more than a mere parroting of conventional formulas. They express a genuine suffering, longing and hope. But precisely because they are so genuine, their 'marginal' place in the overall *Gestalt* of the doctrinal systems as well as the spiritual and devotional lives of their authors becomes all the more blatant. Mrs Shatz-Uffenheimer's assertion[13] to the effect that in Hasidism the basic concepts of traditional Jewish theology concerning *galuth* ('exile') and *ge'ullah* ('redemption') have ceased to possess historical significance and have 'acquired a purely spiritual connotation', and denote spiritual states, seems to go too far and to violate the texts by 'over-interpreting' in another direction, thereby tending to spoil an essentially correct insight. The shift of emphasis is there—and it is enough to make all the difference. A careful reading of, for example, *No'am Elimelekh* by R. Elimelekh of Lyzensk (1717–87) shows to what extent a great Hasidic master can express awareness of 'this bitter exile' and even of

12 *The Messianic Idea*, p. 184.
13 *Loc. cit.*

the impossibility of attaining full spiritual perfection in a pre-messianic world, without messianism ever becoming central to his life and teaching. No doubt 'complete holiness and communion with God' are possible only after the advent of the Messiah—but meanwhile his spiritual energies are bent not on hastening this advent but on achieving that degree of perfection which is possible in the present circumstances. The same type of spirituality is exhibited in *Me'or Eynayim* by R. Menahem Nahum of Tchernobyl (1730–89). The spiritual state of communion known as *gadluth* is transient in the present dispensation; only in the messianic kingdom will it be permanent and general.[14] Exile and absence of mystico-spiritual perfection are interdependent because Israel's lack of *gadluth* prolongs the exile and the labour of cosmic restoration.[15] In fact, the labours of the hasidic saint (*tsaddik*) contribute towards hastening the messianic advent,[16] etc. Yet not even the sharpest ear can possibly detect in R. Menahem Nahum's teaching that note of messianic urgency and immediacy that is the hallmark of acute (i.e. short term) messianism. The centre of gravity has shifted to the sphere of mystico-spiritual states of perfection and communion.

One of the most interesting texts in this respect is the homily of R. Ephraim of Sedylkov (*c.* 1737–*c.* 1800)—a grandson of the founder of the Hasidic movement. R. Israel Ba'al Shem Tob—on Gen. 28: 16.[17]

(*a*) 'And Jacob awoke from his sleep, and he said, Surely the Lord is in this place and I knew it not' . . . It is known that the exile is called 'sleep', that is, the state when God removes himself and hides his face . . . as it is said [Dt. 31: 18] 'And I [Hebr. *anokhi*] will surely hide my face'. And redemption is when God reveals himself through the light of the Torah as is said 'Awake, awake, for thy light has come',[18] that is, that he will awake from sleep because the light of the Torah and the revelation of God . . . have come. And this is the meaning of [Dt. 31: 81] 'and I [*anokhi*] will surely hide my face', that is to say that I will hide the Torah and the light thereof which is contained in the [word] *anokhi* [this being the first word of the Ten Commandments, 'I am the Lord thy God'] which is the same as the

14 *Me'or Eynayim*, ed. Slavita (1798), f. 2b.

15 *Ibid.*, f. 9b.

16 *Ibid.*, f. 10b.

17 The passage has been quoted by both Scholem, *The Messianic Idea*, pp. 200–1, and Schatz-Uffenheimer, *loc. cit.*, pp. 209–10, but I feel that it is more complex than has been allowed so far. I give the repetitious and cumbersome text in a slightly condensed form (indicated by square brackets) and with omissions, and I must appeal to the reader's confidence in the reliability of my rendering.

18 A pseudo-quotation from Isaiah, conflated from Isa. 51: 17 and 60: 1.

hiding of my face . . . and this is the meaning of 'I am the Lord thy God' [Ex. 20: 2], that is to say, the 'I' [*anokhi*] which is the totality of the Torah—i.e. the Tetragrammaton [the Ineffable Name of God]—which is the revelation of God's name through the revelation of the light of the Torah . . . And this is indicated by the verse 'and Jacob awoke from his sleep', that is to say, from exile which is likened to sleep as [it is said Ps. 126: 1, When the Lord turned again the captivity of Zion] 'we were like them that dream' . . .

(*b*) It can also be explained by way of the saying in the *Tiqqunim* [i.e. the Zohar, on the verse Ex. 3: 2], 'And the angel of the Lord appeared unto him in a flame of fire' of prophecy, as this was the manner of the first redemption [i.e. from Egypt], whereas the ultimate redemption will be in the [superior] flame of the fire of the Torah, and this will be the perfect redemption, after which there will be no more exile. And this is hinted at in the verse 'and Jacob awoke from his sleep (*mishenatho*)', which [has been homiletically interpreted by the rabbis as if it] means *mi-mishnatho*, 'through his learning', that is to say that the last redemption will come in the flame of the [full revelation of the] Torah . . . [but] 'I knew it not' . . . until now . . . because the first redemption was [only] in the [inferior] flame of the fire of prophecy . . .

(*c*) Or it may be explained 'And Jacob awoke from his sleep and said, Surely the Lord is in this place and I knew it not' . . . as above, for exile is likened to a dream . . . and as man, when he is asleep, sees in his dream imaginary things that are false—for the dream is a thing imagined and not truth—so also exile as such is likened to sleep and dream, where it is impossible to know what is truth and the true end . . . [and so also is our way of serving God confusedly]. Redemption consists in God enlightening our eyes that all will see the absolute truth and will depart from exile which is falsehood. And this applies individually to each and everybody in the mystery of [the verse, Ps. 69: 18] 'draw nigh unto my soul, and redeem it' . . . For when man is sunk in falsehood then he is in exile, which is likened to sleep and dream, but when God helps him to purify his meditations and thoughts . . . [so that they are concentrated] on God alone . . . in a clear and brilliant light . . . then all his dreams are true, for everything which he sees is truth, and everything which is truth he will see, because he has departed from exile and from falsehood . . .

The curious thing about this passage is the author's way of introducing the theme of exile and redemption without any obvious constraint to do so. If he had expounded a scriptural passage mentioning 'exile' and 'redemption', then one could have argued that the author 'spiritualises' his text by giving it a mystical twist and interpreting exile and redemption in terms of spiritual states of darkness and illumination. But this is not the case here, and from a purely logical point of view the author could easily have proffered his spiritual exegesis by way of a simple mystical allegory of Jacob's sleeping and awakening.[19] The motif exile–redemption is dragged in without apparent necessity or justification, the only necessity and justification being the thoroughly Jewish conditioning of the author's mind and idiom: even when he wants to make a mystico-spiritual point he resorts to the vocabulary of messianic theology.

This observation leads to a second point. R. Ephraim suggests three successive interpretations which *prima facie* do not appear to be so very different one from the other. In fact there is a subtle shift in his argument. The exposition in sections (*a*) and (*b*)[20] is ambiguous. It does not really turn exile and redemption into symbols of spiritual darkness and illumination. On the contrary, it interprets sleep and awakening in terms of exile = darkness and redemption = illumination in a manner which presents the two realities symbolised as interconnected and equally real. It is not that exile is a symbol or allegory for spiritual darkness, and redemption for illumination. Both are real, and both pairs are symbolized by the images of sleep and awakening. Exile implies darkness, and only the final redemption will bring full illumination. The exposition in section (*c*) is already couched in words which suggest that illumination is the real theme, and exile and redemption but figures of speech.

R. Ephraim does not simply 'allegorise' exile and redemption. On the contrary, he introduces these terms into a context where they are actually superfluous. It is precisely the strength of the messianic idiom in his homily that highlights the basically unmessianic and essentially 'spiritual' character of his concerns. Indeed, messianism was neither liquidated nor discarded by the early Hasidic masters. It was very much there, but not as an actute, pivotal and consuming concern; it had moved to a different *locus standi* in their spiritual universe. The most accurate definition of this development is Professor Scholem's term 'neutralisation of messianism'.

19 Sleeping and awakening are, of course, well known and widespread metaphors in many religious (and not exclusively mystical) texts. Their association with (spiritual) exile and redemption from exile is a standard Gnostic motif: cf. Jonas, *Gnosis und Spätantiker Geist* I (1964), pp. 113–39.

20 The subdivision is my own.

Additional note 9a (see p. 309)
Also the modern practitioners of 'content analysis' seem to have arrived at the conclusion that frequency in a text is no sufficient criterion for measuring the force of attitudes, beliefs and views; cf., for example, the symposium *Trends in Content Analysis*, ed. I. de Sola Pool (1959), and especially the chapter by A. George, 'Quantitative and qualitative approaches to content analysis'.

22

Geo Widengren

Salvation in Iranian religion

1. In Iranian languages the notion of salvation is expressed by means of the root *baog-* and its derivatives.[1]

If we turn to Zoroastrianism, we find that liberation from the evil powers met with in man's existence as well as in the universe, i.e. on both the anthropological and the cosmological plane, is achieved thanks to a continuous fight against Evil. 'Relentless struggle' may be said to be the keynote of the doctrine of Zoroaster and his followers. In the Gathas, Zoroaster repeatedly exhorts his disciples to carry out this fight. The hostile powers in the world, the Good One and the Evil One, will meet for a decisive battle. To whom will Ahura give the victory? This is the question asked by Zoroaster (*Y* 44: 15). Through man's own deeds his own ego will bring him to an existence, corresponding to his own deeds, he says (*Y* 31: 20). Emphasis is always put on man's own deeds resulting from his free choice between good and evil. The militant character of Zoroaster's religion is especially clear from his exhortation to his disciples to defend themselves against their enemies with their weapon, *snaiϑiš* (*Y* 31: 18).[2] Because of this fighting spirit of Zoroastrianism it is in accordance with Zoroaster's whole doctrine that the idea of 'salvation' in the proper sense of the term is completely absent from the Gathas. No trace of the root *baog-* is found there.

However, in some Avestic texts of a later date the root *baog-* does appear. We thus find it in *Yt* 4: 3, *Yt* 14: 46 and *Aogemadaēčā* 57*f*. Of these texts both *Yt* 14 and *Aogemadaēčā* are without any doubt originally to be located in non-Zoroastrian circles.[3] Therefore these passages,

1 Cf. *AirWb*, col. 916*f*.
2 Cf. Widengren, *Die Religionen Irans* (1965), p. 65.
3 Cf. Nyberg, *Die Religionen des alten Iran* (1938), p. 301, and *Vayu* 1, ed. Wikander (1941), pp. 102*ff*. In this connection we should also mention the epithet *buxtiš* given to *Vayu Yt* 15: 47. As I suggested in *Hochgottglaube im*

in themselves not very significant, cannot be adduced as illustrating the idea of salvation in Zoroastrianism. As *Yt* 4: 3 has not much to give, our general impression of the absence of the idea of salvation in original Zoroastrianism is not altered. We shall, however, give a short account of the content of the passages enumerated.

Yt 4: 3 says that certain Yazatas save the righteous man from the Nasu, the female demon associated with the dead body, and from some categories of anti-Zoroastrian organisations.[4] The form *būǰaṱ* of *baog-* in this text has the more general sense of 'rescue' and carries no religious connotation, in contradistinction to what is generally associated with the term 'salvation' in a religious context. The passage in *Aogemadaēčā* 57*f.* belongs more to the sphere of salvation, for it is said there that no one is saved from Astōvīdōtuš, the deity or possibly demon of death. It is, however, characteristic that in this case no salvation is said to be possible. Finally, the passage *Yt* 14: 46 speaks of formulas capable of rescuing a man whose head is already forfeited. Here the context is clearly magical.[5]

In still later Zoroastrianism we meet with the conception of salvation in the biography of Zoroaster in *Dēnkard* VII. Some examples taken from this text will illustrate the appearance of terms and ideas expressing 'salvation'. It is said (VII: iv, 73) that Ohrmazd sent out some (messengers) to Vištāsp in order to save the religion, reveal its truth and knowledge, and dissipate Vištāsp's doubts, 'dēn bōxtan u-š rāstīh ⟨ut⟩ dānišnīh paitākēnītan ut Vištāsp-šāh . . . apēgumānēnītan'.[6] The same idea of a salvation of the religion is alluded to in VII: v, 5, when it is related that Āturpāt i Mahraspandān subjected himself to an

---

alten Iran (1938), this name must mean 'Saviour', and not, as Bartholomae, *Airb*, col. 967, proposed, 'Healer'. This suggestion of mine was accepted by Wikander, *Vayu*, p. 88. The substantive *buxtiš* should accordingly be derived from the root *baog-*.

4 Such categories are: the army, *haēnā*, and those who carry the banner, *drafša*, and (with emendation) the tyrannical leaders of the societies, *sāstar*. These are obviously designations of members belonging to secret societies or warrior societies; cf. Wikander, *Der arische Männerbund* (1938), and Widengren, *Der Feudalismus im alten Iran* (1969), chapter I.

5 The formula, here called *vāčō*, 'words', are in themselves efficient without any help from a deity. This is the characteristic attitude of magic; cf. Widengren, *Religionsrhänomenologie* (1969), p. 8.

6 Text quotations from the Zoroaster biography in *Dēnkard* are in accordance with the posthumous publication of Molé, *La Légende de Zoroastre selon les textes pehlevis* (1967).

ordeal in order to save the religion.[7] It is further stated that of those who will praise the Mazdayasnian religion during the fifth and the sixth hundred winters, none will save his soul, except through the 'coming of the Four' 'ōyšān kē pat pančom ut šašom satōkzim Dēn i mazdēsnān stāyēnd ōyšān nē kas ruvān bōžēnd bē pat rasišn i 4'.[8]

2. If we now turn to Zervanism, the situation is quite different. We have to admit that Zervanism, in spite of much research, associated above all with the names of Nyberg and Zaehner, is still a somewhat elusive entity.[9] But by general agreement we nevertheless possess many Pahlavi texts the Zervanite character of which is perfectly conspicuous. To such texts belong *Zātspram, Bundahišn* and *Mēnōk i Xrat.*[10]

In many passages in these Pahlavi texts, where Zurvān is mentioned as the deity of time and destiny, salvation (*bōžišn*) is met with in various contexts. In *Zātspram,* where more of the authentic Zervanite type is preserved,[11] the name of the personal god Zurvān is still found, but in the corresponding passages of *Bundahišn* the impersonal designation *zamān,* Time, is met with.[12] It is significant that we find a passage describing the death of Gayōmart in both *Bundahišn* and *Zātspram.* A comparison of the decisive wording is of relevance for our theme.[13]

7 This is the well known story, for which cf. Widengren, *Die Religionen Irans,* pp. 253*f*.

8 There is a slip in the translation, *rasišn* being translated as 'vérité'. The glossary s.v. *rasišn* is, however, quite correct and refers also to this passage. The coming of the Four presumably refers to the coming of the four Sōšyants. In *Dēnkard* IX it is spoken of Zoroaster's 'coming', *rasišn,* to be an Apostle, *aštak,* of Ahura Mazdā; cf. Widengren, *The Great Vohu Manah* (1945), p. 63. The Four would be Zoroaster and his three sons. They always constitute a group of four saviours. There may be ultimately some connection between this group of four and the four aspects of Zervan, but this problem cannot be tackled here.

9 Cf. Nyberg, 'Questions de cosmogonie et de cosmologie mazdéennes.' *Journal Asiatique* CCXIV (1929), CCXIX (1931); Zaehner, *Zurvan: a Zoroastrian Dilemma* (1955).

10 Both Nyberg and Zaehner agree on this point.

11 Cf. Widengren, 'The death of Gayōmart', in *Myths and Symbols: Studies in honor of Mircea Eliade* (1969), pp. 184*f*.

12 Cf. Widengren, 'The death of Gayōmart', pp. 183 and 193. We may also compare *Bundahišn* I with *Zātspram* I, as I have done in my article 'Zervanitische Texts aus dem Avesta in der Pahlavi-Überlieferung', in *Festscrift für W. Eilers* (1967).

13 Cf. Widengren, 'The death of Gayōmart', pp. 183 and 184*f*.

Bundahišn	*Zātspram*
It is said that in the beginning of the creation, when the Evil Spirit came to attack, Time decided for thirty years the life and rulership of Gayōmart.	For it was the decision of the decree-deciding Zurvān in the beginning at the coming of Ahriman: 'For thirty winters I decree for the valiant Gayōmart the salvation of life [soul].'

We observe here that in the *Bundahišn* text *zamān* is mentioned, but in *Zātspram* Zurvān, and further that *Zātspram* speaks of the salvation of the life (or Soul) of Gayōmart, 'hān i ǰān bōžišn'. Accordingly, we find in the more authentic Zervanite passage the idea of the salvation of the soul, 'ǰān < vyāna', or 'life' of primordial man.[14] In *Bundahišn*, on the other hand, we come across a text the poetical structure of which was first discovered by Nyberg. Zaehner does not think that this passage is a poem, but after careful consideration I am still of the opinion that Nyberg was right. After repeated endeavours to reconstruct the original text—behind which I presume an Avestic text may be looked for—I would like to present the following text and translation:[15]

zamān ožomandtar hač har dōān dāmān zamān handāčak ō kār ut dātastān	Twelve syllables
zamān hač ayāpakān ayāpaktar zamān hač pursišnīkān pursišnīktar	Eleven syllables
zamān inmān apakanīhēt brīn pat zamān pistak frāč skīhēt	Nine syllables
kas hač oy nē boxtēt nē kā ō ul vāzēt	Six syllables

14 For *vyāna*, cf. Wikander, *Vayu*, pp. 84*f.* where it is rightly emphasised that both the verb *an-* and its derivatives are extremely rare in the Avestal whereas *giyān* < *vyāna* is often met with in Pahlavi literature. As we shall see, however, *giyān* is not so often met with in purely Zoroastrian texts as *ruvān*. My observations in this article supplement my all too brief remarks in *Die Religionen Irans*, pp. 20 and 84.

15 *Bundahišn*, ed. Anklesaria, pp. 10, 8–11, 1. The detailed commentary needed on this difficult text cannot be given in this connection. Especially is the second line difficult, because if we accept the reading *handāčak*, proposed by Zaehner, a reading which has much to recommend it, we do not obtain the same number of syllables as in the first line, despite the fact that in all the other couplets except the last (where the alternation between eleven and nine is easier to explain) we have the same number of syllables. The alternation between twelve and eleven syllables seems rather awkward, but this problem must be left for the future.

nē ō nikūnīh čāhē kanēt — Nine syllables
nē kā ažēr xān iāpān frōt vartēt — Eleven syllables

Time is mightier than the two creations,
Time is the measure of action and order.

Time is more understanding than those who understand,
Time is more informed than those who are informed.

The Time of the house is thrown away,
Through the decision of Time the adorned is crushed.

Nobody can be saved from it,
Not if he flies upwards,

Not if he digs a pit below,
Not if he turns away beneath the well of waters.

In Zervanism it is accordingly emphasised that no one can be saved from the mighty Time, *zamān*. Originally we have to surmise that in this passage it was not the impersonal designation of *zamān* but the personal name of Zurvān that was used, as is the case in other places in Pahlavi texts, where *zamān* has been substituted for an original personal being, Zurvān. This has already been remarked above. As already observed, the text *MX* is characterised by strong Zervanite ideas. It is therefore of interest in this connection to note some passages where it speaks of salvation; salvation, moreover, of the soul. It is noteworthy, however, that the designation of 'soul' in the following passage is *ruvān*, and not *ǰān* (< *giyān*).

MX II: 196*f*.: 'mēnōk i āsnōxrat ō dānāk guft ku ēt i-t pat dārišn i tan ut bōžišn i ruvān rāi pursīt', etc. 'The Spirit of the innate Wisdom said to the knowing one: That which you have asked about the preservation of the body and the salvation of the soul,' etc. The question here is how to ensure the preservation and well-being of the body without doing damage to the soul, but instead acquiring the salvation of the soul, 'bōžišn i ruvān' (cf. also *MX* II: 2 in this connection). Here the body, *tan*, and the soul, *ruvān*, are opposite notions, but *MX* is so far adapted to Zoroastrian conceptions about the value of the body that it tries to solve the problem of saving the soul, without declaring in any way that the body lacks value. Accordingly, *MX* is not a pure Zervanite text, but, as previous research has proved, only influenced by Zervanite belief.

We have observed that the designation of the soul in the passage quoted is *ruvān*. The same is true of another passage, *MX* II: 67, where we find the expression 'ruvān bōxtan', corresponding well with 'bōžišn i ruvān'. More interesting for our problem is the following statement (*MX* xxxix: 23): '. . . and in wisdom he is the more complete who is able to save his own soul', 'ut pat xrat bundaktar kē hān i xvēš ruvān bōxtan tuvān'. Wisdom, *xrat*, is accordingly the prerequisite for being able to save one's own soul. We should observe that in the passages quoted from *MX* it is always the soul, here called *ruvān*, that has to be saved. This is, as it were, the *positive* aspect of salvation. The *negative* aspect is that one has to be saved from some evil power. *MX* xliii: 14 says, after enumerating the parts of the spiritual armour that it is necessary to put on:[16] '. . . in this manner it is possible to come to Paradise and the vision of the gods,[17] and to save [one's soul] from Ahriman, the wicked, and hell, the evil-smelling', 'pat ēn advēnak ō vahišt ut vēnišn i yazatān matan, ut hač Ahriman i druvand ut dōšaxv i duš-gand bōxtan šāhēt'. Here we see that the souls are saved *from* Ahriman and hell, and thus able to attain paradise and the gods. That in this case too it is the soul that is saved from Hell is expressly stated (*MX* lvii: 9), where we read: '. . . and the souls of the righteous, in being saved from hell to the *Garōdmān* of paradise arrive better, thanks to the power and protection of wisdom', 'ut ruvān i ahravān pat bōxtan hač dōšaxv ō vahišt garōtmān nērōk ut panāh i xrat rāi apērtar rasênd'.

3. On some Sasanian gems and seals, as well as in some Pahlavi texts, we come across the following names, which are of interest in connection with the problem of salvation:

Sēbōxt	Saved by the Three
Čahārbōxt	Saved by the Four
Haftānbōxt	Saved by the Seven

Who are these deities alluded to by the designations of Sē, Čahār and Haftān? The last of these terms causes no difficulties, for it can hardly mean anything but the seven planets. These seven planets, according

16 For the symbol of spiritual armour in *MX* cf. Widengren, *Iranisch-semitische Kulturbegegnung in parthischer Zeit* (1960), pp. 38*f*., where it is demonstrated that this passage reveals some traces of the Parthian dialect and accordingly emanates from north-western Iran, the home of the Median Magians, the representatives of Zervanism.

17 At the time when *MX* was conceived *yazatān* did not mean 'God', as West translates, but was a real plural, as we can see from the Sasanian inscriptions.

to *MX* VIII, are the seven generals on the side of Ahriman.[18] In *KN* VI, where the name of Haftānbōxt is found, the bearer of this name is the enemy of Ardašēr, whose army suffers a defeat through him. There is a mythical background to this story into which we cannot enter here.[19] It is essential only to observe that the seven are collectively an evil power and that the bearer of the name 'Saved by the Seven' is in the service of the evil powers, being the 'Lord of the Worm', *i Kirm xvatāi*. This Worm is the mythical monster killed by Ardašēr, according to *KN*. However, the name 'Saved by the Seven' indicates a positive evaluation of the seven. It is obvious that *MX*, in placing the seven planets on the side of Ahriman, has adopted the dualistic Zoroastrian ideas and that originally the seven planets were quite simply the agents of the deity of time and destiny, Zurvān.[20] The names of Sēbōxt and Čahārbōxt, on the other hand, can be placed within the Zervanite doctrine of the highest deity itself. The word 'Three' obviously refers to the well known three aspects of Zurvān, aspects much discussed in recent research,[21] i.e. Ašōqar, Frašōqar and Zarōqar. They are aspects of the highest god, Zurvān, but at the same time independent gods.[22] The Four, again, is the name of these three aspects *plus* the god Zurvān himself, who is the quadriform god.[23]

We have, further, quite a series of names formed on the same pattern: Āturbōxt, Māhbōxt, Vāibōxt, Vādbōxt and Yazdānbōxt.[24] These deities, including the general term *Yazdān* in the meaning of 'gods', are found in the later Zoroastrianism. It is not possible to assign them especially to Zervanism.

More important for our theme are the names Mihrbōg and Mihr-

18 Cf. Nyberg, *Journal Asiatique* CCXIV (1929), pp. 198*f.* and Zaehner, *op. cit.*, pp. 368*f.*

19 Cf. Widengren, *Die Religionen Irans*, p. 313, and 'La légende royale de l'Iran antique', in *Hommage à Georges Dumézil* (1960), p. 229, note 2, with references.

20 It is difficult to find a reason why the seven planets should be evil, but the twelve Zodiacal signs good. Zaehner (*op. cit.*, pp. 161*f.*) has clearly shown that both categories are agents of Time, and accordingly both evil and good.

21 Cf. Widengren, *Die Religionen Irans*, pp. 286*f.* with references to the investigations of Bailey, Nyberg and Zaehner.

22 Cf. the Syriac texts quoted by Zaehner, *op. cit.*, pp. 435, 439, 440, 441. These texts speak of them as 'elements' or 'gods'.

23 Cf. especially Nyberg, *Journal Asiatique* CCXIX (1931), pp. 47*ff.*: 'Le dieu quadriforme'.

24 These names are indexed in Horn and Steindorf, *Sasanidische Siegelsteine* (1891), p. 31.

bōžēt.[25] Formed like the first of these two is Mātbōg.[26] These names have the meaning of 'Having salvation through Mithra' and 'Having salvation through the Mother'. In consequence, Mithra is associated with the idea of salvation; Mithra is the divine element in the theophoric name of the usual type in *-bōxt*, e.g. Mihrbōxt. Accordingly, Mithra, as the saviour god, is more represented than other deities in theophoric names from a later period. He is also represented in such names from an older period, namely in the name of Bagabuxša, where Baga means Mithra, who is the *baga par excellence*.[27] More difficult is the name written in Greek, *Μιϑϱο βουζάνης*. It was previously assumed that this name—to be reconstructed as Mihrbōžan, a form actually found in inscriptions dating from the post-Achaemenian period[28]—also meant 'Having salvation through Mithra'. This view, however, was contested by Benveniste with some weighty arguments,[29] and we may therefore omit it from our discussion. The picture is not altered in consequence. Mithra and Māt—i.e. Anāhitā, the Mother Goddess in Iran[30]—both belong to Zervanism. Accordingly, in the Zervanite system the following deities are represented in theophoric names expressing the idea of salvation: Zervan himself, his three aspects, Mithra, and Anāhitā. Of these deities, Mithra is most represented in the proper names as the saviour god, a fact well in agreement with his general character in the Mithraic mysteries, as emphasised by Cumont.[31]

We may observe one remarkable absence in this connection. It is well known that Ahura Mazdā belongs, as one of the divine Twins, to the Zervanite system. Nevertheless, he is *not* met with in the proper names as a saviour god. He is not associated in these names with the idea of salvation, but has ceded this place to Mithra, who may have been regarded as the more active god. We shall discuss this problem in the next section when dealing with Manichaeism.

3. When we pass to Manichaeism we find—not unexpectedly—that 'salvation', *bōžišn*, 'saviour', *bōxtār* (Mp.) or *bōxtāgar* (Mparth), and 'to

25 Cf. Gignoux, *Glossaire des inscriptions Pehlevies et Parthes* (1972), p. 58a, for Mihrbōg; and Horn and Steindorf, *op. cit.*, p. 31, for Mihrbozet.

26 Cf. Widengren, *Die Religionen Irans*, p. 119.

27 *Ibid.*

28 Cf. Gignoux, *op. cit.*, p. 58a.

29 Cf. Benveniste, *Titres et noms propres en iranien ancien* (1966), pp. 112*ff*.

30 Cf. Widengren, *Die Religionen Irans*, p. 227.

31 Cf. Cumont, *Die Mysterien des Mithra*, third edition (1923), p. 127.

save', *bōxtan*, are quite dominant terms.[32] They express the innermost intention of Manichaeism, which is above all a religion of salvation.[33]

In Manichaeism salvation has to do with human souls, who are equated with the elements of light, which need to be rescued from the admixture with darkness.[34] The word generally used for 'soul' is *giyān*. However, some illustrations of the word *ruvān* (or Mparth, *arvān*) will be given in the following. Accordingly, we meet with two terms, *giyān* and *ruvān*, exactly as in Zervanism. One is saved from the evil and 'comes' to the soul, 'bōxtan ē až anāgīh ud madan ē ō giyān', *M* 9. I. V. 4t = *MirM* II, p. 7 [298]. A hymn is called 'Bring together the souls to salvation', 'amvardēd giyānān ō bōg', *M.* 7 R. I. 16 = *MirM* III, p. 25 [870] (Mparth.). In the publication *MirM* III, which contains Parthian texts, we find fifteen passages where *giyān* is used, against only two with *ruvān*. However, *ruvān* is used in alternation with *giyān*, seemingly without any shift of meaning. A few examples will illustrate the usage of this word.

It is said of the Saviour: 'He opened the gate of salvation to the happy souls', 'višādiš bar moxšīg ō ruvānān farruxān', *M* 42. V. I. 54–6 = *MirM* III, p. 35 [880] (Parthian). The Indian loan word *moxš* (Skr. *mokṣa*) has given rise to the adjective *moxšīg* used in this context. Another passage is *M* 74. ḥ. 9: 'And mayest thou be saved in the soul', 'ud pad ruvān bōxtag bavāi' (Saleman, *Manich. Stud.* I, p. 15). In a passage addressed to the divine Mani, he is asked to save the penitent's soul, 'bag Mārī Mānī man arvān bōž', *M* 176. V. 10–11 (*ibid.*, p. 21).

In Manichaeism we further find a third term, *grīv*, in connection with salvation. This word may be translated as the Ego of the human individual (in German translated as *das Ich*), because its etymology does not indicate any special connection with the idea of a soul.[35] This designation, *grīv*, which plays a great role in Manichaean texts, is also associated with the idea of salvation. As an illustration we may quote the following two passages: 'Blessed, so that he may be saved, who will save my Ego from distress', 'āfrīd ku bōxtag bavāh kē man grīv

32 Cf. the glossaries in *MirM* I–III and Saleman, *Manich. Stud.* (1908), Henning, *Ein manichäisches Bet- und Beichtbuch* (1937), and Boyce, *The Manichaean Hymn Cycles in Parthian* (1954).

33 Cf. Widengren, *Mani and Manichaeism* (1965), pp. 63*f.*, and Puech, *Le Manichéisme* (1949), pp. 70–2.

34 Cf. Widengren, *Mani and Manichaeism*, pp. 54–6; Puech, *op. cit.*, pp. 79*f.*

35 Cf *AirWb*, col. 530. There is no doubt that the basic meaning is 'neck'. In Pahlavi we find the word *grīvpān* as a designation of protective armour. In Avesta the word *grīvā* is used of daēvic beings—which is significant.

bōžāh až vidang', *M* 7. II. V. II. 208–11 = *MirM* III, p. 29 [874]. And from the Parthian hymn cycles the following text may be quoted: 'My Ego is saved from all the sins' (*Angad Rōšnān* VIII: 2 a = Boyce, *Hymn Cycles*, pp. 168–9). We might adduce many other examples of this usage.[36] As *grīv*, however, obviously designates the whole personality rather than the soul, we are left with two designations in Manichaeism for the soul as an object of the process of salvation: *giyān* and *ruvān*. This use of two terms creates a certain problem: why were two terms used here? Do these two terms belong to different religious milieus or do they possess one and the same background?

In the inscriptions of Kartēr, the creator of the Sasanian State religion, we meet with the name of *bōxtruvān* 'he whose soul is saved' as a name of honour given to Kartēr.[37] It is significant that the term *giyān* is absent from the Sasanian inscriptions. How is this presence of *ruvān* and absence of *giyān* to be explained?

In answering this question we may proceed from Wikander's observation that in Avesta *vyāna* is rarely met with and obviously belongs to the vocabulary of non-Zoroastrian circles.[38] It would seem that the same term in its Pahlavi form *giyān*, was still absent in Parthian and Sasanian times from the Zoroastrian religious language. I think it is significant that in Zoroaster's biography *ruvān* is the word used for 'soul', but that *giyān* is used, on the one hand, as the complement of *tan*, the body, and on the other in the expression *giyān čašm*, 'the eye of the soul', the visionary faculty.[39]

There can be no doubt that in an eschatological context *ruvān* is the usual Zoroastrian word for 'soul'. We may refer to such texts as *HN* and *Bundahišn* XXX.

In *Zātspram* the word *giyān* is, as we have seen, found in the description of the death of Gayōmart. But on the other hand the term *giyān* is not found in the likewise Zervanite text *MX*. In the description of man given in *Zātspram* XXIX–XXX both *giyān* and *ruvān* are met with, but here as designations of different notions of the soul, clearly associated with different aspects of the spiritual parts of man.[40] It may be that we have to seek the solution of our problem in this circumstance. For

36 Cf. Boyce, *op. cit.*, p. 188a.

37 Cf. Gignoux, *op. cit.*, p. 21a.

38 Cf. note 14 above.

39 Cf. the passages indexed in Molé *op. cit.*, glossary, p. 282b; *Dēnkard* VII: iv, 62 (*giyān–tan*), and VII: iv, 84 (*giyān čašm*). It is also used in the general sense of 'life'.

40 Cf. Bailey, *Zoroastrian Problems* (1943), the texts published as appendix v.

it is possible that the elaborated anthropology of *Zātspram* included elements deriving from various quarters, and thus assimilated with it also the term *giyān* < *vyāna*, coming from some non-Zoroastrian religion in Iran. It is even possible that in the original Zervanite system this term was the one regularly used for 'soul', not only as the vital soul, but also as the higher spiritual element in man, the element that should be the object of salvation. The occurrence of *ruvān* in *MX* would then be a result of Zoroastrian influence. That *giyān* in Manichaean texts is the dominant word would then be easy to explain against the background of the strong influence exercised on Mani by Zervanism.[41] But all this requires a more thorough investigation than it has been possible to carry out in the space of this paper.

It is easier to say why we find the soul associated with salvation in Zervanism but not in original Zoroastrianism: it is to be explained by the fact that Zervanism takes an altogether hostile attitude to the body and sexual life.[42] Because of this attitude it would be quite natural to attach weight only to the salvation of the human soul. This tendency is, of course, further accentuated in Manichaeism.

This short investigation has brought out a clear difference between original Zoroastrianism on the one hand and Zervanism–Manichaeism on the other. It has further raised some problems concerning terminology as far as the salvation of the soul is concerned, but not been able to indicate more than a possible solution of these problems. We have found that the deity who is associated above all with the idea of salvation is Mithra. In this connection it calls for notice that in the West we find that Mithra is the saviour, for he is called in Latin inscriptions *salutaris* (*salus* = *sotería*); the same idea is met with on the eastern boundaries of Iranian dominance among the Saka tribes who conquered the north-western part of India, by whom Mithra, as the sun god, is called *bōžaka*, 'saviour'.[43]

As we have said, it is quite natural that Mithra more than other deities should have been the saviour god. But the absence of any association with the notion of salvation in the case of Ahura Mazdā—at least as

41 Cf. Widengren, *Mani and Manichaeism*, pp. 137–9.

42 Cf. Widengren, 'Primordial man and prostitute', in *Studies in Mysticism and Religion presented to Gershom Sholem* (1967), pp. 348, 352; and especially Zaehner, *op. cit.*, pp. 183–92.

43 Cf. Vermaseren, *Corpus inscriptionum et monumentorum religionis Mithriacae* I (1956), Nos. 333, 348, where we find the epithet *salutaris* applied to Mithra. As to the term *bōžaka*, cf. Widengren, *Die Religionen Irans*, p. 334.

far as our present evidence goes—needs at least some reflection. Would it be possible here to establish a connection with Manichaeism, where Mihryazd is the most active of the three successive saviours? It is also remarkable that in some textual traditions the third Messenger may be called Mithra, whereas in Manichaeism the name of Ohrmizd is given to the first of these figures, Primordial Man, who, after all, plays a rather passive role (for even if he proceeds to engage in battle with the evil powers, he is defeated and has to be saved himself). In a way, therefore, he is rather the object than the subject of salvation. He accordingly corresponds with the part played in the Zervanite tradition by Gayōmart, who fought against Ahriman and his supporters, but was conquered and killed. Now S. Hartman has presented evidence to show that there are certain correspondences in the Zoroastrian tradition between Ohrmazd and Gayōmart.[44] If this be true, it would further explain the fact that Ahura Mazdā is absent from the list of gods associated with salvation, whereas the other deities in Zervanism are present. In this connection we should also refer to the well known aspects of the weakness and even stupidity of Ohrmazd in certain Zervanite traditions. But all this includes difficult problems, impossible to try to solve within the scope of this paper.

44 Cf. Hartman, *Gayōmart* (1953), pp. 92–100.

John Parry

Bibliography of works by S. G. F. Brandon

1944

Review of G. Dumézil, *Jupiter, Mars, Quirinus* (*Journal of Theological Studies* XLV).

1948

'The crisis of A.D. 70', *Hibbert Journal* XLVI.
'The logic of New Testament criticism', *Hibbert Journal* XLVII.
'The historical element in Christianity', *Modern Churchman* XXXVIII.

1949

'Modern interpretations of history and their challenge', *Modern Churchman* XXXIX.
Reviews of H. J. Schoeps, *Die Tempelzerstörung des Jahres 70 in der jüdischen Religionsgeschichte*; J. Seznec, *La Survivance des dieux antiques* (*Modern Churchman* XXIX).

1950

'Tübingen vindicated?' *Hibbert Journal* XLI.
Letter re Robert Eisler, Ph.D., D.Sc., D.Litt., *Modern Churchman* XL.

1951

Time and Mankind, Hutchinson, London.
The fall of Jerusalem and the Christian Church, SPCK, London.
'History, challenge of theology', *Hibbert Journal* L.
'Recent interpretations of Christian origins', *Modern Churchman* XLI.
'The primitive Church in its relation to Judaism', *Modern Churchman* XLI.
Letter on the martyrdom of St James, *Modern Churchman* XLI.
Reviews of E. Brunner, *Christianity and civilisation*; J. Baillie, *The belief in progress*; E. O. James, *The concepts of deity* (*Modern Churchman* XLI).

1952

'The present state of biblical studies', *Modern Churchman* XLII.

1953

'Myth and the Gospel', *Hibbert Journal* LI.
'Professor Simon on Christian origins', *Modern Churchman* XLIII.

'"Demythologising" the Gospel: the significance of Professor Bultmann's undertaking', *Modern Churchman* XLIII.

Reviews of J. Finegan, *The archaeology of world religions*; H. Weisinger, *Tragedy and the paradox of the fortunate Fall* (*Hibbert Journal* LI).

1954

'A plea for the comparative study of religion', *Modern Churchman* XLIV.

Reviews of E. C. Dewick, *The Christian attitude to other religions*; A. W. Watts, *Myth and ritual in Christianity* (*Hibbert Journal* LII).

1955

'Mithraism and its challenge to Christianity', *Hibbert Journal* LIII.

'Divine kings and dying gods', *Hibbert Journal* LIII.

'The Markan Apocalypse', *Modern Churchman* XLIV.

'The concept of man in non-Christian religions', *Modern Churchman* XLV.

Reviews of A. G. Widgery, *What is religion?* (*Modern Churchman* XLV); S. H. Hooke, *Babylonian and Assyrian religion* (*Folklore* LXV); S. Radhakrishnan, *The principal Upanishads*; P. R. Damle, *Philosophical essays* (*Philosophy* XXX).

1956

'The historical element in primitive Christianity', *Numen* II.

'De-eschatologising Christian doctrine', *Hibbert Journal* LIV.

'Modern trends in Old Testament studies', *Modern Churchman* XLVI.

1957

The fall of Jerusalem and the Christian Church, second edition.

The formation of Christian dogma, translated from a shortened form of M. Werner's *Die Entstehung des christlichen Dogmas*.

'Three recent studies in comparative religion', *Hibbert Journal* LV.

'The effect of the destruction of Jerusalem in A.D. 70 on primitive Christian soteriology', *Atti dell' VIII Congresso Internazionale di Storia delle Religioni*.

Reviews of C. H. Ratschow, *Magie und Religion* (*Journal of Semitic Studies* II); H. Kraemer, *Religion and the Christian faith* (*View–Review* VII).

1958

'The myth and ritual theory critically considered', in *Myth, ritual and kingship*, ed. S. H. Hooke, London.

'Salvation, Mithraic and Christian', *Hibbert Journal* LVI.

'The idea of the soul: a comparative study', *Modern Churchman* I, new series.

'The fall of Jerusalem, A.D. 70', *History Today* VIII.

'A problem of the Osirian judgment of the dead', *Numen* V.

Reviews of E. O. James, *Prehistoric religion* (*Hibbert Journal* LVI; *Modern Churchman* I, new series); E. Drioton *et al.*, *Les Religions de l'Orient ancien* (*Bulletin of the School of Oriental and African Studies* XXI); F. Steiner, *Taboo* (*British*

Journal of Sociology IX); F. F. Bruce, *Second thoughts on the Dead Sea scrolls* (*Modern Churchman* I, new series); P. Carrington, *The early Christian Church*; L. Paul, *Nature into history*; L. Jacobs, *We have reason to believe* (*Modern Churchman* I, new series).

1959

'Recent study of the sources for the life of Jesus', *Modern Churchman* II.

'Josephus: renegade or patriot?' *History Today* VIII.

'The origin of religion', *Hibbert Journal* LVII.

'The effect of the destruction of Jerusalem in A.D. 70 on primitive Christian soteriology', in *La Regalità Sacra*, ed. U. Bianchi, Leiden.

'A faith for the present age', *Modern Churchman* II.

'Jowett, Benjamin' in *Die Religion in Geschichte und Gegenwart*, III, third edition, ed. K. Galling.

Reviews of A. C. Bouquet, *The Christian faith and non-Christian religions*; *Man and time*, ed. J. Campbell; M. Eliade, *Patterns in comparative religion*; D. W. Gundry, *Religions*; J. Wach, *The comparative study of religions* (*Hibbert Journal* LVII); N. Smart, *Reasons and faiths* (*Journal of Theological Studies* X); F. H. Cleobury, *The armour of Saul*; G. Every, *Lamb to the slaughter* (*Modern Churchman* II); J. J. Bachofen, *Die Unsterblichkeitslehre der orphischen Theologie Römische Grablampen* (*Man* LIX).

1960

'The ritual perpetuation of the past', *Numen* VI.

'The Gnostic problem in early Christianity', *History Today* X.

'Osiris, the royal mortuary god of Egypt', *History Today* X.

'Survey of recent Continental theology', *Hibbert Journal* LVIII.

'The perennial problem of Paul', *Hibbert Journal* LVIII.

'Death and the relevance of the Christian conception of God', *Modern Churchman* III.

'Is there a New Testament theology?' *Modern Churchman* III.

'The Gnostic problem', *Modern Churchman* III.

'Modernismus' in *Die Religion in Geschichte und Gegenwart*, IV, third edition, ed. K. Galling.

Reviews of E. L. Allen, *Christianity among the religions*; R. C. Zaehner, *The concise encyclopaedia of living faiths* (*Hibbert Journal* LVIII); S. Sauneron *et al.*, *La Naissance du monde*; *id.*, *Les Songes et leur interpretation* (*Bulletin of the School of Oriental and African Studies* XXIII); G. H. C. MacGregor and A. C. Purdy, *Jew and Greek: tutors unto Christ*; R. H. Grant and D. N. Freedman, *The secret sayings of Jesus* (*The Guardian*, 2 March); J. M. Allegro, *The treasure of the copper scroll*; E. O. James, *The ancient gods*; W. Corswant, *A dictionary of life in Bible times*; H. B. Parkes, *Gods and men* (*History Today* X). Short notices of S. E. Johnson, *Jesus in his own time*; W. P. Witcutt, *The rise and fall of the individual*; A. Toynbee, *Christianity among the religions of the world*; J. Jeremias, *Die Kindertaufe in der ersten vier Jahrhunderten*; *id.*, *Heiligengräber in Jesu Umwelt* (*Modern Churchman* III).

1961

'The date of the Markan Gospel', *New Testament Studies* VII.
'The personification of death in some ancient religions', *Bulletin of the John Rylands Library* XLIII.
'The epic of Gilgamesh: a Mesopotamian philosophy', *History Today* XI.
'The Jewish philosophy of history', *History Today* XI.
'In the beginning: the Hebrew Creation myths in their contemporary setting', *History Today* XI.
'The Book of Job in the history of religions', *History Today* XI.
'Recent Continental theology', *Hibbert Journal* LIX.
'The Gnostics and their problems', *Modern Churchman* IV.
'Clio, a sphinx', *Modern Churchman* IV.
Reviews of R. M. Grant, *Gnosticism and early Christianity*; J. Maringer, *The gods of prehistoric man* (*Hibbert Journal* LIX); F. G. Brattan, *A history of the Bible*; R. C. Zaehner, *The dawn and twilight of Zoroastrianism* (*History Today* XI); J. Yoyotte *et al.*, *Les Pèlerinages*; *id.*, *Le Jugement des morts* (*Bulletin of the School of Oriental and African Studies* XXIV); *La Regalità Sacra, The sacral kingship*, ed. U. Bianchi (*Journal of Semitic Studies* VI); F. V. Filson, *A commentary on the Gospel according to St Matthew*; G. Parrinder, *Worship in the world's religions* (*Modern Churchman* IV); P. Winter, *On the trial of Jesus* (*The Guardian*, 3 November).

1962

Man and his destiny in the great religions, Manchester University Press.
'Jesus and the Zealots', *Annual of Leeds University Oriental Society* II.
'Paul—the problem figure of early Christianity', *History Today* XII.
'Herod the Great of Judaea', *History Today* XII.
'Akhenaten, the heretic king of Egypt', *History Today* XII.
'Further quest for the historical Jesus', *Modern Churchman* V.
'A new portrait of Paul', *Hibbert Journal* LX.
'The personification of death in early Christianity', proceedings of the tenth Internationaler Kongress für Religionsgeschichte, Marburg.
Reviews of E. Doblhofer, *Voices in stone*; M. Eliade, *Images and symbols*; E. O. James, *Seasonal feasts and festivals*; R. J. H. Shutt, *Studies in Josephus* (*Hibbert Journal* LX); S. C. Neill, *Christian faith and other faiths*; J. Pépin, *Les Deux Approches du Christianisme* (*Journal of Theological Studies* XIII); L. Paul, *The son of Man*; H. Stephan, *Geschichte der deutschen evangelischen Theologie seit dem deutschen Idealismus*; A. J. Toynbee, *A study of history*, XII, *Reconsiderations*; G. Leff, *Gregory of Rimini* (*Modern Churchman* V); J. Jocz, *The spiritual*

history of Israel (*The Guardian*, 7 March); *History of Religions* I, No. I (*Bulletin of the School of Oriental and African Studies* xxv).

1963

Creation legends of the ancient Near East, Hodder & Stoughton, London.

The saviour god: essays presented to Professor E. O. James to commemorate his seventy-fifth birthday (ed.), Manchester University Press.

'The ritual technique of salvation in some ancient Near Eastern religions', in *The saviour god.*

'Did the Roman world need Christianity?' *Modern Churchman* VI.

'Zarathustra and the dualism of Iran', *History Today* XIII.

'The Devil in faith and history', *History Today* XIII.

Reviews of G. Parrinder, *Comparative religion* (*Journal of Theological Studies* XIV); T. W. Manson, *Studies in the Gospels and Epistles*; *New Testament essays: studies in memory of T. W. Manson*, ed. A. J. B. Higgins; H. Montefiore, *Josephus and the New Testament*; E. Conze, *Buddhist thought in India* (*Modern Churchman* VI); H. Kraft, *Kaiser Konstantins religiöse Entwicklung* (*Erasmus* xv); P. Derchain *et al.*, *La Lune: mythes et rites* (*Bulletin of the School of Oriental and African Studies* XXVI); E. Renan, *The life of Jesus*; Dean Farrar, *Life of Christ*; H. Zahrnt, *The historical Jesus*; R. Aron, *Jesus of Nazareth: the hidden years*; W. Barclay, *Jesus as they saw him* (*The Guardian*, 26 February): J. Carmichael, *The death of Jesus*; J. Knox, *The Church and the reality of Christ* (*The Guardian*, I November).

1964

'The political factor in some ancient Near Eastern cosmogonies', in *Promise and fulfilment: essays presented to S. H. Hooke*, ed. F. F. Bruce, Edinburgh.

'The Millennium (non-Christian)', in *Encyclopaedia Britannica.*

'Angels: the history of an idea', *History Today* XIII.

'The idea of the soul', (I) 'In the West', (2) 'In the East', *History Today* XIV.

'The judgment of the dead', *History Today* XIV.

'Religious education', in *World Book Encyclopaedia.*

Reviews of G. Parrinder, *Witchcraft, European and African*; *What religion is in the words of Swami Vivekanada*, ed. J. Yale; S. Spencer, *Mysticism in world religion* (*Modern Churchman* VII); Y. Yadin, *The art of warfare in biblical lands* (*History Today* XIV); G. A. Williamson, *The world of Josephus* (*History Today* XIV); *The Guardian*, 25 September; J. Cazeneuve *et al.*, *Les Danses sacrées* (*Bulletin of the school of Orental and African Studies* XXVII).

1965

History, time and deity, Manchester University Press.

'B.C. and A.D.: the Christian philosophy of history', *History Today* XV.

'The Zealots: the Jewish resistance movement against Rome', *History Today* XV.

'The ancient Egyptian doctrine of immortality', *Expository Times* LXXVI.
'Matthaean Christianity', *Modern Churchman* VIII.
'The significance of time in some ancient initiatory rituals', in *Initiation*, ed. C. J. Bleeker, Brill, Leiden.
Reviews of H. Dumoulin, *A history of Zen Buddhism*; M. Goguel, *The primitive Church*; C. Rice, *The Persian sufis*; E. O. James, *The worship of the sky god*; W. M. Watt, *Truth in the religions*; S. C. Neill, *The interpretation of the New Testament*; A. J. Toynbee, *A study of history* VII (*Modern Churchman* VIII); H. W. F. Saggs, *Everyday life in Babylonia and Assyria*; F. V. Filson, *A New Testament history* (*History Today* XV); *The seed of wisdom: essays in honour of T. J. Meek*, ed. W. S. McCullough (*Journal of Semitic Studies* X); H. J. Schonfield, *The Passover plot* (*Financial Times*, 3 November).

1966

'The origin of death in some Near Eastern religions', *Religious Studies* I.
'Time and the destiny of man', in *Voices of time*, ed. E. J. Fraser, New York.
'The trial of Jesus', *History Today* XVI.
Reviews of W. Förster, *Palestinian Judaism in New Testament times*; A. Grillmeier, *Christ in Christian tradition*; W. H. C. Frend, *Martyrdom and persecution in the early Church*; E. Best, *The temptation and the Passion: the Markan soteriology*; E. B. Schnapper, *The inward Odyssey* (*Modern Churchman* IX); W. A. Ward, *The spirit of ancient Egypt*; *Religion*, ed. P. Ramsay (*Journal of Semitic Studies* XI).

1967

Jesus and the Zealots, Manchester University Press.
The judgment of the dead, Weidenfeld & Nicolson, London.
'The trial of Jesus', *Horizon* IX.
'The origins of religion in theory and archaeology', *History Today* XVII.
Review of S. Saunerson *et al.*, *Le Monde du sorcier* (*Bulletin of the School of Oriental and African Studies* XXX).
'The death of James the Just: a new interpretation', in *Studies in mysticism and religion presented to G. G. Scholem*, Jerusalem.

1968

'Pontius Pilate in history and legend', *History Today* XVIII.
'Jesus and the Zealots', *Studia Evangelica* IV.
'Magic and the black art', *Modern Churchman* XI.
'The holy book, the holy tradition and the holy ikon', in *Holy Book and holy tradition*, ed. F. F. Bruce and E. G. Rupp, Manchester.
'St Paul and his opponents', *Horizon* X.
Reviews of P. C. Hodgson, *The formation of historical theology*; *id.*, *The story of*

the Wise Men; H. Ringgren and Å. V. Ström, *Religions of mankind yesterday and today*; N. Perrin, *Rediscovering the teaching of Jesus*; rejoinder to review of *Jesus and the Zealots* (*Modern Churchman* XI); E. O. James, *The tree of life* (*Religious Studies* III, 2); J. Hawkes, *Dawn of the gods*; K. M. Kenyon, *Jerusalem* (*History Today* XVIII).

1969

The trial of Jesus of Nazareth, Batsford, London, and Stein & Day, New York.
Religion in ancient history, Scribner's, New York.
'The weighing of the soul', in *Myths and symbols: studies in honor of Mircea Eliade*, Chicago.
'The history of the idea of the Church', in *Dictionary of the history of ideas*, ed. P. P. Wiener, New York.
'Ritual: its nature and function in religion', in *ibid.*
'Ideas of the origin of religion', in *ibid.*
'Ancient Near Eastern cosmogonies', in *The origin of cosmos and man*, ed. M. Dhavamony, Gregorian University Press, Rome.
'The origin of religion in the light of recent research', *Ekklestiastikos Pharos*.
'The *siccarii*', in *Encyclopaedia Judaica*, Jerusalem.
'The Zealots', in *ibid.*
'Testimonium Flavianum', *History Today* XIX.
'A new awareness of time and history', in *Religious pluralism and world community* ed. E. J. Jurji, Leiden.
'Saviour and judge: two examples of divine ambivalence', in *Liber amicorum discipulorumque C. J. Bleeker*, London.
Reviews of C. H. Dodd, *More New Testament studies* (*Modern Churchman* XII); C. Aldred, *Akhenaten, pharaoh of Egypt: a new study*; P. Winter, 'Josephus on Jesus', *Journal of Historical Studies* (*History Today* XIX); C. J. Edmonds, *A pilgrimage to Lalish* (*Journal of the Royal Asiatic Society*).

1970

Dictionary of comparative religion (ed. and chief contributor), Weidenfeld & Nicolson, London, and Scribner's, New York.
Ancient empires (ed. and chief contributor), Weidenfeld & Nicolson, London.
'The defeat of Cestius Gallus, A.D. 66', *History Today* XX.
'Ideas of God, from prehistory to the early Middle Ages', in *Dictionary of the history of ideas*, ed. P. P. Wiener, New York.
'The Zealots and the ancient Jewish resistance against Rome', in *The fourth dimension of warfare*, ed. M. Elliott-Bateman, Manchester.
Articles on 'Altars', 'Animism', 'Aphrodite', 'Baptism', '*Book of the Dead*', 'Bridges', 'Creation myths', 'Caves', 'Charon', 'Death, personification of', 'Dreams, in the ancient world', 'Evil, origin of', 'Ebionites', 'Egypt' 'Election', 'Eye goddess', in *Man, Myth and Magic*.

'Jerusalem, A.D. 70; upon the nineteenth centenary of the fall of the city', *History Today* XI.
'Redemption in ancient Egypt and in early Christianity', in *Types of redemption*, ed. R. J. Z. Werblowsky and C. J. Bleeker, Leiden.
'The epic of Gilgamesh', in *The epic of man to 1506*, ed. L. S. Stavrianos, New Jersey.
Reviews of Sir Malcolm Knox, *A layman's quest* (*Modern Churchman* XIII); F. F. Bruce, *New Testament history*; *The crucible of Christianity*, ed. A. Toynbee (*History Today* XX); K. Cragg, *The privilege of man* (*Bulletin of the school of Oriental and African Studies* XXXIII). J. Campbell, *The flight of the wild gander*; T. H. Gaster, *Myth, legend and custom in the Old Testament* (*New York Review of Books*, 7 May).

1971

The trial of Jesus of Nazareth (paperback), Paladin Books, London.
'The portrait of Christ: its origin and evolution', *History Today* XI.
'Time consciousness as the basic factor in human culture', *Documenta Geigy*.
'The deification of time', *Studium Generale* XXIII.
'The trial of Jesus', *Judaism* XX.
'Jesus and the Zealots: aftermath', *Bulletin of the John Rylands Library*, LIV.
Articles on 'The "Good Shepherd"', 'Harranian religion', 'Headless spirits', 'Heresy', 'History, philosophy of', 'Iconography', 'Imhotep', 'Jesus', 'Job', 'Judgment of the dead', 'Man', 'Mary', 'Mummification', 'New Testament apocrypha', 'Oil', 'Osiris', in *Man, Myth and Magic*.
'Sin and Salvation', in *Dictionary of the history of ideas*, ed. P. P. Wiener, New York.
'The Church as an institution', in *ibid*.
'Salvation', in *Encyclopaedia Britannica*.
Reviews of C. H. Dodd, *The founder of Christianity* (*The Guardian*, 25 February); C. Hill, *Antichrist in seventeenth-century England*; J. B. Segal, *Edessa*; R. E. Witt, *Isis in the Graeco-Roman world* (*History Today* XI).

1972

Articles on 'St Paul', 'Phoenicians and Carthaginians', 'Religion', Revelation', 'Sacraments', 'Scarab', 'Stars', 'Tammuz', 'Time', 'St Uncumber', 'Vegetation spirits', 'War', 'Yahweh', 'Zealots', in *Man, Myth and Magic*.
'The proleptic aspect of the iconography of the Egyptian "judgment of the dead"', in *Ex orbe religionum: studia G. Widengren*, Leiden.

Forthcoming

Man and God in art and ritual, Scribner's, New York.
'Death rites and customs', in *Dictionary of the history of ideas*, ed. P. P. Wiener, New York.
'The idea of God', in *ibid*.

Subscribers

Frank Andrew, March
Markus Barth, Riehen
A. R. Bates, Manchester
C. F. Beckingham, London
Jan Bergman, Linköping
Ugo Bianchi, Bologna
Haralds Biezais, Åbo
Marco Boni, Bologna
Gerald Bonner, Durham
Gerald L. Borchert, Sioux Falls, South Dakota
Mr and Mrs D. L. Brandon, Ravensthorpe, Peterborough
F. F. Bruce, Manchester
T. A. Burkill, Salisbury, Rhodesia
R. F. G. Burnish, Slough
Dennis R. Bury, Birmingham
John H. Chamberlayne, Tonbridge
Eberhard Cold, Kronshagen, Kiel
Sir W. Mansfield Cooper, Meldreth, Royston
M. H. Cressey, Birmingham
Hubert Cunliffe-Jones, Manchester
H. R. Ellis Davidson, Barton, Cambridge
Rosemary F. Dorey, Warmwell, Dorchester
H. J. W. Drijvers, Groningen
Heinrich Dumoulin, Tokyo
Eldon Jay Epp, Cleveland, Ohio
Owen E. Evans, Bangor
Valerie E. Fisher, Bournemouth
Thomas Forrest-Kelly, Appley Bridge
E. D. Francis, New Haven
Christian R. Gaba, Cape Coast, Ghana
C. Scibona Giuffre, Messina
Karen Elizabeth Gordon, Pentre, Broughton
R. L. Gordon, Norwich
Stuart G. Hall, Nottingham

Raymond J. Hammer, Birmingham
Nora Edythe Harkness, Hostert
K. D. D. Henderson, Steeple Langford, Salisbury
O. V. Henkel, The Hague
A. J. B. Higgins, Lampeter
Joanna Hill (*née* Reading), Morden
Olle Hjern, Stockholm
Charles L. Horn, Minneapolis
G. F. Hudson, Oxford
Elizabeth M. Jackson, Winsford
A. R. Johnson, Alderley, Wotton under Edge
T. L. Jones, Manchester
J. P. Kane, Manchester
F. Kenworthy, Manchester
H. Paul Kingdon, Almondsbury, Bristol
Günter Lanczkowski, Heidelberg
H. C. Lefever, London
S. Levin, Johannesburg
T. O. Ling, Manchester
David W. MacDowall, Berkhamsted
John Macquarrie, Oxford
George W. Mac Rae, Cambridge, Mass.
Goro Mayeda, Tokyo
J. Stuart McKenzie, Knutsford
William Meany, Maynooth
Jaques-E. Menard, Strasbourg
Peter and Fritha Middlemiss, Manchester
John A. Midgley, Altrincham
Berta Millroth, Solna, Stockholm
Jan Nielse, Soroe
David A. Pailin, Manchester
Styl Papadimas, Katerini
Robert Peters, Birmingham
J. R. Porter, Exeter
Eric H. Pyle, Glasgow
L. K. Rawlinson, Nelson
John Reumann, Philadelphia, Pennsylvania
M. G. Robson (*née* Walmsley), Burton on Trent
Sten Rodhe, Malmö
J. W. Rogerson, Durham

D. H. Salman, Montreal
D. Howard Smith, Storth, Milnthorpe
Maurice Temple Smith, London
H. C. Snape, Bampton, Oxford
Mr and Mrs Rowland Swales, Knutsford
C. G. Sykes, Reading
S. W. Sykes, Cambridge
Theophilus M. Taylor, Topsham, Vermont
J. Heywood Thomas, Durham
Jan A. M. van Moll, Belmont
W. C. van Unnik, Bilthoven
Rosemarie Wedell, Manchester
Cyril G. Williams, Ottawa
T. S. M. Williams, Oxford

Libraries

Basel Mission library
Brotherton Library, University of Leeds
Catholic Central Library, London
Catholic University of Leuven
Clifford E. Barbour Library, Pittsburgh Theological Seminary
Concordia Seminary, St Louis, Missouri
Congregational College, Whalley Range, Manchester
Edge Hill College of Education, Ormskirk
Gardner A. Sage Library, New Brunswick Theological Seminary
Library of Jewish Sciences, Bar Ilan University
McAlister Library, Fuller Theological Seminary, Pasadena, California
Mansfield College, Oxford
Pontificio Istituto Biblico, Rome
Poulton le Fylde College of Education, Blackpool
St Mark's Library, General Theological Seminary, New York
School of Theology at Claremont, California
University College, Dublin
University of Bristol
University of Dundee
University of Glasgow
University of Heidelberg
University of Kiel
University of Lancaster

University of London
University of St Andrews
University of Utrecht
Georg-August University, Göttingen
Victoria University, Toronto
Warburg Institute, London
Westminster Theological Seminary, Philadelphia, Pennsylvania